T0214169

IFIP Advances in Information and Communication Technology

570

Editor-in-Chief

Kai Rannenberg, Goethe University Frankfurt, Germany

IFIP – The International Federation for Information Processing

IFIP was founded in 1960 under the auspices of UNESCO, following the first World Computer Congress held in Paris the previous year. A federation for societies working in information processing, IFIP's aim is two-fold: to support information processing in the countries of its members and to encourage technology transfer to developing nations. As its mission statement clearly states:

IFIP is the global non-profit federation of societies of ICT professionals that aims at achieving a worldwide professional and socially responsible development and application of information and communication technologies.

IFIP is a non-profit-making organization, run almost solely by 2500 volunteers. It operates through a number of technical committees and working groups, which organize events and publications. IFIP's events range from large international open conferences to working conferences and local seminars.

The flagship event is the IFIP World Computer Congress, at which both invited and contributed papers are presented. Contributed papers are rigorously refereed and the rejection rate is high.

As with the Congress, participation in the open conferences is open to all and papers may be invited or submitted. Again, submitted papers are stringently refereed.

The working conferences are structured differently. They are usually run by a working group and attendance is generally smaller and occasionally by invitation only. Their purpose is to create an atmosphere conducive to innovation and development. Refereeing is also rigorous and papers are subjected to extensive group discussion.

Publications arising from IFIP events vary. The papers presented at the IFIP World Computer Congress and at open conferences are published as conference proceedings, while the results of the working conferences are often published as collections of selected and edited papers.

IFIP distinguishes three types of institutional membership: Country Representative Members, Members at Large, and Associate Members. The type of organization that can apply for membership is a wide variety and includes national or international societies of individual computer scientists/ICT professionals, associations or federations of such societies, government institutions/government related organizations, national or international research institutes or consortia, universities, academies of sciences, companies, national or international associations or federations of companies.

More information about this series at http://www.springer.com/series/6102

Jason Staggs · Sujeet Shenoi (Eds.)

Critical Infrastructure Protection XIII

13th IFIP WG 11.10 International Conference, ICCIP 2019
Arlington, VA, USA, March 11–12, 2019
Revised Selected Papers

 Springer

Editors
Jason Staggs
Tandy School of Computer Science
University of Tulsa
Tulsa, OK, USA

Sujeet Shenoi
Tandy School of Computer Science
University of Tulsa
Tulsa, OK, USA

ISSN 1868-4238   ISSN 1868-422X (electronic)
IFIP Advances in Information and Communication Technology
ISBN 978-3-030-34649-2   ISBN 978-3-030-34647-8 (eBook)
https://doi.org/10.1007/978-3-030-34647-8

This Springer imprint is published by the registered company Springer Nature Switzerland AG
The registered company address is: Gewerbestrasse 11, 6330 Cham, Switzerland

Contents

Contributing Authors   ix

Preface   xv

PART I   THEMES AND ISSUES

1
Quantifying the Costs of Data Breaches   3
Siddharth Dongre, Sumita Mishra, Carol Romanowski and Manan
Buddhadev

PART II   INFRASTRUCTURE PROTECTION

2
A Comparative Analysis Approach for Deriving Failure Scenarios   19
   in the Natural Gas Distribution Infrastructure
Michael Locasto and David Balenson

3
An Attack-Fault Tree Analysis of a Movable Railroad Bridge   51
Matthew Jablonski, Yongxin Wang, Chaitanya Yavvari,
Zezhou Wang, Xiang Liu, Keith Holt and Duminda Wijesekera

4
Converting an Electric Power Utility Network to Defend Against   73
   Crafted Inputs
Michael Millian, Prashant Anantharaman, Sergey Bratus, Sean
Smith and Michael Locasto

5
Cyber Security Modeling of Non-Critical Nuclear Power Plant Digi-   87
   tal Instrumentation
Trevor MacLean, Robert Borrelli and Michael Haney

PART III   VEHICLE INFRASTRUCTURE SECURITY

6

Electronic Control Unit Discrimination Using Wired Signal Distinct   103
    Native Attributes
Rahn Lassiter, Scott Graham, Timothy Carbino and Stephen Dunlap

7

Vehicle Identification and Route Reconstruction via TPMS Data   123
    Leakage
Kenneth Hacker, Scott Graham and Stephen Dunlap

8

Modeling Liability Data Collection Systems for Intelligent Trans-   137
    portation Infrastructure Using Hyperledger Fabric
Luis Cintron, Scott Graham, Douglas Hodson and Barry Mullins

PART IV   TELECOMMUNICATIONS INFRASTRUCTURE SECURITY

9

Securing Wireless Coprocessors from Attacks in the Internet of   159
    Things
Jason Staggs and Sujeet Shenoi

10

Vulnerability Assessment of InfiniBand Networking   179
Daryl Schmitt, Scott Graham, Patrick Sweeney and Robert Mills

PART V   CYBER-PHYSICAL SYSTEMS SECURITY

11

Leveraging Cyber-Physical System Honeypots to Enhance Threat   209
    Intelligence
Michael Haney

12

Dynamic Repair of Mission-Critical Applications with Runtime Snap-   235
    Ins
J. Peter Brady, Sergey Bratus and Sean Smith

13

Data-Driven Field Mapping of Security Logs for Integrated Monitoring   253
Seungoh Choi, Yesol Kim, Jeong-Han Yun, Byung-Gil Min and HyoungChun Kim

PART VI   INDUSTRIAL CONTROL SYSTEMS SECURITY

14
Modeling and Machine-Checking Bump-in-the-Wire Security for   271
    Industrial Control Systems
Mehdi Sabraoui, Jeffrey Hieb, Adrian Lauf and James Graham

15
Defining Attack Patterns for Industrial Control Systems   289
Raymond Chan, Kam-Pui Chow and Chun-Fai Chan

16
An Incident Response Model for Industrial Control System Foren-   311
    sics Based on Historical Events
Ken Yau, Kam-Pui Chow and Siu-Ming Yiu

Contributing Authors

Prashant Anantharaman is a Ph.D. student in Computer Science at Dartmouth College, Hanover, New Hampshire. His research interests include smart grid and Internet of Things protocol security, and eliminating input-handling vulnerabilities in code.

David Balenson is a Senior Computer Scientist in the Infrastructure Security Group at SRI International in Arlington, Virginia. His research interests include critical infrastructure protection, experimentation and testing, and technology transition.

Robert Borrelli is an Assistant Professor of Nuclear Engineering at the University of Idaho, Idaho Falls, Idaho. His research interests include assessing and safeguarding advanced nuclear fuel cycles, including securing industrial control systems.

J. Peter Brady is a Ph.D. student in Computer Science at Dartmouth College, Hanover, New Hampshire. His research interests include improving systems and data security via the application of formal verification techniques.

Sergey Bratus is a Research Associate Professor of Computer Science at Dartmouth College, Hanover, New Hampshire. His research interests include computing system exploitation and its formalization as a distinct research and engineering discipline.

Manan Buddhadev is a Software Engineer at Microsoft Corporation, Redmond, Washington. His research interests include natural language processing and data privacy.

Timothy Carbino is an Adjunct Assistant Professor of Electrical Engineering at the Air Force Institute of Technology, Wright-Patterson Air Force Base, Ohio. His research interests include digital communications protocols, physical layer device fingerprinting and critical infrastructure protection.

Chun-Fai Chan is a Ph.D. student in Computer Science at the University of Hong Kong, Hong Kong, China. His research interests include penetration testing, digital forensics and Internet of Things security.

Raymond Chan is a Lecturer of Information and Communications Technology at Singapore Institute of Technology, Singapore. His research interests include cyber security, digital forensics and critical infrastructure protection.

Seungoh Choi is a Senior Researcher at the Affiliated Institute of ETRI, Daejeon, South Korea. His research interests include critical infrastructure protection and network security.

Kam-Pui Chow is an Associate Professor of Computer Science at the University of Hong Kong, Hong Kong, China. His research interests include information security, digital forensics, live system forensics and digital surveillance.

Luis Cintron recently completed his M.S. degree in Computer Engineering at the Air Force Institute of Technology, Wright-Patterson Air Force Base, Ohio. His research interests include embedded systems, critical infrastructure protection, distributed computing applications and software engineering.

Siddharth Dongre is an M.S. student in Computing Security at Rochester Institute of Technology, Rochester, New York. His research interests include data privacy and security, and their applications in critical infrastructure protection.

Stephen Dunlap is a Cyber Security Research Engineer at the Air Force Institute of Technology, Wright-Patterson Air Force Base, Ohio. His research interests include embedded systems security, cyber-physical systems security and critical infrastructure protection.

James Graham is a Co-Founder and the Chief Executive Officer of True Secure SCADA, Goshen, Kentucky. His research interests include information security, digital forensics, critical infrastructure protection, high performance computing and intelligent systems.

Scott Graham is an Associate Professor of Computer Engineering at the Air Force Institute of Technology, Wright-Patterson Air Force Base, Ohio. His research interests include vehicle cyber security, critical infrastructure protection and embedded systems security.

Kenneth Hacker recently completed his M.S. degree in Computer Engineering at the Air Force Institute of Technology, Wright-Patterson Air Force Base, Ohio. His research interests include automotive embedded systems, critical infrastructure protection and distributed computing applications.

Michael Haney is an Assistant Professor of Computer Science at the University of Idaho, Idaho Falls, Idaho; and a Cyber Security Researcher at Idaho National Laboratory, Idaho Falls, Idaho. His research interests include critical infrastructure protection and active defenses for industrial control systems.

Jeffrey Hieb is an Assistant Professor of Engineering Fundamentals at the University of Louisville, Louisville, Kentucky. His research interests include information security, honeypots, digital forensics, secure operating systems and engineering education.

Douglas Hodson is an Associate Professor of Computer Engineering at the Air Force Institute of Technology, Wright-Patterson Air Force Base, Ohio. His research interests include computer engineering, software engineering, real-time distributed simulation and quantum communications.

Keith Holt is the Vice President of Northeast Division Rail Systems at HNTB Corporation, Philadelphia, Pennsylvania; and a retired Deputy Chief Engineer at Amtrak, Philadelphia, Pennsylvania. His research interests are in the area of rail systems.

Matthew Jablonski is a Ph.D. student in Information Technology at George Mason University, Fairfax, Virginia. His research interests include attack modeling, secure system design and transportation systems security.

HyoungChun Kim is a Principal Researcher at the Affiliated Institute of ETRI, Daejeon, South Korea. His research interests include cyber security and critical infrastructure protection.

Yesol Kim is a Researcher at the Affiliated Institute of ETRI, Daejeon, South Korea. Her research interests include cyber security and industrial control systems security.

Rahn Lassiter recently completed his M.S. degree in Electrical Engineering at the Air Force Institute of Technology, Wright-Patterson Air Force Base, Ohio. His research interests include digital communications protocols, physical layer device fingerprinting and critical infrastructure protection.

Adrian Lauf is an Assistant Professor of Computer Engineering and Computer Science at the University of Louisville, Louisville, Kentucky. His research interests include the integration of embedded computing, networking and security applications in airborne robotics.

Xiang Liu is an Assistant Professor of Civil and Environmental Engineering at Rutgers University, Piscataway, New Jersey. His research interests include rail systems safety and security.

Michael Locasto is a Principal Computer Scientist at SRI International, New York. His research focuses on understanding software faults and developing fixes.

Trevor MacLean is an M.E. student in Mechanical Engineering at the University of Idaho, Idaho Falls, Idaho. His research interests include industrial control systems security, especially in the nuclear sector.

Michael Millian is a Ph.D. student in Computer Science at Dartmouth College, Hanover, New Hampshire. His research interests include language-theoretic security for network-level and bootloader-level protocols.

Robert Mills is a Professor of Electrical Engineering at the Air Force Institute of Technology, Wright-Patterson Air Force Base, Ohio. His research interests include network security and management, cyber situational awareness and electronic warfare.

Byung-Gil Min is a Senior Researcher at the Affiliated Institute of ETRI, Daejeon, South Korea. His research interests include security monitoring, industrial control systems and critical infrastructure protection.

Sumita Mishra is a Professor of Computing Security at Rochester Institute of Technology, Rochester, New York. Her research interests include critical infrastructure protection, smart grid privacy and resource-constrained network security.

Barry Mullins is a Professor of Computer Engineering at the Air Force Institute of Technology, Wright-Patterson Air Force Base, Ohio. His research interests include cyber-physical systems security, cyber operations, critical infrastructure protection, computer, network and embedded systems security, wired and wireless networking, and code reverse engineering.

Carol Romanowski is a Professor of Computer Science at Rochester Institute of Technology, Rochester, New York. Her research interests include applications of data science and data mining to critical infrastructure protection, cyber security and engineering design.

Mehdi Sabraoui is a Ph.D. student in Computer Science and Engineering at the University of Louisville, Louisville, Kentucky. His research interests include the formal modeling and verification of security in industrial control systems.

Daryl Schmitt recently completed his M.S. degree in Computer Science at the Air Force Institute of Technology, Wright-Patterson Air Force Base, Ohio. His research interests include network security and management, cyber situational awareness and cyber defense.

Sujeet Shenoi is the F.P. Walter Professor of Computer Science and a Professor of Chemical Engineering at the University of Tulsa, Tulsa, Oklahoma. His research interests include critical infrastructure protection, industrial control systems and digital forensics.

Sean Smith is a Professor of Computer Science at Dartmouth College, Hanover, New Hampshire. His research interests include industrial Internet of Things security, trusted computing and human-computer interaction security.

Jason Staggs is an Adjunct Assistant Professor of Computer Science at the University of Tulsa, Tulsa, Oklahoma. His research interests include telecommunications networks, industrial control systems, critical infrastructure protection, security engineering and digital forensics.

Patrick Sweeney is an Assistant Professor of Computer Engineering at the Air Force Institute of Technology, Wright-Patterson Air Force Base, Ohio. His research interests include avionics security, critical infrastructure protection and embedded systems security.

Yongxin Wang is a Ph.D. student in Computer Science at George Mason University, Fairfax, Virginia. His research interests include applications of cyber security and sensor systems to transportation systems.

Zezhou Wang is a Ph.D. student in Civil Engineering at Rutgers University, Piscataway, New Jersey. His research interests include rail systems safety and security.

Duminda Wijesekera is a Professor of Computer Science at George Mason University, Fairfax, Virginia; and a Visiting Research Scientist at the National Institute of Standards and Technology, Gaithersburg, Maryland. His research interests include cyber security, digital forensics and transportation systems.

Ken Yau is a Ph.D. student in Computer Science at the University of Hong Kong, Hong Kong, China. His research interests are in the area of digital forensics, with an emphasis on industrial control system forensics.

Chaitanya Yavvari recently completed his Ph.D. degree in Computer Science at George Mason University, Fairfax, Virginia. His research areas include cyber security, and transportation systems safety and security.

Siu-Ming Yiu is an Associate Professor of Computer Science at the University of Hong Kong, Hong Kong, China. His research interests include security, cryptography, digital forensics and bioinformatics.

Jeong-Han Yun is a Senior Researcher at the Affiliated Institute of ETRI, Daejeon, South Korea. His research interests include network security, cyber security and industrial control systems security.

Preface

The information infrastructure – comprising computers, embedded devices, networks and software systems – is vital to operations in every sector: chemicals, commercial facilities, communications, critical manufacturing, dams, defense industrial base, emergency services, energy, financial services, food and agriculture, government facilities, healthcare and public health, information technology, nuclear reactors, materials and waste, transportation systems, and water and wastewater systems. Global business and industry, governments, indeed society itself, cannot function if major components of the critical information infrastructure are degraded, disabled or destroyed.

This book, *Critical Infrastructure Protection XIII*, is the thirteenth volume in the annual series produced by IFIP Working Group 11.10 on Critical Infrastructure Protection, an active international community of scientists, engineers, practitioners and policy makers dedicated to advancing research, development and implementation efforts related to critical infrastructure protection. The book presents original research results and innovative applications in the area of critical infrastructure protection. Also, it highlights the importance of weaving science, technology and policy in crafting sophisticated, yet practical, solutions that will help secure information, computer and network assets in the various critical infrastructure sectors.

This volume contains sixteen revised and edited papers from the Thirteenth Annual IFIP Working Group 11.10 International Conference on Critical Infrastructure Protection, held at SRI International in Arlington, Virginia, USA on March 11–12, 2019. The papers were refereed by members of IFIP Working Group 11.10 and other internationally-recognized experts in critical infrastructure protection. The post-conference manuscripts submitted by the authors were rewritten to accommodate the suggestions provided by the conference attendees. They were subsequently revised by the editors to produce the final chapters published in this volume.

The chapters are organized into six sections: (i) themes and issues; (ii) infrastructure protection; (iii) vehicle infrastructure security; (iv) telecommunications infrastructure security; (v) cyber-physical systems security; and (vi) industrial control systems security. The coverage of topics showcases the richness and vitality of the discipline, and offers promising avenues for future research in critical infrastructure protection.

This book is the result of the combined efforts of several individuals and organizations. In particular, we thank David Balenson for his tireless work on behalf of IFIP Working Group 11.10. We gratefully acknowledge the Institute for Information Infrastructure Protection (I3P), managed by George Washington University, for its sponsorship of IFIP Working Group 11.10. We also thank the National Science Foundation, U.S. Department of Homeland Security, National Security Agency and SRI International for their support of IFIP Working Group 11.10 and its activities. Finally, we wish to note that all opinions, findings, conclusions and recommendations in the chapters of this book are those of the authors and do not necessarily reflect the views of their employers or funding agencies.

JASON STAGGS AND SUJEET SHENOI

I

THEMES AND ISSUES

Chapter 1

QUANTIFYING THE COSTS OF DATA BREACHES

Siddharth Dongre, Sumita Mishra, Carol Romanowski and Manan Buddhadev

Abstract   Recent years have seen increases in the number of data breaches. This chapter attempts to quantify the impacts of data breaches in terms of the monetary costs incurred by providers and consumers. This is important because data breaches are a major factor when allocating funds for security controls. Case studies involving the Equifax incident in 2017 and the Target incident in 2013 are employed to demonstrate that the cost impacts of data breaches are significant for providers as well as consumers. The cost components in the overall cost function for providers and consumers are presented. Guided by open-source data, the cost components in the provider portion of the cost function are expressed as best-fit functions of time since the data breach. An important point in the cost quantification is that equal weights are assigned to the costs incurred by the provider and the consumers.

Keywords: Data breaches, cost analysis, providers, consumers

1.   Introduction

The average cost of data breaches has increased by 6.4% during the past year, with an average increase of 4.8% in the cost of each stolen record [9]. These statistics point to a general increase in the cost impacts of data breaches. Clearly, it is imperative to understand the many aspects of data breaches in terms of their cost impacts.

A data breach is defined as an incident that leads to the loss or exposure of sensitive information. The focus of this chapter is on specific data breaches that have exposed personal information such as social security numbers, driver's license information, dates of birth, credit card numbers, telephone numbers and residential addresses, and/or other information that malicious entities could use to perpetrate activities such as identity theft and credit card fraud.

© IFIP International Federation for Information Processing 2019
Published by Springer Nature Switzerland AG 2019
J. Staggs and S. Shenoi (Eds.): Critical Infrastructure Protection XIII, IFIP AICT 570, pp. 3–16, 2019.
https://doi.org/10.1007/978-3-030-34647-8_1

The root causes of data breaches vary from incident to incident. Most data breaches occur due to vulnerabilities in web applications hosted by providers or through cyber-espionage activities [9]. Since the majority of breaches have these two vectors, their costs appear to be more significant to providers than consumers.

Acquisiti et al. [1] have analyzed the impact of privacy breaches on the market value of providers. Their research demonstrates that a data breach has a statistically-significant negative impact on the market value of a company on the day that the breach is announced.

Romanosky [21] has analyzed the causes and costs of cyber incidents in an attempt to understand how companies should improve their security postures in order to reduce the risk of data breaches. He states that public concerns regarding data breaches are excessive compared with the financial impacts on companies.

Most research efforts, including the work of Acquisiti et al. [1] and Romanosky [21], analyze the cost impacts of data breaches on providers. Limited research has focused on the cost impacts on consumers. In contrast, the research described in this chapter considers the cost impacts from the perspectives of providers and consumers. Both providers and consumers have to pay to mitigate the negative effects of data breaches. For example, the Equifax data breach of 2017 cost the company approximately $439 million [18], but numerous Equifax consumers also paid a price by becoming victims of identity theft [16] that exposed them to financial losses.

This chapter presents a mathematical formulation that expresses the cost impacts of data breaches. The costs incurred by the provider and consumers have different components, all of which vary with time. Therefore, a cost function for a provider and consumers is developed, which incorporates multiple cost components and weights for the components that vary with time. In the case of providers, the component weights are derived from real data pertaining to the Equifax data breach of 2017 and the Target data breach of 2013. The two case studies were selected because they had significant, direct impacts on providers and consumers, and open-source data related to the breaches and their impacts was available.

2.   Cost Function

The cost impacts of a data breach can be broadly expressed as a function of time $C(T)$. Specifically, this cost function is the sum of the costs incurred by the provider and by consumers, $C_p(T)$ and $C_c(T)$, respectively, which are also functions of time. The time T denotes the number of months elapsed since the breach was discovered. Unique weights $W_p \in [0, 1]$ and $W_c \in [0, 1]$ are assigned to the costs incurred by the provider and by consumers, respectively, based on the relative impacts of the two cost perspectives. Thus, the costs incurred due to a data breach at time T months after the breach is given by:

$$C(T) = W_p C_p(T) + W_c C_c(T) \tag{1}$$

Each term in Equation (1) is expressed as the sum of the individual cost components for the provider and consumers, $C_{pi}(T)$ and $C_{cj}(T)$, where $1 \leq i \leq N$ and $1 \leq j \leq M$, and N and M are the numbers of cost components incorporated for the provider and consumers, respectively.

Thus, the costs incurred by the provider and by consumers are given by:

$$C_p(T) = \sum_{i=1}^{N} C_{pi}(T) \tag{2}$$

$$C_c(T) = \sum_{j=1}^{M} C_{cj}(T) \tag{3}$$

Each term $C_{pi}(T)$ and $C_{cj}(T)$ can be further expressed as the sum of the costs incurred each month, which varies with time $t \in [0, T]$ expressed in months:

$$C_{pi}(T) = \sum_{t=0}^{T} C_{pi}(t) \tag{4}$$

$$C_{cj}(T) = \sum_{t=0}^{T} C_{cj}(t) \tag{5}$$

Equations (1) through (5) can be combined to yield the following overall cost function for the provider and consumers:

$$C(T) = W_p \sum_{i=1}^{N} \sum_{t=0}^{T} C_{pi}(t) + W_c \sum_{j=1}^{M} \sum_{t=0}^{T} C_{cj}(t) \tag{6}$$

where the weights are based on well-defined cost component values C_{pi} and C_{cj} for the provider and consumers, respectively. These cost component values vary on a case by case basis. In this work, the cost component values are assigned based on case studies involving the 2017 Equifax and 2013 Target data breaches.

3.   2017 Equifax Data Breach

Equifax is one of the leading credit reporting agencies along with TransUnion and Experian. It provides important services that determine the creditworthiness of consumers based on their credit histories. The information provided by Equifax is used by lenders to decide whether or not to issue credit lines to consumers and to determine the appropriate credit limits.

In July 2017, Equifax became the victim of one of the largest data breaches in history [7]. The breach was traced to a vulnerability in Equifax's web application systems, which were developed using the Apache Struts 2 framework [13].

In March 2017, a few months before the breach, Apache announced a vulnerability in its technology. However, many users, including Equifax, did not apply the patch. The vulnerability enabled an unknown entity to remotely access Equifax's web application servers and run malicious programs, eventually extracting sensitive data belonging to more than 145 million consumers. Credit card numbers of more than 209,000 consumers were compromised. Private information such as social security numbers, driver's license numbers and dates of birth were also exposed.

Equifax reportedly handled the data breach in an irresponsible manner. It did not notify the affected consumers until two months after the breach was discovered. Equifax executives sold nearly $2 million in stock before the breach was disclosed; however, a special company committee cleared the executives upon finding that they did not know about the breach when they made the transactions [4].

Equifax stock lost billions of dollars within a few months of the announcement of the breach, demonstrating the major impacts that data breaches can have on providers. However, numerous innocent consumers became victims of identity theft and credit card fraud as a result of the breach. Indeed, the Equifax breach is a lesson about the significant impacts that data breaches can have on consumers.

3.1   Components Affecting Data Breach Costs

An analysis of corporate filings and news reports in the aftermath of the Equifax data breach identified several components that may affect the costs incurred by providers. Data from Equifax quarterly reports was used to derive the cost function for each component. The cost function formulas were obtained by applying machine learning algorithms to the available data.

Earnings Loss from Customer Dissatisfaction. Equifax reported that its earnings were affected by customer dissatisfaction – its net income fell 27% to $96.3 million in the third quarter of 2017 [2]. It is safe to assume that the loss in earnings due to customer dissatisfaction is the highest immediately after a breach and decreases gradually over time.

The four data points in Figure 1 show Equifax's net income (earnings loss) figures for four consecutive quarters after the breach. Based on the variation of net income (earnings loss) C_{p1} in millions of dollars over time t in months, the following best-fit function was obtained to express the costs due to customer dissatisfaction as a function of time:

$$C_{p1}(t) = 165.39 - 33t + 3.42t^2 \tag{7}$$

where the parameters $a = 165.39$, $b = -33$ and $c = 3.42$ are specific to the provider, in this case, Equifax.

Market Capitalization Loss from Investor Nervousness. After the breach was publicly announced, Equifax stock value fell sharply because nervous shareholders sold their holdings. Equifax's market capitalization

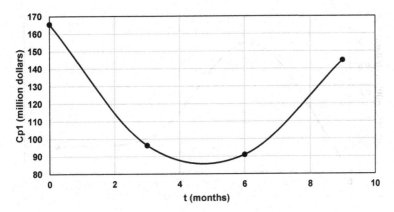

Figure 1. Variation in Equifax's costs (earnings loss) from customer dissatisfaction.

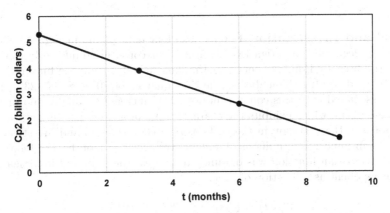

Figure 2. Variation in Equifax's market capitalization loss.

dropped by \$5.3 billion [19]. However, after the initial slump, the stock value gradually increased over the next three quarters.

The four data points in Figure 2 show Equifax's market capitalization losses from four consecutive quarterly reports after the breach. The costs associated with this component decrease linearly with time. Based on the variation in the market capitalization loss C_{p2} in billions of dollars over time t in months, the following best-fit function was obtained to express the costs due to investor nervousness as a function of time:

$$C_{p2}(t) = 5.3 - 0.44t \tag{8}$$

where the parameters $c = 5.3$ and $m = -0.44$ are specific to Equifax.

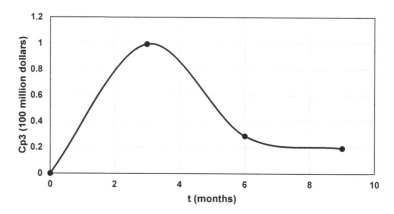

Figure 3. Variation in Equifax's legal and investigation fees.

Legal and Investigation F es. The four data points in Figure 3 show Equifax's legal and investiga' on fees from four consecutive quarterly reports after the breach. Equifax spent $99.4 million in fees during the final quarter of 2017 and $28.9 milli n during the first quarter of 2018 [8, 17, 23]. The costs associated with this component start low, increase gradually and finally decrease again, which exhibits the characteristics of a Gaussian curve.

Based on the variation in the costs associated with legal and investigation fees C_{p3} in hundreds of millions of dollars over time t in months, the following best-fit Gaussian function was obtained to express the legal and investigation fees component as a function of time:

$$C_{p3}(t) = 1.38 \times e^{-(t-3.93)^2/2(1.17)^2} \tag{9}$$

where the parameters $a = 1.38$, $b = -3.93$ and $c = 1.17$ are specific to Equifax.

Customer Services. The four data points in Figure 4 show Equifax's customer services costs from four consecutive quarterly reports after the breach. Equifax paid approximately $64.4 million for customer support services during the final quarter of 2017 and the payments went down to $4.1 million during the first quarter of 2018 [23]. This cost component decreases gradually with time in a manner similar to earnings loss due to customer dissatisfaction. Based on the variation in the costs associated with customer services C_{p4} in millions of dollars over time t in months, the following best-fit function was obtained to express the customer services cost component as a function of time:

$$C_{p4}(t) = -0.14 + \frac{64.54}{2^{t/0.76}} \tag{10}$$

where the parameters $a = -0.14$, $b = 64.54$ and $c = 0.76$ are specific to Equifax.

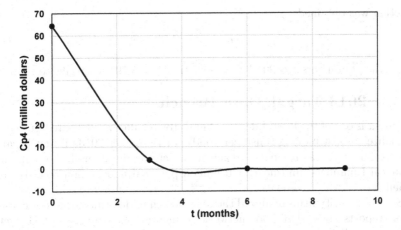

Figure 4. Variation in Equifax's customer services costs.

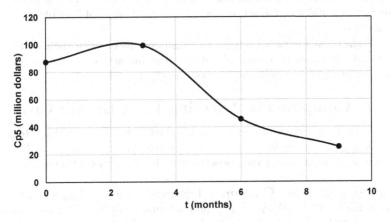

Figure 5. Variation in Equifax's information technology security upgrade costs.

Information Technology Security Upgrades. The four data points in Figure 5 show Equifax's information technology security upgrade costs from four consecutive quarterly reports after the breach. Immediately after the breach was announced, Equifax incurred a one-time charge of $87.5 million, which was presumably spent on incident response and disaster recovery [2]. During the last quarter of 2017, a portion of the $99.4 million spent on fees was due to information technology security upgrades; the upgrade costs dropped to $45.7 million during the first quarter of 2018 [23]. This cost component starts high immediately after the data breach and decreases gradually.

Based on the variation in information technology security upgrade costs C_{p5} in millions of dollars over time t in months, the following best-fit Gaussian function was obtained:

$$C_{p5}(t) = 99.65 \times e^{-(t-1.79)^2/2(3.79)^2} \tag{11}$$

where the parameters $a = 99.65$, $b = -1.79$ and $c = 3.79$ are specific to Equifax.

4.   2013 Target Data Breach

Target is one of the largest departmental store chains in the United States. It specializes in fast-moving consumer goods. In December 2013, Target became the victim of a massive data breach in which nearly 40 million credit and debit card numbers, and nearly 70 million personal information records were stolen [22].

Several security firms analyzed the data breach to determine the root causes. Their reports state that poor network segmentation, a mistake on Target's part and malicious actions by an adversary contributed to the massive data breach. The adversary reportedly installed BlackPOS malware on point-of-sale terminals to collect sensitive user information, especially credit and debit card numbers. The stolen information was discovered being sold on black market websites [11].

The data breach exposed numerous consumers to identity theft and credit card fraud. It is another example of how the impacts of a data breach on consumers are just as significant as those on the provider.

4.1   Components Affecting Data Breach Costs

Since the Target data breach was announced, several reports have been released that estimate the losses incurred by the company. This section discusses the components that affect the costs incurred by Target as a provider.

Earnings Loss from Customer Dissatisfaction. Target's profits reportedly fell by \$440 million during the final quarter of 2013, i.e., immediately after the data breach [15]. In the final quarter of 2014, Target reported a net loss of \$2.6 billion during the one year after the breach [20]. It can be assumed that this cost component (earnings loss) reached its maximum value in the first quarter after the data breach and decreased sharply over the course of a year.

The four data points in Figure 6 show Target's net income (earnings loss) figures for four consecutive quarters after the breach. Based on the variation of net income (earnings loss) C_{p1} in billions of dollars over time t in months, the following best-fit Gaussian curve was obtained to express the cost due to customer dissatisfaction as a function of time:

$$C_{p1}(t) = 0.91 \times e^{-(t-7.22)^2/2(3.81)^2} \tag{12}$$

where the parameters $a = 0.91$, $b = -7.22$ and $c = 3.81$ are specific to Target.

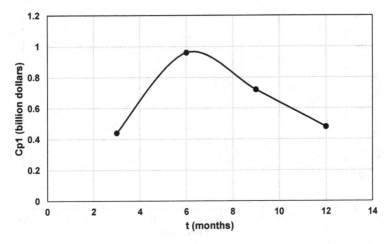

Figure 6. Variation in Target's costs (earnings loss) from customer dissatisfaction.

Legal Fees and Lawsuit Settlements. Target reportedly made settlements totaling more than $153.9 million through May 2017, almost four years after the breach. The major costs incurred by Target during this period were [14]:

- $10 million to settle a class action lawsuit by consumers in March 2015.

- $19 million to MasterCard in April 2015.

- $67 million to Visa in August 2015.

- $39.4 million to banks and credit unions in December 2015.

- $18.5 million to settle actions by 47 state governments in May 2017.

Figure 7 shows the variation in Target's lawsuit settlement costs over a two-year period starting eighteen months after the breach. It is a classic example of how the costs incurred by a provider due to legal actions arising from a data breach are considerable over a long period of time. However, due to the unpredictable nature of legal settlements, it is difficult to express the associated costs as a function of time. The only statement that can be made is that the legal costs are significant over a long period of time.

Other Expenses. Target's 2016 annual financial report estimated that its total costs due to the data breach were $292 million. The annual breakdowns were $17 million in 2013, $145 million in 2014 and $39 million in 2015; information about the 2016 costs was not provided [14]. These figures cover the expenses incurred for incident response and forensics, disaster recovery and information security upgrades.

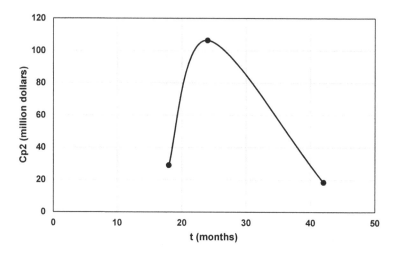

Figure 7.   Variation in Target's lawsuit settlement costs over four years.

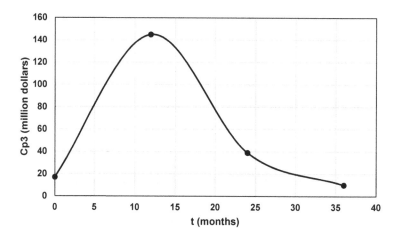

Figure 8.   Variation in Target's other costs over three years.

Figure 8 shows the variation in Target's other costs (for incident response and forensics, disaster recovery and information security upgrades) over a three-year period following the data breach. Based on the variation in the other costs C_{p3} in millions of dollars over time t in months, the following best-fit Gaussian function was obtained to express the cost component as a function of time:

$$C_{p3}(t) = 148.57 \times e^{-(t-13.44)^2/2(6.47)^2} \tag{13}$$

where the parameters $a = 148.57$, $b = -13.44$ and $c = 6.47$ are specific to Target.

5.   Cost Impacts on Consumers

Data breaches expose sensitive consumer information such as social security numbers, driver's license information, dates of birth, credit card numbers, telephone numbers and residential addresses. Consumer information of this nature can be exploited to perpetrate identity theft and other fraudulent activities that can have devastating financial impacts on consumers.

It is posited that consumers as a whole incur costs that are comparable to those incurred by the provider as a result of data breaches. Therefore, the weights assigned to the costs incurred by the provider and consumers in Equation (6) are equal, i.e., $W_p = W_c = 0.5$. Thus, the overall cost function is given by:

$$C(T) = 0.5 \sum_{i=1}^{N} \sum_{t=0}^{T} C_{pi}(t) + 0.5 \sum_{j=1}^{M} \sum_{t=0}^{T} C_{cj}(t) \tag{14}$$

The following sections discuss four components of the cost function for consumers.

5.1   Identity Theft and Credit Card Fraud Costs

Many consumers whose personal data has been exposed by a breach become unwitting victims of identity theft and credit card fraud. In 2016, 15.4 million consumers were victims of identity theft or fraud and they collectively lost more than \$16.2 billion. These figures went up in 2017 with 16.7 million victims losing \$16.8 billion in total. On average, every consumer who becomes a victim of identity theft or fraud loses more than \$1,000 a year [10]. The costs include notary fees and fax, copying, postage, mileage and calling charges incurred to address identity theft or fraud. The costs also include loss of income as a result of taking time off from work to handle the problems.

5.2   Protection and Monitoring Costs

The exposure of personal information puts consumers at risk of becoming targets of identity theft and credit card fraud. Consumers are urged to enroll in credit monitoring and identity protection services, which cost \$120 to \$300 annually [3].

5.3   Legal Fees

Victims of data breaches have the right to file lawsuits against providers that may be responsible for the breaches. Attorney expenses vary, but are they still relatively high [5]. Consumers who live in small towns and rural areas may be charged \$100 to \$200 per hour by experienced attorneys. In metropolitan areas, attorney fees are \$200 to \$400 per hour. Attorney fees for complicated data breach cases that require technical expertise are even higher.

5.4   Other Costs

Consumers who are victims of data breaches are highly susceptible to identity theft and credit card fraud. Most victims are unaware that fraudulent activities are being perpetrated until it is too late; there are cases where even minors have become victims of identity theft or fraud [6].

Identity theft victims should consider freezing their credit, which prohibits credit reporting companies from disclosing their credit histories. This also prevents malicious entities from opening fake credit card accounts in their names. Credit freeze requests can cost consumers \$2 to \$10 per credit reporting agency [24]; several states now ensure that credit freeze requests are free [12].

Consumers who become victims of identity theft face the following severe consequences:

- Difficulty securing credit cards and loans.

- Difficulty securing home mortgages and home rentals.

- High credit card interest rates.

- Difficulty securing jobs.

- Psychological impacts such as distress and anxiety.

6.   Conclusions

This research is the first attempt to quantify the costs of data breaches for providers and consumers. This is important because data breaches are a major factor when allocating funds for security controls. The cost components in the overall cost function for the provider and consumers have been identified. Guided by open-source data, the cost components in the provider portion of the cost function have been expressed as best-fit functions of time elapsed since the data breach. An important point in the cost quantification is that equal weights are assigned to the costs incurred by the provider and the consumers.

Future research will attempt to formulate cost components in the consumer cost function as functions of time. This effort will be theoretical as opposed to empirical because of the lack of data pertaining to consumer costs over time.

References

[1] A. Acquisti, A. Friedman and R. Telang, Is there a cost to privacy breaches? An event study, *Proceedings of the Twenty-Seventh International Conference on Information Systems*, article no. 94, 2006.

[2] Agence France-Presse, Massive data breach has cost Equifax nearly $90 million, November 11, 2017.

[3] Consumer Reports, Don't get taken guarding your ID. Do-it-yourself safeguards are just as effective as paid services, September 8, 2014.

[4] Federal Trade Commission, The Equifax Data Breach, Washington, DC (`www.ftc.gov/equifax-data-breach`), 2018.

[5] D. Goguen, How, and How Much, Do Lawyers Charge? Lawyers.com (`www.lawyers.com/legal-info/research/how-and-how-much-do-lawyers-charge.html`), 2019.

[6] K. Grant, Identity theft isn't just an adult problem. Kids are victims, too, *CNBC*, April 24, 2018.

[7] S. Gressin, The Equifax Data Breach: What to Do, Federal Trade Commission, Washington, DC (`www.consumer.ftc.gov/blog/2017/09/equifax-data-breach-what-do`), September 8, 2017.

[8] M. Heller, Equifax hack could cost well over $600M, *CFO Magazine*, March 5, 2018.

[9] IBM Security and Ponemon Institute, 2018 Cost of a Data Breach Study: Global Overview, Cambridge, Massachusetts and North Traverse City, Michigan (`www.ibm.com/security/data-breach`), 2018.

[10] Javelin, Identity fraud hits all time high with 16.7 million U.S. victims in 2017, according to new Javelin Strategy and Research study, Press Release, San Francisco, California (`www.javelinstrategy.com/press-release/identity-fraud-hits-all-time-high-167-million-us-victims-2017-according-new-javelin`), February 6, 2018.

[11] B. Krebs, Who's selling credit cards from Target? *Krebs on Security* (`www.krebsonsecurity.com/2013/12/whos-selling-credit-cards-from-target`), December 24, 2013.

[12] K. Lobosco, Congress just made credit freezes free, *CNN*, May 22, 2018.

[13] J. Luszcz, Apache Struts 2: How technical and development gaps caused the Equifax Breach, *Network Security*, vol. 2018(1), pp. 5–8, 2018.

[14] V. Lynch, Cost of 2013 Target data breach nears $300 million, *Hashed Out* (`www.thesslstore.com/blog/2013-target-data-breach-settled`), May 26, 2017.

[15] Marketwatch, Target's profits down $440M after data breach, *New York Post*, February 26, 2014.

[16] K. McCoy, Equifax data breach: What's changed since last year's huge hack of personal information? *USA Today*, September 7, 2018.

[17] J. McCrank and J. Finkle, Equifax breach could be most costly in corporate history, *Reuters*, March 2, 2018.

[18] PYMNTS, Equifax breach to cost total of $439M (`www.pymnts.com/news/security-and-risk/2018/equifax-cost-275m`), March 5, 2018.

[19] V. Reklaitis, Equifax's stock has fallen 31% since breach disclosure, erasing $5 billion in market cap, *MarketWatch*, September 14, 2017.

[20] J. Roman, Target breach costs: $162 million. Response expenses continue to grow following 2013 incident, *BankInfoSecurity* (`www.bankinfo security.com/target-breach-costs-162-million-a-7951`), February 25 2015.

[21] S. Romanosky, Examining the costs and causes of cyber incidents, *Journal of Cybersecurity*, vol. 2(2), pp. 121–135, 2016.

[22] X. Shu, K. Tian, A. Ciambrone and D. Yao, Breaking the Target: An Analysis of the Target Data Breach and Lessons Learned, arXiv:1701.04940 (`arxiv.org/abs/1701.04940`), 2017.

[23] Titanadmin, The cost of the Equifax data breach? $242 million and rising, SpamTitan, Tampa, Florida (`www.spamtitan.com/blog/cost-of-the-equifax-data-breach-242-million-rising`), April 27, 2018.

[24] F. Williams, How credit freezes work and what they cost, Credit-Cards.com, Austin, Texas (`www.creditcards.com/credit-card-news/credit-report-freeze-1282.php`), September 13, 2017.

II

INFRASTRUCTURE PROTECTION

Chapter 2

A COMPARATIVE ANALYSIS APPROACH FOR DERIVING FAILURE SCENARIOS IN THE NATURAL GAS DISTRIBUTION INFRASTRUCTURE

Michael Locasto and David Balenson

Abstract   An important question facing critical infrastructure owners and operators is how their assets could be made to fail by the various threat actors. Designing, enumerating and analyzing failure scenarios helps explore the assumptions made on the operational side, the value of current mitigations and the need for certain types of protection mechanisms. This chapter describes the formulation of 55 failure scenarios in the natural gas distribution infrastructure. These failure scenarios highlight a range of potential threats across the natural gas infrastructure, from transmission to distribution and home metering. The chapter also describes a multi-pronged approach used to develop failure scenarios for the gas sector and compares them against the scenarios developed for the electric sector. The focus is on the concepts underlying the failure scenarios and their use, the threat model they encompass, and the assumptions, lessons learned and caveats underpinning their creation.

Keywords: Natural gas distribution infrastructure, failure scenarios, cyber security

1.   Introduction

Failure scenarios are an important consideration when analyzing the cyber security postures of critical information infrastructure assets. This chapter describes a process for developing cyber security failure scenarios in the natural gas distribution network. The process took shape in a project performed with the Gas Technology Institute/Operations Technology Development (GTI/OTD) Cybersecurity Collaborative. During the project planning and prioritization efforts, it was determined that the specification of failure scenarios would help understand the cyber security implications in the natural gas distribution landscape. The effort was kicked off by exploring the

© IFIP International Federation for Information Processing 2019
Published by Springer Nature Switzerland AG 2019
J. Staggs and S. Shenoi (Eds.): Critical Infrastructure Protection XIII, IFIP AICT 570, pp. 19–50, 2019.
https://doi.org/10.1007/978-3-030-34647-8_2

use and adaptation of the National Electric Sector Cybersecurity Organization Resource (NESCOR) Electric Sector Failure Scenarios and Impact Analysis (Version 3.0) [11] to the natural gas distribution environment.

This chapter reviews the process for designing and generating failure scenarios – a process that necessarily begins with acquiring a thorough understanding of the equipment, protocols and facilities used in the natural gas distribution network. It describes the failure scenarios and their categories, the threat model they encompass and the assumptions, lessons learned and caveats underpinning their creation.

In addition to a significant domain familiarization process, the effort involved adapting existing frameworks for describing failure modes and potential compromises from another critical infrastructure sector (i.e., electric power). The NESCOR failure scenarios developed for the electric sector [11] were employed as a template. However, the translation between the two sectors was not straightforward and certain categories of infrastructure did not map at all. Attempting to translate the electric sector failure scenarios to the natural gas infrastructure provided valuable insights about the assumptions and differences between the two sectors. In large part, the gas sector failure scenarios are not restatements of the NESCOR scenarios. Even the closely related automated meter reading category, has some notable differences. Indeed, it was more natural and productive to develop specialized scenarios that tightly reflect natural gas sector equipment, protocols and facilities.

In addition to specifying a procedure for generating interesting and useful scenarios, this chapter provides a differential comparison between the natural gas and electricity domains with the goal of providing a roadmap for similar efforts in other domains. The advantage of differential conceptualization is the efficient enumeration of failure scenarios in another domain because the comparison highlights the parts of the process that can be generalized and the parts that require time and investment in learning about the target domain. This outcome should reduce the amount of effort required to conduct future analyses because one of the least mechanical and most difficult tasks is to acquire adequate domain expertise to define realistic failure scenarios and identify meaningful impacts. Furthermore, the explicit observations help identify surprising differences and considerations in two closely-related sectors, helping calibrate and temper expectations about how certain concepts, settings, vulnerabilities and impacts translate between sectors.

2.   Failure Scenarios

According to the NESCOR document [11]:

> *"A cyber security failure scenario is a realistic event in which the failure to maintain confidentiality, integrity and/or availability of sector cyber assets creates a negative impact on the generation, transmission and/or delivery of power."*

This definition requires one minor edit – replacing power with natural gas – to apply to the natural gas distribution network.

Table 1. Example failure scenarios.

Scenario	Description	Vulnerabilities	Impact
AMR.18	Competitor observes gas consumption at a store or factory	Insecure cleartext protocols permit any party to observe usage data	Competitive advantage and insight into a direct competitor
O.3	Attacker gains access to odorizer controller and modifies setpoints to increase the amount of odorant injected, resulting in over-odorization of the gas	Network and software compromise, supply chain attack, or infected maintenance or vendor laptop used to manipulate set-points and possibly disable or modify sensor readings or alarms	Increase in service calls as customers report suspected leaks

A scenario is actually not a single event; it is a complex mixture of conditions and events. Scenarios are not limited to direct failures induced by malicious cyber actors. Indeed, scenarios include malicious and non-malicious events [11]:

- Failures due to equipment functionality compromises.

- Failures due to data integrity attacks.

- Communications failures.

- Human error.

- Interference with the equipment lifecycle.

- Natural disasters that impact the cyber security posture.

Failure scenarios are not equivalent to single vulnerabilities or specific software errors that should have been or can be remedied by a simple checklist or adherence to best practices. By considering the mixture of causes listed above, failure scenarios can provide a rich ground for analyses and a variety of other uses that are discussed later. Failure scenarios offer a structured approach for representing the potential impacts of different categories of threat actors and provide an analysis tool for evaluating the utility and sufficiency of existing mitigations.

Table 1 highlights two failure scenarios to provide readers with an idea about the structure of failure scenarios.

As discussed later, the NESCOR report gathers scenarios into similar themes called categories that map to electric power system functions such as demand-response. The natural gas distribution network scenarios are also gathered into categories, but the categories are more closely mapped to facilities and components of infrastructure rather than functions.

3.   Benefits of Failure Scenarios

Failure scenarios can be used in a number of ways, including for risk assessment, planning, procurement, training, tabletop exercises and security testing. While the value proposition for employing failure scenarios as an analytical tool for the natural gas distribution infrastructure encompasses all these uses, the scenario development effort focused on three principal benefits:

- **Assess Sufficiency of Current Safety and Security Measures:** Natural gas distribution companies are aware of critical infrastructure threats. In some cases, companies have electric and gas portions of the business, and cyber security considerations are an active area of planning, protection and analysis. However, a common consideration is whether the current mitigations are sufficient. To help assess whether vendor or internal tools and procedures are adequate, companies need an analytical methodology that directs their attention to relevant threats, vulnerabilities and impacts.

- **Assess Risk/Reward of Incorporating Intelligent Electronic Devices:** The natural gas industry is at an inflection point where automation is set to increase. Companies are making decisions about which portions of their infrastructure have priority during the normal equipment replacement cycle. The industry is also undergoing a generational shift, where experienced engineers are retiring or are on the cusp of retirement. One approach to compensating for this reduction is by introducing automation that is managed by junior engineers.

- **Nurture Ties between IT and OT Personnel:** It is important for information technology (IT) and operational technology (OT) personnel to work together on cyber security implementation and preparedness. The value of such an engagement has been demonstrated by partnerships such as the Linking the Oil and Gas Industry to Improve Cybersecurity (LOGIIC) Consortium [3, 25] and the Trustworthy Cyber Infrastructure for the Power Grid (TCIPG) and Cyber Resilient Energy Delivery (CREDC) Consortia [4, 24] that involve academia, government and industry. Trust cannot be built overnight. A key benefit of working with natural gas utilities to specify failure scenarios was that it provided a mechanism for collaboration, interaction and mutual understanding between engineers and cyber security experts. The failure scenarios were also integrated in a tabletop exercise and used to prioritize cyber security planning activities within the GTI/OTD Cybersecurity Collaborative.

3.1   Cyber Security Analysis

Critical infrastructure, industrial control systems and operational technology present unique challenges for cyber security techniques and practice. These specialized domains have legal and regulatory requirements and performance constraints that affect the application of cyber security. Straightforward applications of existing information technology security mechanisms do not always work. Sometimes it requires a minor porting effort; sometimes, although the technology may function out-of-the-box, it does not offer the same benefits as in an information technology environment; at other times, it requires a completely new method or major redesign; and yet other times, it is completely unworkable due to the unique demands of the operational environment. Nevertheless, these complex cyber-physical systems likely contain unintended, latent errors in their software, hardware and procedures, and therefore require monitoring and protection techniques that are suited to the domain. Some of the potential faults, flaws and vulnerabilities exist because of specific combinations of software and equipment, or might only be exercised under very special conditions.

Thus, a critical question for infrastructure owners and operators is how their assets could be made to fail by a variety of threat actors exercising unanalyzed – indeed previously non-existent – system states that result from injecting computerized monitoring and control into physical processes. Asset owners need to comprehend the nature of the threats to the operational technology environment and how and where cyber security protection, detection and control mechanisms should be deployed. Understanding how a system will break or could be made to break are difficult tasks during the hard work of conceiving how the system should properly operate in the first place [8, 9].

Such a conceptualization activity is even harder when applied to systems of systems or where there may be cascading effects due to interdependencies within and across the energy or other critical infrastructures – as there are between natural gas and electric power. To wit, natural gas is used to generate electricity and bulk electric power is used to run some compressor stations that move natural gas. Likewise, if a cyber attack on a communications infrastructure can cause or exacerbate an impact on electricity, gas or both, then because of these interconnections, an event at one location could cascade to multiple events at different locations. The emergent effects that loss of power and storm damage have on the cellular communications infrastructure were evident after Hurricane Sandy: while the cellular infrastructure was mostly undamaged, communications ramped up dramatically due to an increase in calls (because the Internet and other powered infrastructure were out or damaged) and cell tower energy reserves were expended much faster than anticipated. The Liberty Eclipse Exercise [13] has investigated the cyber security concerns surrounding this type of interdependency between natural gas and electric power.

3.2   Understanding Mitigations

Natural gas utilities are looking for procedures that can help avoid significant disruptions of gas flow and destruction of property and infrastructure. Utilities can use product assessments to understand the value of existing mitigations. This process entails iterating through a series of commodity point solutions from a variety of vendors to assess the promised coverage.

A complementary approach for exploring the parameters related to the value of mitigations and utility preparedness is to specify failure modes of concern and work backward to the types of threats that might induce the failures. In short, a framework that categorizes failures is a useful assessment tool for determining the utility and appropriateness of cyber security tools and mechanisms. Designing, enumerating and analyzing failure scenarios can help explore the assumptions made on the operational side, the value of current mitigations and the need for certain types of protection mechanisms. Failure scenarios provide a combination of flexibility, abstraction (e.g., a baseline for further discussion and exploration) and specificity that compare well with analysis techniques that rely on models derived from vulnerability enumeration (e.g., attack trees) and attacker tactics.

4.   Caveats and Assumptions

This work has multiple audiences: researchers, practitioners, engineers and regulators. As such, it is important to clearly state the caveats and assumptions that underlie the approach. To the operational technology community, the scenarios are a form of future-gazing and a suspension of disbelief ("our system doesn't work like that" or "our system can't be compromised in that way") might be necessary. It is worth noting that there is a first time for everything and so-called "system failures" arise exactly because a number of seemingly unrelated and unlikely events occur together.

The capabilities and components considered in this work are taken from a representative, notional architecture of the natural gas distribution network. They are not intended to capture or imply existing weaknesses in company infrastructures nor do they directly account for multiple levels of mitigations that may be in place.

The scenarios discussed here do not constitute implied claims or guarantees of successful exploitation nor do they imply that utilities have unmitigated vulnerabilities, are out of compliance with regulations or could be compromised. Some failure scenarios may require significant resources from a potential adversary whereas others may involve an insider taking advantage of an existing crisis or low probability event.

As such, this work does not seek to provide a cookbook for attackers nor is it intended to be a checklist for security defenses. Also, the enumeration of scenarios is not expected to be complete. Furthermore, the goal is not to find holes that utilities have not considered or to claim that specific mitigations in place would not work, but rather to explore what might happen if some of the mitigations were to fail.

Mitigations include redundant communications, private networks, multiple layers of access control and clear separation of duties (e.g., mostly operate locally, not from the central operations center). Mitigations, however, may fail for any number of reasons: software bugs, expired keys, social engineering, human laziness and complacency, unusable technology or a combination of these shortcomings. Vigilance about the hygiene of operational facilities (e.g., no BYOD policy, vetted upgrades and no removable media) is difficult to maintain at a high level.

Finally, a failure mode need not result in catastrophic damage to an installation, environmental impact or loss of life. It may also relate to compromises of the integrity, confidentiality and availability of information/operational technology assets, as well as the loss of business information and company reputation.

5.   NESCOR Failure Scenarios Report

The most relevant starting point in the effort to develop a representative set of failure scenarios in the natural gas distribution network was the NESCOR document [11], which was produced by a broad collaboration between the Electric Power Research Institute, industry experts, asset owners and academia. The NESCOR document has several contributions that make it an attractive template for adaptation. It clearly identifies the major categories of operations across the electric power grid, specifies a comprehensive threat model and lists impacts and potential mitigations.

Version 3 of the NESCOR report from December 2015 contains 129 scenarios across eight categories:

- **Advanced Metering Infrastructure (AMI):** 32 scenarios.

- **Distributed Energy Resources (DER):** 26 scenarios.

- **Wide-Area Monitoring, Protection and Control (WAMPAC):** 12 scenarios.

- **Electric Transportation (ET):** 16 scenarios.

- **Demand-Response (DR):** 7 scenarios.

- **Distribution Grid Management (DGM):** 16 scenarios.

- **Generation:** 16 scenarios.

- **Generic:** 4 scenarios.

The template has four components for each failure scenario: (i) scenario description; (ii) relevant vulnerabilities; (iii) impact; and (iv) potential mitigations. The NESCOR report lists a threat model that covers cyber threats ranging from intentional and malicious actions to accidental failures. The following threats identified in the report apply equally well to the natural gas distribution infrastructure:

- Adversaries with intent, driven by money, politics, religion, activist causes, recreation, recognition or malevolence.

- Adversary activity may include spying or have direct operational impact.

- Insiders or outsiders, groups or individuals.

- Failures of people, processes and technology, including human error.

- Loss of resources, in particular, key employees and the communications infrastructure.

- Accidents.

- Natural hazards as they impact cyber security (e.g., flooding, foundations, pipelines above and below grade, and wind/blowing gas).

The NESCOR document also lists a number of specific impacts for the failure scenarios that apply to the natural gas distribution infrastructure. These include loss of power, equipment damage, human casualties, revenue loss, customer privacy violations and loss of public confidence.

6.   Approach

Significant work is required to derive failure scenarios in different critical infrastructure verticals. During the effort, it was discovered that the adaptation was not necessarily sped up by attempting faithful replication of existing failure scenario specifications. Instead, a comparative analysis was conducted to understand and then deconstruct the essential elements of scenarios. When appropriate, certain scenarios that did not easily translate or provide adequate fidelity were discarded. Ultimately, the set of failure scenarios must be relevant (i.e., speak to the threats that concern gas distribution utilities) and realistic (i.e., not be too generic). The bottom line is that the mapping is neither easy nor straightforward. Effort is needed to identify the real risks with respect to the actual infrastructure – some risks are out of scope, others are irrelevant and some are of concern only in the far future.

The goal was not to dramatically expand the number of scenarios by tweaking minor properties, such as constructing two variants of the same scenario by placing the attacker at different locations, or having an attacker who is a trusted insider in one variant and an external attacker who steals legitimate credentials in another instance. For variety and as realism dictated, only attacker and scenario properties that made sense and were relevant to mitigation were considered.

The following four complementary approaches were employed to generate failure scenarios:

- Directly translate the applicable categories of the NESCOR failure scenarios report (AMI, DER, WAMPAC, DR, ET and DGM).

- Learn from experienced operators about real and hypothetical failure scenarios.

- Review the relevant incident reports produced by the Pipeline and Hazardous Materials Safety Administration (PHMSA) [15] and Transport Canada Pipeline [18], and posit cyber contributions to physical failures.

- Conduct mental walkthroughs of standard network security threats on a notional architecture along with the Transportation Security Administration (TSA) Pipeline Security Guidelines [19–21, 23].

During the first approach, only advanced metering infrastructure (AMI) and wide-area monitoring, protection and control (WAMPAC) translated easily. Distributed energy resources (DER) did not translate well because residential customers do not generate natural gas. Demand-response (DR) was not applicable; although some smart home appliances (furnaces, dryers, ovens, stoves and water heaters) run on natural gas, there is not the same requirement for responsive demand (or load) shedding in the power grid. Although natural gas distribution sometimes has peak demand (i.e., winter) concerns, the scale and degree of control are not as significant as in the smart grid. The concept exists, but largely as a manual process and coordination with large industrial customers, not residential customers. Electric transportation (ET) did not translate well because natural gas refueling does not have the same semantics (in terms of planning optimal recharging or supporting customer chargeback); instead, the cyber risks are very similar to those faced by common gasoline refueling. However, some aspects of distributed grid management (DGM) can be adapted due to custody exchanges and multiple downstream customers supplied by large providers.

With the rough narrative examples provided by the approaches listed above, the procedure for generating failure scenario descriptions (i.e., fleshing out the template) involved:

- Prerequisites:

    - Reasonable notional architecture for each setting (inventory of devices, processes, people).

- End result:

    - Not necessarily catastrophic system-wide total loss; outcomes may vary in scope and severity.

- Key spectrum of setting variations to generate concrete examples:

    - Natural or attacker-induced failure of a single component.
    - Sequence of events targeting multiple components.

    – Sequence of events plus interference with protection/remediation efforts.

For this last piece, attacker actions were drawn from two sources. The first included standard network security threats and the second specific types of attacks against the natural gas infrastructure. This helps bridge the gap between general threats and domain-specific threats. Another alternative might be to adapt a model of attacker tactics, techniques and procedures such as MITRE's ATT&CK Matrix [10, 17], which provides a structured menu of attacker actions and tactics for achieving capabilities in a target infrastructure.

Given the focus on remotely-commanded infrastructure, attackers typically engage in the following passive and/or active operations against network communications:

- Eavesdropping (threat to confidentiality).

- Injecting manufactured messages (valid and nonsensical).

- Dropping messages (all, selected and random).

- Network congestion leading to dropped messages (denial of service).

- Redirecting messages to unintended destinations and to self.

- Rewriting messages to legitimate recipients with fabricated data and commands.

While methods such as cryptography and strong authentication can be applied to protect against some of these attacks, they are difficult to deploy and manage in operational technology environments. Specialized threats to the domain include network and software compromises, supply chain attacks and infected maintenance and vendor laptops. Specific risks include attacker actions as well as conditions that facilitate attacker operations:

- Infiltrate the central or backup gas operations center and access on-site programmable logic controllers (PLCs).

- Obtain physical access to the facility, embed malware in the system or in auxiliary systems (e.g., heating, ventilation and air conditioning (HVAC) systems, pumps and monitoring systems).

- Compromise the vendor and supply chain.

- Introduce unauthorized USB, CD and DVD drives in the local control center or gas operations center.

- Scramble GPS receivers.

- Conduct local snooping in the wireless radio frequency (RF) and electromagnetic (EM) domains.

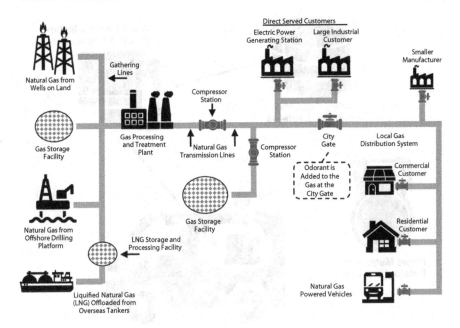

Figure 1. Natural gas distribution network.

- Subvert software upgrade procedures.

- Leverage the lack of operator visibility into supervisory control and data acquisition (SCADA) device internals and operating software.

- Physically link to unattended infrastructure assets and establish remote connections (e.g., modem to programmable logic controller to meter).

7. Analysis of Scenarios by Category

Defining meaningful failure scenarios requires a realistic architecture of the natural gas distribution network. Figure 1 shows the notional architecture [14]. Natural gas extraction and production occur on the left-hand side of the figure and the gas flows toward customers on the right-hand side. Along the way, long-range gas transmission is supported by major compressor stations along the pipeline routes. Compression plays the dual role of moving the product and storing it in the pipeline system (a concept referred to as "linepack"). Separate dedicated storage facilities may be used. High-pressure transmission pipelines transition to lower-pressure distribution lines at major tap points called gate stations (or "city gate" stations) and large industrial customers such as heavy manufacturing and electric power generation facilities. Local distribution lines step down the gas pressure to lower street-level values that depend on the age

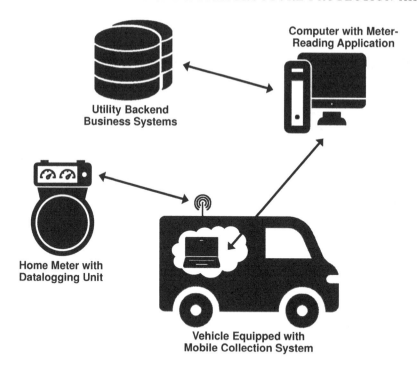

Figure 2.   Vehicle-mounted automated meter reading system.

and condition of the local piping and the needs of customers ranging from residential to commercial (e.g., schools, offices and hospitals).

The failure scenarios are organized into categories that are mapped to the major natural gas distribution network components mentioned above. A total of 55 scenarios are specified. The scenarios are categorized as follows:

- **Automated Meter Reading (AMR):** 18 scenarios (AMR.1–AMR.18).

- City Gate Station

  - **Facility Information (FI):** 11 scenarios (FI.1–FI.11).
  - **Shutoff Valve (SV):** 7 scenarios (SV.1–SV.7).
  - **Metering (M):** 5 scenarios (M.1–M.5).
  - **Odorizer (O):** 4 scenarios (O.1–O.4).
  - **Heating Plant (HP):** 3 scenarios (HP.1–HP.3).

- **Compressor Station (CS):** 7 scenarios (CS.1–CS.7).

The natural gas distribution network failure scenarios largely follow the structure of the NESCOR failure scenarios developed for the electric sector. Each failure scenario has a description, relevant vulnerabilities and an impact. The specification of potential mitigations is the subject of future work.

7.1 Automated Meter Reading

Automated meter reading, which is conducted for billing purposes at residential, commercial and industrial sites, employs specialized handheld, vehicle mounted or airborne reader devices. Figure 2 shows a vehicle-mounted automated meter reading system. The mobile collection system connects to a home meter with a data logging unit to obtain the meter reading. The data is received by a computer with a meter reading application that sends the data to utility backend business systems.

The meters are usually battery powered; their serial numbers are not secrets and can be discovered via scanning. Communications are transmitted in the clear. The protocols employ non-cryptographic checksums for error correction.

Typical home appliances that rely on natural gas are furnaces, stoves and water heaters. Meters that support automated reading generally have limited power and computational resources. However, future designs will support advanced functionality and demand-response management (as in the smart grid), and would possibly employ Internet of Things (IoT) protocols to communicate directly with home appliances. Future meters are also expected to support dynamic pricing and remote shutoff (e.g., for safety).

Tables 2 through 4 present the eighteen automated meter reading failure scenarios (AMR.1–AMR.18). The scenarios focus on current deployments involving the communications hardware and software in the meter, service vehicle and utility. Automated meter reading failures impact billing and customer relations, and reader device maintenance (e.g., battery life), but not natural gas operations or emergency response.

7.2 City Gate Stations

City gate stations are crucial points in the natural gas distribution network because they are locations where a custody transfer takes place and gas pressure is regulated from the transmission level to the distribution level. As custody transfer points, gate stations require the coordination of the operational practices of organizations, business relationships and physical processes involved in transporting natural gas. Gas may also be odorized and scrubbed depending on the installation and utility.

The infrastructure at a gate station includes shutoff valves, metering devices, odorizers and a heating plant, all of which can be susceptible to cyber-induced failures. Additionally, facility information pertaining to a gate station can lead to failures. The failure scenarios associated with gate stations are structured around these key infrastructure components.

Facility Information. Facility information refers to the physical setting/infrastructure (e.g., security plans, facility designs) and related information technology assets (e.g., access credentials) pertaining to a gate station or other facility. Several failure scenarios involve the unauthorized disclosure of protected critical infrastructure information (PCII) [26], security sensitive information

Table 2.   Automated meter reading failure scenarios.

Scenario	Description	Vulnerabilities	Impact
AMR.1	Authorized employee performs unauthorized meter data acquisition system (MDAS) disconnect	Insecure RF channel; limited key management	Reduced consumer confidence; lost revenue for the supplier
AMR.2	Authorized employee manipulates meter data management system (MDMS) data to over/under charge	Unauthorized access to MDMS; no cryptographic integrity; malware	Mischarging; effort to correct billing errors
AMR.3	Invalid access used to install malware enabling remote Internet control	Supply chain; infect readers and/or endpoints	Collection and/or disclosure of customer data
AMR.4	Overused key captured on a meter channel enables usage data manipulation	Applies if crypto is employed; lack of crypto enables manipulation	Untrustworthy data collection; time to remedy errors
AMR.5	Mass meter rekeying when a common key is compromised	Key is extracted from protocol messages or via physical access to units	Effort required to rekey or replace infrastructure; ongoing risk of manipulation
AMR.6	One compromised meter in a network blocks others; interference in the channel	Meters or readers contain malware; local blocking of radio source	Time to rescan customer sites
AMR.7	Deployed meters containing undesirable functionality need repair	Bug and security patching	Time and expense to upgrade meters
AMR.8	False meter data induces unnecessary analytics on the corporate side	Compromised transmitters or homeowner	Data recovery and restoration from backup

Table 3. Automated meter reading failure scenarios (continued).

Scenario	Description	Vulnerabilities	Impact
AMR.9	Invalid messages to meters impact customers and utility	Physical signal or pulse to disable temporarily or permanently	Meter unavailability; battery replacement
AMR.10	Incorrect consumption information impacts utility revenue	Unprotected communications medium enables spoofing or shielding	Effort required to rekey or replace infrastructure; ongoing risk of manipulation
AMR.11	Improper firewall or network access control between reader and corporate network	Readers and/or mobile units are compromised	Significant loss of customer data; access to billing systems
AMR.12	Breach of cellular provider network exposes AMR access	Not under utility control	Loss of customer data
AMR.13	Inadequate security for backend AMR data receivers enables malicious activity	Exposure of networked equipment and data repositories	Replacement costs of equipment and receivers
AMR.14	Malicious creation of duplicate serial numbers or identifiers prevents valid AMR messages	Fake reader; fake tower (for reader-to-office communications)	Effort to reacquire data
AMR.15	Unauthorized devices create denial of service and prevent valid AMR queries and replies	Unprotected communications medium enables spoofing or shielding	Effort to track down or localize problem; law enforcement involvement; reacquire data
AMR.16	Stolen field service tools expose AMR infrastructure	Unattended or unlocked trucks	Loss or exposure of customer data; access to backend
AMR.17	Threat agent performs unauthorized firmware alteration	Update channels for readers and truck communications equipment	Denial of service; battery drain in meters; data disclosure/collection

Table 4. Automated meter reading failure scenarios (continued).

Scenario	Description	Vulnerabilities	Impact
AMR.18	Competitor observes gas consumption at a store or factory	Insecure cleartext protocols permit any party to observe usage data	Competitive advantage and insight into a direct competitor

(SSI) [22] and/or critical energy/electric infrastructure information (CEII) [5] relating to natural gas distribution network facilities.

Tables 5 and 6 present the eleven facility information failure scenarios (FI.1–FI.11).

Shutoff Valves. Gate stations implement a physical process that steps down or regulates the nominal transmission pipeline pressure to distribution pipeline pressure, which is roughly 10% of the transmission pressure. A key safety component in these facilities is an automatic shutoff valve (ASV) or remote control valve (RCV) that permits the gate station to be isolated from the large transmission pipeline in case of a failure or incident in the gate station.

A shutoff valve also provides local, completely manual shutoff in the case of communications or power loss to the motor unit. The operational impact varies on how many valves are compromised. Compromises may have little impact on the system or they could be devastating. Larger impacts may occur if the shutoff valves cannot be operated during an incident, such as system over-pressurization or an explosion.

Table 7 presents the seven shutoff valve failure scenarios (SV.1–SV.7).

Metering. Metering is a critical responsibility of the gate station because it is a handoff point for custody of gas transiting the pipeline.

Several variations in metering setups exist. These include independent meters before and after a tap compared with the distribution company's independent meter on the tap, or jointly-instrumented meters on transmission company pipe. Shared infrastructure assets can present management challenges in coordinating the cyber security practices of the collaborating organizations.

Metering failure scenarios mainly impact other equipment and may require additional operational information or access. Regulators and other equipment have physical safety mechanisms that prevent them from operating outside of safe conditions. Some scenarios require physical access to a station, which may trigger security alarms. In some cases, an attacker may have to corrupt the distribution meter system as well as the transmission meter system, which may be monitored and compared by the utility and the transmission company.

Table 8 presents the five metering failure scenarios (M.1–M.5).

Table 5. Facility information failure scenarios.

Scenario	Description	Vulnerabilities	Impact
FI.1	Risk of disclosure of the relationship between cyber assets and physical infrastructure	Data inference across public sources; observation and surveillance of public facilities	Unauthorized disclosure of PCII and SSI information related to facility location and cyber properties
FI.2	Theft or loss of detailed security plans or facility designs	Inadequate or compromised physical and/or data controls	Unauthorized disclosure of PCII and SSI information related to security plans or facility designs
FI.3	Theft or loss of access credentials	Compromised credentials	Unauthorized access and/or unauthorized disclosure of PCII and SSI information
FI.4	Risk of recording and disclosure of security and safety practices and procedures	Surreptitious observation and surveillance	Unauthorized disclosure of PCII and SSI information related to security and safety practices and procedures
FI.5	Unauthorized, unintentional disclosure by an insider of security and safety system properties, capabilities, configurations and operating procedures	Insider threat – disgruntled or compromised employees	Unauthorized disclosure of PCII and SSI information related to security and safety systems
FI.6	Use of electronic means, tools and online data sources to map physical components of cyber and security systems	Electronic observations and surveillance combined with public information	Unauthorized disclosure of PCII and SSI information related to cyber and security systems

Table 6.   Facility information failure scenarios (continued).

Scenario	Description	Vulnerabilities	Impact
FI.7	Extraction of GPS coordinates, settings or other specific location information allows mapping of equipment to physical infrastructure locations	Incorrect configuration, software vulnerabilities or weak access control of wireless routable devices	Linking physical locations with specific system identification and vulnerability information leads to leaked CEII and increased attacker capabilities and situational awareness
FI.8	Passive RF monitoring may provide details about communications protocols and infrastructure	RF side channels	Unauthorized disclosure of PCII and SSI information related to communications protocols and infrastructure
FI.9	Corruption and denial of service of security cameras and related systems	Compromised or blinded security cameras or related systems	Hide attack or event requiring attention or hide information needed to respond
FI.10	Attacker pivots through the security camera communications infrastructure	Common physical communications medium used for control and security; compromised third-party communications system	Attacker gains access to both communications streams
FI.11	Unexplained failure of computer communications drops alarms or alerts for a period of time, obscuring the root cause of an incident	Failed communications link	Dropped alarms or alerts obscure the root cause of the incident

Table 7. Shutoff valve failure scenarios.

Scenario	Description	Vulnerabilities	Impact
SV.1	Unauthorized remote user invokes mechanical valve closure	Stolen or lost credentials	Isolated gate station from the transmission system
SV.2	Unauthorized insider invokes unsafe mechanical valve open operation from local human-machine interface (HMI)	Rogue employee accesses unlocked screen or uses an observed password	Unsafe valve operation
SV.3	Damage, disable or remove software functions related to valve control by the PLC	Network and software compromise, supply chain attack, or infected maintenance or vendor laptop	Modified control logic that ignores open or close commands
SV.4	Issue spurious (i.e., valve closed) status messages to mimic an uncommanded shutoff event	Network and software compromise, supply chain attack, or infected maintenance or vendor laptop	Depleted trust in the system causes wasted effort
SV.5	Misleading status messages about legitimate commanded valve closure	Network and software compromise, supply chain attack, or infected maintenance or vendor laptop	Reduced confidence in the equipment or alarm fatigue
SV.6	Unsafe or incomplete assumptions about system state resulting in incorrect attribution of the root cause of alarms	Manipulation of sensor data (selective blocking, partial operation injection or rewriting)	Loss of cyber situational awareness and loss of trust in the system
SV.7	Failure to re-open valve after legitimate event	Corrupt control logic to prevent control messages from reaching the valve motor; spoof or drop legitimate acknowledgement messages to the HMI or gas operations center	Valve appears unresponsive

Table 8.   Metering failure scenarios.

Scenario	Description	Vulnerabilities	Impact
M.1	Unauthorized remote user injects false pressure reading in SCADA traffic to the PLC in the local control room	Network and software compromise, supply chain attack, or infected maintenance or vendor laptop	Potentially dangerous physical operation of a regulator or other critical system
M.2	Unauthorized remote user injects false readings or blocks existing messages from receipt at the local control room or remote gas operations center	Network and software compromise, supply chain attack, or infected maintenance or vendor laptop	Reporting false good parameter values can lead to a silent pipe or heater breakdown; reporting false bad parameter values can cause delays while sensor readings are checked
M.3	Disable power supply to meter probes	Network and software compromise, supply chain attack, or infected maintenance or vendor laptop	Disabled data streams to the supplier and distributor
M.4	Unnecessary maintenance caused by spurious unexplained failures of sensor probes	Network and software compromise, supply chain attack, or infected maintenance or vendor laptop	Arbitrary, unpredictable and unexplained errors may cause unnecessary maintenance, repairs or replacement
M.5	Meter readings inconsistent with the linepack models of the transmission operator	Corrupted modeling data or software along with compromised readings from several major gate stations	Could significantly disrupt a major transmission pipeline

Odorizer. In some cases, gas is not odorized during transmission. This is because transporting odorant to remote locations and injecting it in the "middle" of a transmission pipeline may be impractical. Odorant is usually added closer to exit points such as city gates and close-to-terminal compressor stations. Although odorant is often added at a city gate station by a distribution company, in some cases, distribution companies rely on the transmission pipeline operator to inject odorant, but perform an independent verification. The addition of odorant provides an important safety property for consumers.

Table 9. Odorizer failure scenarios.

Scenario	Description	Vulnerabilities	Impact
O.1	Attacker gains access to HMI and reports lower-than-expected or higher-than-expected measurements of odorant in the system	Network and software compromise, supply chain attack, or infected maintenance or vendor laptop used to modify displayed sensor readings	Unnecessary increase or decrease in the level of odorant injected into the system
O.2	Attacker gains access to HMI and hides all sensor readings related to odorant levels in the storage tanks and outflowing gas	Network and software compromise, supply chain attack, or infected maintenance or vendor laptop used to hide displayed sensor readings	Unnecessary maintenance check or possible halt to operations; customers unable to notice gas leaks if enough odorant is not present
O.3	Attacker gains access to odorizer controller and modifies setpoints to increase the amount of odorant injected, resulting in over-odorization of the gas	Network and software compromise, supply chain attack, or infected maintenance or vendor laptop used to manipulate setpoints and possibly disable or modify sensor readings or alarms	Increase in service calls as customers report suspected leaks
O.4	Attacker gains access to odorizer controller and modifies setpoints to decrease the amount of odorant injected, resulting in under-odorization of the gas	Network and software compromise, supply chain attack, or infected maintenance or vendor laptop used to manipulate setpoints and possibly disable or modify sensor readings or alarms	Customers unable to notice existing or induced leaks; escalation of explosive events leading to property damage or loss of life

Table 9 presents the four odorizer failure scenarios (O.1–O.4).

Heating Plant. A critical part of the city gate is the heating plant, which enables safe operations by keeping the gas temperature above the freezing point of water as the gas pressure drops during transmission. The potential for freez-

Table 10.   Heating plant failure scenarios.

Scenario	Description	Vulnerabilities	Impact
HP.1	Attacker targets and modifies thermostat readings	Network and software compromise, supply chain attack, or infected maintenance or vendor laptop used to modify settings or forge readings	Decreased heating may lead to low gas temperature in regulator piping; overheating may cause inefficient heat exchange or trigger nuisance alarms
HP.2	Remote attacker modifies settings or readings of flow meters for the heat exchange medium	Network and software compromise, supply chain attack, or infected maintenance or vendor laptop used to modify settings or forge readings	Increased flow may lead to overheating; reduced flow may lead to decreased heating
HP.3	Remote attacker shuts off pumps or circulation motors that permit the heat exchange medium from entering the boilers or flowing to the regulator piping	Network and software compromise, supply chain attack, or infected maintenance or vendor laptop used to shut off pumps or motors	Lack of flow may lead to damaged regulator or automatic safety shutdown of regulator

ing exists due to the presence of water in the gas, which is also maintained at the desired level by instrumentation and filtering at the city gate. Should the heating plant fail or be taken out of service, the gate station would have to be isolated from the transmission pipeline, causing loss of revenue and downstream effects on customers large and small, even in the presence of failover or redundant supply to the distribution system from other gate stations.

While heating plants operate relatively simple physical processes, their supporting infrastructure components are targets for attacks. These include thermostats, pumps and flow meters for the heating medium (e.g., glycol).

A heating plant may also be co-located with backup power generation (fed by the gas pipeline) that provides the gate station "hotel" power. Heating plant designs and implementations differ, but the failure scenarios assume there is a programmable logic controller connected in the SCADA network.

Table 10 presents the three heating plant failure scenarios (HP.1–HP.3).

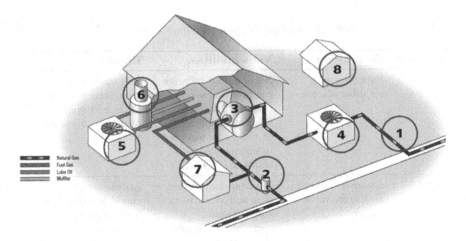

Figure 3. Compressor station yard.

7.3   Compressor Station

Compressor stations have several failure scenarios because they perform a significant physical process and incorporate multiple infrastructure components and smart electronic systems that support, monitor and protect the core process, which may also have a feedback relationship with the electric power grid.

Compressor stations are located at points in the gas system where the gas line pressure must be increased to either increase linepack (i.e., the *de facto* storage of a volume of gas) or push gas downstream through the system. While compressors are present in both transmission and distribution pipelines, they feature prominently in transmission pipelines. As a consequence, compressor station failures in transmission pipelines would have greater impact.

Figure 3 shows a schematic diagram of a compressor station yard (from Spectra Energy). It comprises station yard piping (1), filter separators/scrubbers (2), multiple compressor units (3), gas cooling system (4), lubricating oil system (5), mufflers (exhaust silencers) (6), fuel gas system (7) and backup generators (8).

A compressor station may draw on a larger volume but lower pressure part of the distribution network to concentrate and supply a dense area or several large customers. A compressor station may be paired with a regulator unit to step down pressure if gas needs to be moved from the higher-pressure part of the system back to the lower-pressure portion. The relatively minor difference in pressure places fewer demands on heating; the pressure change may be only about 100 psi, so the temperature change is negligible, roughly 7°F.

Tables 11 and 12 present the seven compressor station failure scenarios (CS.1–CS.7).

Table 11. Compressor station failure scenarios.

Scenario	Description	Vulnerabilities	Impact
CS.1	Suppression of scrubber alarms	Network and software compromise, supply chain attack, or infected maintenance or vendor laptop used to obscure failure states of scrubbers	Full tanks may go unnoticed; overflow tanks may spill hazardous material
CS.2	Attacker induces anti-surge valve failure	Physical damage to pipe and/or network and software compromise, supply chain attack, or infected maintenance or vendor laptop used to modify PLC readings	Anti-surge valve is closed or prevented from opening; uncontrolled surge event causes damage or destruction of pipe and/or compressor
CS.3	Remote attacker modifies gas quality readings back to the control center	Network and software compromise, supply chain attack, or infected maintenance or vendor laptop used to modify gas quality readings	Hide source of problems with feed to downstream or hide source of condensates in pipe; damage or destruction of pipe and/or compressor
CS.4	Remote attacker modifies firmware or control points of gas quality sensors	Network and software compromise, supply chain attack, or infected maintenance or vendor laptop used to modify firmware or control points	Hide source of problems with feed to downstream or hide source of condensates in pipe; damage or destruction of pipe and/or compressor
CS.5	Failure of compressor process cooling system	Induced or natural failure of process cooling system combined with suppression of high-temperature alarms	Loss of compression; physical damage or destruction

Table 12. Compressor station failure scenarios (continued).

Scenario	Description	Vulnerabilities	Impact
CS.6	Failure of electric power supply to compressor turbines that rely on electric power (as primary source and/or for monitoring and control)	Failure of primary electric power combined with induced or eventual failure of backup generators due to fuel exhaustion	Loss of compression
CS.7	Use of HVAC, auxiliary building control systems or vendor systems as pivot points	Software vulnerabilities, supply chain attacks, poor access control hygiene for vendor/service systems	Establishment of a foothold by the attacker in the environment

8.   Lessons Learned

The major lessons of this project relate to performing scenario translations and the cyber security findings.

Lesson 1. During domain translation, it was observed that natural gas distribution incorporates fewer intelligent electronic devices than the electric grid. System properties and business concerns are different because gas and electricity are different physical commodities and their transmission involves significantly different physical processes. Additionally, some parts of the NESCOR report categories simply do not translate because there is no analogous infrastructure component on the gas side or an analogous component exists but has little or no cyber elements.

Lesson 2. Learning about the infrastructure takes time and significant effort. Developing realistic scenarios requires substantial knowledge that must be acquired from domain experts. This requires building trust with utility operators and reviewing authoritative sources such as TSA guidelines, PHMSA reports, device data sheets, vendor case studies about facility installations, and research conducted by academic programs in petroleum engineering and related fields. This engagement facilitated the creation of the notional architecture that provided the setting for failure scenario development.

Lesson 3. When using the failure scenarios, utility personnel should not think in terms of a checklist of mitigations as suggested by current regulatory and TSA guidance, but whether they have an ongoing process for checking security properties that provides easy-to-understand evidence that a monitoring system is working as intended; in other words, whether or not the cyber security mechanisms in place are operating correctly and observing the cyber-relevant behaviors of the operational technology devices. Because failure scenarios are not meant to be a cookbook for attacks and they rest on the assumption that mitigations could fail, utilities must have a process and not just a checklist that enumerates defenses against specific attacks.

Lesson 4. There is a distinct advantage to being more mechanical. Part of the difficulty in specifying failure scenarios was finding enough details about where computational elements and control processors were located, the equipment to which they were connected and the communications channels that provided access to them. Important pieces of the infrastructure are largely mechanical (e.g., regulators large and small involve physical components and isolated controls).

As the natural gas industry looks toward the future, there will likely be an impetus to embed intelligent electronic devices at a density and rate comparable to the electric power sector. However, before anything is done, the natural gas industry must assess whether this will introduce unjustified risk. Computational elements have latent behaviors that simply do not exist in the case of mechanical equipment.

9.   Real-World Application of Failure Scenarios

Significant questions about the utility of the failure scenarios are whether they can be applied in real situations and whether they are tied to real-world concerns. A potential objection to generating and using failure scenarios is that they might be too artificial, and thus lack realism and fail to be beneficial to utilities. The scenario development process compensated for this by engaging with utility personnel and incorporating input from government safety investigation incident reports in the failure scenarios. Indeed, the application of the failure scenarios in the natural gas industry demonstrated that they can model both realistic and real-world scenarios.

One use case is to retroactively study real incidents in terms of combinations of failure scenarios, in essence introducing a synthetic cyber adversary into a real incident. Operators and engineers can model a real incident with a sequence of failure scenarios and re-execute the incident under a what-if analysis while substituting failure scenario elements in the incident timeline.

For example, the San Bruno incident of September 2010 involved the rupture of a 30-inch-diameter intrastate transmission pipeline due to an accidental over-pressurization of a "substandard and poorly welded pipe section with a visible seam weld flaw" [12]. This physical material failure was compounded by a number of contributing factors, including side-effects of electrical work that induced false low pressure readings and caused regulator valves to open fully.

Fake pressure readings introduced by an adversary underpin many of the shutoff valve and metering failure scenarios presented in this chapter. During the San Bruno incident, SCADA systems and communications were crucially

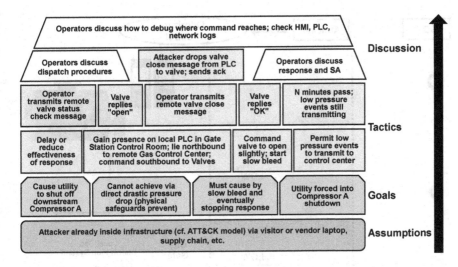

Figure 4. Example tabletop scenario.

important to providing situational awareness. At times during and leading up to the San Bruno pipeline rupture, SCADA system data was not available or reliable due to the side-effects of the repair work; this also affected some control valve positions. Interested readers are directed to the National Transportation Safety Board (NTSB) report on the San Bruno incident [12], especially Sections 1.1.2 and 1.9.1 to note the many opportunities for disrupting SCADA systems that could result in the loss of situational awareness.

Another use case of the failure scenarios is the creation of tabletop exercises. A "low pressure" tabletop exercise scenario was constructed based on real-world events (pipeline incident reports) and some failure scenarios. Figure 4 shows the assumptions, goals and tactics drawn from a small subset of the failure scenarios (FI.10, SV.2, SV.4 and SV.5). These failure scenarios provided the context that supported major discussion topics in the tabletop exercise.

Another way to add realism to a failure scenario is to instantiate it. This can be accomplished in a number of ways, such as in a high-fidelity simulator, by acquiring real equipment or by running it in a test laboratory environment. However, the first step is to provide a concise diagram of the various components.

Figure 5 presents an instantiation of Scenario O.4 of the odorizer, which includes the principal subjects (i.e., actors), objects and an example control and status message exchange. In Scenario O.4, the attacker gains access to the odorizer controller and reduces the amount of odorant that is injected, resulting in under-odorization (see Table 9 for the associated vulnerabilities and impacts). The risk is that real leaks go undetected for a longer period of time than warranted, thus "batching up" and causing a burst of failures over time.

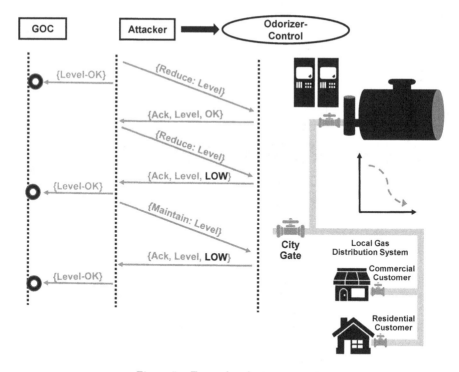

Figure 5.   Example odorizer scenario.

A future line of work is to specify a common graphical language to diagram failure scenarios. Ultimately, this would be another structured way to specify failure scenarios that bind abstract objects such as the odorizer controller and the SCADA protocol to specific products and protocols. Diagramming scenarios provides additional details that tie the abstract scenarios to real-world equipment and communications protocols along with adversary actions.

10.   Related Work

The failure scenarios for the electric sector discussed in the NESCOR report [11] provided the inspiration and model for this research. Indeed, the focus of this chapter has been a comparative analysis of the failure scenarios for the gas sector and the NESCOR scenarios for the electric sector.

A recent (March 2018) TSA document [21] provides best practices and guidance that extend over the entire gas distribution enterprise. Some of the facility information scenarios described in this work were drawn from the TSA best practices and guidance.

Failure mode modeling is a common practice in reliable systems engineering that is often used to design dependable computing systems. Failure mode and effects analysis (FMEA) is a systematic approach for collecting and analyzing the conditions under which system components might experience failure. Effective failure mode and effects analyses are informed by experience with statistical evidence pertaining to the prior behavior and failures of similar systems.

A closely-related piece of work is the Waterfall Security Solutions review of 20 prototypical attacks on industrial control networks [28]. The review sketches a number of scenarios in an example water control system. A significant benefit is the consideration of attackers with differing capabilities and placements in a notional architecture and standard defenses against attacks that originate from a number of locations in the topology.

Attack graphs have been an active area of cyber security research for decades. Seminal work [2, 16] introduced the notion of linking vulnerabilities across a network of host computers to provide a structured method for assessing attack impacts. Hawrylak et al. [6] have applied these notions to an industrial control system environment. Recent work by Wang et al. [27] extends the concept to consider probabilistic modeling, which is related to the use of failure scenarios as an analysis and "what if" tool for utilities.

The Lockheed-Martin "cyber kill chain" concept [7] identifies the phases that cyber attackers must complete to achieve their objectives, which enables defenders to map their courses of action to adversary kill chain indicators. Similarly, the MITRE ATT&CK model [10, 17] provides a structured menu of attacker actions and tactics aimed at achieving specific capabilities in a target infrastructure. The model was originally developed as a community resource for enterprise environments, but MITRE is currently working on applying ATT&CK to industrial control systems in the electric power, gas, water and transportation sectors [1]. The failure scenarios described in this chapter do not seek to provide a cookbook for attackers nor are they intended to be a checklist for security defenses. However, future work may leverage ATT&CK to provide more specificity to the failure scenarios, especially for activities such as tabletop exercises.

11. Conclusions

One of the most important questions facing critical infrastructure owners and operators is how their assets could be made to fail by cyber threat actors. The 55 failure scenarios in the natural gas distribution infrastructure presented in this chapter were created to provide a cyber security analysis framework for natural gas utilities. Designing, enumerating and analyzing failure scenarios help explore the assumptions made on the operational side, the value of current cyber defenses and the need for new protection mechanisms.

In addition to describing the multi-pronged approach used to develop the failure scenarios for the gas sector, the chapter compares them against scenarios developed for the electric sector. The focus is on the concepts underlying the failure scenarios and their use, the threat model they encompass and the assumptions, lessons learned and caveats underpinning their creation. The scenario development process and the differential comparison between the natural gas and electricity domains provide a roadmap for developing failure scenarios in other critical infrastructure sectors.

Future research will extend the scenarios by adding more specificity, expanding them to other areas of the natural gas infrastructure and exploring interdependencies within natural gas systems and between natural gas and other sectors. Attempts will also be made to measure the coverage of the failure scenarios. Additionally, efforts will focus on a more comprehensive mapping of real-world incidents against the failure scenario library as it increases in coverage and specificity.

Any opinions, findings, conclusions or recommendations expressed in this chapter are those of the authors and do not necessarily reflect the views of the U.S. Department of Homeland Security, and should not be interpreted as necessarily representing the official policies or endorsements, either expressed or implied, of the U.S. Department of Homeland Security or the U.S. Government.

Acknowledgements

This work was sponsored by the U.S. Department of Homeland Security Science and Technology Directorate (DHS S&T) under Contract No. HSHQDC-16-C-00034. The authors thank DHS S&T Program Manager, Mr. Gregory Wigton, and the GTI Program Manager, Mr. James Marean, for their guidance and support. Thanks also due to the member utilities in the GTI/OTD Cybersecurity Collaborative for providing valuable insights into the natural gas distribution infrastructure and potential failure scenarios. Additionally, the authors thank the project participants from the Pacific Northwest National Laboratory (PNNL) and MITRE Corporation.

References

[1] O. Alexander, ICS ATT&CK, presented at the *Thirty-Third Annual Computer Security Applications Conference*, 2017.

[2] P. Ammann, D. Wijesekera and S. Kaushik, Scalable, graph-based network vulnerability analysis, *Proceedings of the Ninth ACM Conference on Computer and Communications Security*, pp. 217–224, 2002.

[3] Automation Federation, LOGIIC: Improving Cybersecurity in the Oil and Natural Gas Sector, Research Triangle Park, North Carolina (www.automationfederation.org/Logiic/Logiic), 2019.

[4] Cyber Resilient Energy Delivery Consortium, Information Trust Institute, University of Illinois at Urbana-Champaign, Urbana, Illinois (cred-c.org), 2019.

[5] Federal Energy Regulatory Commission, Critical Energy/Electric Infrastructure Information (CEII), Washington, DC (www.ferc.gov/legal/ceii-foia/ceii.asp), 2019.

[6] P. Hawrylak, M. Haney, M. Papa and J. Hale, Using hybrid attack graphs to model cyber-physical attacks in the smart grid, *Proceedings of the Fifth International Symposium on Resilient Control Systems*, pp. 161–164, 2012.

[7] E. Hutchins, M. Cloppert and R. Amin, Intelligence-driven computer network defense informed by analysis of adversary campaigns and intrusion kill chains, *Proceedings of the Sixth International Conference on Information Warfare and Security*, pp. 113–125, 2011.

[8] M. Locasto, Helping students Own their own code, *IEEE Security and Privacy*, vol. 7(3), pp. 53–56, 2009.

[9] M. Locasto and M. Little, A failure-based discipline of trustworthy information systems, *IEEE Security and Privacy*, vol. 9(4), pp. 71–75, 2011.

[10] MITRE Corporation, ATT&CK Matrix for Enterprise, Bedford, Massachusetts (attack.mitre.org), 2019.

[11] National Electric Sector Cybersecurity Organization Resource, Electric Sector Failure Scenarios and Impact Analyses – Version 3.0, Washington, DC (smartgrid.epri.com/doc/NESCOR%20Failure%20Scenarios%20v3% 2012-11-15.pdf), 2015.

[12] National Transportation Safety Board, Pacific Gas and Electric Company Natural Gas Transmission Pipeline Rupture and Fire, San Bruno, California, September 9, 2010, Pipeline Accident Report NTSB/PAR-11/01, Washington, DC, 2011.

[13] Office of Electricity, Liberty Eclipse Exercise Summary Report, U.S. Department of Energy, Washington, DC (www.energy.gov/oe/articles/ liberty-eclipse-exercise-summary-report), 2017.

[14] Pipeline and Hazardous Materials Safety Administration, Natural Gas Pipeline Systems, U.S. Department of Transportation, Washington, DC (primis.phmsa.dot.gov/comm/naturalgaspipelinesystems.htm), 2019.

[15] Pipeline and Hazardous Materials Safety Administration, Pipeline Failure Investigation Reports, U.S. Department of Transportation, Washington, DC (www.phmsa.dot.gov/safety-reports/pipeline-failure- investigation-reports), 2019.

[16] O. Sheyner, J. Haines, S. Jha, R. Lippmann and J. Wing, Automated generation and analysis of attack graphs, *Proceedings of the IEEE Symposium on Security and Privacy*, pp. 273–284, 2002.

[17] B. Strom, A. Applebaum, D. Miller, K. Nickels, A. Pennington and C. Thomas, MITRE ATT&CK: Design and Philosophy, MITRE Product MP 18-0944-11, MITRE Corporation, McLean, Virginia, 2018.

[18] Transportation Safety Board of Canada, Pipeline Transportation Safety Investigations and Reports, Gatineau, Canada (www.bst-tsb.gc.ca/eng/ rapports-reports/pipeline/index.asp), 2019.

[19] Transportation Security Administration, Pipeline Security and Incident Recovery Protocol Plan, Pentagon City, Virginia, 2010.

[20] Transportation Security Administration, Pipeline Security Smart Practice Observations, Pentagon City, Virginia, 2011.

[21] Transportation Security Administration, Pipeline Security Guidelines, Pentagon City, Virginia, 2018.

[22] Transportation Security Administration, Sensitive Security Information, Pentagon City, Virginia (`www.tsa.gov/for-industry/sensitive-security-information`), 2019.

[23] Transportation Security Administration, Surface Transportation, Pentagon City, Virginia (`www.tsa.gov/for-industry/surface-transportation`), 2019.

[24] Trustworthy Cyber Infrastructure for the Power Grid, Information Trust Institute, University of Illinois at Urbana-Champaign, Urbana, Illinois (`tcipg.org`), 2019.

[25] U.S. Department of Homeland Security, LOGIIC: Linking the Oil and Gas Industry to Improve Cybersecurity, Science and Technology Directorate, Washington, DC (`www.dhs.gov/science-and-technology/logiic#`), 2016.

[26] U.S. Department of Homeland Security, Protected Critical Infrastructure Information (PCII) Program, Washington, DC (`www.dhs.gov/pcii-program`), 2019.

[27] L. Wang, T. Islam, T. Long, A. Singhal and S. Jajodia, An attack graph-based probabilistic security metric, in *Data and Applications Security XXII*, V. Atluri (Ed.), Springer, Berlin Heidelberg, Germany, pp. 283–296, 2008.

[28] Waterfall Security Solutions, The Top 20 Cyber Attacks on Industrial Control Systems, Rosh Ha'ayin, Israel (`waterfall-security.com/20-attacks`), 2018.

Chapter 3

AN ATTACK-FAULT TREE ANALYSIS OF A MOVABLE RAILROAD BRIDGE

Matthew Jablonski, Yongxin Wang, Chaitanya Yavvari, Zezhou Wang, Xiang Liu, Keith Holt and Duminda Wijesekera

Abstract   Mechanical and electrical components of movable bridges are engineered to move heavy concrete and steel structures in order to allow water traffic and rail and/or vehicular traffic to pass many times a day despite harsh weather conditions, storm surges and earthquakes. The bridge spans must also support varying rail and/or vehicular traffic loads.

This chapter considers known and theoretical risks posed by movable bridge system attacks and faults in a single stochastic model based on attack-fault trees. Risks associated with railroad swing bridges are presented, along with the attack-fault tree model and the analysis results.

Keywords: Cyber-physical systems, movable bridges, attack-fault tree analysis

1.   Introduction

Movable bridges constructed over waterways are specifically designed to allow traffic flows on and over waterways. Most movable bridges, which are called "heavy movable structures," maneuver many tons of steel and concrete under the control of modern controllers even under difficult weather conditions.

Bridges have been targets of attacks since ancient times. From castle drawbridges to supply line bridges in Europe during World War II, pitched battles have been fought over bridges. In this post-Stuxnet era, new risks are posed by attacks on programmable logic controllers and networked industrial control systems – the cyber-physical components that control movable bridges. Consequently, securing a modern movable bridge requires the consideration of faults in the physical, mechanical and control aspects of the bridge as well as the cyber security of electro-mechanical components that actuate the movements of physical components.

© IFIP International Federation for Information Processing 2019
Published by Springer Nature Switzerland AG 2019
J. Staggs and S. Shenoi (Eds.): Critical Infrastructure Protection XIII, IFIP AICT 570, pp. 51–71, 2019.
https://doi.org/10.1007/978-3-030-34647-8_3

Figure 1. An open BNSF railroad swing bridge [18].

Faults and vulnerabilities in a system are typically studied by collecting and analyzing data about failure modes. Design corrections are then instituted and the resulting reports are shared with the community to mitigate hazards and risks. Unfortunately, a repository of reports pertaining to movable bridges does not exist for three reasons. First, although they may share some common components, no two movable bridge systems are built the same and operate under the same environmental conditions. Second, the faults and the methods for handling outages vary, but this information is not recorded in a centralized public repository. Third, no cyber attacks have as yet been reported against movable bridges, although attacks against other control systems could be re-purposed to target similar components in movable bridges. To address the lack of data, this chapter models the impacts of failures on movable bridges with a focus on railroad swing bridges (Figure 1).

A literature review indicates that intentional attacks and accidental faults cause movable bridge failures; therefore, a comprehensive model of attacks and faults that result in failures is needed. This work employs the combined attack-fault tree model of Kumar and Stoelinga [16]. This model was built on previous work on attack trees and fault trees to support qualitative and quantitative analyses of combined system security and safety properties. The model is leveraged to create an attack-fault tree for a swing bridge, following which each node in the model is translated to a stochastic timed automaton used by the UPPAAL Statistical Model Checker [7]. A qualitative analysis of the attack-fault tree can be used to identify the root causes of swing bridge system failures whereas a quantitative analysis allows for the incorporation of likelihood values, costs and impacts of disruptions; these two types of analyses are important components of a risk analysis. The utility of the attack-fault tree model in movable swing bridge risk assessments is also discussed.

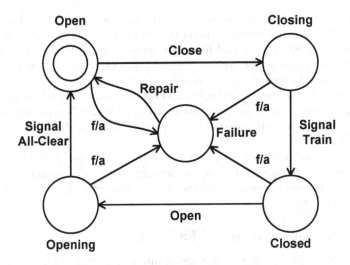

Figure 2. Finite-state machine model of a movable bridge.

This research has two main contributions. The first contribution is a thorough security and safety analysis of a movable swing bridge using an attack-fault tree model. Although the focus is on cyber attacks, physical attacks are also considered because bridges, by their very nature, have open physical access. The second contribution is the application of the attack-fault tree model to a real-world system.

2. Functionality and Failures

This section presents a model of swing bridge functionality and potential system failures. The discussion clarifies the risks of attacks and faults that impact railroad swing bridge operations.

2.1 Functionality Model and Usage Scenarios

A swing bridge is considered to be open when the bridge is rotated parallel to the navigable water traffic direction, enabling water traffic to flow and halting overland traffic. The bridge is considered to be closed when it is aligned with the overland tracks, halting water traffic while enabling overland traffic to flow. These operational states and their transitions are modeled as a finite-state machine shown in Figure 2. It is assumed that a railroad swing bridge is open by default to favor water traffic, and is closed when needed to accommodate passing trains.

When a bridge in the open state needs to transition to the closed state, an operator signals a close request to the bridge control system. At this point, marine craft are alerted via radio, lighting and/or alarms and given time to steer clear of the bridge. Gates may be lowered to prevent the flow of overland traffic. The control system also checks overland traffic control sensors to avoid unsafe operations. After all the sensor checks are completed, the drive system mechanically walks the pinions around the curved rack, rotating the pivot pier and bridge span 90 degrees. End lifts are then secured, wedges are pushed into place (in the case of center bearing systems), the centering device is engaged and the track is locked on both ends of the bridge [15].

The bridge is now closed, and lights and signals are used to inform operators to permit overland traffic to flow. After overland traffic has passed over the bridge for some time, the process is reversed to move the bridge back to the default open state.

The functional use cases of a swing bridge are modeled as a Moore finite state machine with four states – open, closing, closed and opening – as shown in Figure 2. Failure states are introduced when the bridge is in these states or transitioning between the states.

2.2   Classification of Failures

A movable swing bridge is a "binary dynamic and repairable system" [5]. It is binary because its failures are modeled using Boolean variables, dynamic because the order of component failures impacts the system failures and repairable because faulty, degraded and failed components can be replaced. According to this classification, a swing bridge may also be in a failure state, which is defined as a stopped and dysfunctional state, where it remains for a period of period until repairs have occurred and normal functionality can resume. If the bridge fails in the open or closed states, then the passage of overland or water traffic, respectively, is halted.

3.   Attack-Fault Tree for a Movable Swing Bridge

Attacks and faults can result in failure states. The swing bridge attack-fault tree segments in Figures 3 and 4 show both types of failures in a single model. As a top-down failure analysis formalism, an attack-fault tree is a directed acyclic graph that analyzes the top-level safety or security goal and refines it into smaller sub-goals. In the case of the bridge model, the top-level goal $[G_0]$ is "prevent bridge movement," which corresponds to the definition of failure.

An attack-fault tree comprises gates and leaves. Figure 5 shows the five standard, dynamic fault tree gates: (i) AND. (ii) OR; (iii) FDEP (functional dependency); (iv) SAND (sequential AND); and (v) SPARE (spare inputs). The leaves in an attack-fault tree are either basic attack steps or basic component failures, corresponding to attacks and faults, respectively. The leaves are represented as stochastic timed automata (described later in this chapter). Interested readers are referred to [16] for details about attack-fault trees and their use in quantitative security and safety analyses.

It is assumed that a generic swing bridge uses programmable logic controllers for control automation; wireless networks and manual overrides for interconnections and operator control, respectively; an AC-powered electric motor and

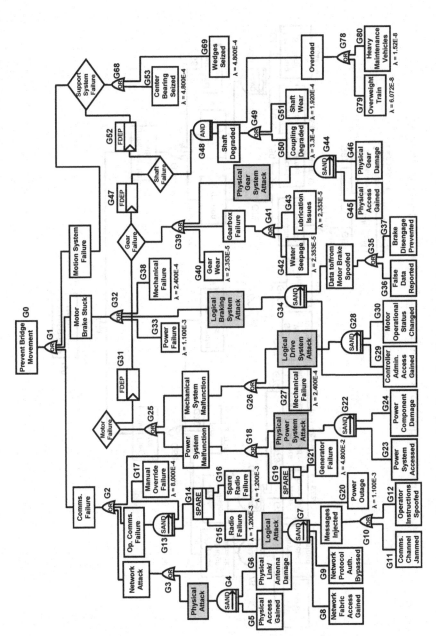

Figure 3. Attack-fault tree for the mechanical and electrical subsystems.

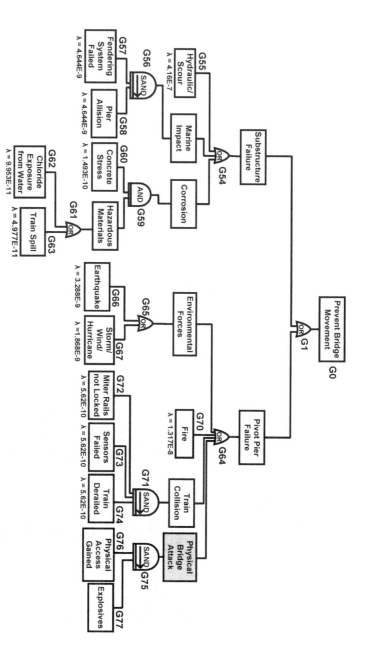

Figure 4.   Attack-fault tree for the superstructure and substructure subsystems.

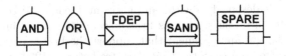

Figure 5. Attack-fault tree gates.

motor brake; a simple mechanical miter rail system that does not require separate electronic controls; and modern power systems.

Attacks or faults can take any one of the following five paths to realize the top-level goal $[G_0]$:

- $[G_2]$: Communications failures prevent local or remote operators from moving the bridge.

- $[G_{32}]$: Stuck electric motor brake prevents bridge movement.

- $[G_{68}]$: Support system failure prevents the motion system from functioning.

- $[G_{54}]$: Substructure failure causes a major bridge outage.

- $[G_{64}]$: Pivot pier failure causes a major bridge outage.

Figure 3 shows paths $[G_2]$, $[G_{32}]$ and $[G_{68}]$. Figure 4 shows paths $[G_{54}]$ and $[G_{64}]$. All five paths could result in $[G_0]$.

4. Movable Swing Bridge Components

This section describes the basic components and subsystems of a movable swing bridge [15]. An overview of swing bridge subsystems is provided in order to discuss the attacks and faults in the attack-fault tree. Certain basic attack steps and basic component failures are highlighted during the discussion. Note that swing bridges are falling out of style in favor of lift bridges because their central piers cut waterways in half, which can prevent the passage of large ships.

4.1 Superstructure and Substructure

A swing bridge superstructure consists of a pivot pier $[G_{64}]$, which is centered in a navigable water channel (Figure 1). The pivot pier is typically fixed in the middle of the rotating span, enabling it to remain balanced as it rotates. Fires $[G_{70}]$, vehicular collisions $[G_{74}]$ and environmental forces $[G_{66}, G_{67}]$ are some of the primary causes of failures in a bridge superstructure system [6]. Additionally, between World War I and the Vietnam War, bridge destruction $[G_{76}, G_{77}]$ was an effective measure used by local populations to limit large armed force movements into their territories [10].

A swing bridge substructure $[G_{54}]$, which includes the foundation for the pivot pier (a round or square concrete base that vertically stretches above the water line), is designed to withstand horizontal loads and keep the bridge centered. Hydraulics issues, such as bridge scour [G_{55}] resulting from water scooping out the soil and sediment that support the bridge pier, caused 60% of complete bridge failures in the United States between 1950 and 1990 [6]. A timber or crib fendering system [G_{57}] is often installed to prevent ships from striking the center pier or to guide them away from the pier. Allisions [G_{58}] that result from marine vessels striking the pier base are the second greatest risk to the substructure and foundation of the bridge [6]. Concrete stress [G_{60}] causes cracks that could be further weakened by chloride from sea water [G_{62}] or by spills [G_{63}].

4.2   Mechanical and Electrical Systems

This subsection describes the mechanical and electrical systems that work together in modern swing bridge systems to control bridge movement. Potential attacks and faults are also identified.

Support Systems.   Modern swing bridges use mechanical bearing designs from the mid-nineteenth century, such as the center bearing, rim bearing and combined bearing designs. This research focuses on bearing systems because they are the most common. A system that uses a center bearing [G_{53}] has a circular disk with a convex spherical surface fixed to the bottom of the pivot pier, which supports the weight of the bridge while sitting on top of a fixed convex disk on which the bridge rotates. When the bridge is rotated on top of the disk, it moves along a circular track around the inside base of the pivot pier that distributes the weight and balances the structure when the bridge turns; this requires regular lubrication. Wedges [G_{69}] or some other support system are used to prop up the bridge when supporting live traffic loads; these often require additional electro-mechanical components.

Drive Systems.   The support system is rotated using a drive system [G_{52}, $FDEP$], which is engineered to reduce friction, limit the impact of resistance during movement and reduce the amount of torque output generated by the motor. A shaft [G_{50}] is used to connect the support system to the drive system; it is generally connected to the rack and pinion system via a grid-type coupler [G_{50}]. Additional force on the bridge span caused by overweight vehicles could result in damage to a worn shaft or rack and pinion system [G_{79}, G_{80}]. Gear drives [G_{40}] may have open or enclosed gearing for rotating the shaft [$G_{47}, FDEP$]. Possible gearbox faults are water seepage [G_{42}] and poor lubrication [G_{43}]. The drive system [$G_{31}, FDEP$] is powered by an electric motor [G_{27}] that produces the torque needed to drive the system. Motor brakes [G_{32}, G_{38}] are spring set and electrically released.

The electric motor and electric brakes, which connect mechanical and electric components [G_{18}, G_{33}] in the bridge system, could be exploited via logical or physical attacks [$G_{29}, G_{30}, G_{36}, G_{37}$]. The electrical drive control system in a modern movable bridge is designed to handle the sequencing of all the moving components to ensure proper bridge control. Programmable logic controllers (PLCs) are connected to a control network that gives local and/or remote operators the ability to instruct the bridge to open or close. Each electric motor typically has a dedicated drive controller that controls variables such as speed and torque for bridge rotation. The sequencing involves instructing the networked drive controllers used to manage the electric motor(s) and motor brake(s), controlling the bridge lighting and instructing interlocking system actuators.

Local operators may open and close the bridge using radios $[G_{15}, G_{16}]$ or a control panel $[G_{17}]$ in the bridge operator's house, which is generally located in the middle of the swing bridge span. Remote network access is typically provided via a wide-area network to a back office controlled by the transportation authority. A bridge without remote access is considered to be in "dark territory." Networked components $[G_2]$ in the bridge system could be attacked logically $[G_8, G_9, G_{11}, G_{12}]$ or physically $[G_5, G_6]$ and should, therefore, be carefully designed and installed with security in mind.

Interlocking Systems. The rotational movement requires a separate interlocking system that aligns the swing span with the connecting spans in order to fully close the bridge. The interlocking system has three functions: (i) ensure that the opening bridge does not become unbalanced and remains stable; (ii) ensure that the closed bridge does not become unbalanced due to a live load; and (iii) center the bridge and ensure that it does not over-rotate. The first two functions are performed by an end lift system, which relieves the dynamic stresses caused when the bridge begins to move and helps withstand the static stresses caused by passing traffic when the bridge is closed. The third function is performed by centering devices that ensure that the bridge does not over-rotate in the horizontal plane.

After the bridge is in the proper horizontal position, the railroad tracks are closed to enable a train to pass. Miter rails are most commonly used to lock the tracks; they are lowered at the end of each side of the span via a joint when the bridge is being locked into place and they are lifted when the bridge begins to open. Depending on the bridge design, the interlocking system may have electrical requirements similar to the drive control system.

Electrical Power System. Modern movable bridges are controlled by solid-state electrical power systems that incorporate silicon-controlled rectifier (SCR) technology made up of power distribution panels, switches, circuit breakers, fuses, ground fault relays, over-current protection relays, cabling, etc. Specialized submarine cables run underwater to the center pier to bring power to the operator's house located in the swing span. Modern bridges use AC and DC motors. Due to their complexity, power systems have the highest failure rates $[G_{20}]$ of any swing bridge system [11]. Consequently, the American Railway Engineering and Maintenance-of-Way Association (AREMA) mandates an emergency auxiliary power supply such as a generator $[G_{21}]$.

5.   Quantitative Analysis Methodology

The quantitative analysis employed the UPPAAL Statistical Model Checker (64-bit v4.1.19) [7] to transform the leaves of the attack-fault tree to stochastic automata that simulate failures [16]. This section describes the automaton parameters for the basic attack steps (BAS) and basic component failures (BCF) used in the simulation.

5.1   Attack Leaf Automata

Each basic attack step leaf in an attack chain is modeled as a stochastic timed automaton. When an attack is activated, the attacker waits until (s)he is able to afford a cost f to proceed. After the attacker proceeds, the attack is undetected with probability $w_1/(w_1 + w_2)$ or detected with probability $w_2/(w_1 + w_2)$. The attack stops if it is detected; otherwise, the attack is either ongoing or activated. An ongoing attack is detected over time with an exponential probability rate λ_1 at a cost v per day to the attacker. An activated attack is detected over time with an exponential probability rate λ at a cost v per day to the attacker.

After an attack is executed, it succeeds with probability $p/(p+q)$ and causes damage d to the bridge or the attack fails with probability $q/(p + q)$. These probabilities are based on the attacker's skills, which are specified in an attacker profile. The advantage of this approach is that it is possible to determine the ratio of cost to the attacker against the damage done to the bridge.

Table 1 provides information about each basic attack step leaf in the attack-fault tree segments in Figures 3 and 4. The w_1 and w_2 detection rates in the table are configured to be high (discussed later in the What-If scenario). The configuration assumes that detection occurs at a higher rate when an attacker is attempting to gain access but at a lower rate after access is gained. The attack labels and their categorizations as logical and physical attacks are relevant to the attack profiles.

The security analysis modeled the attacks in UPPAAL using the As-Is and What-If scenarios [16]. In the As-Is scenario, detection capabilities were eliminated to establish a baseline for a successful attack based on an attacker profile. In the What-If scenario, the w_1 and w_2 detection rates were set to high. This enabled the determination of the effectiveness of the detection mechanisms at preventing attacks.

5.2   Fault Leaf Automata

Exponential probability distributions with means λ are used to model the failure rates, where the probability of a failure at time t is $P(t) = 1 - e^{-\lambda t}$. A stochastic automaton is employed to simulate each basic component failure as described in [16]. Each automaton has a λ-value that expresses the exponential failure rate of the failing node (component). After a period of time, damage d occurs to the system, which transitions to the failed state and sends a message to a higher attack-fault tree gate that the component has failed. Each fault leaf in

Table 1. Basic attack step leaf information.

Attack	Label	Path	Type	Description
Cut Network	A_1	$[G_5] \to$ $[G_6]$	Physical	$[G_5]$: $w_1 = 60$, $w_2 = 40$, $f = 20$, $v = 2$, $d = 5$, $\lambda = 0.0011$, $\lambda_1 = 0.0011$ $[G_6]$: $w_1 = 80$, $w_2 = 20$, $f = 5$, $v = 1$, $d = 50$, $\lambda = 0.00301$, $\lambda_1 = 0$
Jam Network Comms.	A_2	$[G_8] \to$ $[G_9] \to$ $[G_{11}]$	Logical	$[G_8]$: $w_1 = 60$, $w_2 = 40$, $f = 20$, $v = 2$, $d = 5$, $\lambda = 0.001188$, $\lambda_1 = 0.001188$ $[G_9]$: $w_1 = 60$, $w_2 = 40$, $f = 10$, $v = 1$, $d = 50$, $\lambda = 0.0011$, $\lambda_1 = 0.0011$ $[G_{11}]$: $w_1 = 80$, $w_2 = 20$, $f = 10$, $v = 1$, $d = 100$, $\lambda = 0.001$, $\lambda_1 = 0$
Inject Packets	A_3	$[G_8] \to$ $[G_9] \to$ $[G_{12}]$	Logical	$[G_{12}]$: $w_1 = 80$, $w_2 = 20$, $f = 30$, $v = 2$, $d = 250$, $\lambda = 0.001$, $\lambda_1 = 0$
Cut Power	A_4	$[G_{23}] \to$ $[G_{24}]$	Physical	$[G_{23}]$: $w_1 = 60$, $w_2 = 40$, $f = 50$, $v = 3$, $d = 100$, $\lambda = 0.00092$, $\lambda_1 = 0.00092$ $[G_{24}]$: $w_1 = 80$, $w_2 = 20$, $f = 10$, $v = 2$, $d = 350$, $\lambda = 0.001$, $\lambda_1 = 0$
Stop Drive	A_5	$[G_{29}] \to$ $[G_{30}]$	Logical	$[G_{29}]$: $w_1 = 60$, $w_2 = 40$, $f = 40$, $v = 3$, $d = 100$, $\lambda = 0.000596$, $\lambda_1 = 0.000596$ $[G_{30}]$: $w_1 = 80$, $w_2 = 20$, $f = 30$, $v = 2$, $d = 500$, $\lambda = 0.0005$, $\lambda_1 = 0$
Tamper with Brake	A_6	$[G_{29}] \to$ $[G_{36}]$	Logical	$[G_{36}]$: $w_1 = 80$, $w_2 = 20$, $f = 40$, $v = 4$, $d = 500$, $\lambda = 0.0005$, $\lambda_1 = 0$
Stop Brake	A_7	$[G_{29}] \to$ $[G_{37}]$	Logical	$[G_{37}]$: $w_1 = 80$, $w_2 = 20$, $f = 25$, $v = 2$, $d = 500$, $\lambda = 0.0005$, $\lambda_1 = 0$
Break Gear	A_8	$[G_{45}] \to$ $[G_{46}]$	Physical	$[G_{45}]$: $w_1 = 60$, $w_2 = 40$, $f = 20$, $v = 4$, $d = 5$, $\lambda = 0.0011$, $\lambda_1 = 0.0011$ $[G_{46}]$: $w_1 = 80$, $w_2 = 20$, $f = 40$, $v = 8$, $d = 200$, $\lambda = 0.001092$, $\lambda_1 = 0$
Cause Explosion	A_9	$[G_{76}] \to$ $[G_{77}]$	Physical	$[G_{76}]$: $w_1 = 65$, $w_2 = 35$, $f = 50$, $v = 4$, $d = 5$, $\lambda = 0.00037$, $\lambda_1 = 0.00037$ $[G_{77}]$: $w_1 = 80$, $w_2 = 20$, $f = 100$, $v = 10$, $d = 5000$, $\lambda = 0.000178$, $\lambda_1 = 0$

Figures 3 and 4 has its own automaton and the gates are stepped through during the UPPAAL simulation. Table 2 lists the sources of the λ-values corresponding to the basic component failures. All the failure rates are eventually expressed in terms of days so that the faults and attacks in the simulation have consistent time units. Note that the MTBF acronym in Table 2 denotes the mean time between failures.

Table 2.   Basic component failure leaf sources and computation notes.

Failures	Source	Computation Notes
$[G_{15}], [G_{16}], [G_{17}]$	—	Assume MTBF is 20,000 hours based on a product review
$[G_{20}], [G_{33}]$	[11]	Assume annual failure rate is 0.4
$[G_{21}]$	[14]	Assume MTBF is 500 hours
$[G_{27}], [G_{38}]$	[20]	Assume failure rate is ten per million hours
$[G_{40}], [G_{42}], [G_{43}]$	[1]	Assume MTBF is 40,000 hours based on L10 life at the rated torque
$[G_{50}]$	[20]	Assume failure rate is eight per million hours at a 15-year renewal interval
$[G_{51}]$	[20]	Assume failure rate is 14 per million hours at a 15-year renewal interval
$[G_{53}]$	[20]	Assume failure rate is 20 per million hours at a 15-year renewal interval
$[G_{55}], [G_{57}], [G_{58}],$ $[G_{66}], [G_{67}], [G_{70}]$ $[G_{72}], [G_{73}], [G_{74}]$ $[G_{79}], [G_{80}]$	[6]	Assume or derive an annual failure rate
$[G_{60}], [G_{62}], [G_{63}]$	[8]	Assume failure rate is 1.09×10^{-7} per year based on concrete stress and corrosion data
$[G_{69}]$	—	Assume failure rate is 20 per million hours

6.   Attack-Fault Tree Analysis

Simulations were conducted to quantify the impacts of attacks and faults on swing bridge operations. During each test, UPPAAL stepped through a number of runs until the results became statistically significant (or insignificant) to provide feedback on the results. A run was stopped and considered to be a hit if the goal $[G_0]$ was reached within a specified time frame. If the time expired before the goal $[G_0]$ was reached, then the run was considered to be a miss. Statistical significance was assessed using 95% confidence intervals.

6.1   Critical Fault Path Analysis

The first set of simulations was conducted to analyze the probability of disruption over time. Figure 6 shows the probabilities of disruption over time for five scenarios. This helps identify the paths that result in maximum disruption to the railroad bridge over a ten-year period. After one year, the Only Faults scenario yielded a fault probability $P(t \leq 365)$ of 0.75. After two years, the

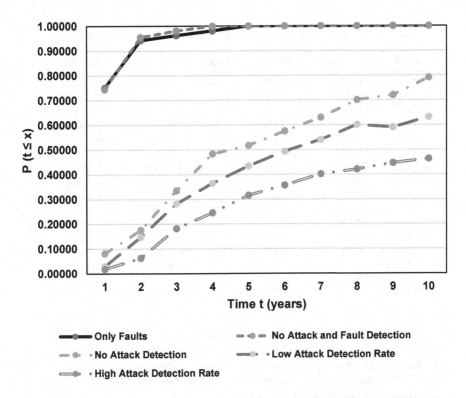

Figure 6. Probability of disruption at time t (95% confidence interval).

Only Faults scenario yielded a higher fault probability $P(t \leq 730)$ of 0.942. Scenarios with No Attack Detection, Low Attack Detection Rate and High Attack Detection Rate yielded two-year probabilities of 0.175, 0.147 and 0.0631, respectively.

The next set of simulations sought to identify the critical path in the attack-fault tree. This involved repeated simulations while disabling each basic component failure leaf in the attack-fault tree for a one-year period, where the Only Faults scenario yielded a fault probability $P(t \leq 365)$ of 0.75. After considering all the leaves, the percentage differences between the new results and the baseline value were computed.

Table 3 shows the results for all the basic component failure leaves. The results demonstrate that the power-related leaves pose the greatest risk to bridge failure. The G_{33} leaf corresponding to motor brake power failure yielded the greatest difference of -25.200% at $P(t \leq 365) = 0.561$, followed by G_{21} corresponding to generator failure with a difference of -21.730% and G_{20} corresponding to power outage with a difference of -19.870%. Note that G_{20} and G_{21} share the same critical failure path because the power generator should take

Table 3. Fault disruption percentages measured for all leaves (0.750).

Leaf	$P(t \leq 365)$	Difference	Leaf	$P(t \leq 365)$	Difference
G_{15}	0.720	-4.000%	G_{57}	0.748	-0.270%
G_{16}	0.693	-7.600%	G_{58}	0.734	-2.130%
G_{17}	0.724	-3.470%	G_{60}	0.749	-0.130%
G_{20}	0.601	-19.870%	G_{62}	0.716	-4.530%
G_{21}	0.587	-21.730%	G_{63}	0.748	-0.270%
G_{27}	0.702	-6.400%	G_{66}	0.758	1.070%
G_{33}	0.561	-25.200%	G_{67}	0.728	-2.930%
G_{38}	0.699	-6.800%	G_{69}	0.689	-8.130%
G_{40}	0.718	-4.270%	G_{70}	0.749	-0.130%
G_{42}	0.731	-2.530%	G_{72}	0.737	-1.730%
G_{43}	0.724	-3.470%	G_{73}	0.724	-3.470%
G_{50}	0.722	-3.730%	G_{74}	0.752	0.270%
G_{51}	0.708	-5.600%	G_{79}	0.722	-3.730%
G_{53}	0.697	-7.070%	G_{80}	0.735	-2.000%
G_{55}	0.735	-2.000%			

over in the event of a power failure. Generators are not built to last forever, but they have low exponential failure rates ($\lambda = 0.0042$). This may indicate a weakness in the model. Without some power system repair capabilities, the purpose of having a backup power system is defeated if its uptime (reliability) is less than the time between power failures.

6.2   Attacker Profile Analysis

Attacker profiles based on the attack-fault tree were created to evaluate various strategies against simulated adversaries. In particular, three attacker profiles were created to evaluate the effectiveness of adding security controls:

- **Nate:** Nation state attacker; Budget = $\$10,000 \times 10^3$; Success rate for logical attacks $p = 90\%$; Success rate for physical attacks $p = 90\%$.

- **Mallory:** Hacker; Budget = $\$5,000 \times 10^3$; Success rate for logical attacks $p = 80\%$; Success rate for physical attacks $p = 60\%$.

- **Chuck:** External attacker; Budget = $\$3,000 \times 10^3$; Success rate for logical attacks $p = 60\%$; Success rate for physical attacks $p = 80\%$.

Table 4 compares the results obtained for the As-Is and What-If scenarios by running the three attack profiles against the attack-fault tree over a ten-year time period.

In the As-Is scenario, Nate had a 36% chance of conducting a successful attack compared with 12.7% for Mallory and 10.2% for Chuck. Although Nate spent twice as much money on average in conducting a successful attack in

Table 4. As-Is versus What-If scenario results over ten years.

	Nate	Mallory	Chuck
As-Is Scenario			
Probability $P(t \leq 3,650)$	0.360	0.127	0.102
Mean Time $E(t)$ (days)	828.469	606.163	410.418
Mean Cost $E(cost)$ (10^3 dollars)	4,158.215	2,388.666	1,706.83
Mean Damage $E(damage)$ (10^3 dollars)	1,066.595	1,058.763	442.77
Successful Attacks	133	22	14
Runs	371	182	150
What-If Scenario			
Probability $P(t \leq 3,650)$	0.226	0.0454	0.0515
Mean Time $E(t)$ (days)	982.201	628.984	971.847
Mean Cost $E(cost)$ (10^3 dollars)	4,409.470	1,650.969	1,776.107
Mean Damage $E(damage)$ (10^3 dollars)	1,361.609	752.78	670.127
Successful Attacks	65	4	5
Runs	287	88	97

the average case as Mallory ($\$4,158.215 \times 10^3$ versus $\$2,388.666 \times 10^3$), they caused roughly the same amount of average damage per attack ($\$1,066.595 \times 10^3$ versus $\$1,058.763 \times 10^3$). This similarity suggests that logical attacks were likely to be more successful because Mallory had a higher probability of successful attacks. Meanwhile, Chuck spent an average of $\$1,706.83 \times 10^3$ per successful attack, resulting in an average of $\$442.77 \times 10^3$ in damage per successful attack. This also confirms that logical attacks are more likely to occur given the resources because Chuck is more likely to succeed with physical attacks. Time comparisons show that Nate (828.469 days) took longer on average than Mallory (606.163 days) and Chuck (410.418 days).

In the What-If scenario, the detection values for w_1 and w_2 were reconfigured as shown in Table 1. The percentages of successful attacks declined for Nate by −37.22%, Mallory by −64.25% and Chuck by −49.51%, demonstrating the utility of implementing detection mechanisms for all three attacker profiles. Nate's average time for attacks increased by 18.56% and cost increased by 6.04%, but he presumably took greater risks with his additional resources because the damage inflicted also increased by 27.66%. The simulation for Nate was executed ten additional times and similar results were obtained, confirming that the results were not anomalous. In contrast, Mallory saw an increase in the average time required to conduct successful attacks of only 3.76%, but decreases in cost of −30.88% and damage of −28.8%. Chuck saw a very large increase in the average time required to conduct successful attacks of 136.79%, only a slight increase in the average cost of 4.06%, but a large increase in damage of 51.35%. These results indicate that additional detection mechanisms would be more useful against strictly logical attackers (Mallory) than adversaries who are stronger at physical attacks (Nate and Chuck).

Table 5. Analysis of attack disruptions measured against $P(t \leq 3,650) = 0.341$.

Attack	$P(t \leq 3,650)$	Difference	Attack	$P(t \leq 3,650)$	Difference
A_1	0.275	−19.365%	A_6	0.347	1.858%
A_2	0.343	0.8072%	A_7	0.349	2.38%
A_3	0.343	0.8072%	A_8	0.358	5.234%
A_4	0.341	0%	A_9	0.339	−0.5234%
A_5	0.330	−3.244%			

6.3   Critical Attack Path Analysis

The observation that attackers with strengths in logical attacks may be at a disadvantage influenced the identification of critical attack paths in the attack-fault tree that might provide an explanation. This was accomplished by re-executing the No Attack Detection scenario discussed in Section 6.1 with Nate as the attacker.

The executions were configured to run for ten years without any detection mechanisms in place. After running through a baseline test with all the basic attack step leaves enabled, the differences in the new results with probability $P(t \leq 3,650) = 0.341$ were computed.

Table 5 shows the results for all the attack paths. The physical attack A_1, which physically cut network links, is critical because it has the highest difference: a −19.365% drop in the probability of successful attacks. This explains why physical attackers fared better in the What-If scenario. Upon applying detection methods of similar strength to both logical and physical attacks, adversaries who were stronger at physical attacks (Nate and Chuck) were still able to increase the amount of damage caused. This was due to their ability to perform attack A_1 that cut bridge network links with higher success rates.

7.   Related Work

Previous work [27] introduced the security and safety risks facing movable railroad bridges and leveraged dynamic attack trees and fault trees to map possible vulnerabilities. Two separate models, one involving security and the other involving safety, were developed after researching control systems for a specific swing bridge. The previous work also revealed that many of the attacks and faults tended to overlap.

In contrast, the research described in this chapter integrates attacks and faults in a single model. The integrated attack-fault tree model was recently introduced by Kumar and Stoelinga [16], who used it to analyze a number of example systems. However, this chapter describes the first real-world application of the integrated attack-fault tree model, as well as the first application to a bridge system.

7.1   Historical Swing Bridge Failures

As discussed in the introductory section, data about swing bridge failures is limited due to a variety of factors. This research began by compiling data about swing bridge failures that was used to create the attack-fault tree.

The following additional information, categorized by the impacted swing bridge subsystems, is highly relevant to the faults considered in the model:

- **Superstructure System:** In 2014, a fire at a 104-year-old portal swing bridge in New York City cut power to the bridge. The resulting 70-minute outage delayed or cancelled 52 trains [17].

- **Substructure System:** The Gasparilla Island Swing Bridge in Charlotte County, Florida was recently replaced because its concrete girders from 1958 were structurally deteriorating, leading to high risks of failure due to storm surges and vehicular impacts [24]. Incident data about bridge allisions by marine vessels is posted by the U.S. Coast Guard [26].

- **Support System:** Older swing bridge center bearing designs are prone to instability when the bridges are unbalanced. As a result, a number of swing bridge renovation projects have been undertaken recently to address the problem, including the Court Street Bridge in Hackensack, New Jersey [3] and the East Haddam Swing Bridge in Connecticut [9]. In 2010, the Somerleyton Swing Bridge in Norfolk, England suffered a catastrophic failure due to a bearing system failure [22].

  Wedge faults have led to several prolonged swing bridge outages. In 2017, degraded wedges impacted operations of the Little Current Swing Bridge in Ontario, Canada [4]. In 2014, a complete wedge failure resulted in significant downtime of the Walk Bridge in Norwalk, Connecticut [23].

- **Drive System:** In 2010, a gearbox failure in the Whitby Swing Bridge in North Yorkshire, England terminated bridge operations for one week [2].

- **Interlocking System:** In 1996, Amtrak Train No. 12 derailed on the Portal Bridge near Secaucus, New Jersey due to defective miter rails $[G_{72}, G_{73}, G_{74}]$ [19]. In 2014, the Walk Bridge in Norwalk, Connecticut was closed due to an interlocking problem with its miter rails [23].

- **Electrical System:** An interesting story from 2002 about the Old Saybrook Bridge is recounted in [21]. This bascule bridge had electrical components dating back to its original design and construction in 1907. Troubleshooting the failed electrical system was an extremely complex task.

7.2   Rules and Regulations

Several rules and regulations govern the management of movable bridges in the United States. The U.S. Coast Guard oversees movable bridge operations on navigable waterways. Organizations such as the American Association of Railroads (AAR) and the American Association of State Highway and Transportation Officials (AASHTO) promulgate national standards and requirements for movable bridge construction, maintenance and inspection. In addition, the following federal regulations govern movable bridge operations:

- **Movable Bridge, Interlocking of Signal Appliances with Bridge Devices (49 CFR 236.312 [12]):** This section specifies rules and restrictions governing the passage of trains over movable bridges.

- **Movable Bridge Locking (49 CFR 236.387 [13]):** This section mandates that movable bridges shall be inspected once a year.

- **Bridge Lighting and Other Signals (33 CFR Chapter 1, Sub-Chapter j, Part 118 [25]):** This section mandates the lighting requirements required for signaling the status of movable bridge operations on navigable waters.

8.   Conclusions

Movable bridges have been used for hundreds of years, but they continue to evolve in their designs and implementations. Numerous movable bridges are being upgraded by automating and networking their components, which adds a new layer of risk to these vital transportation infrastructure assets. The research described in this chapter has leveraged the attack-fault tree model to integrate the physical risks involved in operating railroad swing bridges in the face of risks posed by physical attacks on bridge subsystems and cyber attacks on control systems.

The attack-fault tree approach integrates attacks and faults in a single model that supports the use of stochastic timed automata to identify the critical failure paths for a movable swing bridge. In particular, the integrated model reveals that physical network attacks and power faults are the best ways to disrupt movable swing bridge operations. Moreover, by stepping through the model, it was determined that superstructure and substructure system faults are statistical anomalies as far as the integrated attack-fault model is concerned. Thus, future research should focus on the attack surfaces and mechanical and electrical system failures.

The principal conclusion of this research is that the attack-fault tree approach is effective at identifying critical attack and fault paths at a high level. However, the swing bridge analysis reveals that the model falls short in some ways. In the case of a swing bridge, many faults can only occur only while the bridge is moving and other faults can occur only when the bridge is closed. The state of the system is, therefore, important, but the attack-fault tree model does not take the system state into account. For example, components such as electric motors and gears have failure rates that are established only when the system is in use. A movable bridge is in motion only for a few minutes at a time and these components spend the majority of their time at rest. Additionally, the attack-fault tree allows for the incorporation of attack chains, but it does not necessarily consider the specific system configurations included in previous attack tree models. The attack-fault tree model also abstracts security control solutions as simple detection mechanisms, which reduces its applications in real-world environments.

Note that the views and opinions expressed herein are those of the authors and do not necessarily state or reflect the views and opinions of the Federal Railroad Administration or U.S. Department of Transportation, and shall not be used for advertising or product endorsement purposes.

Acknowledgements

This research was supported by Grant No. DTFR5317C00018 from the Federal Railroad Administration, U.S. Department of Transportation. The authors thank Mr. Francesco Bedini Jacobini and Mr. Jared Withers from the Federal Railroad Administration for their advice and assistance.

References

[1] G. Antony, How to determine the MTBF of gearboxes, *Power Transmission Engineering*, pp. 32–37, April 2008.

[2] BBC News, Swing bridge reopens in Whitby after gearbox failure, July 30, 2010.

[3] L. Burgos, Machinery rehabilitation of the Court Street Bridge over the Hackensack River, Hackensack, New Jersey, presented at the *Heavy Movable Structures Fourteenth Bienniel Symposium*, 2012.

[4] CBC News, Delays at swing bridge in Little Current due to repairs says MTO, July 7, 2017.

[5] P. Chaux, J. Roussel, J. Lesage, G. Deleuze and M. Bouissou, Towards a unified definition of minimal cut sequences, *Proceedings of the Fourth IFAC Workshop on Dependable Control of Discrete Systems*, paper no. 1, 2013.

[6] W. Cook, Bridge Failure Rates, Consequences and Predictive Trends, Ph.D. Dissertation, Department of Civil and Environmental Engineering, Utah State University, Logan, Utah, 2014.

[7] A. David, K. Larsen, A. Legay, M. Mikucionis and D. Poulsen, UPPAAL SMC tutorial, *International Journal on Software Tools for Technology Transfer*, vol. 17(4), pp. 397–415, 2015.

[8] C. Davis-McDaniel, Fault-Tree Model for Bridge Collapse Analysis, M.S. Thesis, Department of Civil Engineering, Clemson University, Clemson, South Carolina, 2011.

[9] J. DeWolf, History of Connecticut's Short-Term Strain Program for Evaluation of Steel Bridges, Report No. CT-2251-F-09-6, Connecticut Department of Transportation, Storrs, Connecticut, 2009.

[10] H. Douthit, The Use and Effectiveness of Sabotage as a Means of Unconventional Warfare – An Historical Perspective from World War I through Viet Nam, M.S. Thesis, School of Systems and Logistics, Air Force Institute of Technology, Wright-Patterson Air Force Base, Ohio, 1987.

[11] R. Eacker and M. Bardsley, Electrical reliability analysis for transit applications, *Proceedings of the ASME/IEEE Joint Railroad Conference*, pp. 81–88, 2002.

[12] Federal Railroad Administration, Code of Federal Regulations, Title 49, Section 236.312 – Movable Bridge, Interlocking of Signal Appliances with Bridge Devices, Department of Transportation, Washington, DC, 2018.

[13] Federal Railroad Administration, Code of Federal Regulations, Title 49, Section 236.387 – Movable Bridge Locking, Department of Transportation, Washington, DC, 2018.

[14] G. Hansen, E. Frame and E. Sattler, Generator Set Durability Testing, Interim Report TFLRF No. 419, U.S. Army TARDEC Fuels and Lubricants Research Facility, Southwest Research Institute, San Antonio, Texas, 2012.

[15] T. Koglin, *Movable Bridge Engineering*, John Wiley and Sons, Hoboken, New Jersey, 2003.

[16] R. Kumar and M. Stoelinga, Quantitative security and safety analysis with attack-fault trees, *Proceedings of the Eighteenth IEEE International Symposium on High Assurance Systems Engineering*, pp. 25–32, 2017.

[17] P. McGeehan, 104-year-old portal bridge presents $900 million problem for rail commuters, *The New York Times*, September 25, 2014.

[18] S. Morgan, Burlington Northern Railroad Bridge 9.6, *Wikipedia* (`en.wiki pedia.org/wiki/Burlington_Northern_Railroad_Bridge_9.6#/media /File:BNSF_Bridge_9.6_swing_span_turning.jpg`), June 25, 2011.

[19] National Transportation Safety Board, Derailment of Amtrak Train No. 12 and Sideswipe of Amtrak Train No. 79 on Portal Bridge near Secaucus, New Jersey, November 23, 1996, Railroad Special Investigation Report, Notation 6813B, Washington, DC, 1996.

[20] Naval Surface Warfare Center (Carderock Division), *Handbook of Reliability Prediction Procedures for Mechanical Equipment*, West Bethesda, Maryland, 2010.

[21] P. O'Neill and A. Ostrovsky, Failure and quick recovery of movable bridge on the Acela Line, presented at the *Heavy Movable Structures Ninth Biennial Movable Bridge Symposium*, 2002.

[22] M. Rimmer, Somerleyton Swing Bridge, Report by Waterways Strategy Officer, Navigation Committee, 2 September 2010, Agenda Item No. 8, Broads Authority, Norwich, United Kingdom, 2010.

[23] Short Term Action Team, Connecticut DOT BR. NO. 04288R Walk Bridge over Norwalk River, Norwalk, Connecticut, Emergency Repair and Reliability Report FINAL July 17, 2014, Connecticut Department of Transportation, Newington, Connecticut, 2014.

[24] H. Sinson, Gasparilla Island Swing Bridge replacement, presented at the *Heavy Movable Structures Sixteenth Biennial Movable Bridge Symposium*, 2016.

[25] United States Coast Guard, Code of Federal Regulations, Title 33 – Navigation and Navigable Waters, Washington, DC, 2010.

[26] United States Coast Guard, Homeport, Washington, DC (`homeport.uscg.mil`), 2019.

[27] Y. Wang, M. Jablonski, C. Yavvari, Z. Wang, X. Liu, K. Holt and D. Wijesekera, Safety and security analysis for movable railroad bridges, presented at the *ASME Joint Rail Conference*, 2019.

Chapter 4

CONVERTING AN ELECTRIC POWER UTILITY NETWORK TO DEFEND AGAINST CRAFTED INPUTS

Michael Millian, Prashant Anantharaman, Sergey Bratus, Sean Smith and Michael Locasto

Abstract   This chapter proposes a roadmap that employs secure parsers to eliminate the possibility of input-handling vulnerabilities in industrial control systems. Industrial control systems are responsible for maintaining the integrity of power grids. Complex communications networks constitute the backbones of these systems. Communications in industrial control networks must be processed correctly and they should not crash devices or enable attackers to access networked devices. Language-theoretic security is the practice of comprehensive input handling using secure parsers. This chapter demonstrates that the existing collection of secure parsers for industrial control protocols can cover the communications needs of industrial control networks. It discusses the merits of guarding industrial control networks using secure parsers, proposes a triage procedure for implementation and summarizes the security benefits and lessons learned.

Keywords: Industrial control networks, input handling, language-theoretic parsers

1.   Introduction

Industrial control systems are increasingly connected to the Internet, either directly or via connections to Internet-connected devices. Industrial control protocols are used to interact with actuators and sensors that help operate important infrastructure assets such as the power grid. The risks posed by the cyber-physical nature of industrial control devices coupled with their network connectivity render the task of securing industrial control network communications a very high priority.

The principal goal of this research is to eliminate input-handling vulnerabilities in industrial control networks. Input-handling vulnerabilities are a class of

© IFIP International Federation for Information Processing 2019
Published by Springer Nature Switzerland AG 2019
J. Staggs and S. Shenoi (Eds.): Critical Infrastructure Protection XIII, IFIP AICT 570, pp. 73–85, 2019.
https://doi.org/10.1007/978-3-030-34647-8_4

vulnerabilities with a long history and many modern examples [5–7, 19]. Previous work has shown that industrial control networks are not immune to these vulnerabilities – between 2013 and 2014 alone, more that 30 input-handling vulnerabilities were discovered in implementations of the DNP3 protocol in industrial control devices [2].

However, eradicating input-handling vulnerabilities presents some challenges. First, while a language-theoretic security approach has been applied to build secure parsers for industrial control protocols, the results have thus far been limited to academic research as opposed to production systems. Indeed, the adoption of these protocol implementations in real systems has been minimal. This research attempts to address the issue by clarifying the benefits and explaining how to use secure parsers.

In particular, a notional architecture of an industrial control network that employs secure parsers is presented. The notional architecture is a general network model that incorporates the components found in industrial control networks. The model loosely maps a real-world network without being tied to a single utility. It is shown that secure parsers cover the communications edges of this model. Indeed, all communications can be guarded using these parsers.

The second challenge is that industrial control networks employ a large variety of protocols. Securing a protocol implementation requires a careful examination of the protocol specification. Device manufacturers often subset or fork existing protocols, resulting in new protocols that must be analyzed thoroughly. Device manufacturers also implement proprietary protocols that significantly complicate protocol analysis. To address this challenge, best practices are proposed for creating new parsers and for subsetting or forking existing protocols.

The third challenge is updating industrial control devices. Because these devices perform vital operations, taking them offline or interrupting their ability to communicate are not viable options. Nevertheless, protocols that contain unsafe features must be made to meet language-theoretic security standards. This is accomplished by employing a triage procedure that enables industrial control devices to continue to operate during the transition.

The proposed approach focuses on subsetting existing industrial control protocols. A subset of a protocol is just the protocol with certain messages excluded. For example, an opcode is removed if the payload for the opcode is unsafe. No features are added to a protocol; rather, unsafe features are removed. As a result, all the industrial control devices that understand a protocol can understand the safe subset of the protocol.

2.   Background and Prior Work

Input-handling vulnerabilities have plagued networked systems since their creation. Several well-known bugs – Heartbleed [6], Shellshock [18], Rosetta Flash [17] and Apple's goto bug [5] – involve input-handling vulnerabilities. Any program that accepts inputs must validate the inputs holistically to ensure that they comply with the protocol specifications. An input-handling vulnerability stems from a protocol violation. Typically this is due to a programmer error, such as forgetting to check a condition. Sometimes, an input-handling vulnerability may arise not from a protocol violation *per se*, but from a deeper flaw in the protocol.

Many bugs have parsing errors at their root. Some work has been done to demonstrate this in specific domains (e.g., USB [12]), but no large-scale effort has been expended to label all parsing bugs as such. Another domain-specific work found more than 30 input-handling vulnerabilities in DNP3 protocol implementations [2]. In fact, only a few implementations were found to be free of vulnerabilities. They were immune because they employed very constrained subsets of DNP3 that significantly reduced their attack surfaces. This result supports the position that protocol subsetting can eliminate input-handling vulnerabilities.

The impacts of input-handling vulnerabilities range from device crashes to attackers gaining access to networks. Heartbleed enabled attackers to exfiltrate data; Apple's goto bug allowed man-in-the-middle attacks; Shellshock gave attackers direct access to systems. Given the ubiquity of input-handling vulnerabilities, it is imprudent to believe that industrial control networks, protocols and devices are immune to input-handling vulnerabilities. Device crashes may pose mild threats in information technology environments. Not so in industrial control networks where device crashes can disrupt critical infrastructure assets. Without question, it is imperative to ensure that industrial control networks are rendered immune to input-handling vulnerabilities.

2.1　Language-Theoretic Security

Language-theoretic security postulates that all inputs received by a program must be validated in their entirety by a parser developed from a formal grammar before any and all uses of the inputs by program internals. A program that receives an unanticipated input could be driven to a state that its developers did not anticipate. A language-theoretic-security-hardened parser ensures that input validation code is explicitly and clearly based on a formal grammar, that the validation code is logically separate from the code that processes the inputs, and that a program can never operate on inputs that have not been verified exhaustively. There is no room for inputs that are "almost correct" because these inputs cannot be meaningfully distinct from malicious crafted inputs.

In this work, a language denotes a set of allowed inputs. A protocol is specified using a grammar, a set of production rules that create the inputs that constitute the language. A parser is an implementation of the protocol in code.

A parser combinator is employed to construct a parser in a manner that clearly and explicitly represents the protocol. It is a toolkit or framework that produces code that visually resembles the formal grammar instead of multiple if-statements that check conditions. Parser combinators dramatically reduce the possibility of programmer errors (e.g., forgetting to check a condition).

In this research, the Hammer parser combinator tool [16] was used to implement parsers. Hammer was developed with a security focus, which is measured against the Chomsky hierarchy that classifies languages according to their complexity [3]. The language classes range from regular expressions that are recognized/generated by finite state automata to recursively-enumerable languages that are recognized/generated by Turing machines. Note that `regex` tools in Perl, Python and JavaScript are actually more complex than regular expressions. Grammars that are deterministic-context-free or simpler are considered safe; this limit is discussed by Momot et al [14]. Parser combinator toolkits are useful for building parsers for binary protocols and for specifying byte-level constraints about languages. They also provide a way to represent top-down grammars. The Hammer tool parses inputs into abstract syntax trees.

2.2 Industrial Control Systems Security

Industrial control systems differ from traditional information technology systems and, consequently, require different security approaches. Industrial control networks interact with physical devices such as sensors and actuators using short messages with extremely low latency. In contrast, information technology networks transfer data using much larger packets with longer latency. Additionally, industrial control networks are typically deeper than information technology networks.

Much work has focused on ensuring the security of industrial control systems and networks. The prevailing security paradigm is defense-in-depth where security features and tools are added at each layer of the system or network to provide compound protection against external threats [8].

This research leveraging secure parsers complements the defense-in-depth model. Industrial control systems were originally designed for isolated, local use of analog equipment. Over the years, industrial control networks have been upgraded to support automation and remote access. New connections and capabilities pose new threats that industrial control systems were not designed to handle. The proposed approach is fundamentally about ensuring message security during the protocol design phase. It may require modifications of existing protocols if they do not meet the complexity-limitation requirements for security. Because protocol complexity is restricted rather than increased, the proposed approach dovetails with current defense-in-depth strategies. Existing security measures do not have to be replaced, they can work in concert with the proposed approach. Indeed, the approach can be used at every level of the defense-in-depth model to increase the security claims at a given level and between levels.

3. Notional Architecture

This section presents a notional architecture for a language-theoretic-security-compliant industrial control system at a utility. The notional architecture contains the general elements and components of a real-world network in an abstract representation that is not tied to a single utility.

First, the types of devices encountered in an electricity utility are specified, including the devices that are expected to communicate directly and the pro-

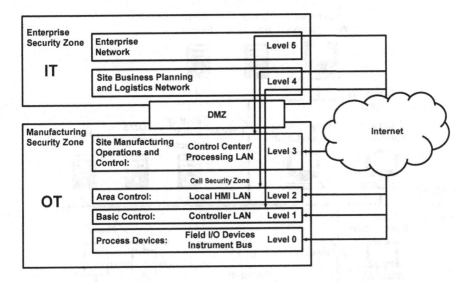

Figure 1. Purdue model architecture (adapted from [11]).

tocols they use for communications. Next, it is shown how secure parsers can provide coverage of the communication needs in the model such that all the communications can be guarded by the parsers.

Figure 1 shows the Purdue model architecture [11], which is annotated with the various paths that an attacker could use to access the industrial control network. The Purdue model has six levels: (i) enterprise network (level 5); (ii) business planning and logistics network (level 4); (iii) site manufacturing operations and control (level 3); (iv) area control (level 2); (v) basic control (level 1); and (vi) process devices (level 0). The levels are divided into several zones, where a zone corresponds to large-scale interconnectivity. Implementing clear boundaries between the zones is a best practice for enforcing multiple layers of defense.

This research focuses mainly on levels 2 through 0, which is called the cell security zone or the SCADA (supervisory control and data acquisition) zone. This zone comprises devices found in an electricity substation as well as devices that are directly involved in managing the substation. Level 2 is concerned with monitoring and controlling physical devices. The devices in this level include control center operation workstations, human-machine interfaces (HMIs), engineering workstations, security event collectors, operations alarm systems, communications front ends, data historians and network/application administrator workstations. Level 1 is concerned with sensing and manipulating physical devices. Devices in this level include dedicated operator workstations, programmable logic controllers (PLCs), control processors, programmable relays, remote terminal units (RTUs) and process-specific microcontrollers. Level 0 contains physical devices such as sensors, actuators, motors, process-specific automation machinery and field instrumentation devices [13].

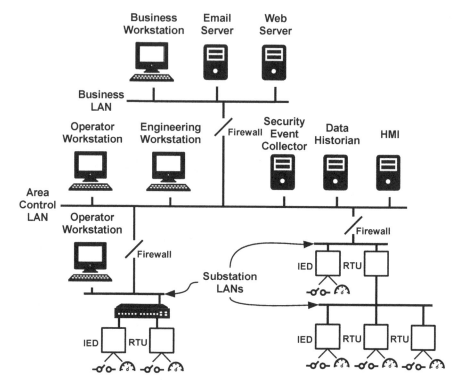

Figure 2. Notional architecture.

During the research, several real and development networks in the SCADA zone were examined. These networks are considered critical infrastructure assets, so detailed information about their network topologies cannot be published. In any case, large variances were observed in device types and layouts from substation to substation. Thus, it has been possible to develop a notional architecture that is not based on a single utility.

Figure 2 shows the notional architecture that is derived from previous models [10, 11, 20] as well as from real and development networks. The architecture is designed to be as generic as possible while still maintaining its utility.

The generic architecture enables the expression of coverage by focusing on a small set of protocols used at the edges (e.g., RTU-RTU, RTU-HMI and control-center-substation) without too much concern about the actual device models. While there are many protocols for a given edge (e.g., RTU-HMI), the notion of coverage means that at least one of the protocols is handled and, therefore, it is feasible to add the protection. Vendor-specific protocols exist, but many vendors provide devices that can handle multiple protocols (i.e., standard languages), so this concept of coverage is practical. Using popular protocols allows easier integration in existing ecosystems. The set of popular protocols considered in this work was determined using informal as well as published surveys [10].

4. Analysis

This section discusses the coverage provided by secure parsers and their benefits and trade-offs.

4.1 Protocol Coverage

At this time, the authors of this chapter have implemented secure input handling for the DNP3, MMS (Manufacturing Message Specification), Modbus, IEC 61850-8-1 (GOOSE), IEEE C37.118 [1], SEL Fast Message, HTTP and Telnet protocols. This section discusses how this selection of protocols offers adequate coverage of industrial control network communications needs.

DNP3, MMS and Modbus are the *de facto* industry communications standards. These protocols allow for communications between the human-machine interface of a master station and remote terminal units, programmable logic controllers and intelligent electronic devices (IEDs). SEL Fast Message is a vendor-specific protocol for SEL devices that handles much of the same communications. GOOSE is used to broadcast or multicast event data fast and reliably in substations; GOOSE messages have a maximum latency of 4 ms. IEEE C37.118 is used to transmit phasor data over wide-area networks. HTTP and Telnet are used for communications between workstations and for configuring devices.

To reiterate, communications from level 2 downwards are covered by the popular DNP3, MMS and Modbus protocols as well as by the vendor-specific SEL Fast Message protocol. Level 1 substation/physical devices are covered by the GOOSE and IEEE C37.118 protocols. Finally, workstation-workstation communications are covered by HTTP and Telnet. By implementing parsers for these industrial control system protocols, a large degree of protection is provided for the majority of low-level (Purdue model) operational technology traffic in most industrial control networks. In particular, secure parsing is provided for the protocols that are responsible for manipulating physical devices, a task that has very high priority.

4.2 Benefits

The major benefit in using a parser combinator tool is the possibility of producing provably-correct code. A programmer implementing a parser should not have to worry about the correctness of a combinator just like a programmer typically does not worry about the correctness of a compiler.

Proofs of correctness of the combinators in Hammer remain to be done. However, as far as this work is concerned, only two possibilities exist – either every combinator is correct or there are bugs in one or more combinators. If a bug is found in a combinator, it can be corrected without having to rewrite the parsers built using the combinator (although they would have to be recompiled using the updated combinator library). This is because each combinator performs a function that is fully understood under formal computational theory, so the function signature of each combinator is set, only the internals may change. After this proof work is complete, every secure parser built with these combinators immediately derives the full benefits of provable security.

The other benefit of the parser combinator is that it reduces the effort undertaken by the programmer who works on a parser. A key observation is that attention should be paid to match the complexity of the parser to the complexity of the protocol and this attention must be baked in during development and implementation. Traditional parser programming involves a number of if-statements that check conditions. It is easy to miss a condition – as in Heartbleed and Apple's goto bug. However, even when a fix is provided, it is still difficult to compare the new parser against the protocol and demonstrate that they match completely [14].

Using a parser combinator simplifies the comparison task, and thus decreases the likelihood of errors, and simplifies the implementation of fixes should errors occur. A parser combinator tool produces code that visually matches the structure of the grammar, rendering the verification of equality trivial. Furthermore, a tool like Hammer does not have combinators that would allow the programming of complex constructions such as Turing machines. If a programmer cannot implement a protocol feature using a parser combinator, then it is an indication that, perhaps, the feature is unsafe and that a subset of the protocol without the feature should be used. Ideally, this practice of subsetting protocols leads to protocols being designed without unsafe features.

The end result of using a parser combinator is a parser that only accepts messages in the protocol specification. The task of implementing protocols safely can thus be broken down to designing protocols and designing parser combinator tools.

Previous work with DNP3 has demonstrated the practicality of the approach for industrial control system protocols [2]. Implementing the DNP3 parser revealed that the specification mentions that the transport layer payload contains at least one byte, but that a zero-length application layer message would cause unhandled exceptions in certain implementations. Each protocol that was implemented contained such features, which were usually handled by if-checks in the parser. The language-theoretic security approach to parser construction considers such packet structure features when writing the parser, significantly decreasing the likelihood that a check is omitted.

4.3   Trade-Offs

The major trade-off that comes with a language-theoretic-security-based parser is the need to subset a protocol when inherently unsafe features are discovered. The cost associated with this modification is the possibility that network devices regularly or occasionally transmit messages using the unsafe features. Experience has shown that such messages are a small, if any, fraction of actual traffic. However, there are situations where the trade-offs could be greater depending on the use cases.

Maintaining unsafe protocol features is dangerous. Unsafe features most often relate to message format as opposed to message content, especially in the case of industrial control networks. Of course, it may be necessary to use certain kinds of messages and there are always development costs involved in making changes. However, the real costs arise from the risks of an attacker crashing devices, exfiltrating data or seizing control of devices.

5. Triage Procedure

This section discusses the roadmap for incorporating language-theoretic-security-hardened parsers in industrial control networks so that electric utilities may realize the security benefits. The roadmap involves a three-step plan for engaging with utilities and vendors. The first step is to develop the secure parsers and incorporate them on a per-device basis in a laboratory setting. The second step is to create a virtual substation in the laboratory. The third step is to work with utilities and vendors to replace parser implementations in device firmware via their product refresh cycles.

5.1 Protocols and Devices

The first step is to write and test parsers for industrial control protocols. At this time, parsers have been implemented for eight protocols: DNP3, MMS, Modbus, IEC 61850-8-1 (GOOSE), IEEE C37.118, SEL Fast Message, HTTP and Telnet. Accomplishing this task in full requires the complete list of protocols used by utilities.

For each protocol of interest, the protocol specification is obtained and a secure parser is written and tested. At first, parser testing is performed using a bump-in-the-wire implementation. A key requirement is to ensure that the messages passed by each parser allow normal device operations.

However, some inherent difficulties exist. Obtaining documentation for industrial control protocols can be difficult. Many protocol specifications have to be purchased – their costs range from a few hundred dollars to several thousand dollars. A protocol specification may not cover the complete protocol; some protocols import other protocols to leverage existing work and offset the design burden (e.g., data encoding formats and protocol data units). The specifications of these embedded protocols might also have to be purchased.

Another challenge is that there is neither uniformity nor good practice when it comes to describing a protocol. Some specifications are all prose and the developer must create the protocol grammars. Even worse are situations where the specifications include state machines or grammars, but their functionalities do not match the prose [2]. This causes divergent implementations depending on how closely the developer reads the documentation. Until protocol specifications improve, close readings of the available specification are essential.

When a protocol has unsafe features, the correct subset of the protocol has to be determined before a parser can be developed. An example of an unsafe feature is nested length fields. Inclusion of nested length fields requires inner length agreement (e.g., the inner length should not exceed the outer length). This constraint cannot be described purely in terms of packet structure using a context-free language because it requires complete parsing of the outer and inner fields to determine agreement. If adherence to the protocol is not maintained by the packet structure of the packet, but left to after-the-fact checks, it is common for one or more checks to be forgotten [5, 6].

After the parsers are written and tested as bump-in-the-wire implementations to ensure that devices can operate as required, the native parsers must be replaced with security parsers on a per-device basis. This action is required because industrial control protocols have maximum latency requirements and parsing every message twice can be expensive. Incorporating a secure parser as the native parser provides security benefits beyond traditional intrusion detection. Intrusion detection systems have difficulty providing insights into encrypted messages, but every message must be decrypted and parsed. Thus, incorporating secure parsers as the only native parsers in a device adds precise security properties.

5.2   Virtual Substation

After implementing the full range of parsers for industrial control protocols and incorporating them in devices, the next step is to create and operate a virtual substation with hardened devices in a laboratory environment. Before deploying the parsers in real critical infrastructure assets, it is necessary to guarantee that the individual devices and the consequences on a network with these devices operating under normal and stress conditions are well understood.

The virtual substation would be a fully-functioning substation that runs in parallel with real-world networks but does not affect the operation of the networks. It could accept real-time data or replayed captures and would operate real or simulated devices. Developers would conduct analyses to ensure correct operations of the virtual substation with no risk to the larger network.

This step can motivate hardened devices via the list of vulnerabilities that the parsers would prevent. It would also demonstrate to utilities and vendors that hardened devices are viable in operational environments.

5.3   Deployment

The final step involves field deployments of the hardened devices. This step must address all the real-world constraints that were not considered in the previous two steps. In particular, industrial control networks are slow to incorporate changes and the changes made may be expected to last for decades. Nevertheless, existing refresh cycles can be leveraged to push language-theoretic-security-based parsers to devices in the form of firmware updates.

5.4   Current Status

The project is currently in the first step in the roadmap. Eight protocol parsers have been developed and tested as bump-in-the-wire implementations in confidential field trials [9]. Parsers for a proprietary JSON-based protocol have also been incorporated in General Electric devices [15].

The parsers will be made available as open source or under similar licenses. Instead of each developer having to implement a parser to read input in a specific format, the project goal is to create a standard library for each parser. It would be very useful if the crypto-idiom "don't roll your own crypto" could be extended to parsers – "don't roll your own parsers." The number of vulnerabilities that have arisen from poor parser code supports this point of view.

Code for the DNP3 and C37.118 parsers is available on GitHub [4]. The remaining parsers will be added to the master repository in the near future.

6.   Conclusions

This chapter has presented the design and implementation of an industrial control network that exclusively employs language-theoretic-security-compliant parser implementations. The collection of secure parsers for industrial control protocols cover the communications needs of industrial control networks while eliminating input-handling vulnerabilities that could be exploited by denial-of-service and remote code execution attacks. The roadmap described in this chapter describes how electric utilities could deploy the security-hardened parsers in their industrial control networks via standard product refresh cycles, reaping the associated security benefits in a cost-effective manner.

Any opinions, findings, conclusions or recommendations expressed in this chapter are those of the authors and do not necessarily reflect the views of the U.S. Air Force, DARPA, United States Government or any agency thereof.

Acknowledgement

This research was supported by the U.S. Air Force and DARPA under Contract No. FA8750-16-C-0179 and by the U.S. Department of Homeland Security under Award No. DE-OE0000780.

References

[1] P. Anantharaman, K. Palani, R. Brantley, G. Brown, S. Bratus and S. Smith, PhasorSec: Protocol security filters for wide-area measurement systems, *Proceedings of the IEEE International Conference on Communications, Control and Computing Technologies for Smart Grids*, 2018.

[2] S. Bratus, A. Crain, S. Hallberg, D. Hirsch, M. Patterson, M. Koo and S. Smith, Implementing a vertically-hardened DNP3 control stack for power applications, *Proceedings of the Second Annual Industrial Control System Security Workshop*, pp. 45–53, 2016.

[3] N. Chomsky, Three models for the description of language, *IRE Transactions on Information Theory*, vol. 2(3), pp. 113–124, 1956.

[4] Dartmouth's PKI/Trust Lab, C37.118PMU and dnp3, GitHub (`github.com/Dartmouth-Trustlab`), 2018.

[5] P. Ducklin, Anatomy of a "goto fail" – Apple's SSL bug explained, plus an unofficial patch for OS X! *Naked Security* (`nakedsecurity.sophos.com/2014/02/24/anatomy-of-a-goto-fail-apples-ssl-bug-explained-plus-an-unofficial-patch`), February 24, 2014.

[6] Z. Durumeric, F. Li, J. Kasten, J. Amann, J. Beekman, M. Payer, N. Weaver, D. Adrian, V. Paxson and M. Bailey, The matter of Heartbleed, *Proceedings of the Internet Measurement Conference*, pp. 475–488, 2014.

[7] J. Freeman, Exploit (& fix) Android "master key," *The Realm of the Avatar Blog* (`www.saurik.com/id/17`), 2013.

[8] B. Galloway and G. Hancke, Introduction to industrial control networks, *IEEE Communications Surveys and Tutorials*, vol. 15(2), pp. 860–880, 2013.

[9] L. Hay Newman, The Hail Mary plan to restart a hacked US electric grid, *Wired*, November 14, 2018.

[10] C. Hurd and M. McCarty, A Survey of Security Tools for the Industrial Control System Environment, INL/EXT-17-42229, Revision 1, Idaho National Laboratory, Idaho Falls, Idaho, 2017.

[11] Industrial Control Systems Cyber Emergency Response Team (ICS-CERT), Recommended Practice: Improving Industrial Control System Cybersecurity with Defense-in-Depth Strategies, Idaho Falls, Idaho, 2016.

[12] P. Johnson, S. Bratus and S. Smith, Protecting against malicious bits on the wire: Automatically generating a USB protocol parser for a production kernel, *Proceedings of the Thirty-Third Annual Computer Security Applications Conference*, pp. 528–541, 2017.

[13] R. Lee, Detecting the Siemens S7 worm and similar capabilities, *SANS Industrial Control Systems Security Blog* (`blogs.sans.org/industrial-control-systems/2016/05`), May 8, 2016.

[14] F. Momot, S. Bratus, S. Hallberg and M. Patterson, The seven turrets of Babel: A taxonomy of LangSec errors and how to expunge them, *Proceedings of the IEEE Cybersecurity Development Conference*, pp. 45–52, 2016.

[15] Office of Cybersecurity, Energy Security and Emergency Response, From Innovation to Practice: Re-Designing Energy Delivery Systems to Survive Cyber Attacks, U.S. Department of Energy, Washington, DC (`www.energy.gov/sites/prod/files/2018/09/f55/CEDS%20From%20Innovation%20to%20Practice%20FINAL_0.pdf`), July 2018.

[16] M. Patterson, Parser combinations for binary formats, in C; Yes, in C; What? Don't look at me like that, GitHub (`github.com/Upstanding Hackers/hammer`), 2017.

[17] M. Spagnuolo, Abusing JSONP with Rosetta Flash, *Michele Spagnuolo Blog* (miki.it/blog/2014/7/8/abusing-jsonp-with-rosetta-flash), July 8, 2014.

[18] Symantec Security Response, ShellShock: All you need to know about the Bash Bug vulnerability, *Symantec Security Response Blog* (www.symantec.com/connect/blogs/shellshock-all-you-need-know-about-bash-bug-vulnerability), September 25, 2014.

[19] K. Torpey, The DAO disaster illustrates differing philosophies in Bitcoin and Ethereum, *CoinGecko Buzz* (www.coingecko.com/buzz/dao-disaster-differing-philosophies-bitcoin-ethereum), July 4, 2016.

[20] C. Veitch, J. Henry, B. Richardson and D. Hart, Microgrid Cyber Security Reference Architecture, Version 1.0, Sandia Report SAND2013-5472, Sandia National Laboratories, Albuquerque, New Mexico, 2013.

Chapter 5

CYBER SECURITY MODELING OF NON-CRITICAL NUCLEAR POWER PLANT DIGITAL INSTRUMENTATION

Trevor MacLean, Robert Borrelli and Michael Haney

Abstract   This chapter examines potential attack vectors that exist in a nuclear power plant and correlates the likelihood of an attack from each vector. The focus is on the boron monitoring system, which directly affects the reactivity in the core; cyber attacks on this system can lead to increased core wear, unsafe reactivity levels and poor power performance. A mockup model is developed using open-source software and hardware, which is tested to evaluate the potential of cyber attacks. A man-in-the-middle attack is implemented to demonstrate a cyber attack and its potential effects. Additionally, a redundancy-based cyber attack mitigation method is implemented using a hardware device that compares the input/output values of multiple programmable logic controllers. The approach for modeling general attack and defense steps is applicable to industrial control systems in the energy sector.

Keywords: Nuclear power plants, digital instrumentation and control, security

1.   Introduction

Cyber security vulnerabilities are an ever-present risk to industrial control systems. As nuclear power plants experience increased digitization of control systems, potential attack vectors will propagate. Critical systems in nuclear power plants have multilayered defenses to prevent malicious actors from causing catastrophic damage. A multilayered defensive approach to all plant operations maintains safety at an increased cost or risk of lost energy production. In the case of non-critical systems (i.e., systems that are not directly involved in the nuclear reactions in the core) and systems designed to be passively safe (e.g., natural convection cooling of a reactor during a power loss incident), lost production caused by an unnecessary shutdown of the power plant or tolerating the equipment deficiency with a less efficient contingency backup method

ⓒ IFIP International Federation for Information Processing 2019
Published by Springer Nature Switzerland AG 2019
J. Staggs and S. Shenoi (Eds.): Critical Infrastructure Protection XIII, IFIP AICT 570, pp. 87–100, 2019.
https://doi.org/10.1007/978-3-030-34647-8_5

can cause unintentional harm to humans and/or the environment. Non-critical and passively-safe systems are designed for continuous operation without direct human interactions. Although operations could be secured to accommodate all equipment deficiencies to maintain safety at all costs, the most efficient, but still safe, method is to operate a non-critical or passively-safe system with a fault detection program and perform automated or rapid repairs without operational impacts by utilizing concurrently-operating systems.

This chapter discusses how cyber attacks have interfered with nuclear power plants in the past. It reviews nuclear power plant components and attack paths. A mockup testbed is developed for a non-critical boron monitoring system against which a cyber attack is launched and an attack mitigation strategy involving failure detection and operator alerts is demonstrated. The modeling of general attack and defense steps is applicable to industrial control systems in nuclear power plants as well as in other types of power plants in the energy sector.

2.　　Background and Literature Review

Cyber attacks focused on gaining or interrupting control of industrial control systems are becoming increasingly prevalent. Kim [11] discusses cyber attacks that compromised plant operations at Ohio's Davis-Besse Nuclear Power Plant in 2003, Browns Ferry Nuclear Power Plant in 2006 and Iran's Natanz uranium hexafluoride centrifuge facility in 2010. Each of these compromised plants had one or more previously-unidentified vulnerabilities – "zero-day" vulnerabilities [11] – that were exploited to result in a security breach or cause equipment damage. The Ohio Davis-Besse Nuclear Plant's network server was infected by the Microsoft SQL Slammer worm that disabled a safety monitoring system. Excessive network traffic caused by a failing programmable logic controller caused the variable frequency drives of recirculation pumps in the Browns Ferry Nuclear Power Plant to be disabled. A man-in-the-middle attack by the Stuxnet worm on Iran's Natanz facility allowed the centrifuges to operate normally, except under specific conditions when critical system values were modified while reporting normal conditions to operators via the human-machine interfaces (HMIs).

Industrial control systems are often controlled by programmable logic controllers due to their modular input/output (I/O) options and ability to operate in harsh environments. Programmable logic controllers typically have minimalized operating systems and often no security software, which render them vulnerable to cyber attacks, such as the Stuxnet computer worm or via the manipulation of controller I/O pins as described in [1]. Potential ways to influence I/O pin values are via configuration manipulation attacks, control-flow attacks and code manipulation attacks. The manipulation of I/O pins, called a pin control attack [1], involves reconfiguring pin assignments so that output pins are changed to input pins, and vice versa.

Programmable logic controller protocols such as Modbus Serial, Modbus TCP/IP and Distributed Network Protocol 3 (DNP3) are commonly used in

Probability of Cyber Attack on Availability	Severity of Impact				
	Insignificant	Minor	Moderate	Significant	Catastrophic
Near Certain					
Likely	Plant Balance (Monitoring Only)		Cooling Tower; Switch Yard	Plant Balance (Process Control)	
Possible	Condenser	Turbine; Electric Generator	Steam Generator	Spent Fuel Pool; Radiation Monitor; Boron Monitoring System	
Unlikely					
Remote				Nuclear Reactor	Pressure Vessel

Figure 1. Nuclear power plant cyber attack risk matrix.

the energy sector. These protocols are highly susceptible to cyber attacks, including numerous methods for intercepting, interrupting, modifying and fabricating data communications. These attack methods are described in detail in attack taxonomies for Modbus [9] and DNP3 [6], where each attack method has multiple sub-categories of attacks.

3.   Risk-Informed Selection of Attack Paths

In 2012, the National Institute of Standards and Technology published a guide for conducting risk assessments [10]. This guide describes a process for performing risk assessments of information systems, which can be directly applied to various components of a nuclear power plant. Part of the process involves the review of threat sources, threat events, vulnerabilities, likelihoods and impacts. This research has identified the threat sources, threat events and vulnerabilities as nominal attack vectors at a nuclear power plant.

The major systems involved in plant operations were identified and placed in a risk matrix (Figure 1). Each system was assigned a probability of accessibility by a cyber attack and the severity of the attack impact on overall plant operations, plant employees, the public and/or the environment. The specific purpose of each system in the nuclear power plant was considered when assigning the accessibility probability and impact severity values in the risk matrix.

A nuclear power plant comprises safety-critical, important-to-safety and non-safety systems [14]. Safety-critical systems must operate to ensure the safety of plant employees, the public and the environment; a failure of a safety-critical system can cause serious injury to plant personnel and significant harm to the public and the environment. Important-to-safety systems impact the safety of plant personnel but would not have impacts as large as safety-critical systems. Non-safety systems are the remaining systems in a nuclear power plant that do not pose significant impacts to plant employees, the public and/or the environment.

This research examined the safety-critical and important-to-safety systems and the safety and security measures in place at a nuclear power plant. Safety-critical systems often have their risks mitigated through engineered controls, such as control rods that are physically unable to be retracted (which prevents the system from going critical rapidly). Therefore, these systems were determined to have lower likelihoods of successful cyber attacks. However, the consequences of successful attacks on safety-critical and important-to-safety systems would be severe because of the potential to affect the lives of plant personnel and the public, and the environment through contamination and radiation exposure. Figure 1 expresses such scenarios – the nuclear reactor and pressure vessel have remote cyber attack probabilities, but significant or catastrophic impact severity values.

Other non-safety-critical systems in the nuclear power plant would have lower severity levels in the risk matrix because cyber attacks on these systems would impact plant operational time, but would not cause significant hazards to plant employees, the public and the environment. The lower level of scrutiny placed on non-safety-critical systems can lead to an increase in cyber attack probability because these systems do not have the same level of protection as safety-critical systems.

The probabilities of cyber attacks listed are based on the accessibility of the control system to an attacker, either directly or via network access. For example, the switchyard has a high cyber attack probability because the power plant connections to external power utility lines cannot be air-gapped. The severity scale is based on the impact that the failed system would have on plant operations and employees, the public and the environment. Returning to the switchyard example, mitigating the consequences of an attack would require power from emergency backup generators. The use of emergency generators would not impact the public, but it would impact plant employees and plant operation; therefore, the switchyard is rated as having moderate severity.

Based on the data in Figure 1, the project scope was narrowed to focus on the spent fuel pool, switchyard, balance of plant systems and boron monitoring system, all of which are high risk systems because of their accessibility to external attacks (i.e., not air-gapped) and because of significant impact to plant operations if the cyber-physical systems were to be compromised. The spent fuel pool, switchyard and boron monitoring system have significant severity because failures could lead to unstable plant conditions or loss of plant control. The switchyard, although rated as having moderate severity, is a likely target of cyber attacks because of the accessibility of the switchyard by external entities and the inability to provide power to the plant without external sources after a successful attack.

Poresky et al. [12] describe cyber security strategies and vulnerability mitigation methods for advanced nuclear reactors. Research related to spent fuel pools, including patents such as [4], reveals that passive cooling is actively pursued to mitigate concerns about the failure of an active spent fuel pool cooling system. Based on the available information about passively-cooled spent fuel pools, the scope of this research was narrowed further to include only the switchyard, balance of plant systems and boron monitoring system.

Gergely et al. [8] describe risk mitigation methods for industrial control systems, including a fail-safe programmable logic controller that detects failures and places the system in a safe (non-operating) state. They also discuss fail-operate programmable logic controllers that detect failures and resort to backup systems for continuity of operations. However, the drawback of fail-operate systems is that they tend to degrade system performance.

Therefore, based on the analysis related to Figure 1 and previous research [4, 12], the boron monitoring system was selected as the system to model and analyze in this research. The boron monitoring system is rated as significant on the severity scale and possible on the accessibility scale. Modeling and analysis of the switchyard and balance of plant systems are topics for future research.

4. Boron Monitoring System

The boron monitoring system measures the boron levels in the reactor cooling loop. This system can directly affect the reactivity ("fissionability") or changes to the time-dependent neutron population in the core and cause undesirable operating conditions, leading to increased core wear, unsafe (high) reactivity levels and poor power performance. Using an outside vendor to design and implement a boron monitoring system introduces additional paths for cyber attacks compared with a boron monitoring system designed and implemented in-house. Therefore, the monitoring system is assigned a possible value on the cyber attack accessibility scale.

Multiple companies offer boron monitoring systems that incorporate programmable logic controllers. Examples include the Rolls-Royce Boronline and Mirion Technologies BM 501 Boron Meter. These products have similar components – a neutron emitting source and a neutron detector placed around an in-place pipe or in a storage tank in the nuclear power plant. The boron monitoring system is fail-safe because it is designed to place the reactor in a safe state if it were to fail.

4.1 Experimental Setup

This research demonstrates a cyber attack that compromises a programmable logic controller in a boron monitoring system and the mitigation of the attack. OpenPLC [2] and Raspberry Pis were selected to create a mock boron monitoring system. OpenPLC was selected because of its open-source software and hardware – its development platform is compliant with the IEC 61131-3 standard, supports SCADA protocols and interfaces with open-source human-machine interfaces and the ScadaBR SCADA simulator [3, 13]. Raspberry

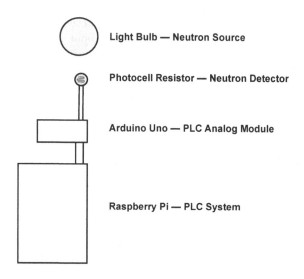

Figure 2.   Conceptual model of the boron monitoring system.

Pis were employed because their I/O pins can be used to simulate the boron monitoring system.

Figure 2 shows a mockup of the boron monitoring system. It incorporates a Raspberry Pi with the OpenPLC software to emulate a programmable logic controller, an Arduino Uno to emulate a programmable logic controller analog module that feeds analog values to the Raspberry Pi, a photoresistor to represent a neutron detector and a light source to represent a neutron source. The neutron detector and neutron source are unique to the boron monitoring system whereas the programmable logic controller and analog module are commonly used in other industry sectors.

In order to launch and mitigate cyber attacks, three programmable logic controllers were set up in parallel using a 2-out-of-3 logic circuit arrangement to compare signals of interest. This method of risk mitigation [5] uses AND and OR integrated circuits to compare the signals received from the three programmable logic controllers and outputs the signal that matches at least two of the three inputs. The 2-out-of-3 circuit with three programmable logic controllers operating in parallel helps prevent performance loss and downtime if an individual programmable logic controller were to fail. By incorporating a method that identifies a compromised programmable logic controller in real-time and implementing a self-healing protocol [5] for continuity of operations, repairs can be performed and malicious software can be purged without interrupting the overall function of the boron monitoring system.

The 2-out-of-3 circuit compares the high and low photoresistor values for the three programmable logic controllers. The output of the 2-out-of-3 circuit is the majority value expressing the presence (high) or absence (low) of

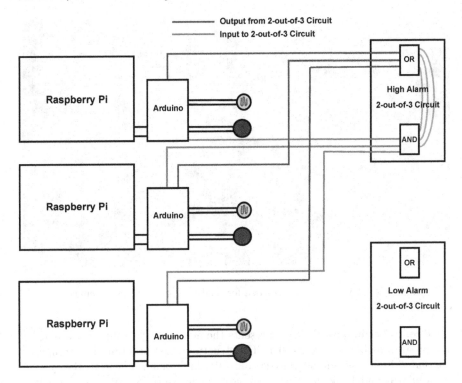

Figure 3. Schematic diagram of the boron monitoring system testbed.

neutrons reaching the detector. An alarm is sent to plant operators when a programmable logic controller has an anomalous output value.

Figure 3 shows a schematic diagram of the testbed with the implemented 2-out-of-3 circuit. The diagram shows the three programmable logic controllers, three Raspberry Pis and three Arduino Unos (analog system models), each with a photoresistor and cyber attack trigger. Each system outputs an alarm when a high or low level light is detected, corresponding to high or low boron levels, respectively. These alarm signals are wired to a 2-out-of-3 circuit to check for system continuity, which ultimately determines the overall system state of the light (boron) levels.

Figure 4 shows the cyber-physical testbed for analyzing cyber attack scenarios. Three different models of Raspberry Pi were incorporated in the testbed to ensure that performance differences would not produce differing results.

The testbed was programmed using the structured text programmable logic controller programming language via the OpenPLCEditor software [2]. The program checks the value read from each photoresistor and compares it against the predetermined high and low levels. When the photoresistor value is too high or too low an alarm signal is sent to the 2-out-of-3 circuit. The output of the 2-out-of-3 circuit is used as a system state alarm input to the programmable

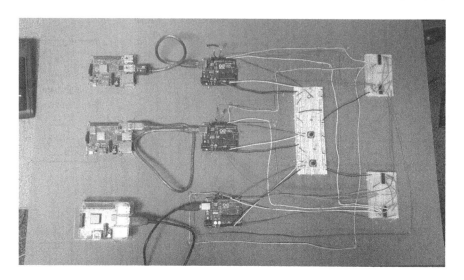

Figure 4. Cyber-physical testbed for analyzing cyber attack scenarios.

logic controller in question; it represents the actual boron value monitored by
the programmable logic controller. The structured text program then compares
the individual programmable logic controller high or low alarm to the system
state alarm and triggers a programmable logic controller system alarm if a
difference is detected.

```
IF Photoresistor < 21000 THEN
        LowAlarm := TRUE;
ELSIF Photoresistor > 37000 THEN
        HighAlarm := TRUE;
ELSIF Photoresistor > 21000 & Photoresistor < 37000 THEN
        LowAlarm := FALSE;
        HighAlarm := FALSE;
ENDIF;

IF OR((HighState <> HighAlarm),(LowState <> LowAlarm)) THEN
        SystemAlarm := TRUE;
ELSE SystemAlarm := FALSE;
ENDIF;
```

Figure 5. Structured text program.

Figure 5 shows the structured text program. The code has six declared
variables. The Photoresistor variable stores the analog value provided by
the photoresistor. HighAlarm and LowAlarm are programmable-logic-controller-

specific output variables that denote whether the controller receives high or low light readings from the photoresistor. The `HighState` and `LowState` variables store the value received from the 2-out-of-3 circuit output and represent the value of at least two of the three programmable logic controllers. Finally, the `System Alarm` output variable holds the result of the comparisons of the `HighState` and `HighAlarm` variables and the `LowState` and `LowAlarm` variables.

4.2   Cyber Attack Simulation

In order to simulate an attack on the programmable logic controller, the source code of the slave device was modified to enable the photoresistor values to be changed before sending them to the controller. This corresponds to a man-in-the-middle attack on a Modbus communications system.

The testbed incorporates a pushbutton as a trigger for launching the attack; however, this could be any exploit on the programmable logic controller. When the pushbutton trigger is activated, the code functions identical to the default code, except when a value is assigned to the analog pin fed by the photoresistor. Specifically, the photoresistor analog pin value is set to a predetermined value of low, which corresponds to the system diluting the boron concentration to enable more neutrons to reach the detector from the neutron source. This attack results in an inadequate level of boron in the cooling system that could lead to an abnormal increase in the radiation levels and require the nuclear reactor to be tripped.

4.3   Experimental Results

Since the focus is on the cyber security vulnerability in a single programmable logic controller and the integrity of a system with multiple programmable logic controllers operating in parallel, the concern is not about the boron monitoring system state being high or low, but about the differences between the programmable logic controller alarm values. During normal operations, all the programmable logic controller states should match, reporting either low, high or no alarm.

Figure 6 shows the programmable logic controllers operating under normal conditions with matching low boron states. Since all the programmable logic controller values match, no programmable logic controller alarms are illuminated in the right-hand side of Figure 6.

Figure 7 shows the programmable logic controllers operating under normal conditions with matching high boron states. During normal operations, the boron measuring system would ideally have the correct amount of boron in the cooling loop. Therefore, the low, high and programmable logic controller alarms would not be illuminated. However, in Figure 7, although the high system state alarms are illuminated for all the programmable logic controllers, the boron monitoring system is considered to be operating properly and should be able to correct the high boron alarms. Since all the programmable logic controller

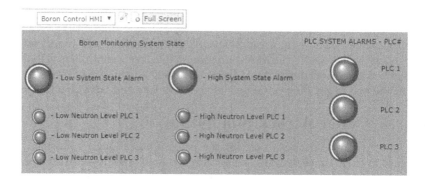

Figure 6.   Human-machine interface with no alarm.

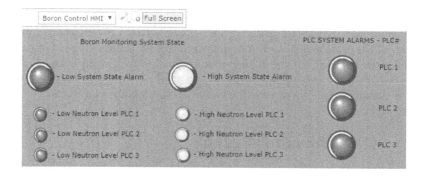

Figure 7.   Human-machine interface with a high alarm.

values match, no programmable logic controller alarms are illuminated in the right-hand side of Figure 7.

In order to validate the operation of the 2-out-of-3 circuit, light was blocked from the photoresistors associated with two programmable logic controllers (PLC 2 and PLC 3), causing them to have low values. Since the PLC 1 value does not match the low PLC 2 and PLC 3 values, the alarm of the non-conforming PLC 1 is triggered (Figure 8).

On the other hand, in Figure 9, extra light was provided to the two photoresistors associated with PLC 1 and PLC 2, causing them to have high values. Since the PLC 3 value does not match the high PLC 1 and PLC 2 values, the alarm of the non-conforming PLC 3 is triggered.

With the testbed operating as expected under normal conditions, a simulated cyber attack was executed to see if the testbed could identify that a programmable logic controller was reading an incorrect value compared with the remaining programming logic controllers. This was accomplished by installing

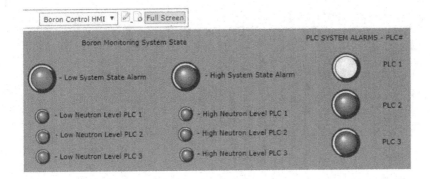

Figure 8. Human-machine interface with two low alarms.

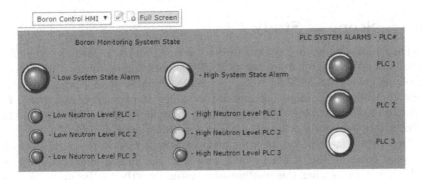

Figure 9. Human-machine interface with two high alarms.

a pushbutton that overwrites the photoresistor value of a programmable logic controller with a significantly lower value.

Without the 2-out-of-3 circuit, the low neutron level alarm is activated for PLC 1, which tells the monitoring system to dilute the boron concentration. However, when the 2-out-of-3 circuit is operational during the cyber attack, the low alarm for PLC 1 is tripped and, because the PLC 1 value does not match the values of PLC 2 and PLC 3, the PLC 1 alarm is activated. With a proper contingency procedure in place, either the system operator would be notified or contingency recovery code would be executed to address the problem with PLC 1.

Figure 10 shows the situation when the pushbutton cyber attack trigger is activated for PLC 1 to overwrite the incoming photoresistor value with the low value. The cyber attack activates the low neutron level alarm for PLC 1. Due to the disparity between the PLC 1 value and the PLC 2 and PLC 3 values, instead of the monitoring system diluting the boron concentration, the PLC 1 alarm is triggered.

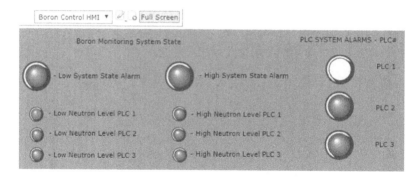

Figure 10.   Human-machine interface with active cyber attack alarms.

5.   Scope of Study

The boron monitoring system testbed is constrained to identify cyber attacks and differentiate situations involving malfunctioning devices from those involving cyber attacks. Therefore, the testbed reports when a programmable logic controller value does not match the values of its two counterparts. In order to implement robust cyber security, a method should be implemented to differentiate between a cyber attack and a malfunctioning sensor.

The current method for initiating and executing a man-in-the-middle attack does not cover up the malicious value passed to the human-machine interface. Indeed, not presenting the photoresistor value directly to the operator is a significant system vulnerability.

To create a more realistic and difficult-to-detect cyber attack, the man-in-the-middle attack should change the value of an output device (e.g., valve controlling a boron solution based on the control logic) while still reporting the output from the photoresistor as an acceptable, non-alarming value to the human-machine interface. In this way an operator would not receive an alarm despite the system operating in an alarmed state.

6.   Conclusions

The review of nuclear power plant components and the subsequent assignment of qualitative risk measures to the components facilitated the identification of non-critical systems that pose significant safety and/or economic risks. The focus on the boron monitoring system is important because cyber attacks on this system can lead to increased core wear, unsafe reactivity levels and poor power performance. The mockup of the boron monitoring system using open-source software and inexpensive hardware components enabled the execution of a man-in-the-middle attack that demonstrated a system vulnerability and its mitigation using a mixed analog/digital solution. Similar methods can provide energy sector asset owners, operators and regulators insights into risk management and compliance regimes for securing industrial control system environments from evolving cyber threats.

A growing trend in the modernization of nuclear power plants is splitting digital and analog instrumentation and control [12]. Future research will investigate the cyber security implications of this modernization on non-critical nuclear power plant instrumentation, including the implementation of mitigation techniques involving field programmable gate arrays [7], fault-tolerant operations and self-repairing designs [12]. Additionally, future research will investigate other cyber attacks such as baseline response replay and direct slave control [9] to verify the effectiveness of the mitigation techniques. Creating testbeds for the switchyard and balance of plant systems, and incorporating split digital and analog instrumentation and control systems, would advance protection efforts for non-critical nuclear power plant instrumentation, helping identify potential vulnerabilities and mitigation approaches.

References

[1] A. Abbasi, M. Hashemi, E. Zambon and S. Etalle, Stealth low-level manipulation of programmable logic controller I/O by pin control exploitation, in *Critical Information Infrastructures Security*, G. Havarneanu, R. Setola, H. Nassopoulos and S. Wolthusen (Eds.), Springer, Cham, Switzerland, pp. 1–12, 2017.

[2] T. Alves, OpenPLC (`www.openplcproject.com`), 2019.

[3] T. Alves and T. Morris, OpenPLC: An IEC 61131-3 compliant open source industrial controller for cyber security research, *Computers and Security*, vol. 78, pp. 364–379, 2018.

[4] J. Dederer, W. Brown and F. Vereb, Alternate Passive Spent Fuel Pool Cooling Systems and Methods, U.S. Patent No. 9646726 B2, May 9, 2017.

[5] M. Denzel, M. Ryan and E. Ritter, A malware-tolerant, self-healing industrial control system framework, in *ICT Systems Security and Privacy Protection*, S. De Capitani di Vimercati and F. Martinelli (Eds.), Springer, Cham, Switzerland, pp. 46–60, 2017.

[6] S. East, J. Butts, M. Papa and S. Shenoi, A taxonomy of attacks on the DNP3 protocol, in *Critical Infrastructure Protection III*, C. Palmer and S. Shenoi (Eds.), Springer, Berlin Heidelberg, Germany, pp. 67–81, 2009.

[7] M. Elakrat and J. Jung, Development of a field programmable gate array based encryption module to mitigate man-in-the-middle attacks on nuclear power plant data communication networks, *Nuclear Engineering and Technology*, vol. 50(5), pp. 780–787, 2018.

[8] E. Gergely, D. Spoiala, V. Spoiala, H. Silaghi and Z. Nagy, Design framework for risk mitigation in industrial PLC control, *Proceedings of the IEEE International Conference on Automation, Quality and Testing, Robotics*, pp. 198–202, 2008.

[9] P. Huitsing, R. Chandia, M. Papa and S. Shenoi, Attack taxonomies for the Modbus protocols, *International Journal of Critical Infrastructure Protection*, vol. 1, pp. 37–44, 2008.

[10] Joint Task Force Transformation Initiative, Guide for Conducting Risk Assessments, NIST Special Publication 800-30, Revision 1, National Institute of Standards and Technology, Gaithersburg, Maryland, 2012.

[11] D. Kim, Cyber security issues imposed on nuclear power plants, *Annals of Nuclear Energy*, vol. 65, pp. 141–143, 2014.

[12] C. Poresky, C. Andreades, J. Kendrick and P. Peterson, Cyber Security in Nuclear Power Plants: Insights for Advanced Nuclear Technologies, Technical Report UCBTH-17-004, Department of Nuclear Engineering, University of California, Berkeley, Berkeley, California, 2017.

[13] ScadaBR Project Team, ScadaBR (`sourceforge.net/p/scadabr/wiki/Home`), 2019.

[14] J. Song, J. Lee, C. Lee, K. Kwon and D. Lee, A cyber security risk assessment for the design of I&C systems in nuclear power plants, *Nuclear Engineering and Technology*, vol. 44(8), pp. 919–928, 2012.

III

VEHICLE INFRASTRUCTURE SECURITY

Chapter 6

ELECTRONIC CONTROL UNIT DISCRIMINATION USING WIRED SIGNAL DISTINCT NATIVE ATTRIBUTES

Rahn Lassiter, Scott Graham, Timothy Carbino and Stephen Dunlap

Abstract   A controller area network bus is a communications system used in modern automobiles to connect the electronic control units that implement normal vehicular operations as well as advanced autonomous safety and driver comfort features. However, these advancements come at the expense of vehicle security – researchers have shown that automobiles can be hacked by compromising electronic control units or by connecting unauthorized devices to the controller area network bus.

Physical layer device fingerprinting is a promising approach for implementing vehicle security. This chapter presents a fingerprinting method and classification algorithm for electronic control unit discrimination. Cross-lot discrimination is assessed using four Toyota Avalon electronic control units with different lot numbers as authorized devices, and a BeagleBoard, Arduino and CANable as rogue devices. The experiments yielded perfect rejection rates for rogue devices with false credentials and access denial rates exceeding 98% for authorized electronic control units with false credentials. Additionally, an average correct classification of approximately 99% was obtained for authorized devices.

Keywords: CAN bus, electronic unit discrimination, rogue device detection

1.   Introduction

As automobiles become more technologically advanced and connected, they are more susceptible to hacking. Research funded by the U.S. Defense Advanced Research Projects Agency (DARPA) exposed several security vulnerabilities [9, 10]. In particular, using a laptop with wireless connectivity, researchers were able to attack vehicles as they were being driven on highways – remotely turn off the engines, activate the windshield wipers and wiper fluid releases, and

© IFIP International Federation for Information Processing 2019
Published by Springer Nature Switzerland AG 2019
J. Staggs and S. Shenoi (Eds.): Critical Infrastructure Protection XIII, IFIP AICT 570, pp. 103–121, 2019.
https://doi.org/10.1007/978-3-030-34647-8_6

even disable the brakes at speeds below 15 mph. These threats are not limited to automobiles. Heavy vehicles, ships and aircraft are also vulnerable because they have electronic control systems connected in on-board networks.

The technology needed to perform attacks on vehicles is more accessible. In 2014, security researchers developed the CAN Hacking Tool targeting the controller area network (CAN) bus in modern vehicles – the tool costs less than $20 to build; it is the size of an iPhone and can be hooked up to a vehicle within five minutes [15]. Developmental boards such as Arduino and BeagleBoard can be programmed to emulate automobile electronic control units (ECUs) that provide gateways for hackers to compromise CAN bus systems. Although these "hobbyist" experiments may seem harmless, the same technology can be used to carry out serious hacking attacks on vulnerable vehicles.

This research demonstrates that wired signal distinct native attributes (WS-DNA) can be leveraged to detect rogue devices such as the CAN Hacking Tool. The approach uses wired signal distinct native attribute fingerprinting and multiple discriminant analysis with maximum likelihood to identify (classify) and authenticate (verify) devices based on their unique signal variations. The experiments conducted during this research yielded perfect (100%) rejection rates for rogue devices with false credentials and access denial rates exceeding 98% for authorized electronic control units with false credentials. Additionally, an average correct classification of approximately 99% was obtained for authorized devices.

## 2.	CAN Bus

CAN bus is a lightweight, broadcast communications system created in the 1980s by Bosch as a replacement for the older wiring systems used in automobiles [8]. The CAN bus system comprises multiple networked electronic control units that transmit, receive and process critical data such as vehicle speed, engine RPM and even the angle of the steering wheel. The latest CAN 2.0 version used in modern vehicles transmits data at speeds up to 1 Mbps. The CAN bus has two message formats: (i) base frame format; and (ii) extended frame format. This work focuses on devices that transmit data in the base frame format, which is specified in Table 1.

CAN signals are transmitted as non-return-to-zero (NRZ) encoded differential voltages. A differential voltage is the difference between the twisted pair CAN-Hi and CAN-Lo signals [6]. The bits in the base frame format are formed from the differences between the CAN-Hi and CAN-Lo signals [20]. A dominant bit (0) is transmitted when the difference between CAN-Hi and CAN-Lo is approximately 2 volts and a recessive bit (1) is transmitted when the difference between CAN-Hi and CAN-Lo is approximately 0 volts, as shown in Figure 1.

The CAN bus is a broadcast network where electronic control units transmit freely to all devices that are listening, or to devices that request information. An electronic control unit that needs to send data attempts to do so when the CAN bus is in an idle state. If multiple electronic control units transmit

Table 1. Typical base frame format [8].

Bits	Name/Field	Description
1	Start of Frame	Always dominant (0)
11	Identifier	Varies for each electronic control unit; also determines priority
1	Remote Transmission Request	Dominant for data frame (0)
1	Identifier Extension Bit	Difference between base frame and extended frame; dominant for base (0)
1	Reserved Bit	Must be dominant (0)
4	Data Length Code	Determines data length (bytes)
0-64	Data	Transmitted data
15	CRC	Checksum
1	CRC Delimiter	Recessive (1)
1	Acknowledgement Bit	Recessive (1)
1	Acknowledgement Delimiter	Transmitter sends recessive (1)
7	End of Frame	All recessive; end of transmission
7	Interframe Spacing	All recessive; time required to process message

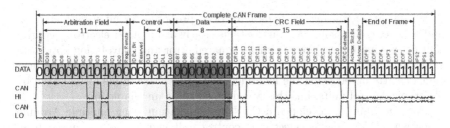

Figure 1. Base frame format [20].

messages at the same time, then the transmissions are synchronized at their start of frame bits and an arbitration occurs in the network.

During synchronization, each identical bit is coherently combined to produce a waveform that has the same voltage for a one or a zero. The device with the lowest identifier number, which indicates higher priority, wins the arbitration and continues to transmit while the device that loses the arbitration stops transmitting as shown in Figure 2. Because of the potential for multiple electronic control units to transmit simultaneously in the arbitration field, Choi et al. [6] determined that the identifier may not be the best region to use to calculate statistical features for fingerprints in a typical CAN bus environment. Instead, they employed the extended identifier in the extended frame format used by electronic control units.

This work focuses on electronic control unit discrimination in a collision-free environment and proposes the use of a region of interest (ROI) after the arbitration field to address the issue of CAN bus collisions. The arbitration field

	SOF	Identifier							
ECU 1	0	0	0	0	1	0	1	0
ECU 2	0	0	0	1	stops transmitting
CAN Bus	0	0	0	0	1	0	1	0

Figure 2.   CAN bus arbitration.

in the base frame comprises identifier bits and the remote transmission request bit whereas the control field comprises the identifier extension bit, reserved bit and four data length code bits as shown in Figure 1. These bits are utilized as the region of interest for fingerprint generation.

3.   Device Fingerprinting

This section discusses related work in the area of device fingerprinting and the radio frequency distinct native attribute (RF-DNA) methodology for device classification and discrimination.

3.1   Related Work

Several fingerprinting methods have been proposed for intrusion detection and security controls in CAN bus systems. Early attempts at electronic control unit discrimination employed a mean-squared error and convolution approach, achieving classification rates ranging from 90% to 100% [14]. Device identification was attempted using the identifier field in the base frame format used by electronic control units, but this was deemed to be unreliable [6].

Cho and Shin [5] developed a CAN bus simulation using multiple Arduino Unos with CAN shields; electronic control unit signals were acquired from real vehicles. Their fingerprinting approach leveraged the internal clocks of electronic control units to identify the transmitting devices. The fingerprints were generated based on the clock offset, clock frequency and clock skew. A recursive least-squares algorithm was used for electronic control unit detection and verification, achieving about 97% success in device detection.

The majority of fingerprinting methods employ statistical properties of signals and machine learning or neural net classifiers to identify unique attributes in the extracted features [1, 6, 11]. Avatefipour et al. [1] used a CAN transceiver and development board setup to simulate the CAN bus and electronic control units. Choi et al. [6] employed CAN boards connected in a physical network to simulate the CAN bus and various electronic control units. Jaynes et al. [11] plugged a device directly into the on-board diagnostics port (OBD-II) in a vehicle for electronic control unit signal acquisition. The three methods used different signal collection methods but similar fingerprint generation techniques and neural network classifiers, yielding correct classifications up to 98.6% in the case of Avatefipour et al. [1], 96.5% in the case of Choi et al. [6] and 86% in the case of Jaynes et al. [11].

3.2   RF-DNA Methodology

The radio frequency distinct native attribute (RF-DNA) methodology was developed to perform tasks such as detecting rogue devices, identifying aging devices and augmenting bit-level security [4, 16, 18, 21]. Radio frequency emissions are captured from devices and distinct native attributes of the emissions are generated based on the statistical features of signal amplitude, frequency and phase [4, 7, 13, 16, 18, 22].

Time-Domain Fingerprinting.   Time-domain (TD) radio frequency fingerprints are generated from the instantaneous responses of signals, which include the instantaneous amplitude, instantaneous frequency and instantaneous phase. A discrete real-valued signal $s(k)$ is broken up into I-Q samples using the Hilbert transform [4]:

$$s(k) = s_I(k) + s_Q(k) \tag{1}$$

where the amplitude $a(k)$, frequency $f(k)$ and phase $\phi(k)$ are computed as:

$$a(k) = \sqrt{s^2(k)} \tag{2}$$

$$\phi(k) = \tan^{-1}[\frac{s_Q(k)}{s_I(k)}] \tag{3}$$

$$f(k) = \frac{1}{2\pi}[\frac{d\phi(k)}{dk}] \tag{4}$$

Features are typically centered and normalized using the mean and maximum values of the respective time-domain responses [21]. An invariant region, such as the preamble, mid-amble or post-amble, is identified as the region of interest. The region of interest is divided into N_R equal subregions. Usually, the entire region of interest is included as a subregion to produce $N_R + 1$ subregions for statistical feature extraction.

Typical features that are extracted include the standard deviation σ, variance σ^2, skewness γ and kurtosis κ. These statistics are computed for a subregion to generate the fingerprint F_{RF_i}. The fingerprints corresponding to a region are concatenated to form the composite fingerprint F_{RF}:

The fingerprints are expressed by the following equations:

$$F_{RF_i}^{RF} = [\sigma_{R_i}, \sigma_{R_i}^2, \gamma_{R_i}, \kappa_{R_i}]_{1\times 4} \tag{5}$$

$$F_{a,\phi,f}^{RF} = [F_{R_1}^{RF} : F_{R_2}^{RF} : F_{R_3}^{RF} : \cdots : F_{R_{N+1}}^{RF}]_{1\times[4(N_R+1)]} \tag{6}$$

$$F_C^{RF} = [F_a^{RF} : F_\phi^{RF} : F_f^{RF}] \tag{7}$$

The features included in an RF-DNA fingerprint comprise the number of responses N_{resp}, number of statistical features N_{stat} and number of subregions N_R. For example, if $N_{resp} = 4$, $N_{stat} = 3$ and $N_R = 9$, then the number of features $N_{feat} = 4 \times 3 \times 9 = 108$ [4].

The wired signal distinct native attribute (WS-DNA) fingerprinting approach, which is based on the RF-DNA process, is adopted in the WS-DNA methodology used in this research. The composite WS-DNA fingerprints are given by:

$$F_C^{WS} = [F_a^{WS} : F_\phi^{WS} : F_f^{WS}] \tag{8}$$

WS-DNA signals are acquired directly from the wire of a transmitting device instead of over-the-air captures of radio frequency emissions from the device as in the case of the RF-DNA methodology [2–4, 12, 17–19].

Multiple Discriminant Analysis Maximum Likelihood. Device fingerprints are compared using a multiple discriminant analysis maximum likelihood (MDA/ML) classifier. Multiple discriminant analysis is a dimensionality reduction algorithm that takes the extracted features or fingerprints and reduces them to $N - 1$ classes, where N is the number of devices. The maximum likelihood classifier assumes that the data has a Gaussian distribution, equal priors and uniform costs. The classifier establishes thresholds based on training fingerprints and assigns each test fingerprint to a class using Bayesian decision criteria [22].

Additionally, K-fold cross-validation is used to increase reliability [4]. Cross-validation is accomplished by: (i) dividing the training fingerprints into K equal blocks; (ii) holding one block out and conducting training with the remaining $K - 1$ blocks; (iii) conducting testing using the block that was held out; and (iv) repeating the process until all the blocks have been held out. The iteration that produces the highest score is used for model development [3, 21].

Device discrimination is a two-step process comprising classification and verification. Classification is a one-vs-many assessment that determines which training fingerprint best matches a testing fingerprint. Verification is a one-vs-one assessment that determines how similar the identity of a claimed fingerprint is to the identity of the actual fingerprint [3, 16].

4.   Experimental Methodology

This section discusses the experimental setup and collection as well as the parameters used in the WS-DNA fingerprinting methodology.

4.1   Device Under Test and Signal Collection

The device under test (DUT) was a steering angle sensor (SAS) from a Toyota Avalon. This electronic control unit transmits a data frame or burst in the base frame format approximately every $260\,\mu s$ as shown in Figure 3. The

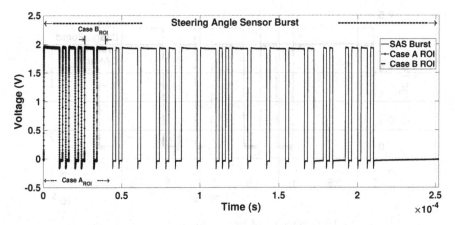

Figure 3. Data frame or burst from a Toyota SAS.

steering angle sensor was chosen for the experiments because it has a relatively high priority on the CAN bus of a Toyota Avalon and because it continuously transmits data with or without user input.

Table 2. Devices under test (four-class cross-lot discrimination).

Device	Device ID	Lot	Average SNR$_C$
1	SAS 1 (A1)	503G	42.9 dB
2	SAS 2 (A2)	823F	42.4 dB
3	SAS 3 (A3)	826I	43.5 dB
4	SAS 4 (A4)	523E	43.4 dB

Four devices ($N_C = 4$ classes), each from a different lot, were used to assess the cross-lot discrimination (Table 2).

Table 3. Rogue devices used for authentication testing.

Rogue Device ID	Description
R1	BeagleBoard; ISO 1050 CAN transceiver
R2	Arduino Uno with CAN shield
R3	CANable

Additionally, three rogue devices ($N_{rg} = 3$) were created to present false credentials during attempts to access the CAN bus as authorized devices. Table 3 provides information about the rogue devices.

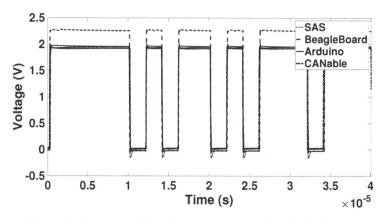

Figure 4. Average region of interest responses for all the devices.

Figure 4 shows the average differential voltage waveform of the region of interest of the steering angle sensors compared with those of the rogue devices. All the devices transmit the same bit-level data and should be accepted as authorized devices on the CAN bus. On average, rogue device R1 has a maximum differential voltage that is 0.2 V greater than those of the other rogue devices as well as the steering angle sensors as shown in Figure 4.

A Keysight InfiniiVision MSOX3054T 5.0 GHz oscilloscope operating at f_s = 1 GSPS was used to collect and store the baseband signals from the Toyota steering angle sensors. A total of 260 ms of signals were collected, which comprised $N_{bursts} \approx 1,000$ bursts. To reduce environmental and collection bias, a random permutation of five collections of $N_{bursts} \approx 200$ bursts for each device were taken over a one-week period at various times and various temperatures. To further reduce experimental variability, each steering angle sensor was locked into the same position so that all the devices transmitted the same 64-bit message and all the devices used the same power supply.

MATLAB was used to process the unfiltered signals and generate WS-DNA fingerprints. Each burst or data frame was extracted by cross-correlating the collected signal with an ideal preamble reference signal and each burst was aligned at the same starting index in a fingerprint generation matrix. Prior to fingerprint generation, a fourth-order baseband Butterworth filter was used to reduce noise. The estimated average collected signal-to-noise ratio (SNR) was computed by taking the ratio of the average power of the region of interest to the average power of the noise region before the start of frame, yielding a signal-to-noise ratio $SNR_C \approx 43.1$ dB.

4.2   Signal-to-Noise Ratio Scaling

Multiple noise realizations were required for fingerprint generation. Although every effort was taken to reduce the effects of environmental noise, additive white Gaussian noise (AWGN) was assumed to be present in signals from the power supply, oscilloscope and collection probes. However, because this noise does not demonstrate the effects of different channel conditions, different iterations of like-filtered, power-scaled independent additive white Gaussian noise were added during post-processing to simulate different channel conditions.

In the experiments, noise was added to produce $-46\,\mathrm{dB} < SNR_\Delta < 0\,\mathrm{dB}$ in 2 dB increments, where SNR_Δ denotes the reduction in the signal-to-noise ratio under the collected conditions as the power of the additive white Gaussian noise was increased. In this work, SNR_{col} (collected conditions) denotes the signal-to-noise ratio where the classification performance is statistically equal to the classification performance at SNR_C. To be clear, the signal-to-noise ratio was never improved. Instead, additive white Gaussian noise was added to each burst until the average correct classification $\%C \approx 1/N_C$ was obtained.

4.3   Fingerprint Generation

Fingerprints were generated for the ideal, collision-free environment to: (i) assess the WS-DNA classification and verification performance using an entire invariant region of interest; and (ii) use a comparable amount of bits as in [6] to provide a performance estimate for the WS-DNA implementation for electronic control units using the extended frame format. This set of fingerprints does not represent a realistic CAN bus scenario because collisions occur frequently, but the fingerprints could be used to establish a baseline for the electronic control units prior to installation in a vehicle. A second set of fingerprints was generated to address the best region of interest for the WS-DNA implementation for electronic control units using the base frame format on the CAN bus in a realistic environment.

- **Case A (Ideal Collision Free Environment):** Time-domain WS-DNA fingerprints were generated using the steering angle sensor preamble with the region of interest comprising the start of frame, arbitration field and control field. Additionally, $N_{samp} = 210$ samples were included before the start of frame bit, resulting in a region of interest with $N_{samp} \approx 40,000$ samples. The region of interest was further divided into $N_R = 54$ contiguous subregions each containing $N_{samp} \approx 740$ samples (Figure 5).

  The total number of features N_{feats} included in the WS-DNA fingerprints is equal to $N_{resp} \times N_{stats} \times N_R + 1$. Thus, $N_{feats} = 3 \times 4 \times 55 = 660$ features. Fingerprints for the $N_{rg} = 3$ rogue devices were generated along with the authorized devices using the same fingerprint generation method.

- **Case B (Realistic CAN Bus Environment):** Time-domain WS-DNA fingerprints were generated to address a typical collision environment for electronic control units using the base frame format, but excluding the start of frame and arbitration field. The region of interest for this scenario

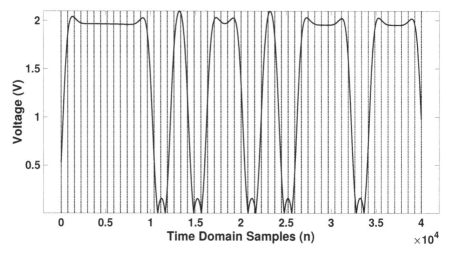

Figure 5.   Region of interest divided into $N_R = 54$ subregions.

included the remote transmission request bit, identifier extension bit, reserved bit and the four data length code bits. The region of interest was divided into $N_R = 45$ subregions, each containing $N_{samp} \approx 306$ samples. The total number of features N_{feats} included in the WS-DNA fingerprints is equal to $N_{resp} \times N_{stats} \times N_R + 1$. Thus, $N_{feats} = 3 \times 4 \times 46 = 552$ features.

4.4   MDA/ML Classification and Verification

This section discusses the use of multiple discriminant analysis with maximum likelihood for device classification and device verification:

- **Device Classification:** A total of $N_{NZ} = 5$ noise realizations were used per signal-to-noise ratio to generate a total of $N_{prints} \approx 5,000$ fingerprints. $N_{trng} = N_{test} \approx 2,500$ interleaved training and testing fingerprints per device were used for classification. Additionally, $K = 5$ was used for cross-validation, which is consistent with previous RF-DNA work [18, 21]. Decision thresholds were established during the training phase and testing fingerprints were classified based on the decision region they fell in during the testing phase.

- **Device Verification:** Device verification was implemented using the Euclidean distance as the measure of similarity and an equal error rate (EER) of 10% as the measure of success. In the experiments, the equal error rate (device dependent metric) was chosen such that true verification rate (TVR) was equal to the rogue rejection rate (RRR). The true verification rate corresponds to the number of attempts by an authorized device that are correctly accepted divided by the total number of attempts. The rogue rejection rate corresponds to the total number of rogue attempts that are correctly rejected divided by the number of attempts.

A probability mass function was generated during training. Device-dependent thresholds $t_V(d)$ were established based on the desired true verification rate and false verification rate (FVR) for authorized device verification and established based on the desired true verification rate and rogue acceptance rate (RAR) for rogue device verification. Note that FVR = 1 − TVR and RAR = 1 − RRR.

During testing, the verification test statistic Z_V was generated from the fingerprint of each unknown device and compared against the threshold t_V. Devices were either granted access or denied access (correctly or incorrectly) depending on how Z_V compared against t_V [3].

Receiver operating characteristic (ROC) curves were generated to present the verification performance using the established verification and acceptance rates. Stem plots were generated to present the results for each of the $N_{test} \approx 5,000$ rogue attempts (for rogue devices R1, R2 and R3) to pass as authorized devices (A1, A2, A3 and A4) [3]. Rogue device acceptance and rejection rates were established using the BeagleBoard, Arduino, CANable and an arbitrarily-chosen fourth device (R4) as rogue devices. The unauthorized rogue devices were excluded from the training so that the classifier would be presented with true rogue devices during the verification phase.

5. Experimental Results

This section presents the results for multiple discriminant analysis with maximum likelihood classification and verification. The classification results are presented using %C versus SNR_Δ plots and confusion matrices. The verification results are presented using ROC curves and stem plots.

5.1 Device Classification

Figures 6 and 7 show the classification results. The confusion matrix results at SNR_{col} are presented in Table 4. All the classification results presented are based on 95% confidence intervals, which are omitted in Figures 6 and 7 for visual clarity because the confidence intervals fall in the vertical extent of the markers.

The results reveal that device SAS 3 has a statistically-significant increase in correct classification over all the other devices from $SNR_\Delta \geq -39\,\text{dB}$ to $SNR_\Delta = -14\,\text{dB}$. Upon further inspection, SAS 3 was verified to have the newest internal components. The classification results for device SAS 2 are statistically equal to the cross-class average. Devices SAS 1 and SAS 4 were incorrectly classified as each other more often than with the other two devices.

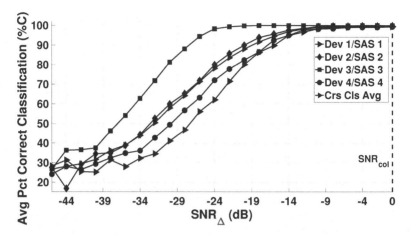

Figure 6. Classification results for $N_C = 4$ classes using the ECU preamble.

These devices were both obtained from used vehicles that were manufactured during the same year.

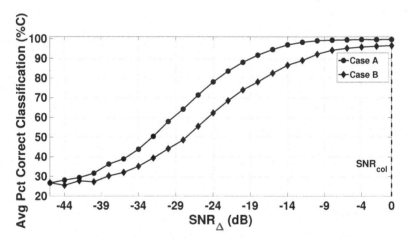

Figure 7. Classification results for cross-class average for Case A and Case B ROIs.

Figure 7 provides a direct comparison of the classification results using the fingerprints generated with the regions of interests used in Case A and Case B. The results are statistically equal at $SNR_\Delta \leq -40$ dB. Moreover, using the preamble as the region of interest yielded statistically better classification for $SNR_\Delta > -40$ dB. This is arguably the result of having more bits and more bit transitions in the region of interest, which provide more useful time-domain discrimination information.

Table 4. Cross-lot discrimination confusion matrix (%) for $N_C = 4$ classes.

	SAS 1	SAS 2	SAS 3	SAS 4
SAS 1	**99.6**/93.76	**0**/1.88	**0**/0	**0.4**/4.36
SAS 2	**0.04**/1	**99.6**/97.8	**0**/0.04	**0**/1.16
SAS 3	**0**/0.56	**0.04**/1.04	**99.92**/97.88	**0.04**/0.52
SAS 4	**0.28**/2.76	**0.2**/1.92	**0**/0.12	**99.52**/95.2

Table 4 shows the cross-lot discrimination confusion matrix for $N_C = 4$ classes; the results are displayed as %C Case A/%C Case B. The bold values in the table correspond to the classification results for Case A and the non-bold values correspond to the classification results for Case B. The classification performance degraded when the arbitration field was excluded from the region of interest. The classification performance values of devices SAS 1 and SAS 4 were reduced by approximately 5% and the classification performance values of devices SAS 2 and SAS 3 were reduced by approximately 2%. SAS 1 and SAS 4 were confused with each other more often than with the other devices; these devices were obtained from used vehicles manufactured during the same year. As the signal-to-noise ratio was degraded, SAS 1 and SAS 4 were incorrectly classified as each other more often than other devices, which may indicate that these devices look more similar to each other as they age.

Greater than 90% correct identification of similar components was achieved using WS-DNA fingerprints generated in Case B. Moreover, correct classification (%C) greater than 90% in realistic implementations was obtained even when the signal-to-noise ratio was degraded by 10 dB.

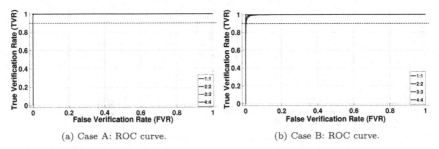

(a) Case A: ROC curve.   (b) Case B: ROC curve.

Figure 8. Authorized device verification ROC curve at SNR_{col}.

5.2   Device Verification

Figure 8 shows the results for authorized device verification. Note that the Euclidean distance was used as the measure of similarity and success was defined as a true verification rate greater than 0.9 and a false verification rate less

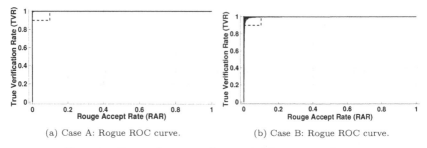

(a) Case A: Rogue ROC curve.   (b) Case B: Rogue ROC curve.

Figure 9.   Rogue device verification ROC curve at SNR_{col}.

than 0.1. The horizontal black dashed lines correspond to the true verification rate benchmark of 0.9, which is consistent with previous RF-DNA work [4, 7, 16, 18, 21]. The solid ROC curves for Case A and Case B indicate that all four devices satisfy the true verification benchmark at the average collected signal-to-noise ratio.

In the rogue device verification scenario, rogue devices presented false credentials and were either accepted or rejected as the device they claimed to be based on the threshold established by the probability mass function generated during training.

Figure 9 shows the results for rogue device verification. The dashed black boxes represent the areas where the true verification rate is greater than 0.9 and the rogue acceptance rate is less than 0.1. The black stars on each line denote the device-dependent equal error rate and the solid curves denote devices that met the success criteria. Consistent with the authorized device verification results, all the devices successfully met the equal error rate success criteria for Case A and Case B.

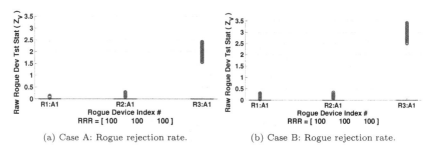

(a) Case A: Rogue rejection rate.   (b) Case B: Rogue rejection rate.

Figure 10.   Rejection rates of rogue devices using valid credentials at SNR_{col}.

Figure 10 shows the rejection rates for unauthorized rogue devices (R1, R2 and R3) using the valid credentials (i.e., ID) of the authorized device A1 at SNR_{col}. The verification results are based on burst-by-burst grant/deny access criteria [4]. Note that the O symbols denote access correctly denied and the X symbols denote access incorrectly granted. The horizontal black lines correspond to the device-dependent equal error rate thresholds.

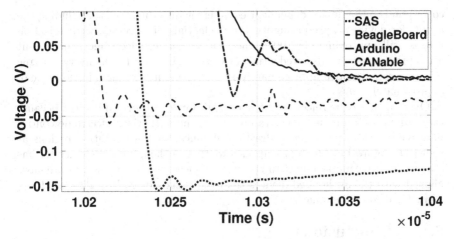

Figure 11. Zoomed-in view of bit transitions in Figure 4.

The rogue devices were rejected 100% of the time in Case A and Case B. The results also indicate that using the smaller region of interest yields rogue device fingerprints that are more similar to the fingerprints of the authorized devices, except for rogue device R3 based on the same vertical and horizontal axes in both figures. Although the rogue rejection rates were perfect for rogue devices R1 and R2, the verification test statistics Z_V generated for these devices were closer to the threshold t_V, indicating a greater similarity in Case B than in Case A.

Rogue device R3 looks less like device SAS 1 in Case B, which is likely due to the symbol and transition misalignment seen in Figure 11, a zoomed-in view of the bit transitions in Figure 4. All the rogue device transitions are slightly misaligned and do not accurately replicate the authorized device transitions.

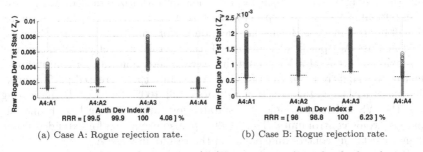

(a) Case A: Rogue rejection rate.   (b) Case B: Rogue rejection rate.

Figure 12. Rejection rates of a device (A4) using the credentials of other devices.

Figure 12 shows the rejection rates when the compromised device SAS 4 (or A4) presented false credentials belonging to the other three authorized devices (A1, A2 and A3). Note that the 0 symbols denote access correctly denied and the X symbols denote access incorrectly granted. The black dashed lines correspond to the device-dependent equal error rate thresholds. Excluding the results for device A4 presenting its own credentials, the average rogue rejection rate is still approximately 100% when an authorized electronic control unit attempts to present false credentials in Case A. In Case B, the average rogue rejection rate dropped approximately 1%, resulting in a rogue rejection rate of approximately 99%.

Overall, the rogue rejection rates are high for unauthorized devices because the devices were unable to accurately match the authorized electronic control unit symbol rate, resulting in drastic differences in the transition regions as shown in Figure 11. The figure also shows that, although rogue device R1 has a higher average amplitude than the other devices, the bit transitions are more aligned with the authorized devices than the rogue device R3. This results in a greater degree of similarity.

6.   Conclusions

Electronic control units in modern automobiles implement normal vehicular operations as well as advanced autonomous safety and driver comfort features. However, the automobiles can be hacked by compromising the electronic control units or by connecting unauthorized devices to the controller area network bus.

The WS-DNA methodology described in this chapter is a viable solution for electronic control unit classification and verification. Although development boards such as Arduino and BeagleBoard can be used to create rogue electronic control units, the differences in their signal transition regions and amplitudes provide enough information to reject these devices when they are compared against authorized electronic control units. When only the message preamble of an electronic control unit was used, 100% of the CAN bus access attempts by three rogue devices were detected. Using an authorized steering angle sensor as a compromised device yielded a rogue device rejection rate greater than 99%, even when a region of interest smaller than the preamble was used. Additionally, the average correct classification of the four authorized devices was greater than 99% at SNR_{col}. As expected, when only seven bits were used as the region of interest in Case B, the classification performance was statistically worse than in Case A. Specifically, in Case B, the average correct classification was approximately 96% at SNR_{col} and the average detection rate for compromised devices was slightly lower than in Case A. Despite the decreased performance, the unauthorized rogue rejection rate was still 100% for Case B, indicating that the WS-DNA methodology is suitable for authenticating base frame format electronic control units. The results are also promising for extended frame format electronic control unit based on the results in Case A.

Security can be established on the CAN bus using the WS-DNA methodology with fingerprints generated from the region of interest used in Case B. A device capable of monitoring and collecting signals could be installed on the CAN bus, programmed with authorized electronic control unit WS-DNA fingerprints as well as an multiple discriminant analysis maximum likelihood classifier. CAN bus traffic could then be collected and analyzed in real-time to detect the presence of compromised or rogue devices in the network.

The WS-DNA methodology can be applied to a range of CAN bus and electronic control unit discrimination problems. Investigating electronic control unit discrimination for the extended frame format could validate the claims made in Case A. Like model discrimination – differentiating between electronic control units from the same manufacturer and with the same lot number – should also be examined, although it is a more difficult aspect of RF-DNA discrimination [3]. Additionally, discriminating between vehicle electronic control units with different functions such as a steering angle sensor, engine control module and telematic control unit would be beneficial. Finally, discriminating between CAN transceivers and evaluating the temperature effects on fingerprinting and discrimination are also promising topics for future research.

The views expressed in this chapter are those of the authors, and do not reflect the official policy or position of the U.S. Air Force, U.S. Department of Defense or U.S. Government. This document has been approved for public release, distribution unlimited (Case #88ABW-2019-0050).

References

[1] O. Avatefipour, A. Hafeez, M. Tayyab and H. Malik, Linking received packets to the transmitter through physical-fingerprinting of controller area network, *Proceedings of the IEEE Workshop on Information Forensics and Security*, 2017.

[2] T. Carbino, Exploitation of Unintentional Ethernet Cable Emissions Using Constellation Based-Distinct Native Attribute (CB-DNA) Fingerprints to Enhance Network Security, Ph.D. Dissertation, Department of Electrical and Computer Engineering, Air Force Institute of Technology, Wright-Patterson Air Force Base, Ohio, 2015.

[3] T. Carbino, M. Temple and J. Lopez, A comparison of PHY-based fingerprinting methods used to enhance network access control, in *ICT Systems Security and Privacy Protection*, H. Federrath and D. Gollmann (Eds.), Springer, Cham, Switzerland, pp. 204–217, 2015.

[4] T. Carbino, M. Temple and J. Lopez, Conditional constellation based distinct native attribute (CB-DNA) fingerprinting for network device authentication, *Proceedings of the IEEE International Conference on Communications*, 2016.

[5] K. Cho and K. Shin, Fingerprinting electronic control units for vehicle intrusion detection, *Proceedings of the Twenty-Fifth USENIX Security Symposium*, pp. 911–927, 2016.

[6] W. Choi, H. Jo, S. Woo, J. Chun, J. Park and D. Lee, Identifying ECUs using inimitable characteristics of signals in controller area networks, *IEEE Transactions on Vehicular Technology*, vol. 67(6), pp. 4757–4770, 2018.

[7] W. Cobb, E. Garcia, M. Temple, R. Baldwin and Y. Kim, Physical layer identification of embedded devices using RF-DNA fingerprinting, *Proceedings of the Military Communications Conference*, pp. 2168–2173, 2010.

[8] S. Corrigan, Introduction to the Controller Area Network (CAN), Application Report SLOA101, Texas Instruments, Dallas, Texas, 2002.

[9] R. Currie, Developments in Car Hacking, Information Security Reading Room, SANS Institute, North Bethesda, Maryland, 2015.

[10] A. Greenberg, Hackers remotely kill a Jeep on the highway – With me in it, *Wired*, July 21, 2015.

[11] M. Jaynes, R. Dantu, R. Varriale and N. Evans, Automating ECU identification for vehicle security, *Proceedings of the Fifteenth IEEE International Conference on Machine Learning and Applications*, pp. 632–635, 2016.

[12] J. Lopez, N. Liefer, C. Busho and M. Temple, Enhancing critical infrastructure and key resources (CIKR) level-0 physical process security using field device distinct native attribute features, *IEEE Transactions on Information Forensics and Security*, vol. 13(5), pp. 1215–1229, 2018.

[13] M. Lukacs, P. Collins and M. Temple, Device identification using active noise interrogation and RF-DNA "fingerprinting" for non-destructive amplifier acceptance testing, *Proceedings of the Seventeenth Annual IEEE Wireless and Microwave Technology Conference*, 2016.

[14] P. Murvay and B. Groza, Source identification using signal characteristics in controller area networks, *IEEE Signal Processing Letters*, vol. 21(4), pp. 395–399, 2014.

[15] P. Paganini, CAN hacking tools, 20 USD to hack a car remotely, *Security Affairs*, February 9, 2014.

[16] D. Reising, M. Temple and J. Jackson, Authorized and rogue device discrimination using dimensionally-reduced RF-DNA fingerprints, *IEEE Transactions on Information Forensics and Security*, vol. 10(6), pp. 1180–1192, 2015.

[17] B. Ross, T. Carbino and S. Stone, Physical-layer discrimination of power line communications, *Proceedings of the International Conference on Computing, Networking and Communications*, pp. 341–345, 2017.

[18] B. Ross, T. Carbino and M. Temple, Home automation simulcasted power line communications network (SPN) discrimination using wired signal distinct native attribute (WS-DNA), *Proceedings of the Twelfth International Conference on Cyber Warfare and Security*, pp. 313–322, 2017.

[19] B. Ross, T. Carbino and M. Temple, Simulcasted power line communications network (SPN) configuration validation for home automation applications using wired signal distinct native attribute (WS-DNA) fingerprinting, *Journal of Information Warfare*, vol. 16(3), pp. 95–118, 2017.

[20] Wikipedia Contributors, CAN-Bus-Frame in Base Format without Stuffbits, *Wikipedia Commons* (`commons.wikimedia.org/wiki/File:CAN-Bus-frame_in_base_format_without_stuffbits.svg`), 2017.

[21] M. Williams, S. Munns, M. Temple and M. Mendenhall, RF-DNA finger-printing for airport WiMax communications security, *Proceedings of the Fourth International Conference on Network and System Security*, pp. 32–39, 2010.

[22] M. Williams, M. Temple and D. Reising, Augmenting bit-level network security using physical layer RF-DNA fingerprinting, *Proceedings of the IEEE Global Telecommunications Conference*, 2010.

Chapter 7

VEHICLE IDENTIFICATION AND ROUTE RECONSTRUCTION VIA TPMS DATA LEAKAGE

Kenneth Hacker, Scott Graham and Stephen Dunlap

Abstract   Tire pressure monitoring systems have become a mandatory feature of modern automobiles, but their presence opens a new attack vector for a potential adversary. These systems have minimal security features, allowing for eavesdropping and data injection with low technical and financial costs.

This chapter explores the potential for tire pressure monitoring systems to provide inputs to a remote sensing network, which leverages the data broadcast by the systems to identify vehicles and track their movements. A traffic simulation is employed to generate vehicle movements and tire pressure monitoring system packets. Experiments demonstrate that the tire pressure monitoring system data can help identify vehicles and reconstruct vehicle routes. They show that a determined adversary could deploy sensors to detect tire pressure monitoring systems and learn about the movements of individual vehicles without any insider information. Potential solutions to this privacy problem are discussed, focusing on low cost changes with the greatest consumer security benefits.

Keywords: TPMS data leakage, vehicle identification, route reconstruction

1.   Introduction

The adoption of a new technology is exciting, with vendors and government regulators eager to lead the way, but often without considering the security risks. Even seemingly insignificant systems can provide avenues for an adversary to gain information or influence. This is the case with vehicular technologies, where manufacturers must balance consumer desires, company goals and safety obligations. Tire pressure monitoring systems (TPMSs), which employ wireless communications to provide tire status information on drivers'

© IFIP International Federation for Information Processing 2019
Published by Springer Nature Switzerland AG 2019
J. Staggs and S. Shenoi (Eds.): Critical Infrastructure Protection XIII, IFIP AICT 570, pp. 123–136, 2019.
https://doi.org/10.1007/978-3-030-34647-8_7

dashboards, are a mandatory safety feature in all new vehicles. However, the wireless signals are neither protected from eavesdroppers nor are they authenticated, enabling a malicious actor to gain access to sensitive data, or worse, manipulate the system.

This chapter discusses potential privacy threats that result from TPMSs being installed in the majority of vehicles on roadways. Experiments were conducted using traffic simulations with realistic TPMS data that an adversary could collect and analyze. The experiments demonstrate that a determined adversary could deploy sensors to identify vehicles using TPMS data and learn about the movements of individual vehicles without any insider information. Potential solutions to this privacy problem are discussed, focusing on low cost changes with the greatest consumer security benefits.

2.   Tire Pressure Monitoring Systems

This section provides an overview of TPMSs, including TPMS legislation, implementation, attacks and security.

2.1   Legislation

In the United States, steps toward mandating TPMSs in new vehicles initiated after a number of traffic fatalities related to defective tires. The Transportation Recall Enhancement, Accountability and Documentation (TREAD) Act of 2000, which was rapidly passed by the U.S. Congress [9], called for a mandatory system that would warn drivers when one or more vehicle tires were significantly underinflated.

The National Highway Traffic Safety Administration [5] drafted more detailed compliance requirements for all new vehicles starting from September 1, 2007. These requirements included reporting to the driver if one or more tires were 25% below minimum pressure within 20 minutes of the pressure dropping. The European Commission [3] mandated TPMSs in all new vehicles after 2012 as part of a major safety and emission-reduction program. As a result, millions of TPMS-equipped vehicles are on the roadways and their percentage is growing as older vehicles are removed from service.

2.2   Implementation

A TPMS unit embedded in the tire of a vehicle periodically reads its pressure and temperature sensors, constructs a network packet, encodes it (e.g., with Manchester encoding) and transmits it using amplitude shift or frequency shift keying to a vehicle TPMS receiver, which forwards it to a central control module for analysis. Tire pressure alerts are sent by the control module directly or indirectly to the dashboard where they are displayed.

The wireless data packets transmitted by most TPMS units are fairly simple. A typical packet includes 32 bits for an ID, eight bits of pressure data, eight bits of temperature data, four bits of status flags and twelve bits for a cyclic redundancy check (CRC).

Unfortunately, the tire pressure and temperature data in the network packets are neither encrypted nor significantly obfuscated, allowing anyone in wireless proximity who captures the packets to read the data. Notably, information is only transmitted in one direction, from the tire device to the vehicle TPMS receiver, in order to conserve battery power for the sensors, which are in the sleep mode for the vast majority of the time.

The main reason for the lack of security in TPMSs is the increased power cost required for encryption and two-way communications. The lifespans of the batteries are five to ten years; size and weight requirements preclude the use of larger batteries [10]. The tire pressure unit, which includes a battery, is usually set in epoxy inside the tire; the individual components are, therefore, not replaceable. As a result, the entire tire pressure unit has to be replaced when the battery is depleted.

2.3   Attacks

In 2010, Rouf et al. [6] published an evaluation of TPMS attack scenarios as part of a case study of in-car wireless networks. They demonstrated that the lack of authentication and integrity checks made spoofing trivial, leading to malicious effects such as displaying false information and warning lights, and disabling the TPMS control unit.

In the same article, Rouf and colleagues [6] discussed the feasibility of tracking vehicles based on their TPMS sensor broadcasts. Given the static IDs of the four tires associated with a vehicle, it is simple to associate them with the identity of a vehicle. In fact, given the data from all four tires of a vehicle – and without considering any other data such as geographic locations – there would have to be more than one billion vehicles on the road to even approach a 1% chance of misidentifying the vehicle.

Creating an eavesdropping infrastructure can be challenging, especially for passive data collection. The low power transmissions from TPMS units require receivers to be positioned close to vehicles, so large numbers of receivers would have to be placed along roadways to ensure that the infrequently-transmitted packets are captured.

A more effective solution may be to stimulate a TPMS transmission using a low frequency activation signal. While this process is more complex and prone to noise, it could guarantee readings at points of interest along roadways.

Rouf and colleagues [6] also compared TPMS-based tracking of vehicles against the other alternative for tracking vehicles – automatic number plate reading. According to their study, tracking via TPMSs would have higher read rates (99% versus 90%) and would not require line-of-sight measurements. However, TPMS-based tracking by law enforcement would require changes to existing laws and regulations.

2.4   Security

Researchers have proposed approaches for rendering TPMS-based tracking and spoofing of vehicles more difficult by obfuscating the packet IDs. Xu et al. [11] have proposed a system incorporating pseudo-IDs, sequence numbers, message authentication codes and session keys, which addresses many of the privacy and integrity problems. However, their system, which requires a three-way handshake to establish keys, does not work with current TPMS sensors because they are not equipped to receive data.

Emura et al. [2] have examined sensor costs and have demonstrated a protocol that could be used under current TPMS constraints. Other researchers [4, 8] have shown that rolling IDs that change between TPMS transmissions are feasible and can defeat tracking methods. The next generation of TPMSs may incorporate these and other upgrades. However, automobile manufacturers are not as yet concerned about TPMS vulnerabilities, so the security problems persist.

3.   Background

This section describes the traffic simulator and the performance metrics used in this research.

3.1   Simulator for Urban Mobility

Simulator for Urban Mobility (SUMO) is an open-source traffic simulation suite that provides several tools for mapping and traffic generation, manipulation and simulation. First released in 2002, SUMO continues to be actively enhanced [1], providing a platform for testing vehicular routing protocols, executing traffic congestion models and generating realistic traffic data that can be used for further research.

SUMO is a microscopic simulator in that the level of simulation goes down to individual vehicles and lanes, with the vehicles acting on their own and responding in a realistic manner. In contrast, macroscopic simulators abstract the individual vehicles into general traffic flows in sections of a map. SUMO models maps as nodes (intersections) and edges (roads) on a Cartesian grid; the maps can be constructed, randomly generated or imported from sources such as OpenStreetMap. Traffic conditions such as the number of lanes, traffic light timings, speed restrictions and more can all be specified or imported. Vehicles can belong to standard classes such as cars, trucks or buses, or customized vehicles can be developed to meet the simulation needs.

Simulations are defined by map and route files. The map establishes the places where a vehicle may travel, along with the road conditions and restrictions. The route defines the points at which a vehicle enters and exits the roadway, the roads on which it travels and its behavior during the trip. The simulation can be modified in real time using the Traffic Control Interface

(TraCI) to observe how changing conditions such as traffic lights or a collision may affect the simulation.

3.2   Measurement Metrics

This chapter discusses algorithms for identifying vehicles and reconstructing their routes. In order to evaluate the effectiveness of the algorithms, metrics are needed to compare their results against truth data in the simulation. Each metric is intended to provide relative assessments of the "goodness" of various configurations.

Data from the simulation is passed to the tire ID association phase, which transforms TPMS observations into vehicle identities. The vehicle identities and associated observations are sent to the route reconstruction phase, which processes the individual observations to create complete routes.

Two metrics were selected: (i) Jaccard distance used in the tire ID association phase; and (ii) graph edit distance used in the route reconstruction phase:

- **Jaccard Distance:** During the tire ID association phase, sets are compared to determine the combinations of IDs that are commonly found together. The Jaccard distance is a set similarity metric that is commonly used for spell checking strings [12]. The Jacquard distance J of two sets A and B is given by:

$$J(A, B) = \frac{|A \cap B|}{|A \cup B|}$$

  The Jaccard distance is used to compare a candidate set of tire IDs against tire IDs observed during a time window at a specific intersection along a route. For example, if the candidate set is {0xa1, 0xb2, 0xc3} and if the set of tire IDs observed during a five-second window at an intersection is {0xcc, 0xdd, 0xff, 0xa1, 0xb2}, then the Jaccard distance is computed as:

$$\frac{|\{0xa1, 0xb2\}|}{|\{0xa1, 0xb2, 0xc3, 0xcc, 0xdd, 0xff\}|} = \frac{2}{6} = 0.33$$

  This score helps determine the best association of tire IDs. Additionally, it is used to compare candidate associations against true sets belonging to vehicles in order to judge their goodness.

- **Graph Edit Distance:** A target route on a road map and a candidate route are modeled as directed graphs where the nodes are intersections and the edges are roads. The graph edit distance, which compares the similarity between two graphs, is widely used in pattern matching [7]. It is employed in the route reconstruction phase to score candidate routes.

The graph edit distance is defined as the minimum number of modifications required to transform the graph corresponding to a candidate route to the target graph. In this work, the modification operations correspond to insertions, deletions or substitutions of nodes or edges. Each modification operation can be weighted differently to reflect the impact of the operation. Specifically, insertions and deletions have weights of one. A substitution has a weight of two because it corresponds to a deletion followed by an insertion.

4.   Simulation Methodology

This section describes the simulation methodology.

4.1   Simulation Setup

The main steps in the simulation setup phase are: (i) geographical map generation; and (ii) traffic generation.

- **Geographical Map Generation:** The map employed in the simulation covered a section of downtown Dayton, Ohio. SUMO provides a tool that uses OpenStreetMap to download real data for an area, which accurately represents traffic lights, speed limits, one-way streets and other elements of traffic flow.

  The map size is a simulation parameter that may be adjusted to serve various purposes. The map size chosen for the simulation was approximately 600 nodes and 1,200 edges. This map was selected for reasons of familiarity and to represent sufficiently diverse traffic conditions that could demonstrate the feasibility of the approach. An urban deployment with a relatively high density of intersections was of particular interest in this study.

- **Traffic Generation:** The SUMO Python script *randomTrips* employed the network description, simulation time, optional seed and traffic density to generate an XML trip file that described every vehicle created along with its source node and destination. The SUMO DUAROUTER tool converted the source/destination pairs to actual routes that described the roads that each vehicle could take during the simulation.

- **Wireless Communications Detection:** SUMO includes a package for wireless communications that can model technologies such as Bluetooth and vehicular ad-hoc networks (VANETs) [1]. Vehicles may be given receivers and transmitters independently, and the assignments can be made explicitly or randomly using a user-specified percentage.

  All the vehicles in the simulation were assumed to have transmitters (i.e., they were equipped with tire pressure sensors). The TPMS detectors were modeled as vehicles equipped with receivers that were parked at intersections. Edge cases, corresponding to situations where multiple intersections were very close to each other, were handled by manually removing overlapping detectors.

When a vehicle enters detector range in the simulation, data is recorded in an XML file associated with the vehicle. At the end of the simulation, this XML file contains considerable details about the vehicle route and travel conditions. Packets may be optionally dropped by eliminating a percentage of detectors, simulating heavy versus sparse detector deployments.

This method of modeling wireless detectors differs from real-world deployments, but it has enough fidelity to achieve the research goals. A real detector would likely be a directional antenna that could only receive data from a few lanes, possibly requiring $2n$ detectors for an n-way intersection. This could actually improve a tracking algorithm by providing travel directions. However, the simulation conducted only considered binary detections at intersections – was a vehicle present at the intersection and at what time? Based on previous research and working within the time constraints, these inputs were deemed adequate for purposes of tire ID association and route reconstruction. The additional benefit is that this type of data could come from detectors other than TPMS sensors (which are of interest as VANET technologies enter the roadways), but the data could still be applied to existing systems such as automatic number plate readers.

4.2   TPMS Packet Generation

In the TPMS packet generation phase, wireless observation data generated by SUMO is post-processed to produce TPMS packets needed for tire ID association. In this phase, most of the data is stripped to prevent sensitive information such as actual vehicle IDs, speeds and routes from being accessed in the later phases.

The TPMS packet generation phase starts with a dictionary containing time and location data for all wireless observations; the data is indexed by the observed vehicle ID. For each unique vehicle, four random 32-bit tire IDs are generated. For each vehicle observation, the simulation must decide which tires have been observed.

A simple probabilistic model was developed based on previous experiments that used a directional antenna to measure the attenuation due to vehicles. The model assumed that transmissions from the two tires closest to a roadside detector (i.e., right-side tire transmissions) would always be detected, and the left-front and left-rear tire transmissions would be detected with probabilities of 50% and 10%, respectively. If a tire is deemed to be detected at an observation point, then the location and timestamp are placed in a new dictionary indexed by the tire ID. This ensures that the resulting data structure does not contain the true vehicle ID, and is at most four times larger than the original data structure.

4.3   Tire ID Association

The main steps in the tire ID association phase are: (i) candidate association creation; and (ii) candidate association scoring:

- **Candidate Association Creation:** This step attempts to associate the observed tire IDs with one another to create a tuple called a candidate (tire ID) association, which ideally belongs to one vehicle. Each tire ID has an associated list of observations that form a route. Because it is unlikely to obtain data about all four tires of a vehicle at every intersection, tire IDs that belong with each other (i.e., from the same car) would have similar, but not necessarily identical, lists of observations.

  All the tire IDs observed at a given location during a certain time window (chosen as one second in the experiments) are examined. For every tire ID, the frequency with which every other tire ID is observed near the selected tire ID is tallied across the entire observed route. In a high-density traffic environment, two vehicles could be close enough to yield overlapping tire IDs. Thus, tire IDs from nearby vehicles have to be filtered.

  This is accomplished by creating sets of the four most frequently observed tire IDs with respect to the tire ID being evaluated. The Jaccard distance metric is used to compare these sets against the sets observed at each location. The set with the highest average Jaccard distance across the route is considered to be an identity and is saved in a scoring matrix. This enables a tunable metric to be used to manipulate the risk/reward of associating more tire IDs. Additionally, because the route for a set of tire IDs may appear to be different even if they belong to the same vehicle, it is possible for an infrequently observed tire ID to appear to be associated with a different set of tire IDs.

  A scoring matrix adds a second layer of filtering to reduce this error. After all the tire IDs are considered independently, the scoring matrix is evaluated to create the final virtual vehicle identities, which are the sets of tire IDs belonging a unique vehicle. If a set of four or fewer tire IDs are consistently grouped with each other, the tire IDs in the set are assumed to belong to a specific vehicle, the set is designated as a candidate association and the tire IDs are removed from further consideration. Otherwise, if a set of more than four tire IDs appear to be related, then four tire IDs that are most frequently associated with each other are assumed to belong to a specific vehicle; this set is also designated as a candidate association.

- **Candidate Association Scoring:** When scoring a candidate association, the tire IDs grouped as corresponding to a vehicle identity should be evaluated with respect to each other instead of attempting to match them against a true vehicle. Additionally, the risk/reward of attempting to add a third or fourth tire ID to the group should increase.

Table 1. Candidate association scores.

Matches	Set Size	Comments	Score
0	4	Four incorrectly associated tires (worst case)	0.14
0	3	Three incorrectly associated tires	0.17
0	2	Two incorrectly associated tires	0.2
0	1	One associated tire is effectively not an association	0.25
1	4	Two correctly associated tires and two unrelated tires	0.33
1	3	Two correctly associated tires and one unrelated tire	0.4
1	2	Two correctly associated tires	0.5
2	4	Three correctly associated tires and one unrelated tire	0.6
2	3	Three correctly associated tires	0.75
3	4	Four correctly associated tires (ideal case)	1.0

The method used to score a candidate association performs a reverse lookup in the truth data to find the true vehicle ID that is associated with each tire ID in the candidate association. This creates a tuple of one to four tire IDs, each of which may correspond to the same vehicle or, in adverse cases, multiple vehicles.

Jaccard similarity is used to compare a candidate association against the most likely true vehicle. As shown in Table 1, in the case of a four-wheeled vehicle, the Jaccard similarity score ranges from 0.14 to 1.0. Note that the first column corresponds to the number of tire IDs in a candidate association that belong to the same vehicle. Thus, the values range from zero (all the tires belong to different vehicles) to three (all the tires belong to the same vehicle).

4.4 Route Reconstruction

The main steps in route reconstruction are: (i) candidate route creation; and (ii) candidate route scoring:

- **Candidate Route Creation:** The output from the tire ID association phase, which is input to the route reconstruction phase, comprises a list of candidate vehicles and their associated observations (location-timestamp pairs). The algorithm used in route reconstruction is assumed to have complete knowledge of the roads in the geographic area where the detectors are placed. This knowledge is encoded in a graph where the intersections are nodes and the roads are edges. The edges are weighted based on the estimated travel times to traverse the edges.

The algorithm examines the observations for a given vehicle and attempts to predict the most likely route corresponding to the observations. This is accomplished by taking two consecutive observations and finding a simple path (without loops) whose estimated travel time is the closest to the difference between the observed times. The complete vehicle route is created by repeating this step for all the observations corresponding to the vehicle. This entire process is repeated until candidate routes are generated for all the vehicles.

- **Candidate Route Scoring:** Because the road network is modeled as a graph, the graph edit distance is the natural choice for quantifying the correctness of candidate routes. The truth data is used to build a directed graph containing only the nodes and edges that are actually traversed by a vehicle. The graph corresponding to the candidate route is compared against the truth graph.

  The candidate route score is computed by tallying the weights corresponding to the minimum number of insertions, deletions or substitutions required to convert one graph to the other. Note that an insertion implies that a node or edge is in the candidate route whereas a deletion implies that an extraneous (incorrect) node or edge exists in the candidate route.

4.5   Simulation Variables

Two variables, detector density and vehicle density, were employed in the simulation experiments. The values of these variables were varied in the simulation runs.

Three detector density values were employed, low, medium and high, corresponding to detectors placed at 10%, 50% and 100% of intersections, respectively. The detector densities were selected to provide insights into the optimal number of detectors that should be used when cost and infrastructure size are considerations.

Three vehicle densities were employed, low, medium and high, corresponding to 200, 500 and 2,000 vehicles, respectively. These densities were manually determined based on how much traffic could be handled without becoming overwhelmingly gridlocked.

5.   Simulation Results

This section presents the tire ID association and route reconstruction results.

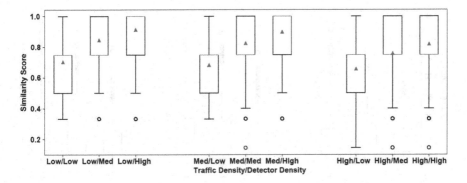

Figure 1. Tire ID association results.

5.1 Tire ID Association Results

A candidate tire ID association was scored based on pairwise matches in a reverse lookup of tire IDs that were believed to be associated with each other. This metric provided a relative measure of goodness as the experimental conditions changed.

Each experimental configuration was run over 150 seeds, which varied the routes and detector placements while keeping the detector and traffic densities constant. The resulting scores are shown in the boxplots of Figure 1. Note that the triangles denote the means of the experiments whereas the circles denote outliers. All the experiments with medium or high detector coverage achieved mean scores greater than 0.75. This demonstrates that the correct 3-tuples were identified frequently and that significant mismatches rarely occurred.

Certain trends that followed expected patterns emerged from the data. The means always improved with increasing detector density because more observations provided more opportunities to discern patterns. Every experiment had at least one case where all four tire IDs were correctly associated; this is likely to occur when there are enough vehicles and long enough routes to observe all the tires. The minimum scores appeared to be affected more by traffic density than detector density, with the worst cases getting worse as the traffic density increased. This is likely the result of traffic congestion, which causes vehicles to gather at intersections, effectively forming caravans. Multiple vehicles passing by a detector in a short window increased the likelihood of errors in tire ID associations. This issue may be alleviated by adjusting the locations of detectors so that important intersections are adequately covered.

5.2 Route Reconstruction Results

A candidate route was scored based on the graph edit distance between the candidate route and the true route travelled by the vehicle. Since every node or edge inserted/deleted incurred a cost of one and every modified node or edge incurred a cost of two, a score of zero corresponded to a perfect route

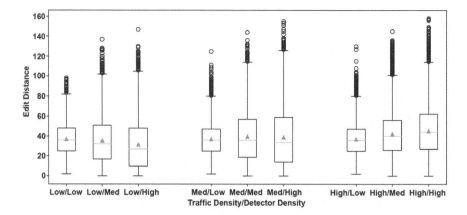

Figure 2.   Route reconstruction results.

reconstruction. Note that, because the routes were random, the length of each route varied and the numbers of nodes and edges travelled did not have constant relations to the physical distance travelled. As such, the graph edit distance was used as a natural metric to observe trends between experiments when maps were modeled as directed graphs. Figure 2 shows the distribution of scores for the route reconstruction experiments.

Expected trends in route reconstruction emerged primarily as a function of detector density. When the detector density was high, some vehicle routes were reconstructed perfectly. In the case of low vehicle density and a high number of detectors, the average score was the best in every experiment. However, when the vehicle density was high, adding more detectors did not improve the average score. This occurred because the heuristic that was used guessed the route between observations based on travel time. As the difference between actual and expected travel times on a given roadway increased, the route reconstruction accuracy decreased. In the high traffic density experiments, traffic congestion greatly increased the travel time over the average, leading the algorithm to assume that vehicles took longer routes. Improved graph tracking heuristics or engaging traffic congestion data could alleviate this issue when unusual road conditions are encountered.

6.   Conclusions

This research has examined the security consequences of TPMSs, highlighting some vulnerabilities and demonstrating their potential negative effects. It extends the seminal work of Rouf et al. [6] by exploring TPMS security concerns in a large simulated environment. The open-source SUMO tool was leveraged to rapidly generate realistic data and conduct extensive simulations to evaluate the feasibility of associating tire pressure ID packets with vehicle identities, and subsequently track vehicles of interest.

The use of intersection-based wireless observations and realistic TPMS detection parameters resulted in high tire ID association rates despite employing a fairly simple algorithm. With knowledge of vehicle identities and timestamped locations, sparse observations could be processed to reconstruct vehicle routes with reasonable, albeit varying, accuracy. The simulation experiments demonstrate that an adversary could deploy current roadside sensors to glean pattern-of-life data for large numbers of vehicles. The low level of effort required to breach privacy should motivate further research into the proper use of the technology and push manufacturers to implement advanced security features.

Future research would be facilitated by creating a SUMO plug-in that would handle TPMSs in a simple and consistent manner. Another avenue is to develop algorithms with new heuristics that would provide improved accuracy and speed. Another potential improvement is the application of machine learning techniques, which appear viable due to the abstract association tasks and the availability of scoring metrics. Finally, the concepts and techniques developed in this research could be applied to other wireless vehicular technologies such as Bluetooth and vehicular ad-hoc networks.

The views expressed in this chapter are those of the authors, and do not reflect the official policy or position of the U.S. Air Force, U.S. Department of Defense or U.S. Government. This document has been approved for public release, distribution unlimited (Case #88ABW-2018-6333).

References

[1] DLR – Institute of Transportation Systems, Eclipse SUMO – Simulation of Urban Mobility, Berlin, Germany (`dlr.de/ts/sumo`), 2019.

[2] K. Emura, T. Hayashi and S. Moriai, Toward securing tire pressure monitoring systems: A case of PRESENT-based implementation, *Proceedings of the International Symposium on Information Theory and its Applications*, pp. 403–407, 2016.

[3] European Commission, Top News from the European Commission, 23 November to 20 December 2009, AGENDA/09/40, Press Release, Brussels, Belgium, November 20, 2009.

[4] D. Kilcoyne, S. Bendelac, J. Ernst and A. Michaels, Tire pressure monitoring system encryption to improve vehicular security, *Proceedings of the IEEE Military Communications Conference*, pp. 1219–1224, 2016.

[5] National Highway Traffic Safety Administration, Federal Motor Vehicle Safety Standards; Tire Pressure Monitoring Systems; Controls and Displays; Final Rule, 49 CFR Part 571, Docket No. NHTSA 2000-8572, RIN 2127-AI33, Washington, DC, 2003.

[6] I. Rouf, R. Miller, H. Mustafa, T. Taylor, S. Oh, W. Xu, M. Gruteser, W. Trappe and I. Seskar, Security and privacy vulnerabilities of in-car wireless networks: A tire pressure monitoring system case study, *Proceedings of the Nineteenth USENIX Conference on Security*, article no. 21, 2010.

[7] A. Sanfeliu and K. Fu, A distance measure between attributed relational graphs for pattern recognition, *IEEE Transactions on Systems, Man and Cybernetics*, vol. SMC-13(3), pp. 353–362, 1983.

[8] C. Solomon and B. Groza, LiMon – Lightweight authentication for tire pressure monitoring sensors, in *Security of Industrial Control Systems and Cyber Physical Systems*, A. Becue, N. Cuppens-Boulahia, F. Cuppens, S. Katsikas and C. Lambrinoudakis (Eds.), Springer, Cham, Switzerland, pp. 95–111, 2016.

[9] U.S. Congress, Transportation Recall Enhancement, Accountability and Documentation (TREAD) Act, Public Law 106-414, 106th Congress, Washington, DC, 2000.

[10] S. Velupillai and L. Guvenc, Tire pressure monitoring [Applications of Control], *IEEE Control Systems*, vol. 27(6), pp. 22–25, 2007.

[11] M. Xu, W. Xu, J. Walker and B. Moore, Lightweight secure communications protocols for in-vehicle sensor networks, *Proceedings of the ACM Workshop on Security, Privacy and Dependability for Cyber Vehicles*, pp. 19–30, 2013.

[12] S. Yadav, A. Reddy, A. Reddy and S. Ranjan, Detecting algorithmically-generated domain-flux attacks with DNS traffic analysis, *IEEE/ACM Transactions on Networking*, vol. 20(5), pp. 1663-1677, 2012.

Chapter 8

MODELING LIABILITY DATA COLLECTION SYSTEMS FOR INTELLIGENT TRANSPORTATION INFRASTRUCTURE USING HYPERLEDGER FABRIC

Luis Cintron, Scott Graham, Douglas Hodson and Barry Mullins

Abstract   Distributed ledger technology is transforming environments where the participating entities have low trust. Employing distributed ledgers for intelligent transportation infrastructure communications and operations enables decentralized collaboration between entities that do not fully trust each other. This chapter models a transportation event data collection system as a Hyperledger Fabric blockchain network and simulates it using a transportation environment modeling tool. Data structures model the data collected about accidents involving vehicles and witness reports from nearby vehicles and road-side units that observed the events. The chaincode developed for the collection, validation and corroboration of the reported data is presented. Network performance results for various configurations are discussed. Optimization of the network configuration parameters resulted in a 48.1% improvement in transaction throughput. The experiments demonstrate that a distributed ledger technology such as Hyperledger Fabric holds promise for the collection of transportation data and the collaboration of applications and services that consume the data.

Keywords: Intelligent transportation infrastructure, distributed ledger, blockchain

1.   Introduction

Intelligent transportation systems are information-intensive tools that facilitate connected, integrated and automated transportation systems in modern transportation infrastructures [28]. Intelligent transportation systems enable vehicles, pedestrians and infrastructure components to communicate and in-

© IFIP International Federation for Information Processing 2019
Published by Springer Nature Switzerland AG 2019
J. Staggs and S. Shenoi (Eds.): Critical Infrastructure Protection XIII, IFIP AICT 570, pp. 137–156, 2019.
https://doi.org/10.1007/978-3-030-34647-8_8

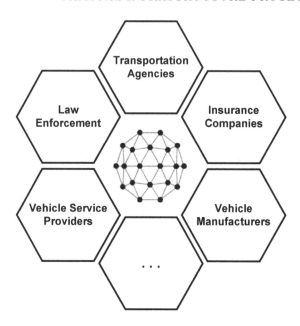

Figure 1. Transportation infrastructure consortium members.

teract with each another and to provide services to infrastructure stakeholders such as government entities and businesses. However, these systems are often isolated and do not communicate with each other due to the lack of network services, ownership/control (company-owned and maintained) and geopolitical limitations (cities, states and countries).

Distributed ledger technology, which has changed the way transactions are conducted in environments with limited or zero trust among peers, can enhance the collection, sharing and storage of data among intelligent transportation systems by providing decentralized collaborative platforms for stakeholders. Indeed, embedding distributed ledger technology in the intelligence transportation ecosystem can address communications and interoperability challenges while providing governance, security and privacy benefits that are not currently available in transportation infrastructures and services.

This chapter describes an approach for standing up a distributed ledger network (DLN) infrastructure that significantly enhances accident event data collection in an intelligent transportation infrastructure. The proposed approach involves standing up a consortium-based distributed ledger network infrastructure to serve as the back-end for multiple intelligent transportation system applications within the same instance. The decentralized network infrastructure, which is developed using the Hyperledger Fabric framework and Hyperledger Composer toolset, is designed to be operated and maintained by a consortium of government and non-government entities such as law enforcement, transportation agencies, insurance companies, vehicle manufacturers and other transportation-related service providers (Figure 1). The infrastructure supports the integration, collaboration and maintenance of relevant data by pre-selected parties in a decentralized and secure manner.

The focus is on a trusted, secure and verifiable repository for data collected by vehicles, infrastructure components and participants, which would extend the accident reconstruction work of Kopylova et al. [10]. Specifically, the distributed ledger network infrastructure would serve as a platform for executing distributed network services for reconstructing events leading up to, during and immediately following vehicle accidents. Sensors mounted on vehicles and road-side units (RSUs) collect data about vehicle parameters (e.g., speed, heading, location) as well as data about other vehicles shared via vehicular ad-hoc network (VANET) vehicle-to-vehicle/vehicle-to-infrastructure communications using the IEEE 1609 family of standards for wireless access in vehicular environments (WAVE). This capability would enhance vehicle forensics and improve processes and tools for identifying the root causes of accidents and the liable parties.

2. Background

Intelligent transportation systems comprise devices and sensors that collect, transmit and analyze data and information to provide services that enhance the quality of and experiences provided by modern transportation infrastructures [25].

The data collection components in intelligent transportation systems include sensors such as cameras, GPS receivers, RFID readers and radar systems that are embedded in vehicles and road-side units. The continuous collection and analysis of observed data enables vehicles to detect and avoid collisions, report traffic conditions and pass on other information witnessed during road events such as accidents. Systems and sensors may share the collected data with other vehicles, road-side units and remote services via proximal vehicular ad-hoc networks or through network communications technologies such as Ethernet and 3G/4G/5G. The transmitted data is analyzed and processed to provide services such as congestion control, automatic toll collection and collision prevention, among others. In other words, intelligent transportation systems rely on information collection and dissemination to provide services to transportation infrastructure stakeholders.

Currently, communications between intelligent transportation systems are hindered by the high cost of operation and maintenance, lack of network capabilities, issues of data ownership/control (company-owned and maintained) and geopolitical limitations (imposed by jurisdictions such as cities, states and countries). As a result, the search for innovative and cost-saving solutions to create a connected ecosystem of intelligent transportation systems is an active area of research in large cities such as New York City [17] and Tampa [26].

Distributed ledger technology enables the maintenance of append-only data structures by untrusted or partially-trusted participants in a decentralized manner [3]. It leverages protocols that provide decentralized communications, tamper-resistant storage of transactions, crash/fault tolerance, and data provenance, as well as other features such as code execution via smart-contracts or chaincode. The resulting deployments are often referred to as distributed ledger networks.

Popular distributed ledger networks, which utilize blockchains [16] or directed acyclic graphs [2] to maintain ledgers, are categorized based on the level of trust required for peers to participate. Public or permissionless distributed ledger networks are accessible to anyone on the Internet and their contents are visible and verifiable by all participants [21]. Access permissions in private or permissioned distributed ledger networks are maintained by single central entities where the network peers are highly trusted. Consortium chains, as described in [5], are partially-decentralized solutions that are hybrids of low-trust (i.e., public blockchains) and single high-trust entity models (i.e., private blockchains) [21]. Such hybrid models enable organizations in a consortium to share transaction records without having to trust all the other organizations in the network or rely on a trusted third party to facilitate communications [9]. The consortium-based distributed ledger network model is a good fit for transportation infrastructure applications due to its privacy-enabling and access control features, distributed execution and low-cost scalability. Ideally, the consortium would comprise government entities such as law enforcement and transportation departments as well as organizations that provide services to the transportation infrastructure or its stakeholders (e.g., vehicle manufacturers, automobile dealers, insurance companies and maintenance service providers).

3.   Related Work

Kopylova et al. [10] have presented an approach for collecting vehicular ad-hoc network data to reconstruct the events that took place before, during and after accidents. The approach leverages vehicles with improved logging mechanisms, vehicular ad-hoc network communications data and a GPS data rectification mechanism that processes data submitted by other entities. All the events are logged in the associated vehicle data recorders that require owner consent or court orders to gain access to the stored data. This data is parsed, filtered and appended to previously-acquired witnessed data in order to perform forensic analyses. Potential problems are that the data stored in the vehicles is at risk of tampering via modification or deletion, and the data may not always be accessible.

Dorri et al. [8] have proposed the use of a blockchain-based distributed ledger network to address scalability issues with centralized systems (e.g., cloud services), preserve the privacy of vehicle owners and passengers, and enhance the security of smart transportation systems. Unlike permissionless public blockchains such as Bitcoin, the approach clusters the network and moves distributed ledger network management to nodes whose sole purpose is to broadcast and verify transactions and append blocks to the ledgers. Important features include hash checks of wireless software updates, secure data exchange with insurance providers and car-sharing services. Security mechanisms in the blockchain design include a chain of block hashes, encryption of transactions and public-key-based authentication of transactions. The distributed network architecture prevents service disruptions caused by distributed denial-of-service attacks by filtering transactions from entities with invalid keys. Unfortunately, Dorri and colleagues have not conducted any experimentation of their approach, even in a simulated transportation environment.

Oham et al. [19] have described a blockchain liability attribution framework for autonomous vehicles based on a consortium of transportation and government organizations. The framework employs two partitions for communications – operational and decision partitions – that collect and share data between different entities and sensors. A qualitative analysis of the framework demonstrates its resilience to malicious activities such as transaction deletion, collusion and spoofing. A performance evaluation focusing on the average verification and validation times for different types of transactions is promising; the results show less overhead compared with the approach of Cebe et al. [7].

In other work, Oham and colleagues [18] have developed a blockchain framework for auto-insurance claims and adjudication for connected and automated vehicles. However, both works by Oham et al. [18, 19] are unclear about how the consensus algorithm operates to ensure network integrity and they omit design considerations for enabling the services to operate within existing intelligent transportation systems. Unlike the other proposals described in this section [7, 18, 19], the implementation described in this chapter leverages an open-source framework that has been tested in production environments, has community and commercial support and continuing upgrades while enabling a number of applications within a single platform.

While previous research describes implementations of distributed ledger networks that enhance intelligent transportation applications, little, if any, work has focused on modeling transportation infrastructure applications or intelligent transportation systems that leverage distributed ledger network frameworks. Additionally, evidence showing how distributed ledger networks can scale to millions of vehicles in public roads and in other transportation environments is minimal. In particular, scalability challenges related to consensus algorithms, performance metrics, and designs and decisions related to operational distributed ledger networks for intelligent transportation systems have not been discussed. Furthermore, the other approaches described in this section have not been analyzed in terms of key parameters such as block size, block timeout and transactions per block that affect overall performance parameters such as transaction throughput and consensus time, which are vital in intelligent transportation ecosystems.

4. Infrastructure Modeling and Implementation

The goal of this work was to model an intelligent transportation infrastructure and applications using a distributed ledger network, specifically, Hyperledger Fabric. Performance metrics were recorded and analyzed to assess the

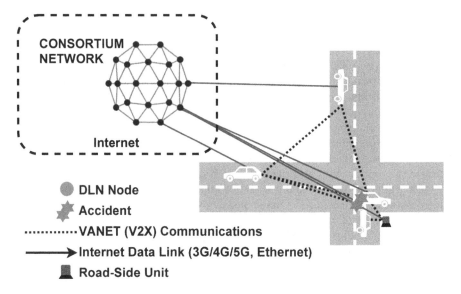

CONSORTIUM NETWORK

Internet

● **DLN Node**
✦ **Accident**
············ **VANET (V2X) Communications**
⟶ **Internet Data Link (3G/4G/5G, Ethernet)**
▮ **Road-Side Unit**

Figure 2. Operational view of an infrastructure with a consortium network.

effectiveness of the network at handling the data volumes encountered in an active intelligent transportation infrastructure. Network and code design parameters that improve responsiveness and throughput are also discussed. Figure 2 shows the operational view of the modeled infrastructure, which incorporates vehicles and road-side units, and their interactions with the consortium network.

4.1   Definitions

The following are the key terms used in the model:

- **Consensus:** Consensus refers to agreement in a distributed ledger network about the next set of transactions and the order in which they are appended to the ledger [15]. Consensus in Hyperledger Fabric takes place among ordering service nodes (commonly referred to as orderers) and is achieved by selecting a leader from among the nodes with a fully synchronized ledger to order the transactions, place them in a block and deliver them to other peer nodes for validation and committal. Apache Kafka was employed for consensus because it is the only implementation provided by Hyperledger Fabric (v1.2) that is suitable for production environments.

- **Channel:** A channel in Hyperledger Fabric is a private blockchain that only channel participants can access and interact with [15]. Participation is managed via authentication and access control policies.

- **Chaincode:** Chaincode is the code/service invoked by an application that interacts with the Hyperledger Fabric network to manage accesses and modifications to the ledger. It is installed on peer nodes to work on one or more available channels [15].

- **Endorsement:** Endorsement in Hyperledger Fabric is the simulation of the execution of a chaincode transaction by a peer node and the communication of the response back to the originator along with the peer node signature to provide proof of a valid execution result [15]. Endorsement policies specify transaction endorsement requirements using Boolean expressions involving the participating organizations [27].

- **Membership Services Provider:** A membership services provider (MSP) supplies cryptographic (public-key infrastructure based) credentials to Hyperledger Fabric participants for authentication and transaction processing [15].

- **Peer Node:** A peer node is a network node that executes the chaincode and maintains a copy of the ledger. Peer nodes designated as endorsers can participate in the endorsements of transactions. Nodes can also be designated as anchors, which enables them to be discovered by and communicate with all the other peer nodes.

4.2 Implementation Platform

The network node simulations were executed in virtual machines (VMs) on a single workstation powered by an Intel CORE i7 vPro (7th Gen) processor (2.9 GHz, four cores, eight logical processors) with 16 GB of RAM. Each Hyperledger Fabric virtual machine node was allocated two logical processors, 2 GB RAM and ran the Ubuntu 16.04 64-bit operating system.

4.3 Frameworks and Tools

Several frameworks and tools, which are part of the Hyperledger collaborative effort hosted by the Linux Foundation, were employed. These frameworks and tools are maintained by technology leaders such as IBM, Intel and SAP. In particular, the following frameworks and tools were used in this research:

- **Hyperledger Fabric:** Hyperledger Fabric (v1.2) is a modular and extensible open-source platform for deploying and operating permissioned distributed ledgers; it is hosted by the Linux Foundation and maintained by IBM [1]. Its modularity enables architects and developers to tailor various layers such as methods for validation, consensus and distributed ledger data structures to meet an organization's needs. Furthermore, Hyperledger Fabric supports the creation of a consortium-based network of peers in which organizations can manage their own user permissions. Hyperledger Fabric served as the distributed ledger network backbone for this research.

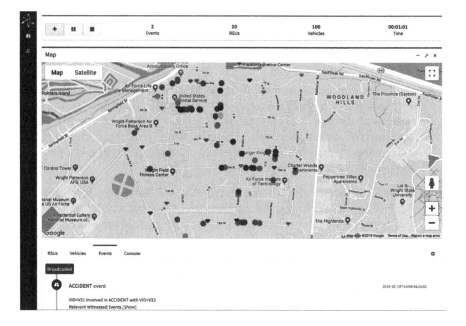

Figure 3. AFIT Lightweight Transportation Modeling Tool user interface

- **Hyperledger Composer:** Hyperledger Composer (v0.20.3) is a toolset that supports the development and execution of blockchain networks and services [13]. It was employed to model and deploy intelligent transportation infrastructure chaincode and network services. Hyperledger Composer incorporates the Playground tool for viewing and interacting with world-state data and performing upgrades to services. It can also spawn a REST server that interfaces with the Hyperledger Fabric network to provide a web application programming interface.

Vehicles, road-side units, and infrastructure behavior and communications were modeled using a custom tool:

- **AFIT Lightweight Transportation Modeling Tool:** This tool provides an intuitive environment for modeling and simulating vehicle movements and their communications with other vehicles and entities in a transportation infrastructure. The tool, developed using JavaScript and NodeJS, can be deployed as a web application or as a standalone application. In the experiments, the tool was used to generate vehicular traffic and accident scenarios, and to function as an application client that interacted with the distributed ledger network (Figure 3).

Table 1.   Baseline Hyperledger Fabric network configuration.

Parameter	Value
Participating Organizations	3
Orderer Nodes	3
Peer Nodes	3
Channels	1
Zookeeper-Kafka Cluster Nodes	3 Zookeeper, 4 Kafka
World-State Database	CouchDB
Block Size	99 MB or 10 Tx/Block
Block Timeout	2 s
Endorsement Policies	ORG1, ORG2, ORG3

4.4   Experimental Network

Table 1 shows the baseline configuration of the Hyperledger Fabric network with a Zookeeper-Kafka node cluster. Figure 4 shows the network topology corresponding to this configuration. Membership services providers and peer containers for each organization were instantiated in the same virtual machine. The peer virtual machines executed the Composer Rest Server to expose the web application programming interface. All the virtual machines were configured with static IP addresses and the Docker container configurations were set to the host network mode.

The number of participating organizations (consortium members) was chosen to be three because it is the minimum number of organizations required to create a partial-trust environment where a blockchain or distributed ledger network would be most beneficial (this is not enforced by Hyperledger Fabric). There are other more efficient ways than a distributed ledger for storing and managing data for a single organization; one possibility is a distributed database. When two organizations collaborate, the collaboration assumes full trust between the organizations and there is no need for endorsement or consensus with regard to data distribution. However, in a consortium of three organizations, the possibility exists that not all the organizations would trust each other, increasing the importance of endorsement, and leader-based or voting-based consensus.

The seven nodes used in the Zookeeper-Kafka cluster configuration is the minimum number needed for Zookeeper-Kafka consensus in Hyperledger Fabric (v1.2). In the case of the Zookeeper nodes, the number should be odd to avoid split-brain scenarios and should be larger than one to avoid a single point of failure [12]; hence, the configuration employed three Zookeeper nodes. In the case of the Kafka nodes, four nodes is the minimum number needed to exhibit crash/fault tolerance [12].

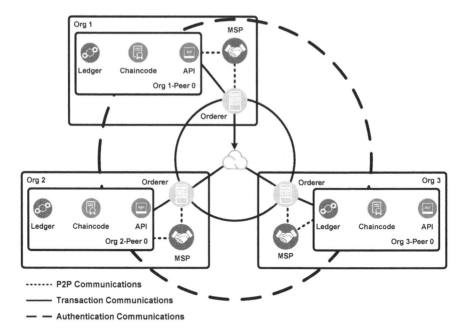

Figure 4. Experimental Hyperledger Fabric network configuration.

4.5 Assumptions

The following assumptions were made in the experiments:

- **Transaction Latency:** Transaction times were measured from the time the client submits a transaction to the network for validation and consensus to the time the corresponding block is created and broadcasted.

- **Signal Loss:** Wireless and wired signal losses were assumed to be minimal and were not modeled in the simulation environment.

- **Vehicle and Sensor Authentication:** Vehicles and road-side units that send or manage transactions were assumed to have appropriate access rights to the services.

- **Traffic Laws:** Vehicles were assumed to not stop at intersections and not adjust their speeds based on roadway speed limits. Also, vehicular traffic lanes were not considered.

- **Obstacles:** Aside from other vehicles in the same path, no other obstacles (e.g., pedestrians or animals) were assumed to exist.

- **Event Data Recording:** Vehicles were assumed to have event data recorders that stored times, vehicle IDs, locations, speeds, headings and

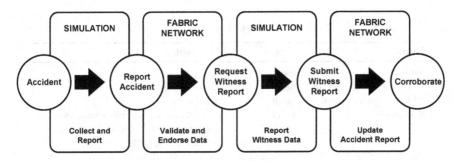

Figure 5. Application event workflow.

misbehavior data of vehicles in range. This capability is typically enabled via on-board units.

- **Vehicle Communications:** Vehicles were assumed to be equipped with the means to establish zero-latency data links with other vehicles and road-side units, and could communicate with Hyperledger Fabric services over the Internet. The inner workings of vehicular network communications as specified by the IEEE 1609 family of standards were not modeled.

5.   Accident Data Collection

This research focused on the storage of accident event reports and witnessed data recorded by vehicles and road-side units in order to create snapshots of events within a window of time before, during and after an accident, providing evidence that could identify the liable parties. Each vehicle in the simulation shared information with other vehicles and the infrastructure via vehicle-to-vehicle or vehicle-to-infrastructure communications channels, and with the transportation distributed ledger network (Figure 4) via connections to the Internet (Figure 2). Vehicles were equipped with event data recorders that logged their sensor data as well as sensor data received from other vehicles. The broadcasted messages contained GPS position, heading and current speed as in other implementations [10]. The vehicular *ad hoc* network parameters, which were based on beacon data in [10], comprised vehicle ID, location, speed and heading.

5.1   Scenario Generation

Each simulation scenario involved a predefined number of vehicles and road-side units in a specified area. Each vehicle was assigned an origin and destination, and the vehicle moved until it arrived at the destination. Only road-side units were assumed to collect data about misbehaving vehicles. Vehicles broadcasted their parameters to other vehicles within a range of 100 m.

Table 2.   Modeled data and attributes.

Name	Type	Attributes
Sensor	asset	id, type
Vehicle extends Sensor	asset	odometer, eventsInvolved
RSU extends Sensor	asset	location
RoadEvent	asset	id, location, eventtimestamp, type, vehiclesInvolved, witnessedData, validated, sourceSensor
RoadEventTx	transaction	Same as RoadEvent
WitnessedData	asset	id, observedVehicle, sourceSensor, roadEventId, location, eventtime, speed, heading, distanceFromsource, behavior, nearbySensors
WitnessDataTx	transaction	Same as WitnessedData

The simulation triggered an accident when two or more vehicles were within the collision distance. At this point, one of the involved vehicles reported the event to the distributed ledger network along with its logged data and the IDs of the other involved vehicles. The distributed ledger network then validated the source vehicle and the involved vehicles, created an accident event report and notified the simulation application after the report was submitted. Next, the simulation application notified all the vehicles in the area about the accident and requested them to report witnessed data within the accident location during the time frame of the accident. Road-side units were also informed about the accident and were requested to report witnessed misbehavior data. Figure 5 shows the event workflow in the experiments.

5.2   Network Data Models

The models used to store data about road events were defined using Hyperledger Composer. Hyperledger Composer employs its own object-oriented modeling language, Composer Modeling Language (CML). Table 2 presents the model definitions. Vehicle and road-side unit owners were not modeled in the experiments, but they could easily be included in an operational environment. Note that the only Composer Modeling Language reference in the initial model definitions is between Sensor and RoadEvent. The received witnessed data was appended to the RoadEvent.WitnessedData collection. This design raised some database concurrency issues, which are discussed below.

5.3   Chaincode

Chaincode was packaged and deployed using Hyperledger Composer. In Hyperledger Composer, chaincode logic is developed using JavaScript in the form of transaction processor functions and it is part of the business network

---

Algorithm 1 : Submit a transaction for a road event.

1: tx ← {sourceId, eventId,time,location,VehiclesInvolved,WitnessedData}
2: **if** SensorExists(tx.sourceId) AND IsValid(tx) **then**
3:     re ← RoadEvent(tx)
4:     re.source ← SensorAssetRegistry.get(tx.sourceId, sensorType)
5:     EventAssetRegistry.add(re)
6:     **for** i = 0 to tx.VehiclesInvolved.length **do**
7:         //create record of vehicle observed to be involved in event
8:         v ← SensorAssetRegistry.get(tx.VehiclesInvolved[i])
9:         v.eventsInvolved.add(re)
10:        SensorAssetRegistry.update(v)
11:     **end for**
12:     emit(RoadEventSubmitted)
13: **else**
14:     emit(InvalidSourceVehicleEvent)
15: **end if**

Algorithm 2 : Submit a witnessed data transaction for a road event.

1: tx ← {sourceId, eventId, WitnessedData}
2: **if** tx.WitnessedData.length > 0 AND SensorExists(tx.sourceId) AND
3: RoadEventExists(tx.eventId) AND IsValid(tx) **then**
4:     wd ← WitnessedData(tx)
5:     WitnessedDataRegistry.add(wd)
6:     emit(WitnessedDataSubmitted)
7: **else**
8:     emit(InvalidWitnessedDataTx)
9: **end if**

---

archive that is deployed to the Hyperledger Fabric network to provide capabilities and services. Transaction processor functions are automatically invoked when transactions are submitted from the application programming interfaces generated by Hyperledger Composer. Additionally, transaction processor functions reference the data models and describe how to use transaction objects to create road event reports and append the witnessed data to the reports. The procedures defined in chaincode must be passed arguments (if required) that are objects of transaction type classes listed in Table 2. The chaincode must validate the existence of sensors that submit transactions and also validate data (e.g., bounds validation) before creating an asset.

Algorithm 1 specifies how a road event report is created.

Algorithm 2 specifies how a road event is updated with witnessed data.

Algorithm 3 specifies how the network validates witnessed data about an event to obtain consensus that the event did indeed occur (i.e., same observed behavior by multiple unrelated parties), and help identify potential misbehavior. This transaction processor function can be triggered by a consortium entity (e.g., insurance company or law enforcement) looking into an event or it could

---

Algorithm 3 : Corroborate witnessed data for a specific road event.

1: re ← {RoadEvent}
2: **for all** WitnessReport observed ∈ RoadEvent re **do**
3:     possibleValidators ← getWitnessReports(ΔT, observed, WitnessReports ∈ re)
4:     **for all** WitnessReport p ∈ possibleValidators **do**
5:         **if** p validates observed **then**
6:             observed.validatedBy ← observed.validatedBy ∪ p.id
7:         **end if**
8:         **if** p.seenInRange(observed) **then**
9:             observed.seenBy ← observed.seenBy ∪ p.id
10:        **end if**
11:    **end for**
12: **end for**
13: validated ← getValidatedReports()
14: seen ← getSeenVehicleReports()
15: possibleSpoofers ← re.WitnessReports − (validated ∩ seen)

---

be triggered automatically after a specified period of time. After the chaincode
is executed on a transaction, the transaction awaits endorsement, following
which it is sent for ordering.

5.4   Analysis of Data

During the initial tests, a number of unsuccessful transactions occurred when
submitting the witnessed data reports and when performing stress tests with
repeated vehicle IDs. The unsuccessful transactions reported "Error trying in-
voke chaincode" and "Error: Peer has rejected transaction with code MVCC_-
READ_CONFLICT." This is due to the multi-version concurrency control employed by Hyperledger Fabric, which requires the state of an object to be read
or written during the commit phase to be the same as when the transaction
was endorsed during the execution phase [4, 20, 27]. The errors were caused by
fast update rates of road event assets with witnessed data from all the other
entities. They were eliminated by creating a new object for each witnessed
data transaction. The solution employs unique IDs to reference the road event
and sensors in a report, an approach analogous to the use of foreign keys in
relational databases.

Scenarios with ten to 100 road events in increments of ten were submitted
within a one second time period. All the submissions were distributed over the
network peers in a round-robin manner. Figure 6 shows the network performance with the baseline configuration. A peak throughput of 10.0 transactions
per second (TPS) and an average of 8.82 transactions per second were measured
in the application layer.

The block size and timeout parameters, and the endorsement policies were
modified based on the optimization recommendations in [27]. The network
configuration shown in Table 3 resulted in the best overall performance.

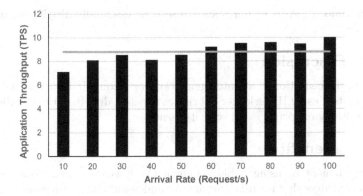

Figure 6. Network performance with the baseline configuration.

Table 3. Optimized Hyperledger Fabric network configuration.

Parameter	Value
Block Size	99 MB or 100 Tx/Block
Block Timeout	1 s
Endorsement Policies	Two of ORG1, ORG2, ORG3

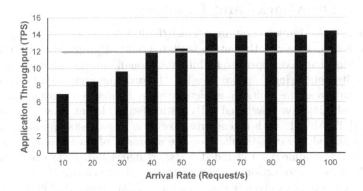

Figure 7. Network performance with the optimized configuration.

Figure 7 shows the network performance with the optimized configuration. A peak throughput of 14.4 transactions per second was measured in the application layer, a 48.1% improvement over the baseline configuration. Moreover, the average response time was reduced by 33.4%. Increasing the transaction arrival rate over the throughput limit over long periods of time often resulted in network timeout errors or unresponsive servers, essentially distributed denial-of-service.

6.   Discussion

The implementation of an intelligent transportation infrastructure data collection system using Hyperledger Fabric has benefits, drawbacks and challenges; it also raises some privacy and security issues:

6.1   Benefits

A key benefit of using a blockchain network is the access to a pseudo-immutable ledger that records transactions and world-state changes in a cryptographically-secure manner. The network provides native auditing services that could ensure the reliability and safety of modern transportation infrastructures.

The modularity of Hyperledger Fabric makes it an attractive framework for implementing a distributed ledger network that can interface with an infrastructure and services. By resolving transactions into a world-state database, stakeholders can execute rich queries to obtain data if they have the proper access rights. Additionally, as a permissioned network framework, its implementation ensures zero participant anonymity because all the identities in the distributed ledger network are authenticated. As a result, participants are always accountable for their actions (e.g., for certificate revocations, traffic violations and accident liability).

6.2   Drawbacks and Challenges

Although the implementation is crash/fault tolerant as a result of using Apache Kafka, it is not Byzantine fault tolerant. Byzantine faults refer to faulty nodes that may appear to be fully functional, but may produce inconsistent results unknowingly or maliciously. The ordering nodes can be rendered resilient to Byzantine faults by implementing a different consensus algorithm. Sousa et al. [24] have developed a Byzantine-fault-tolerant consensus module called BFT-SMART, with a tentative execution of requests approach similar to the practical Byzantine fault tolerance approach of Castro and Liskov [6]. However, this module is not included in Hyperledger Fabric and its performance and reliability in production environments are still unknown.

Storage is a concern given the large amount of data transacted in transportation environments. Since transactions recorded in the blockchain ledger cannot be erased or tampered with, the ledger grows in size quickly. As a result, peer nodes must have adequate storage to accommodate this data, which results in high hosting costs over time for all participants. Consequently, nodes that experience downtime suffer long synchronization times that could extend endorsement downtime and lead to transaction execution failures. Finally, framework components such as those provided by Hyperledger Composer are not mature enough and, therefore, suffer from reliability issues that could result in nonresponsiveness during periods with high transaction arrival rates, as was encountered in the experiments.

Processing times for applications with high-throughput requirements are also a concern. Based on the results obtained in the experimental network, several variables have to be considered when designing a distributed ledger network that would support the processing and storage of data at high rates. In production environments, it is expected that applications relying on a Hyperledger Fabric implementation of a distributed ledger network could handle thousands of vehicles, road-side units and users conducting transactions every minute. Although Thakkar et al. [27] have demonstrated that a Hyperledger Fabric implementation can reach a throughput of 2,800 transactions per second, determining whether or not the solution is adequate for a transportation infrastructure would depend on the requirements of the applications that are deployed.

6.3   Security and Privacy Considerations

Public-key-infrastructure services and access control rules allow secure access to data by privileged users as defined by the consortium. Implementations can enable users (e.g., vehicle owners) to control access to data involving their vehicles. A vehicle public-key infrastructure (VPKI) as defined by the IEEE 1609.2 standard can be supported in a Hyperledger Fabric implementation by integrating vehicle certificate manager services in the membership services providers. Since such an infrastructure relies on providing pseudonymity to vehicles, certificates can be utilized to authenticate vehicles or sign transaction data and increase the trust in data sources without revealing their identities. Designated authorities can always obtain the real identities of vehicle pseudonyms in the case of accidents or legal investigations [22]. Hyperledger Fabric also allows for certificate revocation, preventing participants from accessing data after they have lost their credentials.

Hyperledger Fabric orderers, although not involved in the validation of transactions, could be compromised to gain access to all the transactions received and distributed by the Kafka cluster. These nodes could be compromised to intercept transactions sent and received by the ordering service. If information privacy is required (e.g., for personally-identifiable information), Hyperledger Fabric provides private data channels that create separate private ledgers between parties. Private channel transactions are not sent to an orderer; instead, hashes of the transactions and the timestamps are sent, preventing the orderer from observing transaction content.

The possibility exists that a participant could analyze the shared ledger data to discover traffic patterns, and the origins, destinations and times of vehicles. This information could reveal details such as home addresses, work locations and daily routines of vehicle owners. Therefore, participating organizations must be transparent in the way they handle the data. More importantly, all the stakeholders must be aware that participants could analyze data for purposes other than were intended. By incorporating access control policies in

Hyperledger Fabric, it is possible for vehicle owners to actively prevent certain users and organizations accessing data about their vehicles and behavior.

7. Conclusions

The work described in this chapter extends the approach of Kopylova et al. [10] by employing the Hyperledger Fabric framework and Hyperledger Composer toolset to create a distributed ledger network that provides services for storing, corroborating and querying accident event data in a decentralized and secure manner. Like other proposals [7, 8, 18, 19], the approach relies on vehicle on-board units to collect and disseminate vehicular ad-hoc network data while the vehicles are on the road. Data about accidents and other road events is pushed to the Hyperledger Fabric network, providing irrefutable evidence pertaining to the events for subsequent analyses. This distributed ledger network differs from the other proposals because of its use of the open-source Hyperledger Fabric platform, which supports the execution of multiple applications and channels, as well as seamless integration with existing transportation systems.

The design considerations and improvements discussed in this chapter ensure that the distributed ledger network can scale to handle the large volumes of transactions encountered in transportation infrastructures. Specifically, optimizing the configuration by adjusting block size, block timeout and endorsement policies provides significant performance improvements. However, as with any modern technology, the benefits come with some drawbacks, in this case, primarily privacy risks.

The views expressed in this chapter are those of the authors, and do not reflect the official policy or position of the U.S. Air Force, U.S. Department of Defense or U.S. Government. This document has been approved for public release, distribution unlimited (Case #88ABW-2018-6399).

References

[1] E. Androulaki, A. Barger, V. Bortnikov, C. Cachin, K. Christidis, A. De Caro, D. Enyeart, C. Ferris, G. Laventman, Y. Manevich, S. Muralidharan, C. Murthy, B. Nguyen, M. Sethi, G. Singh, K. Smith, A. Sorniotti, C. Stathakopoulou, M. Vukolic, S. Weed Cocco and J. Yellick, Hyperledger Fabric: A distributed operating system for permissioned blockchains, *Proceedings of the Thirteenth European Conference on Computer Systems*, article no. 30, 2018.

[2] L. Baird, The Swirlds Hashgraph Consensus Algorithm: Fair, Fast, Byzantine Fault Tolerance, Technical Report SWIRLDS-TR-2016-01, Swirlds, College Station, Texas, 2016.

[3] F. Bencic and I. Zarko, Distributed ledger technology: Blockchain compared to directed acyclic graph, *Proceedings of the Thirty-Eighth IEEE International Conference on Distributed Computing Systems*, pp. 1569–1570, 2018.

[4] P. Bernstein and N. Goodman, Multiversion concurrency control – Theory and algorithms, *ACM Transactions on Database Systems*, vol. 8(4), pp. 465–483, 1983.

[5] V. Buterin, On public and private blockchains, *Ethereum Foundation Blog* (blog.ethereum.org/2015/08/07/on-public-and-private-blockchains), August 6, 2015.

[6] M. Castro and B. Liskov, Practical Byzantine fault tolerance, *Proceedings of the Third Symposium on Operating Systems Design and Implementation*, pp. 173–186, 1999.

[7] M. Cebe, E. Erdin, K. Akkaya, H. Aksu and S. Uluagac, Block4Forensic: An integrated lightweight blockchain framework for forensic applications of connected vehicles, *IEEE Communications*, vol. 56(10), pp. 50–57, 2018.

[8] A. Dorri, M. Steger, S. Kanhere and R. Jurdak, Blockchain: A distributed solution to automotive security and privacy, *IEEE Communications*, vol. 55(12), pp. 119–125, 2017.

[9] J. Kang, R. Yu, X. Huang, S. Maharjan, Y. Zhang and E. Hossain, Enabling localized peer-to-peer electricity trading among plug-in hybrid electric vehicles using consortium blockchains, *IEEE Transactions on Industrial Informatics*, vol. 13(6), pp. 3154–3164, 2017.

[10] Y. Kopylova, C. Farkas and W. Xu, Accurate accident reconstruction in VANET, in *Data and Applications Security and Privacy XXV*, Y. Li (Ed.), Springer, Berlin Heidelberg, Germany, pp. 271–279, 2011.

[11] L. Lamport, R. Shostak and M. Pease, The Byzantine generals problem, *ACM Transactions on Programming Languages and Systems*, vol. 4(3), pp. 382–401, 1982.

[12] Linux Foundation, Bringing up a Kafka-Based Ordering Service, San Francisco, California (hyperledger-fabric.readthedocs.io/en/release-1.2/kafka.html), 2019.

[13] Linux Foundation, Hyperledger Composer, San Francisco, California (hyperledger.github.io/composer/latest), 2019.

[14] Linux Foundation, Hyperledger Explorer, San Francisco, California (github.com/hyperledger/blockchain-explorer), 2019.

[15] Linux Foundation, Hyperledger Fabric (1.2) Glossary, San Francisco, California (hyperledger-fabric.readthedocs.io/en/release-1.2/glossary.html), 2019.

[16] S. Nakamoto, Bitcoin: A Peer-to-Peer Electronic Cash System (bitcoin.org/bitcoin.pdf), 2008.

[17] New York City Department of Transportation, NYC Connected Vehicle Project for Safer Transportation, New York (cvp.nyc), 2019.

[18] C. Oham, R. Jurdak, S. Kanhere, A. Dorri and S. Jha, B-FICA: Blockchain-Based Framework for Auto-Insurance Claim and Adjudication, arXiv:1806.06169 (arxiv.org/abs/1806.06169), 2018.

[19] C. Oham, S. Kanhere, R. Jurdak and S. Jha, A Blockchain-Based Liability Attribution Framework for Autonomous Vehicles, arXiv: 1802.05050 (arxiv.org/abs/1802.05050), 2018.

[20] C. Papadimitriou and P. Kanellakis, On concurrency control by multiple versions, *Proceedings of the First ACM SIGACT-SIGMOD Symposium on Principles of Database Systems*, pp. 76–82, 1982.

[21] M. Pilkington, Blockchain technology: Principles and applications, in *Research Handbook on Digital Transformations*, F. Olleros and M. Zhegu (Eds.), Edward Elgar, Northampton, Massachusetts, pp. 225–246, 2016.

[22] Y. Qian, K. Lu and N. Moayeri, A secure VANET MAC protocol for DSRC applications, *Proceedings of the IEEE Global Telecommunications Conference*, 2008.

[23] M. Singh and S. Kim, Blockchain-Based Intelligent Vehicle Data Sharing Framework, arXiv:1708.09721 (arxiv.org/abs/1708.09721), 2017.

[24] J. Sousa, A. Bessani and M. Vukolic, A Byzantine fault-tolerant ordering service for the Hyperledger Fabric blockchain platform, *Proceedings of the Forty-Eighth Annual IEEE/IFIP International Conference on Dependable Systems and Networks*, pp. 51–58, 2018.

[25] A. Sumalee and H. Ho, Smarter and more connected: Future intelligent transportation systems, *IATSS Research*, vol. 42(2), pp. 67–71, 2018.

[26] Tampa Hillsborough Expressway Authority, THEA Connected Vehicle Pilot, Tampa, Florida (www.tampacvpilot.com), 2019.

[27] P. Thakkar, S. Nathan and B. Viswanathan, Performance benchmarking and optimizing the Hyperledger Fabric blockchain platform, *Proceedings of the Twenty-Sixth IEEE International Symposium on Modeling, Analysis and Simulation of Computer and Telecommunication Systems*, pp. 264–276, 2018.

[28] U.S. Department of Transportation, ITS Strategic Plan 2015-2019, FHWA-JPO-14-145, Washington, DC (rosap.ntl.bts.gov/view/dot/3506), 2014.

[29] Y. Yuan and F. Wang, Towards blockchain-based intelligent transportation systems, *Proceedings of the Nineteenth IEEE International Conference on Intelligent Transportation Systems*, pp. 2663–2668, 2016.

IV

TELECOMMUNICATIONS INFRASTRUCTURE SECURITY

Chapter 9

SECURING WIRELESS COPROCESSORS FROM ATTACKS IN THE INTERNET OF THINGS

Jason Staggs and Sujeet Shenoi

Abstract   Wireless communications coprocessors are a vital component of numerous Internet of Things and mobile devices. These subsystems enable devices to communicate directly with peers and supporting network infrastructures. Previous research has shown that wireless communications coprocessors lack fundamental security mechanisms to combat attacks originating from the air-interface and application processor (main CPU). To mitigate the risk of exploitation, methods are needed to retroactively add security mechanisms to communications coprocessors.

This chapter focuses on securing a cellular baseband processor from attacks by hostile applications in the application processor. Such attacks often leverage attention (AT) commands to exploit vulnerabilities in baseband firmware. The attacks are mitigated by installing an AT command intrusion prevention system between the application processor and baseband processor interface.

Keywords: Wireless coprocessor, Internet of Things, intrusion prevention

1.   Introduction

A Statista report [29] estimates that nearly 31 billion Internet of Things (IoT) devices will be in use by 2020. Consumer demand for smart devices has surged, launching a time-to-market race by manufacturers to release Internet of Things devices with rich features at affordable prices. Unfortunately, security has taken a back seat to features, significantly increasing the risks to devices, networks and users [16].

Further complicating matters are the diversity and complexity of wireless protocols and communications systems that interconnect Internet of Things devices [22]. Internet of Things devices use wireless coprocessors and protocols to support communications with smart devices and networks. These communica-

© IFIP International Federation for Information Processing 2019
Published by Springer Nature Switzerland AG 2019
J. Staggs and S. Shenoi (Eds.): Critical Infrastructure Protection XIII, IFIP AICT 570, pp. 159–178, 2019.
https://doi.org/10.1007/978-3-030-34647-8_9

tions coprocessors are normally separate microcontrollers that are independent of the main CPUs. The heterogeneity of wireless communications coprocessors and protocol stacks has inadvertently increased the attack surfaces of Internet of Things and mobile devices. The security problems associated with wireless communications coprocessors are also inherited by devices such as remote terminal units and programmable logic controllers that help operate critical infrastructure assets.

Previous research has demonstrated that wireless communications coprocessors lack rudimentary security measures to combat attacks, especially data execution prevention (DEP), address space layout randomization (ASLR) and basic memory protections [2, 6, 14, 33, 34]. Although it is important to consider attacks that target the main CPUs of devices, it is equally imperative to consider attacks that focus on wireless network coprocessors. Internet of Things and mobile devices must be engineered to be more resilient to attacks that target communications coprocessing units, especially if the security threats posed by insecure devices that plague the Internet [16] and some operational technology environments are to be reduced.

This work focuses on mitigating attacks by applying security defenses to a specific type of wireless communications coprocessor – the cellular baseband processor. Baseband processors, also known as cellular modems, are present in all mobile phones and in many Internet of Things devices and industrial control systems that require cellular wide-area networking connections to the Internet [27]. These independent systems provide direct, unfiltered radio access to public cellular GSM, UMTS and LTE networks, and are attractive targets for attackers who seek to intercept, modify, fabricate or interrupt communications.

Despite concerns about attacks on communications coprocessors, relatively few attempts have been made to secure their external interfaces [20]. This work addresses the gap by mitigating exploitation attempts from the application processor (main CPU) that leverage malformed or unauthorized vendor-specific serial AT commands to target the baseband processor. Such attacks are commonly employed to unlock cell phones, but they can be repurposed to perpetrate nefarious baseband system compromises [13, 14, 30].

This chapter describes a proof-of-concept application-processor-interface-based AT command intrusion prevention system that combats exploitation attempts against the baseband processor. The intrusion prevention system relies on rules (signatures) based on AT command syntax and semantics. The signatures help detect and prevent malicious AT commands and payloads (parameters) from being sent to the baseband processor. The proof-of-concept system incorporates a Raspberry Pi 3 hardware platform for main CPU emulation and a SIM900 GSM module (baseband processor). Empirical testing reveals that the system combats baseband processor attacks from the application processor. Although the system employs hobbyist hardware, the underlying techniques can be applied to Internet of Things and mobile devices by making slight modifications to their operating systems or by adding a dedicated security coprocessor that inspects input/output messages on the data bus.

2. Security of Communications Stacks

The vast majority of Internet of Things and mobile devices incorporate wireless communications processors for wide-area networking and personal area networking radio needs. These independent coprocessors facilitate communications between other smart devices, sensors, motors, relays and supporting telecommunications infrastructure assets (e.g., cellular base stations). Communications technologies such as 802.15.4 (i.e., Zigbee and WirelessHART), 802.11 (i.e., Wi-Fi), Bluetooth and GSM/UMTS/LTE have emerged over the years and are now widely integrated in Internet of Things devices. In many cases, the wireless chipsets operate independently of the main CPUs and, therefore, have their own attack surfaces [17].

Previous research has demonstrated that wireless communications coprocessors lack basic security mechanisms. Although it is important to consider attacks that target the main CPUs of devices, it is imperative that future Internet of Things and mobile devices are engineered to be resilient to attacks that target communications coprocessors. Researchers have identified a number of security problems and vulnerabilities in wireless coprocessors and protocol stacks [2, 6, 33, 34]. Some attacks target vulnerabilities in coprocessor firmware while others target kernel modules or libraries used by the operating systems of the main CPUs to interact with wireless subsystems on the devices [26].

In particular, several vulnerabilities have been identified in Broadcom Wi-Fi chipsets. Beniamini [3–5] demonstrated heap and stack overflow vulnerabilities that lead to remote code execution (RCE) on a common Broadcom Wi-Fi chipset. These vulnerabilities stem from inadequate data field checking by the Wi-Fi coprocessor unit when processing certain 802.11r-2008 (fast BSS transition) authentication frames. Building on Beniamini's work, Artenstein [2] weaponized the exploits by incorporating them in a propagating worm that could target other Wi-Fi chipsets. Meanwhile, Seri and Livne [26] have developed a new attack called "BlueBorne" that targets Bluetooth implementations in operating systems used by billions of Internet of Things and mobile devices. Arguably, the most terrifying wireless chipset attacks involve the exploitation of cellular baseband processors.

Cellular baseband stack exploits have been discussed for nearly a decade [10, 33, 34]. The exploitation of communications coprocessors presents an existential threat to the devices they support, and by extension, the physical environments in which they are used (e.g., industrial Internet of Things and industrial control systems). Novel ideas, techniques and mechanisms are needed to counter the threats to frail and insecure communications coprocessors.

This chapter presents an approach for retrofitting security in one of the external interfaces used by baseband processors in order to mitigate hostile activity originating from the main CPU. Admittedly, this is not a perfect solution to the overall problem, but the approach is useful when security controls have to be implemented in current mobile phones and legacy industrial control systems.

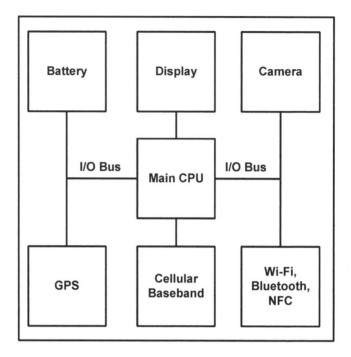

Figure 1. System of systems in a smartphone.

3. Cellular Baseband Processors

Baseband processors – also called cellular modems – are present in Internet of Things devices and mobile phones that require wide-area networking connections to the Internet and other cellular functions. The independent baseband systems, which provide direct, unfiltered access to public cellular networks, are prime targets for attackers interested in intercepting, modifying, fabricating or blocking voice, text, data and signaling traffic.

3.1 Symbiotic System of Systems

Internet of Things devices and modern mobile phones incorporate supporting microcontrollers and subsystems, each serving a dedicated and crucial role. These subsystems are interconnected directly or indirectly over a common data bus, enabling the smart device to provide rich interactions with the external environment via sensors (e.g., camera, microphone, gyroscope and accelerometer) and radios. Because the microcontrollers operate independently of the main CPUs, they have their own firmware that is usually stored in read-only memory (ROM).

Figure 1 presents a logical view of the peripheral systems in a smartphone. Examples include the GPS, camera, battery, Wi-Fi, near-field communications (NFC), Bluetooth and cellular baseband systems.

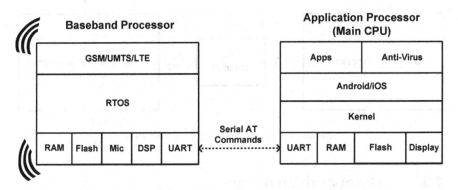

Figure 2. Relationship between the application processor and baseband processor.

Although the systems are viewed as being independent, it is important to note that some of these systems are often encapsulated in a single integrated circuit called a "system on a chip" (SoC). The systems may be housed in a single integrated circuit package, but a common input/output interface is still required for them to exchange commands and data (e.g., UART, CAN, SPI, I2C, USB or shared memory). Just like any other embedded system, each encapsulated system has its own volatile memory (RAM) and non-volatile memory (flash), along with various peripherals. This architecture enables the main CPU to focus on its operating system and user applications, while relying on the independent supporting systems to handle other tasks and provide external data upon request via hardware interrupts. It is common for the tasks performed by these systems to be subject to stringent synchronization and timing constraints, as in the case of a cellular protocol stack that runs on a baseband processor.

The two main components of cellular-enabled Internet of Things and mobile devices are the application processor and baseband processor. Figure 2 shows the relationship between the two processors [8].

The application processor system houses the main CPU and operating system (e.g., Linux, Android, Windows IoT or iOS). User applications and display interfaces execute on the application processor.

The baseband processor system serves as the cellular modem that independently handles cellular network communications between the mobile device and cell towers, including signaling for radio resource management, mobility management, connection management, voice calls, SMS text messages and cellular data. Like the application processor system, the baseband processor system contains dedicated hardware peripherals such as RAM, flash memory and digital signal processor, and provides direct access to the cell phone speaker and microphone [25]. The baseband processor system is analogous to a dial-up modem or Ethernet controller in a personal computer, providing layer 1 modulation and demodulation of carrier signals to encode and decode information over dedicated cellular links.

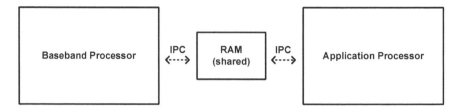

Figure 3. Shared memory architecture.

3.2 Baseband Firmware

In order to manage hardware resources and perform cellular modem tasks, the baseband processor typically runs a bootloader that initializes the hardware and loads a real-time operating system (RTOS) into memory [35]. The real-time operating system executes tasks for the entire cellular network stack (e.g., GSM, UMTS and LTE) [18, 34]. The tasks, which are engineered to provide reliable signal connectivity to carrier networks, generally have the requirement of minimal power consumption during operation.

Although baseband system codebases have been updated over the years to accommodate the latest cellular protocol specifications, significant portions of early GSM, UMTS and LTE codebases are still used in modern baseband stacks. Implementing the 3GPP cellular protocol specifications in software is a complex endeavor that can be ambiguous in some instances. Unfortunately, the messages used by cellular protocol stacks sometimes contain high concentrations of variable length fields that are not handled properly and, thus, can be targeted by fuzzing and vulnerability discovery activities. These factors create a perfect storm for exploiting baseband systems [12, 34].

It is important to note that cellular baseband processors are not limited to mobile phones. In fact, the processors are commonly found in Internet of Things devices such as vehicle telematics units, automated teller machines and smart meters used in electricity, gas and water distribution infrastructures. All these devices typically require low bandwidth connectivity to transmit data.

3.3 Baseband Architectures

Command and data exchange between the application and baseband processors depend on the device architecture. The two architectures are: (i) shared memory architecture; and (ii) independent memory architecture. Figures 3 and 4 illustrate the two architectures [8, 33].

In the shared memory architecture, the application processor and baseband processor address spaces are mapped to the same physical RAM [33]. In this case, a form of interprocess communications is employed to exchange information between baseband and application processes.

The independent memory architecture is more commonly used in Internet of Things devices and modern phones. The architecture requires a dedicated data

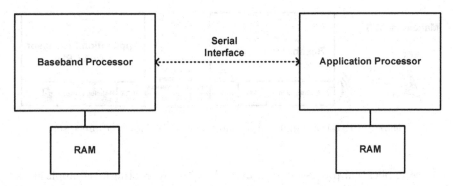

Figure 4. Independent memory architecture.

bus between the application and baseband processors to facilitate communications. Common data bus communications interfaces are UART, SPI, I2C and USB.

3.4 Serial Communications Protocols

Baseband processor command and control protocols vary from device to device. The protocols are used to instruct the baseband to execute cellular functions such as making a call and sending data. The protocols are also used to send information back to the application processor (e.g., notification of an incoming call, SMS or data). Common protocols include standard GSM AT commands [9, 23] and proprietary vendor-specific command protocols [7]. GSM AT commands are similar to the Hayes AT commands used by old dial-up modems [11]. Some baseband processor vendors incorporate additional proprietary commands for extended functionality and debugging; in some instances, they provide backdoors to the application processor [15, 30]. Additionally, the commands are usually sent in the clear and are not authenticated.

4. Securing the Baseband Processor

Despite the increased scrutiny leveled on communications coprocessors as potential attack targets, few attempts have been made to secure their external interfaces [13]. The application processor interface and the air-interface expose the baseband processor to untrusted data and, thus, a number of external threats (Figure 5).

Baseband firmware reverse engineering is required in order to fully appreciate the baseband system security issues. The mobile phone unlocking communities are the most advanced at understanding the complexities involved in baseband processor firmware reverse engineering and exploitation. The application processor interface is routinely leveraged by mobile phone unlocking enthusiasts to exploit vulnerabilities in baseband processors to unlock phones for use in other carrier networks. Although such attacks generally require root access

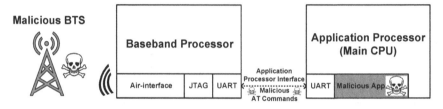

Figure 5.   External input/output interfaces to the baseband processor.

to the application processor (e.g., by jailbreaking or rooting), the application processor has a rich attack surface of its own that could be used to indirectly target the baseband processor.

Tian et al. [30] describe a methodology and analysis framework for identifying and assessing vendor-specific AT commands that are injected via the USB modem interfaces of Android devices. They discovered hundreds of commands that can be used to bypass screen locks, enable developer debugging tools and perform firmware updates. Additionally, they discovered other vendor-specific AT commands that could be used to probe and potentially manipulate baseband processors. Over-the-air remote code execution attacks against the air-interfaces of baseband processors are also a concern because they could be leveraged to compromise the baseband processors remotely.

Some baseband processors incorporate a dedicated JTAG interface that can be used to help reverse engineer and/or read/write to the flash memory of the processor. JTAG is a hardware debugging interface that is commonly used by manufacturers for device testing and verification. Although this interface could provide substantial low-level access to the code, data and operational context of a baseband processor, it is outside the scope of this work. Instead, this section investigates techniques that could be used to retrofit security around the baseband processor to mitigate external attacks from the application processor interface.

4.1   Retrofitting Security

Embedded systems typically have design requirements that stress reliability and efficiency. This is especially true for embedded systems with strict power constraints and those that support human or physical processes (e.g., cell phones, programmable logic controllers and pacemakers) [19]. Unfortunately, security usually comes in second after performance requirements and is often considered only after a serious incident impacts consumers. Reactive approaches to addressing security problems are rarely robust and often have serious ramifications [16]. As a result, proactive measures that incorporate security engineering best practices must be considered early in system design and definitely before system integration.

The longevity of embedded system deployments (e.g., industrial control systems) and the lack of regular firmware updates make them ideal targets for adversaries. The ubiquity of insecure communications interfaces and protocols contributes to inherent vulnerabilities in embedded systems that persist over their lifespans – these are collectively referred to as "forever days."

Retrofitting security in an insecure external communications interface of an embedded system is an active research challenge. Bump-in-the-wire solutions that secure unencrypted IP-based industrial control system protocols such as Modbus/TCP and DNP3 have been developed [32]. Additionally, specialized firewalls have been deployed to perform rigorous message filtering across trust domains in industrial control system environments [21, 31].

In the case of Internet of Things and mobile devices, the interface between the application and baseband processors is fundamentally insecure. The interface transports serial character streams of commands and data that initiate cellular processes in the devices [23, 24]. Unfortunately, this interface enables malware executing on the application processor to target the baseband processor with malicious commands and data.

4.2 AT Command Filtering

Mulliner et al. [20] have developed a "virtual modem" protection mechanism that mitigates malicious injections of cellular signaling traffic from mobile phones. The virtual modem mediates signaling traffic between the application processor and baseband processor. This independent system intercepts and inspects AT commands before forwarding them to the baseband processor.

The virtual modem solution incorporates an AT command filter that enforces a security policy on messages destined for the baseband processor. The policy specifies temporal thresholds on the frequencies of transmitted AT commands. The enforcement of the strict policy on AT commands that initiate critical cellular operations mitigates denial-of-service attacks. However, this solution does not address attacks on the baseband processor itself.

5. Baseband Processor Exploitation

The mobile phone unlocking communities have for years focused on understanding how proprietary baseband processors work in order to bypass network carrier locking restrictions [13]. The Apple iOS and Android communities have acquired substantial expertise in reverse engineering, vulnerability analysis and exploit development for targeting baseband processor firmware. Their focus is on baseband processor exploitation from the perspective of the application processor interface, not the air-interface.

Baseband processor exploitation over the air-interface generally occurs by leveraging remote code execution or denial-of-service vulnerabilities in frail cellular protocol stack implementations. The vulnerabilities are triggered by sending specially-crafted cellular messages (e.g., signaling, voice or data) to the baseband processor. These messages are usually malformed and are constructed to take advantage of inadequate checking of GSM/UMTS message field lengths (e.g., resulting in buffer/heap overflows) or they employ improper variable data types (e.g., resulting in integer overflows) [33, 34]. In contrast, baseband exploitation via the application processor interface typically involves sending crafted AT commands that trigger remote code execution vulnerabilities in the AT command handler code of the baseband processor.

Modern phones support hundreds of AT commands for initiating cellular activities and providing vendor-specific features. This has created large attack surfaces for the baseband and application processors that can be leveraged by attackers to rewrite firmware, bypass security mechanisms, exfiltrate sensitive device data, unlock screens and inject touch events [30].

The approach adopted in this research is to identify suspicious AT commands and create the associated signatures. These AT command signatures are employed in real time to thwart exploitation attempts against the baseband processor.

5.1   AT Command Exploitation Methodology

The iOS and Android unlocking/jailbreaking communities are great sources for information about baseband processor exploitation. This information can also be used to assist in developing reactive and proactive security mechanisms that detect and mitigate attacks against the baseband processor. This work has leveraged the `theiphonewiki.com` community resources to understand baseband processor exploitation from the application processor. It has also drawn on vulnerability and exploit information from `theiphonewiki.com` to develop mitigation techniques.

The first step in unlocking a phone is to understand how and where network carrier locking is implemented. In most cases, this is handled by the baseband processor. Traditionally, a security researcher who intends to unlock a phone unpacks and reverse engineers the baseband firmware of the target phone. Next, the researcher identifies sections of code and data in the firmware where the carrier lock logic is implemented.

A method for remote code execution is then needed to patch the memory of the targeted baseband processor. This can be accomplished by analyzing the AT command interface handler for software vulnerabilities that provide control of the system (e.g., memory corruption). The vulnerabilities are normally triggered (exploited) using anomalous AT commands sent from the application processor. The anomalous AT commands, which are usually valid per specification, are constructed to exploit vulnerabilities in the AT command handler to gain control over the program counter of the baseband processor. In some cases, the AT commands may contain shellcode that is eventually executed in order to unlock the phone. Common memory corruption vulnerabilities that are routinely identified and exploited include stack- and heap-based buffer overflows [1, 13].

Figure 6 shows a proof-of-concept stack overflow exploit employed by the `PurplesnOw` unlock to trigger an AT command vulnerability in the iPhone 3GS X-Gold 608 baseband processor [14]. In the example, the second parameter of

at+xlog=1,"jjjjjjjjjjjjjjjjjjjjjjjjjjjjjjjj44445555PPPP"
j's = junk padding
R4 = 4
R5 = 5
PC = P

Figure 6. iPhone 3GS `PurplesnOw` AT command exploit.

the `+xlog` AT extended command is crafted to gain control of the program counter of the baseband processor.

6. AT Command Intrusion Prevention System

Data entering the baseband processor from an external source should be considered to be untrusted until it is vetted for signs of malicious behavior. A proof-of-concept AT command intrusion prevention system was developed to mitigate exploitation or dynamic vulnerability discovery attempts against the baseband processor that originate from the application processor interface. The intrusion prevention system enables users to define rules (signatures) based on the AT command syntax and semantics. The signatures are used to detect and prevent malicious AT commands and payloads (parameters) from being sent to the baseband processor. Signatures are also specified to detect and prevent fuzzing attempts and unauthorized uses of vendor-specific AT commands.

6.1 AT Command Syntax

The Hayes AT and GSM AT command sets are character-based messaging protocols (strings) that are commonly used by application processors to instruct baseband processors to perform cellular operations. Cellular routines for voice, SMS and data are invoked by AT commands to instruct baseband processors to perform the relevant functions. The AT command specifications cover hundreds of commands. This work focuses on application processor interface protocols that use standard AT and GSM AT commands, as well as proprietary vendor-specific AT commands [30]. Other types of proprietary messaging protocols exist [7]; however, the rigorous treatment of these protocols is the subject of future research.

Several categories of AT command messages, each with its own syntax, have been specified [9, 28]. The three AT command categories considered in this research are basic, extended and s-parameter commands.

- **Basic Commands:** Basic commands have the structure AT<x><n> or AT&<x><n> where <x> is a command and <n> denotes the command parameters.

- **Extended Commands:** Extended commands have the structure AT+<x><n> or AT%<x><n> where <x> is a command and <n> denotes the command parameters.

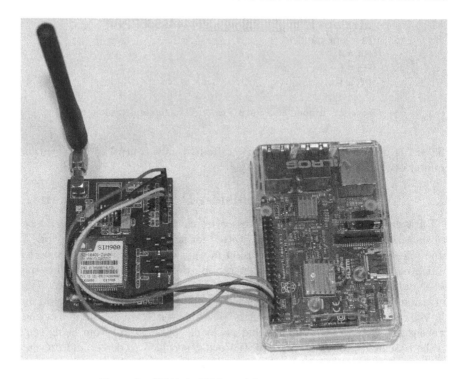

Figure 7. SIM900 GSM module and Raspberry Pi 3.

- **S-Parameter Commands:** S-parameter commands have the structure ATS<n>=<m> where <n> is the index of the s-register to be set and <m> is the value to be assigned.

6.2   Design and Implementation

A SIM900 GSM module and a Raspberry Pi 3 hardware platform running a Linux Debian operating system (Raspbian) were selected to develop the proof-of-concept AT command intrusion prevention system (Figure 7). The SIM900 GSM module was selected as the baseband processor because of its wide support and availability of documentation. The flexibility provided by the Raspberry Pi was leveraged to program it to emulate application processor functionality. The GSM module was connected to the GPIO pins of the Raspberry Pi to facilitate serial UART communications. OpenBTS was used as the test GSM network.

A method is needed to conduct real-time passive analysis of AT commands in transit to the baseband processor. Monitoring the transmission of AT commands requires an understanding of the dataflow from the source (application processor operating system) to the destination (baseband processor real-time operating system). In general, AT command inspection may be performed in three ways, each requiring different levels of device access and intrusiveness: (i) adding an additional security coprocessor tasked with moderating AT commands; (ii) kernel-level modifications; and (iii) user-level library preloading [23, 24]. This research leveraged the library pre-loading technique for AT command inspection because of its ease of implementation.

In order to simulate the cellular functionality of a malicious application or rooted phone, a test application was written for the Raspberry Pi 3 to send arbitrary and malicious AT commands to the SIM900 GSM module. The application sends AT commands to the SIM900 GSM module by creating a file descriptor to the serial device /dev/uart and calling the libc write() function to write a stream of characters to the serial device.

The write() function is hooked to inspect AT commands before being written to the serial device. An easy way to hook a library function in Linux is to use the LD_PRELOAD environment variable [23, 24], which enables a designated shared library to be loaded before any other shared libraries. This precedence technique is leveraged to overwrite stock shared library symbols in order to define an alternative version of write(). This method gains control of the data content passed to the baseband processor.

After hooking the write() function with LD_PRELOAD, control is passed to the intrusion prevention code that checks the AT commands and data. Only verified write() function calls passed with a file descriptor to the baseband processor (UART device) are processed further. If a write() call does not contain a file descriptor that points to a valid serial device, then the function calls the regular libc version of write().

If the altered version of write() is invoked, then the buffer containing the message is parsed by the intrusion prevention system and matched against the predefined rules (signatures). If a rule is triggered by a particular AT command, then the command is dropped and the function simply returns to the calling function the number of bytes that were supposed to be written to the device. This ensures that the intrusion prevention logic is transparent to the underlying application and that the application is unaware that the AT command has been dropped.

Alternatively, if the AT command does not trigger on a rule, it is passed on and written to the UART interface for serial transmission to the baseband processor. The inspection system thus moderates potentially malevolent commands and data sent over an insecure, albeit trusted, serial interface.

Figure 8 illustrates the application-processor-based AT command intrusion prevention process used in the proof-of-concept implementation.

6.3 Intrusion Prevention System

The application-processor-based AT command intrusion prevention system has three components: (i) AT command parser; (ii) rule parser; and (iii) intrusion detection/prevention engine.

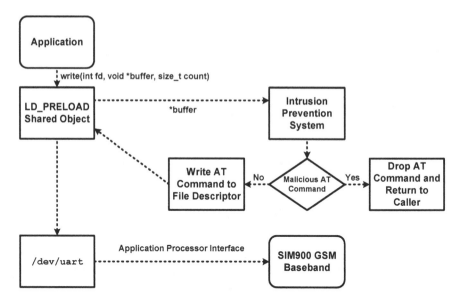

Figure 8. Application-processor-based AT command intrusion prevention system.

The AT command parser parses the command contained in the buffer that is passed to the `write()` call. In addition to performing syntactic checks, an appropriate data structure is created for the AT command (e.g., basic, extended or s-parameter). The data structure, which contains granular attributes that apply to the AT command, is employed when applying the rule-based logic.

The rule parser reads in the rules that are defined in an external configuration file. A rule has the syntax: `<operator> <command><parameter(s)>`. Note that the parameters are operator specific.

Four basic operators are employed by the intrusion prevention system:

- **Length:** This operator provides the length of an AT command parameter. It is useful for flagging AT commands with abnormal parameter lengths (e.g., used to induce stack-based buffer overflows, where the padding size of the exploit is known to be at least a certain length).

  - *Example 1:* `length +xlog 25` blocks the AT `+xlog` command when the parameter length is exactly 25 characters.

  - *Example 2:* `length +xlog >= 25` blocks the AT `+xlog` command when the parameter length is greater than or equal to 25 characters.

- **Match:** This operator matches a substring against the parameters of a specific AT command or all AT commands. If a match occurs, the AT command is blocked. The operator is useful for catching script kiddies or commonly-used shellcode snippets (e.g., used in phone unlocking attempts).

- *Example 1:* `match "baddata"` blocks all commands containing the string `"baddata"` in their parameters.

- *Example 2:* `match +xapp "\0xDE\0xAD\0xBE\0xEF"` blocks +xapp commands containing the shellcode `"\0xDE\0xAD\0xBE\0xEF"` as a parameter.

- **Msg_Sequence:** This operator triggers an alert when a contiguous sequence of AT commands is encountered; the commands are also blocked. It is useful for establishing context-based rules where a single AT command may not be malicious, but a series of commands in the specified order could be malicious.

  - *Example 1:* `msg_sequence +xlog +xlog` triggers an alert on back-to-back occurrences of the +xlog command; the commands are also blocked.

- **Block:** This operator adds an AT command to the blacklist, which causes the command to be dropped as soon as it is encountered. It is useful for blocking vendor-specific AT commands that could be abused by attackers [30].

  - *Example 1:* `block at%imei=` prevents the IMEI of a phone from being changed.

  - *Example 2:* `block at+fus?` prevents a phone from going into the firmware download mode.

  - *Example 3:* `block at+xabbtrace` prevents the baseband trace configuration from being returned.

7. Experimental Analysis and Testing

The application-processor-based AT command intrusion prevention system was subjected to several tests to verify that it could detect and prevent malicious AT command exploitation attempts on the baseband processor without degrading device performance. Specifically, the subscriber should not experience noticeable delays and should be able to use the device as intended (e.g., to make/receive phone calls and send/receive SMS texts and data). Several malicious AT commands were used in the tests, including some that target the X-Gold 608 and 618 baseband processors in older iPhones. These malicious AT commands were selected because of their documentation and use in iPhone baseband unlocks.

Another consideration was to appropriately tune the AT command signatures to minimize false positives and false negatives. Tuning requires the profiling of messages to establish baselines. Signatures that are too general increase the false positive rate and block valid AT commands. Signatures that are too specific increase the false negative rate and fail to block malicious AT commands. Tuning the signatures was determined to be as much art as a science;

a thorough treatment of AT command signature tuning is a topic for future work.

Malicious AT commands used in the tests were obtained from Tian et al. [30] and `theiphonewiki.com`. During the tests, regular cellular communications procedures were performed, including sending and receiving voice calls, SMS messages and streaming data while periodically injecting malicious AT commands.

The following tests were conducted:

- **Test 1:** Injection of a single malicious AT command during a two-minute voice call.

- **Test 2:** Injection of a malicious AT command every 100 ms during a two-minute voice call.

- **Test 3:** Injection of a single malicious AT command while the baseband was not being used (i.e., in the standby mode).

- **Test 4:** Injection of a malicious AT command every 100 ms while the baseband was not being used (i.e., in the standby mode).

- **Test 5:** Injection of a malicious AT command during a streaming data session.

- **Test 6:** Injection of a malicious AT command every 100 ms during a streaming data session.

Table 1 shows the test results along with the rules used to detect and block malicious AT commands. Five malicious or risky AT commands were used in the tests, all of which were successfully detected by the intrusion prevention system. The intrusion prevention functionality did not noticeably impact the normal use of the cellular modem (e.g., making and receiving calls, and sending and receiving SMS messages and packetized data). Additionally, no false positives were observed during tests. Future work will pursue a rigorous testing regimen that considers all the cellular functionality under real-world conditions.

8.   Conclusions

Wireless communications coprocessors provide wide-area and personal-area networking capabilities to Internet of Things and mobile devices. These coprocessors have been the targets of exploitation research in recent years. In particular, the baseband processors, which are responsible for cellular communications, are attractive targets for adversaries interested in intercepting, modifying, interrupting or fabricating voice, text, data and signaling traffic.

This research has made key contributions to securing baseband processors from exploitation attempts by hostile applications that execute on the application processor. Retrofitting an AT command intrusion prevention system between the application processor and baseband processor mitigates the negative effects of malicious AT commands. Because the intrusion prevention

Table 1. Malicious AT command test cases.

AT Command	IPS Rule	Detected
at+xlog=1, "jjjjjjjjjjjjjjjjjjjjjjjjjjj44445555PPPP"	length +xlog >= 30	Yes
at+xapp="aaaaaaaaaaaaaaaaaaaaaaaaaaaaaaaaa aaaa4444555566667777PPPP"	length +xapp >= 50	Yes
at%IMEI="490154203237518"	block at%imei=	Yes
at+fns="000000000000000000000000000000000000000 000000000000000000001111112222333344445555566 66677"	length +fns >=1024	Yes
at+stkprof=1,"064a541c044b1878222803d010700132 0133f8e720470000bf9f154000170100546e56402000000 05c130100266e5640dddddddddeeeeeeeeb890512000000 00010101010202020206113010000c000000";"\x10\x32 \x0F\x27\xBA\x43 \x17\x1C\x0E\xA4\x0B\xA5 \x01\x35\x21\x78\x78\x29\x0C\xD0\xA8\x47 \x0B\x01\x61\x78\xA8\x47\xC0\x46 \xC0\x46 \xC0\x46\xC0\x46\xC9\x18\x11\x70 \x02\x34\x01 \x32\xEF\xE7\xC0\x46\xC0\x46 \x01\x37\x38 \x47\x30\x30\x41\x29\x01\xDA 09pG79pG02480 3A1013101601FBD00004C711140F0B51C4B8026 8BB03601188008911A4C301CA04700250990 ....CONTINUED................... 20xx"	match "\x32\x0F\x27"	Yes

system is vendor agnostic and focuses on analyzing text-based AT commands, the approach is easily implemented to secure baseband processors produced by diverse manufacturers.

Future research will focus on integrating the AT command intrusion prevention technique in Internet of Things and mobile device platforms and operating systems. Additionally, techniques for retrofitting security mechanisms in other vulnerable wireless chipsets will be explored. Finally, efforts will focus on employing cryptographically-sound techniques for firmware attestation to combat threats ranging from unauthorized surveillance to insidious system compromises.

References

[1] Aleph One, Smashing the stack for fun and profit, *Phrack*, vol. 7(49), 1996.

[2] N. Artenstein, Broadpwn: Remotely compromising Android and iOS via a bug in Broadcom's Wi-Fi chipsets, presented at *Black Hat USA*, 2017.

[3] G. Beniamini, Over the Air: Exploiting Broadcom's Wi-Fi Stack (Part 1), Project Zero Team, Google, Mountain View, California (`googleproj ectzero.blogspot.com/2017/04/over-air-exploiting-broadcoms-w i-fi_4.html`), April 4, 2017.

[4] G. Beniamini, Over the Air: Exploiting Broadcom's Wi-Fi Stack (Part 2), Project Zero Team, Google, Mountain View, California (`googleprojectzero.blogspot.com/2017/04/over-air-exploiting-b roadcoms-wi-fi_11.html`), April 11, 2017.

[5] G. Beniamini, Over the Air – Vol.2, Pt. 3: Exploiting the Wi-Fi Stack on Apple Devices, Project Zero Team, Google, Mountain View, California (`googleprojectzero.blogspot.com/2017/10/over-a ir-vol-2-pt-3-exploiting-wi-fi.html`), October 11, 2017.

[6] A. Blanco and M. Eissler, One firmware to monitor 'em all, presented at the *Ekoparty Security Conference*, 2012.

[7] G. Delugre, Reverse engineering a Qualcomm baseband, presented at the *Twenty-Eighth Chaos Communication Congress*, 2011.

[8] J. Drake, P. Fora, Z. Lanier, C. Mulliner, S. Ridley and G. Wicherski, *Android Hacker's Handbook*, John Wiley and Sons, Indianapolis, Indiana, 2014.

[9] European Telecommunications Standards Institute, Digital Cellular Telecommunications System (Phase 2+), AT Command Set for GSM Mobile Equipment (ME), GSM 07.07, Version 5.5.5, TS/SMG-040707Q, Sophia Antipolis, France, 1996.

[10] N. Golde and D. Komaromy, Breaking band: Reverse engineering and exploiting the Shannon baseband, presented at *REcon*, 2016.

[11] History of Computers, The modem of Dennis Hayes and Dale Heatherington (`history-computer.com/ModernComputer/Basis/modem. html`), 2016.

[12] B. Hond, Fuzzing the GSM Protocol, Master's Thesis, Computing Science Program, Radboud University, Nijmegen, The Netherlands, 2011.

[13] iPhone Dev Team, ultrasnOw, *The iPhone Wiki* (www.theiphonewiki. com/wiki/UltrasnOw), 2009.

[14] iPhone Dev Team, PurplesnOw, *The iPhone Wiki* (www.theiphonewiki. com/wiki/PurplesnOw), 2015.

[15] P. Kocialkowski, Samsung Galaxy Back-Door (redmine.replicant.us/ projects/replicant/wiki/SamsungGalaxyBackdoor), February 4, 2014.

[16] B. Krebs, Mirai botnet authors avoid jail time, *Krebs on Security* (krebs onsecurity.com/tag/mirai-botnet), September 19, 2018.

[17] A. Lonzetta, P. Cope, J. Campbell, B. Mohd and T. Hayajneh, Security vulnerabilities in Bluetooth technology as used in IoT, *Journal of Sensor and Actuator Networks*, vol. 7(3), article no. 28, 2018.

[18] L. Miras, The baseband playground, presented at the *Ekoparty Security Conference*, 2011.

[19] M. Moe, Go ahead, hackers. Break my heart, *Wired*, March 14, 2016.

[20] C. Mulliner, S. Liebergeld, M. Lange and J. Seifert, Taming Mr. Hayes: Mitigating signaling based attacks on smartphones, *Proceedings of the Forty-Second Annual IEEE/IFIP International Conference on Dependable Systems and Networks*, 2012.

[21] J. Nivethan and M. Papa, A Linux-based firewall for the DNP3 protocol, *Proceedings of the IEEE Symposium on Technologies for Homeland Security*, 2016.

[22] M. Palattella, N. Accettura, X. Vilajosana, T. Watteyne, L. Grieco, G. Boggia and M. Dohler, Standardized protocol stack for the Internet of (important) Things, *IEEE Communications Surveys and Tutorials*, vol. 15(3), pp. 1389–1406, 2013.

[23] F. Sanglard, Tracing the Baseband: Part 1 (fabiensanglard.net/cell phoneModem/index.php), May 11, 2010.

[24] F. Sanglard, Tracing the Baseband: Part 2 (fabiensanglard.net/cell phoneModem/index2.php), May 11, 2010.

[25] M. Sauter, *From GSM to LTE: An Introduction to Mobile Networks and Mobile Broadband*, John Wiley and Sons, Chichester, United Kingdom, 2014.

[26] B. Seri and A. Livne, Exploiting BlueBorne in Linux-based IoT devices, Armis, Palo Alto, California, 2019.

[27] W. Shaw, *Cybersecuriy for SCADA Systems*, PennWell, Tulsa, Oklahoma, 2006.

[28] SIMCom Wireless Solutions, AT Commands Set, SIM900_ATC_V1.00, Shanghai, China, 2010.

[29] Statista, Internet of Things (IoT) connected devices installed based worldwide from 2015 to 2025 (in billions), Frankfurt, Germany (www.statista. com/statistics/471264/iot-number-of-connected-devices-worldw ide), 2018.

[30] D. Tian, G. Hernandez, J. Choi, V. Frost, C. Ruales, P. Traynor, H. Vijayakumar, L. Harrison, M. Grace and K. Butler, ATtention spanned: Comprehensive vulnerability analysis of AT commands within the Android ecosystem, *Proceedings of the Twenty-Seventh USENIX Security Symposium*, pp. 273–290, 2018.

[31] Tofino Security, Tofino Firewall LSM, Lantzville, Canada (`www.tofino security.com/products/Tofino-Firewall-LSM`), 2017.

[32] P. Tsang and S. Smith, YASIR: A low-latency, high-integrity security retrofit for legacy SCADA systems, *Proceedings of the Twenty-Third IFIP TC 11 International Information Security Conference*, pp. 445–459, 2008.

[33] R. Weinmann, All your baseband are belong to us, presented at the *Hack.lu Conference*, 2010.

[34] R. Weinmann, Baseband attacks: Remote exploitation of memory corruptions in cellular protocol stacks, *Proceedings of the Sixth USENIX Conference on Offensive Technologies*, 2012.

[35] H. Welte, Anatomy of Contemporary GSM Cellphone Hardware (`ondoc. logand.com/d/373/pdf`), 2010.

Chapter 10

VULNERABILITY ASSESSMENT OF INFINIBAND NETWORKING

Daryl Schmitt, Scott Graham, Patrick Sweeney and Robert Mills

Abstract   InfiniBand is an input/output interconnect technology for high performance computing clusters – it is employed in more than one-quarter
of the world's 500 fastest computer systems. Although InfiniBand was
created to provide extremely low network latency with high quality of
service, the cyber security aspects of InfiniBand have yet to be investigated thoroughly. The InfiniBand architecture was designed as a data
center technology that is logically separated from the Internet, so defensive mechanisms such as packet encryption were not implemented.
The security community does not appear to have taken an interest in
InfiniBand, but this is likely to change as attackers branch out from traditional computing devices. This chapter discusses the security implications of InfiniBand features and presents a technical cyber vulnerability
assessment.

Keywords: InfiniBand, networking, vulnerability assessment

1.   Introduction

The cyber threat landscape is becoming more diverse as attackers target
new types of networks, devices and applications. According to Symantec's 2018
Internet Security Threat Report, the number of new mobile malware variants
in 2017 increased by 54% over the number in 2016 [27]. Much more alarming
was the 600% increase in attacks against Internet of Things (IoT) devices. It
is safe to assume that state-sponsored cyber groups are building capabilities
against networks designated by the U.S. Department of Homeland Security as
part of the national critical infrastructure.

Information technology (IT) professionals and cyber defenders alike rely on
signature-based detection methods to provide alerts about anomalous and potentially malicious activities in networks, but this approach cedes the initiative
to the attacker and relegates the defender to a reactive position. Symantec's
findings suggest the need for more proactive measures throughout the com-

Published by Springer Nature Switzerland AG 2019
J. Staggs and S. Shenoi (Eds.): Critical Infrastructure Protection XIII, IFIP AICT 570, pp. 179–205, 2019.
https://doi.org/10.1007/978-3-030-34647-8_10

puting industry and security community. Cyber security experts must explore and evaluate computing equipment in novel ways, especially from the outsider's perspective.

It is unreasonable to expect system engineers and programmers to compete with elite computer hackers, especially those with the backing of nation-states or large criminal organizations. As a result, much of the onus falls on the research community to investigate the cyber hardening and resilience of computing systems that have not been evaluated. Examples include mobile and Internet of Things devices, industrial control systems and networks, and embedded devices that communicate over vehicular networks. Such non-traditional computing devices typically do not have active traffic monitoring in place, much less security professionals to examine logs and alerts. These systems were not designed with cyber security in mind; instead, they were built for user convenience, durability (availability of services) and profitability. Despite these challenges, even small amounts of cyber hardening can greatly increase the costs to attackers and reduce the threats of cyber attacks to critical infrastructure assets.

This chapter focuses on InfiniBand, an advanced input/output interconnect technology used in high-performance computing (HPC). InfiniBand equipment has not been subjected to thorough external security testing because it is not considered to be a likely target for hackers. However, the creators of InfiniBand did realize the need for hardening and resilience. Indeed, they created the technology to address some of the fundamental weaknesses of Ethernet.

High-speed networking hardware is very expensive and InfiniBand customers rightfully expect that their equipment will not be easily compromised by cyber attacks. According to the November 2018 update to the TOP500 list, InfiniBand equipment powers 27% of the 500 most powerful computer systems in the world, but accounts for 37.4% of the total computing performance [28]. As a result, InfiniBand manufacturers have a lot to lose should a newsworthy cyber attack occur on an InfiniBand network.

The desire to put such concerns to rest is evident in a Mellanox white paper titled "Security in Mellanox Technologies InfiniBand Fabrics" [12]. The paper discusses a security review of InfiniBand protocols and highlights certain Mellanox product offerings. A vendor white paper is likely biased; therefore, the vulnerability assessment described here provides an independent and alternative viewpoint. Furthermore, the assessment has a wider scope than the Mellanox effort, which mainly focuses on the protocol, but not much on other aspects of InfiniBand networking. This chapter describes a technical cyber vulnerability assessment, an apparatus for determining the vulnerabilities that are present in a generic InfiniBand network.

2.   Background

This section describes the InfiniBand architecture and the interactions between the architectural components.

Table 1. InfiniBand bandwidth specifications.

InfiniBand Standard	Line Rate	Lines	Total
Quad Data Rate (QDR)	10 Gb/s	4	40 Gb/s
Fourteen Data Rate (FDR)	14 Gb/s	4	56 Gb/s
Enhanced Data Rate (EDR)	25 Gb/s	4	100 Gb/s
High Data Rate (HDR)	50 Gb/s	4	200 Gb/s

2.1 InfiniBand

InfiniBand is a network protocol comparable to Ethernet. It is extremely lightweight and is designed to minimize latency. In the late 1990s, the computing industry recognized that it was facing a tremendous hurdle. Processor speeds were increasing according to Moore's Law, but memory latency and network bandwidth limitations were nullifying processor performance gains. This was not much of a problem for personal computers. However, high-end servers, especially those operating in clusters, needed a solution. In particular, networking (gigabit Ethernet) and storage (fibre channel) cards were pushing the bandwidth limits of motherboard buses and networking cables [11]. The InfiniBand Trade Association (IBTA) was created to come up with a solution.

More than 180 companies assembled in August 1999 to develop the Infini-Band architecture. Individuals from IBM and Intel served as co-chairs of the InfiniBand Trade Association and the steering committee members came from influential companies such as Dell, Compaq, Hewlett-Packard, Microsoft and Sun. With numerous contributors presenting differing needs, the association had to design a flexible system. The specification had to "scale down to cost-effective small server systems as well as scaling up to large, highly robust, enterprise-class facilities" and had to accommodate "new inventions and vendor differentiation" [23]. The InfiniBand Trade Association was striving to design the most secure networks while ensuring the lowest latency and highest application performance [7].

Modern InfiniBand uses individual copper or fiber cables capable of up to 200 Gb/s full bi-directional bandwidth, but the first release was primarily based on 2.5 Gb/s copper [25]. The basic copper link had four wires, a differential signaling pair for each direction. The original specifications called for several speeds: 1x, 4x or 12x copper, and 1x fiber. Table 1 shows the current InfiniBand standards, highlighting the two decades of growth.

InfiniBand was built primarily for high-performing computing clusters that are logically isolated from the open Internet. InfiniBand nodes are capable of communicating across the web, but the Internet backbone could not likely run on InfiniBand due to features such as predetermined static routing. The InfiniBand Trade Association was aware of this, when it said that the "present [router] specification does not cover the routing protocol nor the messages exchanged between routers." True routers are optional in InfiniBand networks;

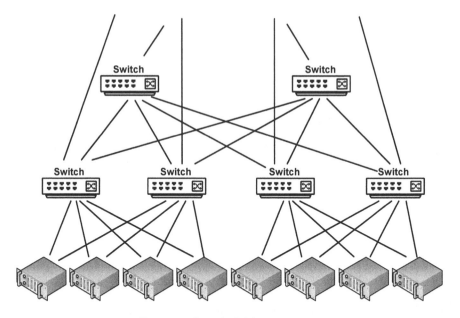

Figure 1. Switched fabric topology.

InfiniBand has been successfully utilized without routers in a production environment between two distant clusters [10]. Nonetheless, InfiniBand is fundamentally a data center technology that is not typically deployed in a network demilitarized zone unless firewalls or other similar access-controlled layers are placed in front of the InfiniBand fabric [12]. The logical segregation provides a fair amount of security, but motivated, well-resourced cyber actors would want to access the valuable data stored inside InfiniBand networks.

2.2 InfiniBand Terminology

InfiniBand is more than just a protocol – the InfiniBand Trade Association envisioned a network infrastructure around it. In fact, the association wanted to improve on the typical hierarchical structure of switches and routers used by Ethernet-based networks.

Figure 1 shows InfiniBand's switched fabric topology, which is a partial mesh that provides connection reliability to interprocessor-communications-based systems by allowing multiple paths between systems. Scalability is supported via fully hot swappable connections managed by a single unit called the subnet manager [11]. InfiniBand hosts have network cards, called host channel adapters (HCAs), which are equivalent to Ethernet network interface cards (NICs). Host channel adapters usually have at least two physical ports so that a node can be connected to two or more InfiniBand switches simultaneously. It would be impractical to create a full mesh by establishing direct links between all devices, but switched fabrics provide a good compromise by enhancing redundancy, load balancing and routing speeds.

Ethernet networks use the dynamic Address Resolution Protocol (ARP) and routing tables to determine how and where to send traffic based on link speeds and congestion. InfiniBand switches do not make routing decisions. Instead, all the shortest paths are calculated by the subnet manager during network initialization and after configuration changes. The subnet manager then pushes forwarding tables to every device in the subnet, including all the compute nodes. Multiple subnet managers may exist, but only one acts as the master. Each host channel adapter and switch have a subnet management agent that enables communications with the subnet manager. The subnet manager sets up and maintains every link in the subnet. Network discovery is performed periodically in InfiniBand, but nodes tend not to be added or removed as often as in Ethernet networks.

Like the Transmission Control Protocol/Internet Protocol (TCP/IP) stack, the InfiniBand protocol stack is based on the seven-layer Open Systems Interconnection (OSI) model. Layer-2 addressing is done via a local identifier (LID), which is dynamically assigned by the subnet manager [10]. The local identifier is a 16-bit value, so a single subnet can support up to 65 K hosts. In contrast, media access control (MAC) addresses used in Ethernet are burned into the network cards by manufacturers. However, these addresses are easily changed via software – a simple command such as `ifconfig eth0 hw ether 02:01:02:03:04:08` accomplishes this in many Linux distributions. This is significant because InfiniBand addresses cannot be easily modified in such a manner.

The layer-3 InfiniBand locators are called global identifiers (GIDs). These are valid IPv6 addresses for the most part. The first half (i.e., 64 of the 128 bits) of each GID is called the global unique identifier (GUID). GUIDs are embedded in the host channel adapter, although there is not just one of them per network card like MAC addresses. Each host channel adapter port has its own GUID. Distinct port addressing helps enforce the static routing, as discussed above.

InfiniBand does not use sockets or virtual ports like Ethernet networks. Instead, InfiniBand connections are established between two endpoints by queue pairs (QPs). Each queue pair consists of a send queue and a receive queue, and each queue pair represents one end of a channel. If an application requires more than one connection, additional queue pairs are created. A send queue and receive queue are collectively referred to as a work queue (WQ).

Work queues put the results of completed work requests (WRs) in an associated completion queue. This includes successfully-completed work requests and unsuccessfully-completed work requests. Completion queues notify applications about ended work requests (status, opcode, size and source) [13]. The user may insert a completion notification routine to be invoked when a new entry is added to a completion queue. This nomenclature lends itself to viewing InfiniBand as a messaging service.

Table 2. InfiniBand transport services.

Class of Service	State	Response Sent
Reliable Connection (RC)	Connection-oriented	Acknowledged
Reliable Datagram (RD)	Multiplexed	Acknowledged
Unreliable Connection (UC)	Connection-oriented	Unacknowledged
Unreliable Datagram (UD)	Connectionless	Unacknowledged
Raw Datagram	Connectionless	Unacknowledged

Keeping applications informed of network activity is vital considering that InfiniBand has a major speed enhancing feature called remote direct memory access (RDMA). Remote direct memory access permits data transfers without interrupting either processor. In order to avoid involving the operating system, applications at each end of a channel must have instant access to queue pairs. This is accomplished by mapping the queue pairs directly to the virtual address space of each application. Thus, the application at each end of the connection has direct, virtual access to the channel connecting it to the application (or storage) at the other end of the channel. This concept is referred to as channel input/output [5]. Because there is no extra copying of data (e.g., to various levels of cache), InfiniBand is referred to as "zero copy" networking.

Reliable connection types send acknowledgements after every transmission. InfiniBand offers stateful and stateless connection types similar to the Transmission Control Protocol (TCP) and User Datagram Protocol (UDP), but these are not as critical in InfiniBand. The reliable connection types in InfiniBand are called reliable connection (RC) and unreliable datagram (UD). The unreliable connection (UC), reliable datagram (RD), raw IPv6 datagram and raw Ethertype datagram transport media exist as well, although these are not as mainstream. Table 2 summarizes the transport options.

In Ethernet networks, most higher-level protocols run over TCP to guarantee 100% packet delivery. Only trivial traffic that can be resent easily (e.g., domain name queries) or traffic that requires high speeds (e.g., streaming video) runs over UDP. Conversely, unreliable datagram is extremely common in InfiniBand. InfiniBand is more efficient at avoiding congestion due to its priority-based flow control. The Ethernet pause frame "stops all traffic indiscriminately" whereas InfiniBand "strictly avoids packet loss by employing link-by-link flow control, which prevents a data packet from being sent from one end of a link if there is insufficient space to receive the packet at the other end of [the] link" [10]. More importantly, the InfiniBand receiver host channel adapter drops all out-of-order packets because it is an error condition as far as the InfiniBand receiver is concerned. This setting can be changed, but the default is to disallow out-of-order delivery.

Possible responses are either a positive acknowledge (Ack) or a negative acknowledge (Nak). A negative acknowledge is triggered under three conditions:

Table 3. Queue pair operations.

Operation	UD	UC	RD	RC
Send (with immediate)	X	X	X	X
Receive	X	X	X	X
RDMA Write (with immediate)		X	X	X
RDMA Read			X	X
Atomic: Fetch and Add			X	X
Atomic: Compare and Swap			X	X
Maximum Message Size	MTU	1 GB	1 GB	1 GB

(i) temporary receiver not ready (RNR Nak); (ii) packet sequence number error (PSN error Nak); and (iii) fatal Nak error code. The reliable connection, unreliable datagram and reliable datagram classes support remote direct memory access and require unique queue pair numbers (QPNs), meaning that no two connections can share the same queue pair numbers simultaneously. Since virtual ports do not exist, this is the primary way that connections can be distinguished from each other. Alternatively, unreliable datagram queue pairs use the same queue pair number, because they can send and receive messages to and from any other unreliable datagram queue pair using the unicast (one-to-one) or multicast (one-to-many) modes; however, only send operations are supported. In addition to remote direct memory access reads and writes, atomic extensions to the remote direct memory access operations also exist. These are essentially a combined write and read remote direct memory access, carrying the data involved as immediate data [23]. Table 3 shows a detailed listing of the available queue pair operations by connection type.

Remote direct memory access has become popular as a result of InfiniBand and it is now used in other I/O interconnects. The reason is that remote direct memory access enables high-throughput, low-latency networking with low CPU utilization. These advantages make it especially useful in massively parallel compute clusters. The Internet Wide-Area RDMA Protocol (iWARP) and RDMA over Converged Ethernet (RoCE) now bring similar capabilities to networks employing Ethernet-based software. The main difference between the two is that iWARP uses a "complex mix of layers, including DDP (direct data placement), a tweak known as MPA (marker PDU aligned) framing, and a separate RDMA Protocol (RDMAP) to deliver RDMA services over TCP/IP" whereas RoCE operates "over standard layer-2 and layer-3 Ethernet switches" [14]. RoCE's superior performance metrics compared with iWARP have made it the market frontrunner.

InfiniBand products (e.g., by Mellanox) support Ethernet by offering Internet Protocol over InfiniBand (IPoIB) and Ethernet over InfiniBand (EoIB) services. IPoIB uses an upper layer protocol (i.e., application layer) driver that enables it to encapsulate IP datagrams over an InfiniBand connected or datagram transport service. EoIB is akin to IPoIB except that it includes the (layer-2) Ethernet header and only runs on UD. EoIB performs an "address translation from Ethernet layer-2 MAC addresses (48-bits long) to InfiniBand layer-2 addresses made of LID/GID and QPN" whereas IPoIB "exposes a 20-byte [hardware] address to the [operating system]" [15]. As a result, EoIB requires additional equipment, specifically a BridgeX gateway that connects an InfiniBand fabric to its external side (i.e., an Ethernet network segment). This may be a reason why EoIB is being phased out; this is evidenced by the fact that it is not mentioned in the latest version of the Mellanox OpenFabrics Enterprise Distribution (OFED) Linux User's Manual. The Ethernet Tunneling over IPoIB (eIPoIB) driver appears to have replaced this functionality.

2.3   InfiniBand Security Features

The InfiniBand architecture provides isolation and protection services using keys. Keys are "values assigned by an administrative entity that are used in messages in order to authenticate that the initiator of a request is an authorized requester and that the initiator has the appropriate privileges for the request being made" [22]. InfiniBand has five types of keys: (i) partition keys (P_-Keys); (ii) memory keys (L_Keys and R_Keys); (iii) queue keys (Q_Keys); (v) management keys (M_Keys); and (vi) baseboard management keys (B_Keys).

A partition key designates a network partition for a channel adapter port. Each port is assigned at least one partition key by the subnet manager; these values point to entries in the port's partition key table. InfiniBand partitions are equivalent to Ethernet virtual local area networks (VLANs), so partition keys are like VLAN tags.

Memory keys are needed for remote direct memory access operations and come in the form of local keys (L_Keys) and remote keys (R_Keys). System memory is registered to provide access to local and remote channel adapters. Registration returns the keys, each of which has the associated access permission (i.e., read-only versus read/write) [3]. The same memory buffer can be registered several times, even with different permissions, and every registration results in a different set of keys.

Queue keys are preshared keys that are used in the datagram connection types (reliable datagram and unreliable datagram). During communications setup, channel adapters exchange queue keys between queue pairs. Receipt of a packet with a different queue key than the one provided to the remote queue pair indicates that the packet is not valid and is, therefore, rejected.

Management and baseboard management keys enforce control of the master subnet manager and subnet baseboard manager, respectively. The baseboard manager component communicates with nodes to provide an in-band mechanism for managing each baseboard configuration [22]. The baseboard manager's purview covers topics such as the retrieval of vital product data (e.g., serial number and manufacturing information), environmental data and adjusting power and cooling resources [24]. The baseboard manager communicates with a baseboard management agent (BMA) on each node, just as the subnet manager does with every subnet manager agent. Every channel adapter port and every switch have a management key and a baseboard management key. These do not need to be identical across all devices, but they must match what the destination is expecting in order to verify that the source of a management packet is correct.

InfiniBand also provides integrity and quality of service (QoS). Integrity is ensured by two cyclic redundancy checksums (CRCs). As the name implies, the 16-bit variant CRC (VCRC) is recalculated at each hop. The 32-bit invariant CRC (ICRC) complements the VCRC by protecting the fields that do not change along the communications pathway. Each packet has a VCRC and an ICRC; a per-block CRC exists as well for each memory block sent in the payload. As for quality of service, packets are assigned a priority between 0 (lowest) to 15 (highest). This priority translates to a virtual lane (VL) through which the packet can transit. Each physical link can support up to sixteen virtual lanes, with VL 15 reserved for management packets.

InfiniBand management is performed in-band, using management datagrams, which are unreliable datagrams with maximum transmission units (MTUs) as low as 256 bytes. Some management datagrams are called subnet management packets, which are unique in several ways. In addition to transiting in VL 15, they are always sent and received on queue pair 0 of each port, and they can use directed routing [23]. Directed routing occurs when a subnet management packet tells a switch which ports to send it on. This is necessary when the forwarding tables have not been initialized.

InfiniBand software derives from the OFED suite from the OpenFabrics Alliance, a collaboration involving major high performance I/O vendors. Mellanox has augmented this package to create its own version of OFED. It supports both InfiniBand and Ethernet (technically, RoCE), although many network cards cannot process both interconnect types [18]. OFED includes custom diagnostic tools for ascertaining the status of the fabric. Two such utilities are `ibstat` and `ibdump`, which are analogous to the traditional Linux `ifconfig` and `tcpdump` utilities, respectively. OFED also includes open-source software called OpenSM, which provides subnet manager functionality.

InfiniBand-supported applications are written using a series of functions called "verbs." The InfiniBand architecture "contains no APIs, defined registers, etc. Instead it is specified as a collection of verbs – abstract representations of the functions that must be present, but may be implemented with any combination and organization of hardware, firmware and software" [23].

For example, the InfiniBand standard does not specify how a queue should be implemented internally in the host channel adapter hardware. Each manufacturer must provide a driver in the OFA Verbs API, whose inputs are function calls and data structures defined in detail by the API. Due to latency requirements, Mellanox programming is done in the C language according to its "RDMA-Aware Networks Programming User Manual" [13]. Example verbs/-functions are `ibv_get_device_list()`, `ibv_reg_mr()` for registering a memory region and `ibv_create_qp()` for creating a queue pair.

Table 4. Ethernet versus InfiniBand features.

Feature	Ethernet	InfiniBand
Network Card	Network interface card (NIC)	Host channel adapter (HCA)
Programming Model	Sockets	Verbs
Layer-2 Addressing	Media access control (MAC) address is statically assigned by the NIC manufacturer	Local identifier (LID) is dynamically assigned by the subnet manager
Layer-3 Addressing	Internet Protocol (IP) address	Global identifier (GID) is a 64-bit subnet ID assigned by the subnet manager plus a 64-bit global unique identifier (GUID) assigned by the HCA manufacturer
Forwarding Tables	Distributed control; each switch discovers neighbors independently	Centralized control by the subnet manager
Packet Capture	Standard operating system tools (e.g., Wireshark and `tcpdump`)	Vendor-specific tools (e.g., `ibdump` from Mellanox)

Table 4 juxtaposes some relevant Ethernet and InfiniBand features.

2.4   Cyber Vulnerability Assessment

A cyber vulnerability assessment (CVA) is an integral part of a good security program. It is the process of identifying and analyzing security vulnerabilities that might exist in a computer system. The term system usually refers to a network or enterprise, but it can be an individual device or component. Vulnerability assessments are typically conducted through "network-based or host-based methods, using automated scanning tools to conduct discovery, testing, analysis and reporting of systems and vulnerabilities. Manual techniques can also be used to identify technical, physical and governance-based vulnerabilities" [8].

A cyber vulnerability assessment has two main phases: (i) planning the vulnerability assessment; and (ii) performing the vulnerability assessment. The planning phase is extremely important, because it entails "gathering all relevant information, defining the scope of activities, defining roles and responsibilities," and more [1]. A cyber vulnerability assessment of a production network entails interviewing system administrators and reviewing appropriate policies and procedures relating to the systems being assessed. However, the experi-

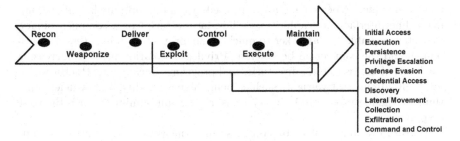

Figure 2. MITRE enterprise tactics.

mental setup comprised just a few Linux hosts connected to a single switch, so the effort is called a technical cyber vulnerability assessment.

The process of defining the scope is almost always up to the customer or network owner. This determines what entities are in play, but the execution strategy is usually up to the assessor. Many cyber experts believe in adopting an attacker's perspective by employing the "hacker methodology." This progression lists the stages of a cyber attack from reconnaissance and enumeration to exfiltrating data and covering tracks. Physical attacks are carried out in much the same manner, but each type of attack does not necessarily incorporate every stage in the progression. Some of the codified models include Lockheed Martin's Cyber Kill Chain [6], MITRE's ATT&CK Matrix [19] and the STRIDE model of Garg and Kohnfelder from Microsoft [26]. This assessment has adopted MITRE's framework because it is widely accepted by the U.S. Government cyber community.

The ATT&CK Matrix begins with gaining initial access to a device. All the adversarial actions taken prior to establishing a foothold in the network are covered by the PRE-ATT&CK Matrix. These steps are extremely important for an actual attacker, but are not relevant here. Indeed, the assumption here is that a host or other device on a generic InfiniBand network could be compromised somehow, but the method or means by which the unintended access might be acquired is tangential to the effort. The full ATT&CK Matrix covers techniques spanning Windows, Macintosh and Linux platforms. Many techniques are operating system dependent. InfiniBand is supported by newer Windows distributions, but the focus here is on Linux-style attacks. No cyber attack model explicitly covers InfiniBand, so the effort sought to discover and document specific techniques using the ATT&CK tactics as guidelines.

The eleven ATT&CK Matrix tactic categories are: (i) initial access; (ii) execution; (iii) persistence; (iv) privilege escalation; (v) defense evasion; (vi) credential access; (vii) discovery; (viii) lateral movement; (ix) collection; (x) exfiltration; and (xi) command and control [19] (Figure 2).

These functions are typically performed in the specified order, although attackers have their own tradecraft and preferences. The available time on target and required stealth also influence the sequence of events. Execution is the means by which cyber effects are produced. Common options include a command line interface, a graphical user interface, a script or a compiled binary. Persistence enables an attacker to quickly and/or easily regain access to a system should the connection be severed. Privilege escalation involves increasing the levels of access to files, directories and programs. Ideally, an attacker would have full administrative rights such as being able to modify, add or delete anything on the filesystem. In Linux systems, the default administrator is the root account.

Defense evasion involves bypassing security measures (e.g., anti-virus software and firewalls) and avoiding detection. Credential access is the process of harvesting usernames, passwords, personal identification numbers, and even cryptographic keys. Discovery involves gaining information about the other systems in the internal network, after which a decision may be made to pivot to another system (lateral movement). Collection is the assembling and staging of the victim's data so that it can be exfiltrated to a location of the attacker's choosing. Lastly, command and control is how an attacker communicates with his or her malicious beacons and implants.

2.5   InfiniBand Security Research

Warren [29] has presented a GUID spoofing attack that altered the values in firmware. This is a significant contribution, but with limited realism because the victim machine (to which the GUID belonged) was taken offline prior to the attack. An attacker who compromises a single host would not be able to shut down another host without first gaining access to it, which negates the benefit of spoofing its address. (The exception might be launching a successful denial-of-service attack.) Nonetheless, this precaution led to a more straightforward proof-of-concept experiment. In Ethernet networks, duplicate MAC addresses in the same subnet can cause network instability. It is unclear how the subnet manager would react to a GUID change in a live network because GUIDs are not supposed to change, unlike LIDs or even GIDs [29].

In a white paper, Mellanox [12] asserts that the InfiniBand architecture "targets one of the main concerns in such environments [a data center LAN] which is security, and has many built-in mandatory features that enable much better isolation and security than current networks and other cluster interconnects." The paper emphasizes that InfiniBand is a layer-2 protocol much like Ethernet, so almost all layer-3 through layer-7 security mechanisms work the same way with InfiniBand. Switch administration is done out-of-band via management ports as opposed to many switches that can be configured remotely. The switches support RADIUS authentication, although it uses MD5 hashes that are now considered to be insecure. Mellanox [12] also contends that hardware-based features such as packet construction and GUID addressing significantly improve security by preventing software applications from gaining control over them and maliciously changing the attributes. It also claims that standard layer-2 attacks such as MAC floods, gratuitous ARP and VLAN hopping are not possible in InfiniBand.

In contrast, Lee et al. [9] believe that the InfiniBand architecture specification omits security, resulting in security vulnerabilities that could be exploited with moderate effort. Lee and colleagues did not orchestrate attacks, but base their arguments on the lack of encryption in InfiniBand. They are concerned that the keys used for authentication and management are sent over the wire in plaintext. The keys could be easily captured by a traffic sniffer and then spoofed to achieve powerful effects. They infer that, having infiltrated an InfiniBand network, a hacker could abuse its extensive computational power and massive storage capacity of the cluster in "another attack and as a repository for illegal content." Although their focus was on data confidentiality, Lee and colleagues proposed a security enhancement to protect against denial-of-service attacks. They constructed a simulation testbed with a stateful partition enforcement mechanism in switches using trap messages; the security mechanism filtered packets with invalid partition keys.

3. Methodology

A test network was created to perform the cyber vulnerability assessment of InfiniBand. Generic equipment and software were employed because the intent was to investigate potential vulnerabilities in core InfiniBand equipment and software, not custom InfiniBand-supported applications. Mellanox products were chosen because it is the largest InfiniBand vendor.

3.1 Equipmental Setup

A minimal network was constructed for the technical cyber vulnerability assessment. It comprised three desktop computers and a Mellanox SX6012 switch. The switch had twelve ports, each capable of 56 Gb/s full bi-directional bandwidth. It also had Ethernet, RS-232 and mini-USB management ports for out-of-band maintenance [16]. The computers were high-performance machines that were built to handle the requirements of the assessment. They had identical hardware and software.

One of the computers was assigned the role of subnet manager. As a result, it ran the OpenSM program in the master mode. In addition, this computer was connected to the switch via an RJ-45-to-DB9 serial cable. This did not affect the normal in-band traffic, although it could provide an attacker with the means to access the switch.

3.2 Approach

A cyber vulnerability assessment of InfiniBand must take a holistic approach, looking at its protocol, physical equipment (hardware), supporting software and network architecture. Hardware vulnerabilities present the most challenges to defenders because they are by far the most difficult to detect. InfiniBand switches and host channel adapters use custom application-specific integrated circuits (ASICs) that are capable of sending and receiving data at rates up to

200 Gb/s per port. The newest Mellanox switch and host channel adapter product lines are Quantum and ConnectX-5, respectively [17]. InfiniBand hardware is cost prohibitive for most businesses and individuals, so these chipsets have not been externally tested or brute forced like, for example, Intel i7 processors. In addition, assembly language or microcode is not available, requiring programmers and users to use vendor-specific tools and APIs. Thus, if hardware vulnerabilities or backdoors were to exist, they would be nearly impossible to discover without insider knowledge. Reverse engineering a microchip begins with an expensive and time-consuming process called delidding, which progressively strips layers off the chip. Images are taken of each chip cross-section using a scanning electron microscope [4]. With more than a billion transistors on a modern ASIC chip, performing these tasks and then analyzing the images is impractical. In any case, a more likely scenario is supply chain tampering rather than a manufacturing or design flaw.

The National Institute of Standards and Technology lists cyber supply chain risks as the "insertion of counterfeits, unauthorized production, tampering, theft, insertion of malicious software and hardware, as well as poor manufacturing and development practices in the cyber supply chain" [20]. In the case of InfiniBand products, this would be an extremely sophisticated attack, probably requiring nation-state support. Malicious variants of integrated circuits could be produced using an embedded rootkit or logic bomb. These could then be substituted for the original chips while the devices are in transit from the manufacturer to the customer. The hope would be that these compromised devices would find their way into facilities or in networks that would otherwise be out of reach of the attacker. Testing for hardware vulnerabilities is such a complex operation that it will not be discussed further in this chapter.

The key component of InfiniBand networking to be evaluated is its architecture. The switched fabric topology is not impervious to attack, but it does have advantages over traditional switched networks. Having more than one physical connection to the rest of the subnet provides redundancy and resilience. If one link were to go down, the endpoint should still be able to communicate through its other channel adapter port. Furthermore, man-in-the-middle attacks are more difficult and generally less successful when potential routes between two endpoints do not share at least one common intermediate node. Valuable intelligence can be gathered when a cyber actor sniffs traffic from a switched port analyzer (SPAN) port on an Ethernet switch; all (or selected) traffic traversing the switch is mirrored on a different port to the host with the listener. InfiniBand nodes are not always connected to a single switch, so in theory only a portion of the packets headed to or from a specific node would transit through the compromised switch.

Switched fabrics also cut down the attack surface by taking away the ability of switches to perform dynamic routing. This is not really a security enhancement of the architecture, but the instantiation by InfiniBand. ARP cache poisoning and routing table overflows are examples of attacks that are not pos-

Table 5. Switched fabric versus shared bus architecture.

Feature	Switched Fabric	Shared Bus
Topology	Switched	Shared Bus
Pin Count	Low	High
Number of End Points	Many	Few
Maximum Signal Length	Kilometers	Inches
Reliability	Yes	No
Scalable	Yes	No
Fault Tolerant	Yes	No

sible because of InfiniBand's predetermined routes. Table 5 summarizes some of the advantages of switched fabrics [11].

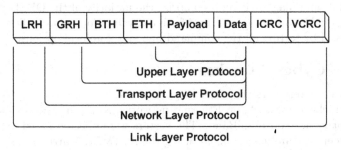

Figure 3. Data packet format.

The InfiniBand protocol follows the OSI model as seen in Figure 3. The local route header (LRH) corresponds to layer 2, the global route header (GRH) layer 3, and the base transport header (BTH) and extended transport header (ETH) comprise layer 4. The LIDs, and service level and virtual lane information are in the local route header. The global route header has the IP version and GIDs, but is omitted entirely during local (within subnet) transmissions. The packet sequence number as well as the queue, partition and memory keys are in the layer-4 headers. The fields in the extended transport header differ based on the base transport header operation or the next header of the local route header. The invariant and variant cyclic redundancy checks (ICRC and VCRC) are the checksums for bits that do not change during the transmission and that are recalculated at each hop, respectively. Breaking the checksum up into two parts makes the packets slightly harder to spoof. However, this design feature was intended to decrease the transmission delay time by limiting the work done by switches.

An obvious security concern with the InfiniBand protocol is the omission of encryption at the link level. Encrypting the payload and possibly some of the metadata contained in the higher levels of encapsulation (protocol data unit headers) can significantly improve data confidentiality. The Ethernet stack offers encryption down to layer 3 via Internet Protocol Security (IPsec), but other common protocols such as Transport Layer Security (TLS) and Secure Shell (SSH) operate at the application layer. The InfiniBand Trade Association chose not to implement encryption because it is computationally expensive and increases latency. Technically, SSH is still available using IP-over-InfiniBand, but even this would not protect the keys.

Another negative, albeit necessary, feature is forced routing. This could enable an attacker to ignore forwarding tables and send a packet along any pathway. Positive security attributes include having virtual lanes, keys (even cleartext ones) and unique queue pair numbers.

Lastly, the InfiniBand supporting software must be examined. The open-source portions of the OFED suite can be modified and recompiled relatively easily to create a new cyber weapon. OpenSM is one such application that is susceptible to exploitation, along with many Linux shell scripts in the filesystem. InfiniBand diagnostic tools comprise the majority of the OFED binaries. Binaries could be overwritten, fuzzed for input validation vulnerabilities and/or brute forced by testing all the command line and graphical options.

3.3   Cyber Attacks

This section discusses the types of cyber attacks that were attempted. Some of the attacks are feasible on Ethernet networks, so the intent was to launch equivalent attacks on InfiniBand. The vectors were selected based on the authors' experience and research, and using the ATT&CK Matrix as a guide. All eleven tactic categories in the matrix do not pertain to InfiniBand. In particular, initial access, persistence, privilege escalation and defense evasion involve methods that are specific to the operating systems being used.

Execution.   Security researchers and the hacking community have created many cyber tools for Ethernet networks. Very few, if any, of these could be applied directly to InfiniBand due to hardware packet crafting, lack of virtual ports, etc., without activating IPoIB or EoIB. Using these protocols is a legitimate technique, but this work does not consider InfiniBand as "running in the Ethernet mode."

- **OFED Diagnostic Tools:** The diagnostic utilities in the OFED suite can help debug the connectivity and status of InfiniBand devices in a fabric. Due to the lack of custom cyber security tools in InfiniBand, these utilities could serve as building blocks for cyber weapons, enabling an attacker to manipulate settings and network traffic. Running standard operating system commands and using the available diagnostic tools are much stealthier techniques than transferring and executing non-native files to an InfiniBand environment. OFED tool usage should not set off any alarms nor should it put the attacker's code at risk of being quarantined or captured.

All the OFED diagnostic tools have to be studied and tested. Individual packet captures have to be taken for each tool to understand the network traffic generated during its execution. All possible combinations of parameters cannot be executed and evaluated. Instead, options that appeared to have dangerous ramifications were chosen and tested (e.g., ibping with the flood option).

- **RDMA Programming:** RDMA programming for InfiniBand, RoCE and iWARP is accomplished via the Verbs API. Mellanox states that its architecture "permits direct user mode access to the hardware" through a "dynamically loaded library" [13]. Networking experts can program with verbs in order to customize and optimize the RDMA network or generate malicious effects.

- **Malicious Firmware Installation:** Firmware is embedded code on a hardware device. The host channel adapter and possibly the switch firmware would be of particular interest. Reprogramming an InfiniBand host channel adapter could enable an attacker to intercept incoming packets and modify outgoing packets. Firmware is chipset dependent, so a code modification would not be guaranteed to work on all InfiniBand host channel adapters. For this and other reasons, the experiments did not delve into firmware, but instead investigated how malicious firmware could be burned on a device.

Credential Access. InfiniBand does not use usernames and passwords for authentication, nor does it require access tokens or tickets like Kerberos. Usernames and passwords are operating system mechanisms meant for human users. In contrast, high-performance computing clusters usually run automated processes, and only matching source addresses and keys enable communications access between nodes. Additionally, administrative privileges are needed to run most InfiniBand tools.

- **Address Spoofing:** Firewalls and intrusion detection/prevention systems typically block traffic and generate alerts based on the source (MAC and/or IP) addresses. Modifying source addresses can enable an attacker to bypass these middleware devices.

  Spoofing can cause a destination computer to grant elevated permissions if no other authentication/authorization mechanisms are in place. Address spoofing can also enable reflected attacks because responses would be sent to the true owner of the spoofed address. Popular hacking tools such as Nmap and Scapy can be used as follows:

  ```
  nmap -S $IP_Address
  ifconfig eth0 hw ether $MAC_Address
  nmap -spoof-mac $MAC_Address
  ```

Address spoofing is an attack on data confidentiality because it can enable an unintended user or computer to gain access to resources that would otherwise be denied. The experiments attempted to duplicate the GUID spoofing accomplished by Warren in 2012 [29]. LID spoofing was investigated as well.

Discovery. A cyber actor can learn the addresses and structure of an internal network in different ways. Typically, discovery is performed passively through traffic analysis and actively through scanning. Traffic analysis utilizes programs such as `tcpdump` and Wireshark whereas scanning uses tools such as `traceroute`, Nmap and Solarwinds.

- **Network Traffic Sniffing:** Traffic sniffing can give an attacker valuable situational awareness about a network. It may not be thought of as an attack in and of itself, but it is an attack on data confidentiality. Monitoring network traffic requires an attacker or attack tool to be positioned between the sender and recipient, unless the interest is in conversations involving one entity. The reason is that messages are not always sent to every device, unless the topology of the network is a shared bus or a network hub is used instead of a switch or router. Broadcast and multicast messages exist in Ethernet and InfiniBand, but these are not private messages. Therefore, switches would tend to be the preferred devices on which to perform sniffing. The experiments explored methods for sniffing InfiniBand traffic.

- **Network Mapping:** The ideal byproduct of the discovery step is a complete and accurate network map. Not every node communicates regularly, so active scanning may be necessary to identify all the connected devices. Even during relatively idle times, Ethernet networks produce a lot of noise in the form of ARP, Network Time Protocol (NTP) and Simple Network Management Protocol (SNMP) traffic. InfiniBand, on the other hand, has very little overhead. A network mapping tool, especially one with a visual display, could provide InfiniBand users and administrators with valuable situational awareness about their networks. A few OFED diagnostic tools deliver this functionality in text-only output form, so efforts focused on augmenting the tools with graphical interfaces.

Lateral Movement. Traditional pivoting is not necessary in an InfiniBand network because remote interactive logins are not used (again, excluding SSH via IPoIB). High-performance computing clusters automate work using scripts and nodes share resources. In a sense, hosts are extensions of each other due to remote direct memory access, far more so than file sharing via server message block (SMB) or the File Transfer Protocol (FTP).

- **Malicious Subnet Manager:** As discussed above, the subnet manager is an extremely powerful entity in an InfiniBand network, analogous to a Windows domain controller, albeit much more primitive. There must be one master subnet manager, but several other nodes can run in the slave or standby mode. The backups perform (vendor-specific) polling to ensure that the master is operational and a failover to one of the backups occurs when the master is not operational [23].

The OpenSM software is open source, so an attacker could download the source code, modify and recompile it [21]. The next step would be to run the weaponized OpenSM on the compromised machine and execute a denial-of-service attack that prevents the master subnet manager from communicating, causing it to be replaced as the master.

A malicious subnet manager could affect the integrity, confidentiality and/or availability of an InfiniBand network. A weaponized version of OpenSM was not created. Instead, the experiments investigated how to cause the master subnet manager to fail remotely.

Collection. Collection is the method used by an attacker to obtain the desired information.

- **Falsified Memory Keys:** Acquiring remote direct memory access memory keys could enable an attacker to read from or write to a remote memory region.

Exfiltration. Exfiltration is loosely interpreted as creating the desired effect instead of merely exfiltrating data from a victim device or network.

- **Denial-of-Service (DoS) Attacks:** Denial-of-service attacks attempt to disable a node or program by various means, including consuming all its resources or shutting it down entirely. This is most often a means to an end, such as enabling an attacker to thwart defenses or migrate to a failover service or situation that may be more advantageous. A common denial-of-service attack is a ping flood, which saturates a victim machine or network link with ping packets to cause legitimate traffic to be dropped or severely stalled. In the experiments, the `ibping` command was executed in a (command line) terminal on one machine, on multiple terminals on one machine and on multiple machines.

4. Experimental Results and Analysis

This section discusses the outcomes of executing the attacks identified in the previous section.

4.1 Malicious Firmware Installation

How this attack is carried out depends on where the malicious firmware is located. Mellanox provides an automatic updater tool named `mlxfwmanager` for Internet-connected devices. The normal syntax is:

```
mlxfwmanager --online -u -d $device
```

Manual firmware installation is accomplished as follows:

```
mlxfwmanager_pci -i fw_file.bin
```

The `mlxfwmanager` binary could be replaced with a malicious version that downloads firmware from a location of the attacker's choosing. This would cause an authorized user to unknowingly install dangerous code. However, the attack would not work if the file hash of the correct firmware was verified from its true source.

Alternatively, the attacker could pull a copy of the malicious firmware via his or her beacon and install it manually. Covering the tracks after the attack could be problematic, although the old version of the firmware could be re-installed after the attack.

4.2   OFED Diagnostic Tools

Table 6 lists the OFED diagnostic tools. A "Yes" in the third column indicates that the tool can be used in a malicious manner, including as a part of a larger cyber weapon. Some of the OFED tools require the user to be running as `root` or as a local administrator.

The tools can run on any node and affect the entire InfiniBand fabric just the same. The result is that every node is critical. Note that Windows-based networks differentiate between local and domain accounts so a local user cannot make changes on a remote node without submitting valid credentials.

The `ibccconfig` is particularly susceptible. The manual page for this command says: "WARNING −− You should understand what you are doing before using this tool. Misuse of this tool could result in a broken fabric." InfiniBand has robust quality of service, but a key point is that every packet is assigned a service level (SL). A table that maps the service level of each port to a virtual lane determines the virtual lane on which a packet will be sent. The Infini-Band architecture specifies a dual priority weighted round robin scheme. In this scheme, each virtual lane is assigned a priority (high or low) and a weight. Within a given priority, data is transmitted from virtual lanes in approximate proportion to their assigned weights (excluding, of course, virtual lanes that have no data to be transmitted).

The `ibccconfig` tool can be abused in several ways. Mapping all the service levels to the same virtual lane will essentially eliminate all priorities. An attacker who wishes to subtly (or not) impede certain traffic could manipulate the virtual lane weights so that the targeted virtual lane is allocated a lower percentage of the total bandwidth. Another attack significantly increments the `HighPriCounter` so that all the low priority lanes rarely get their turn. The impacts of changing the sizes of maximum transmission units are minimal.

4.3   Address Spoofing

As stated above, LIDs and GUIDs/GIDs are the InfiniBand layer-2 and-3 addresses, respectively. Mellanox states that "a node does not determine what

Table 6. OFED diagnostic tools.

Commands(s)	Manual	Exploitable	Function
ibaddr	Yes	No	Simple address resolver
ibdev2netdev	No	No	Device/port status checker
ibdiagnet, iblinkinfo, ibnetdiscover, ibnodes, ibswitches	Yes	Yes	Fabric scanners
ibdiagpath, ibtracert	No, Yes	No	Route tracers
ibdump	Yes	Yes	Traffic sniffer
ibnetsplit	Yes	No	New subnet creator
ibping, ibsysstat	Yes	Yes	Connectivity verifiers
ibportstate	Yes	Yes	Port state querier/modifier
ibqueryerrors, perfquery	Yes Yes	No No	Report port errors
ibroute, dump_fts	Yes, No	Yes	Display forwarding table(s)
ibstat, ibstatus	Yes	No	ifconfig, ipconfig equivalent
ibtopodiff	Yes	No	Topology difference checker
mstflint	Yes	Yes	Firmware burner
saquery, sminfo, smpdump, smpquery, smparquery	Yes (x4), No	Maybe	Issue subnet admininistrator queries
ibcacheedit	Yes	Maybe	Edit ibnetdiscover output
ibccconfig, ibccquery	Yes	Yes, No	Congestion control

the LID should be .... [because] LIDs are assigned by the subnet manager and not the node itself" [12]. Several commands can be issued to print host LID(s): ibaddr, ibdiagnet, ibnodes, ibstat, ibnetdiscover, ibv_devices and ibv_devinfo. Since these addresses are assigned dynamically, it is likely that they are stored in a file instead of in the firmware (like GUIDs). (The /sys/class/infiniband/ directory was ascertained from a Mellanox script elsewhere in the filesystem.) In the case of the personal computer that was tested, these variables were mlx5_0 and mlx5_1, respectively. The files permissions were initially set to read-only for everyone (-r--r--r--) and the owner was root.

The following commands were executed to grant full read/write access:

```
sudo chmod +w /sys/class/infiniband/mlx5_0/ports/1/lid
sudo chmod 777 /sys/class/infiniband/mlx5_0/ports/1/lid
```

The file permissions were changed, but the contents (0x2 corresponding to the LID for the device/port) were not changed after the following attempts to edit them:

```
sudo gedit /sys/class/infiniband/mlx5_0/ports/1/lid
sudo echo 0x9 >> /sys/class/infiniband/mlx5_0/ports/1/lid
```

It is possible that the LID file was locked from an application or it existed in firmware.

Warren [29] altered the GUIDs in host channel adapter firmware using the following commands:

```
mstflint =d $PSID -blank_guids i /usr/share/ib_firmware/
mstflint -d $PSID -guids fake_GUID_1 fake_GUID_2 ...
```

The first command blanks the GUIDs in the firmware and the second command spoofs the GUIDs. Note that PSID (parameter-set identification) is a unique identifier for configuring the firmware.

Warren's work, which was published in 2012, involved an old version of OFED. The firmware location has been changed since. For example, the /usr/ share/ib_firmware/ directory does not exist and a system-wide search did not reveal an obvious replacement. Nevertheless, mstflint still supports GUID changing options.

Another method to spoof addresses involved verbs programming. Infini-Band connections are established via queue pairs. MacArthur et al. [10] state that queue pairs are "comparable to port numbers in TCP and UDP, and make it possible to multiplex many independent flows to the same destination [host channel adapter]." The union ibv_gid *gid output parameter of the ibv_query_gid() function or the return value of the ibv_get_device_guid() method could be changed later. Likewise, the struct ibv_port_attr *port_ attr parameter of the ibv_query_port() function contains the LID of the port (lid) as well as the LID of the subnet manager (sm_lid). Unfortunately, the ibv_create_qp() function fails to create a queue pair when given incorrect inputs because validation occurs whenever an attempt is made to use resources.

4.4 Network Traffic Sniffing

InfiniBand host channel adapters usually have two physical ports to maximize fabric effectiveness. If a host is connected to more than one networking device, then an attacker who has command line access on one of them would most likely not be able to listen in on all the traffic to or from the host. Ethernet and InfiniBand switches are typically configured via out-of-band connections to the management ports. However, many network administrators prefer to have the ability to make changes remotely. As a result, Ethernet switches commonly allow access via Telnet (port 23, unencrypted), SSH (port 22, encrypted) or even through a web browser over HTTP/HTTPS (port 80, unencrypted; or port 443, encrypted). These services do not run on InfiniBand switches and, even if they were, there would be no way to connect to them.

Nevertheless, the `ibdump` tool enables a user to monitor host channel adapter traffic. The traditional `tcpdump` does not work because packets are crafted in hardware, not in software.

After running the following command:

```
ibdump -d $device -w  $filename.pcap
```

the packet capture (PCAP) file was loaded into Wireshark, which has an InfiniBand plugin. The plugin was able to decipher all the bits in the layer-2 to layer-4 headers that are not reserved for vendor-specific fields.

4.5   Network Mapping

Reconnaissance is an important step for defenders and attackers. Network administrators need to discover or confirm what is on their networks and attackers need to survey the network landscape to identify potential targets. Passive mapping, in the form of traffic sniffing, is not an easy option in InfiniBand, because, to be effective, it requires putting a network tap on a switch, installing a hardware splitter and altering forwarding tables to mirror traffic.

Several OFED diagnostic tools were designed to perform discovery and their use should not raise any alarms. However, there are two minor limitations with tools such as `ibdiagnet`, `iblinkinfo` and `ibnetdiscover`. First, the outputs are in text form, which is neither user friendly nor intuitive. Second, they list devices one at a time, not necessarily in the order in which they are connected to each other.

InfiniBand does not have a graphical mapping tool like ZenMap. Adapting the open-source ZenMap Python code to InfiniBand was considered. However, it was deemed to be overkill because of the lack of hosted services and virtual ports in InfiniBand and the fact that the OFED tools provide all the needed network information without multiple parameter options. A relatively simple mapping program was found on GitHub [2], which was enhanced to display hostnames, LIDs and port details in addition to the GUIDs. Figure 4 shows the output of the modified program.

4.6   Malicious Subnet Manager

The `ibportstate` tool was chosen to replace the master subnet manager. The `ibstat` command provides the subnet manager LID, so an attacker can then run a tool such as `ibnetdiscover` to determine the switch or switches to which the subnet manager's host is connected. Next, the corresponding switch port(s) are disabled to shut off all communications to the host, causing the subnet manager to fail during polling. For example, the following command instructs LID 3 to disable its first port:

```
ibportstate 3 1 disable
```

Having disabled the master, the malicious version of OpenSM that is waiting in the slave mode takes over as master assuming there are no other backups.

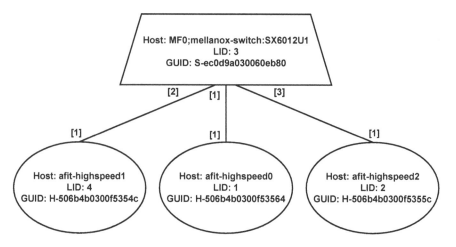

Figure 4. AFIT InfiniBand network.

This process took about ten seconds in the experiments and the switch port(s) were later enabled to restore normal traffic flow. The attack has some limitations, especially if the subnet manager is running on a switch. Disabling all the ports of a switch may be irreversible without physical access.

4.7   Denial-of-Service Attacks

There are several ways to execute denial-of-service attacks. The experiments investigated the use of the `ibping` command with the flood option. The following command sends echo request packets to and receives echo reply packets from LID 4 (victim computer) back-to-back without any delay:

```
ibping -f 4
```

During the experiments, a single instance sent 265 K packets in five seconds, or 53 K per second. Running three terminals simultaneously produced 1.6 M packets in 8.5 seconds, or 217 K per second, when the ends of the capture were removed to account for starting and stopping the commands manually. Four terminals generated 290 K packets per second. Finally, five terminals each were run on two hosts, corresponding to a total of ten simultaneous `ibping` instances. In this case, 4.5 M packets were sent in 9.8 seconds or 582 K per second. The volume seems to scale linearly in the limited sampling. No major packet loss or other harmful effects were observed, but hundreds of instances could result in distributed denial of service.

5.   Conclusions

Although the InfiniBand Trade Association did not make cyber security its top priority when the InfiniBand architecture was designed, it is evident that many InfiniBand features are inherently resistant to tampering and attack. Hardware packet crafting, predetermined routing and redundant pathways in the switched fabric topology contribute to the very low network latency and high availability desired by the high-performance computing community. InfiniBand relies somewhat on external defense mechanisms such as firewalls and other forms of network segregation. However, high performance computing clusters were intended to be located in data warehouses behind demilitarized zones and not to provide services as Internet-facing servers. This was part of the justification for not incorporating packet encryption in InfiniBand or providing support for protocols running over TCP/IP.

Nevertheless, some minor security upgrades could make InfiniBand networks more difficult to exploit without significantly degrading network performance. The subnet manager is a critical component and should have some protections in place should the master fail. A possible solution is file verification, where a node would not become the master if its OpenSM file hash values do not match those of the other standby nodes. Additionally, denial-of-service attacks, such as disabling switch ports from any host or invoking ping floods, should not be allowed even if the user is operating with elevated system privileges.

The views expressed in this chapter are those of the authors, and do not reflect the official policy or position of the U.S. Air Force, U.S. Department of Defense or U.S. Government. This document has been approved for public release, distribution unlimited (Case #88ABW-2018-6395).

References

[1] R. Boyce, Vulnerability Assessments: The Proactive Steps to Secure Your Organization, Information Security Reading Room, SANS Institute, North Bethesda, Maryland, 2001.

[2] cyberang3l, InfiniBand-Graphviz-ualization, GitHub (github.com/cyber ang3l/InfiniBand-Graphviz-ualization), 2016.

[3] D. Deming, InfiniBand software architecture and RDMA, presented at the *Storage Developer Conference*, 2013.

[4] J. Grand, Hardware reverse engineering: Access, analyze and defeat, presented at the *Black Hat DC Workshop*, 2011.

[5] P. Grun, Introduction to InfiniBand for End Users: Industry-Standard Value and Performance for High-Performance Computing and the Enterprise, InfiniBand Trade Association, Beaverton, Oregon, 2010.

[6] E. Hutchins, M. Cloppert and R. Amin, Intelligence-driven computer network defense informed by analysis of adversary campaigns and intrusion kill chains, *Proceedings of the Sixth International Conference on Information Warfare and Security*, 2011.

[7] InfiniBand Trade Association, About InfiniBand, Beaverton, Oregon (www.InfiniBandta.org/about-InfiniBand), 2019.

[8] Information Systems Audit and Control Association, Security Vulnerability Assessment, Rolling Meadows, Illinois (`cybersecurity.isaca.org/info/cyber-aware/images/ISACA_WP_Vulnerability_Assessment_111 7.pdf`), 2017.

[9] M. Lee, E. Kim and M. Yousif, Security enhancement in the InfiniBand architecture, *Proceedings of the Nineteenth IEEE International Parallel and Distributed Processing Symposium*, 2005.

[10] P. MacArthur, Q. Liu, R. Russell, F. Mizero, M. Veeraraghavan and J. Dennis, An integrated tutorial on InfiniBand, verbs and MPI, *IEEE Communications Surveys and Tutorials*, vol. 19(4), pp. 2894–2926, 2017.

[11] Mellanox Technologies, Introduction to InfiniBand, White Paper, Document No. 2003WP, Santa Clara, California (`www.mellanox.com/pdf/whitepapers/IB_Intro_WP_190.pdf`), 2003.

[12] Mellanox Technologies, Security in Mellanox Technologies InfiniBand Fabrics, Technical Overview, White Paper, Document No. 3861WP Rev. 1.0, Sunnyvale, California (`www.mellanox.com/related-docs/whitepapers/WP_Secuirty_In_InfiniBand_Fabrics_Final.pdf`), 2012.

[13] Mellanox Technologies, RDMA Aware Networks Programming User Manual, Rev. 1.7, Sunnyvale, California (`www.mellanox.com/related-docs/prod_software/RDMA_Aware_Programming_user_manual.pdf`), 2015.

[14] Mellanox Technologies, RoCE vs. iWARP Competitive Analysis, White Paper, Document No. 15-4514WP Rev. 2.0, Sunnyvale, California (`www.mellanox.com/related-docs/whitepapers/WP_RoCE_vs_iWARP.pdf`), 2017.

[15] Mellanox Technologies, Mellanox OFED for Linux User Manual, Revision 4.4, Software Version 4.4-1.0.0.0, Sunnyvale, California (`www.mellanox.com/related-docs/prod_software/Mellanox_OFED_Linux_User_Manual_v4_4.pdf`), 2018.

[16] Mellanox Technologies, SX6012 Switch, Product Brief, Sunnyvale, California (`www.mellanox.com/related-docs/prod_ib_switch_systems/PB_SX6012.pdf`), 2018.

[17] Mellanox Technologies, ConnectX-5 Single/Dual-Port Adapter Supporting 100Gb/s with VPI, Sunnyvale, California (`www.mellanox.com/page/products_dyn?product_family=258&mtag=connectx_5_vpi_card`), 2019.

[18] Mellanox Technologies, Mellanox OpenFabrics Enterprise Distribution for Linux (MLNX_OFED), Sunnyvale, California (`www.mellanox.com/page/products_dyn?product_family=26`), 2019.

[19] MITRE Corporation, ATT&CK Matrix for Enterprise, Bedford, Massachusetts (`attack.mitre.org`), 2019.

[20] National Institute of Standards and Technology, Cyber Supply Chain Risk Management, Gaithersburg, Maryland (`csrc.nist.gov/Projects/cyber-supply-chain-risk-management`), 2019.

[21] OpenFabrics Alliance, Index of /downloads/management (`www.openfabrics.org/downloads/management`), 2017.

[22] Oracle, Delivering Application Performance with Oracle's InfiniBand Technology: A Standards-Based Interconnect for Application Scalability and Network Consolidation, Version 2.0, Technical White Paper, Redwood Shores, California, 2012.

[23] G. Pfister, An introduction to the InfiniBand architecture, in *High Performance Mass Storage and Parallel I/O: Technologies and Applications*, R. Buyya and T. Cortes (Eds.), John Wiley and Sons, New York, pp. 617–632, 2001.

[24] QLogic, Fabric Manager User Guide, Firmware Version 6.0, D000007-007 C, Aliso Viejo, California, 2010.

[25] S. Rubenoff, HDR 200G InfiniBand: Empowering Next Generation Data Centers, *insideHPC*, February 25, 2018.

[26] A. Shostack, *Threat Modeling: Designing for Security*, John Wiley and Sons, Indianapolis, Indiana, 2014.

[27] Symantec, Internet Security Threat Report, Volume 23, Mountain View, California, 2018.

[28] TOP500, List Statistics, Sinsheim, Germany (`www.top500.org/statis tics/list`), November 2018.

[29] A. Warren, InfiniBand Fabric and Userland Attacks, Information Security Reading Room, SANS Institute, North Bethesda, Maryland, 2012.

V

CYBER-PHYSICAL
SYSTEMS SECURITY

Chapter 11

LEVERAGING CYBER-PHYSICAL SYSTEM HONEYPOTS TO ENHANCE THREAT INTELLIGENCE

Michael Haney

Abstract   Honeypots and related deception technologies have long been used to capture and study malicious activity in networks. However, clear requirements for developing effective honeypots for active defense of cyber-physical systems have not been discussed in the literature. This chapter proposes a next generation industrial control system honeynet. Enumerated requirements and a reference framework are presented that bring together the best available honeypot technologies and new adaptations of existing tools to produce a honeynet suitable for detecting targeted attacks against cyber-physical systems. The framework supports high-fidelity simulations and high interactions with attackers while delaying the discovery of the deception. Data control, capture, collection and analysis are supported by a novel and effective honeywall system. A hybrid honeynet, using virtualized and real programmable logic controllers that interact with a physical process model, is presented. The benefits provided by the framework along with the challenges to consider during honeynet deployment and operation are also discussed.

Keywords: Cyber-physical systems, honeypots, threat intelligence

1.   Introduction

There is growing evidence that attackers, whether individual miscreants, hactivists, terrorists or state-sponsored actors, are increasingly targeting industrial control systems via Internet-connected computers to wreak havoc on critical infrastructure assets [4, 6, 24, 30, 47, 49, 54]. According to recent U.S. government reports [21, 48], attacks and intrusions as well as fingerprinting and scanning activities against U.S. critical infrastructure assets continue to rise. In 2013, more than 250 incidents were reported and analyzed by the U.S. Industrial Control Systems Cyber Emergency Response Team (ICS-CERT) [21],

© IFIP International Federation for Information Processing 2019
Published by Springer Nature Switzerland AG 2019
J. Staggs and S. Shenoi (Eds.): Critical Infrastructure Protection XIII, IFIP AICT 570, pp. 209–233, 2019.
https://doi.org/10.1007/978-3-030-34647-8_11

primarily in the enterprise networks of industrial companies. In 2017, the U.S. National Cybersecurity and Communications Integration Center (NCCIC) [48] detected 447 separate incidents and received roughly 106,000 reports of incidents affecting communications, enterprise and process control systems. In July 2017, officials from the U.S. Department of Homeland Security and the Federal Bureau of Investigation briefed a number of nuclear and other power systems operators on ongoing cyber threats [35].

The U.S. Department of Homeland Security reports that many incidents are not detected due to the lack of adequate detection and logging capabilities, and because details of detected incidents are insufficient. Much of the dramatic rise in incident reporting is the result of increased awareness, detection technologies and information sharing efforts across government and the private sector. It is unclear whether the prevailing industrial safety mechanisms are or will be adequate against complex attack vectors and varying attacker motivations. Current diagnostic tools are deficient at identifying compound exposure interactions, creating pathways by which control systems may be attacked or emergency and safety systems may be defeated or co-opted for use against control systems. This environment makes threat intelligence a vital area of cyber security research.

Several proposals have been made to adapt traditional information technology security techniques and systems to the operational technologies in cyberphysical system (CPS) environments. While these proposals may meet the common requirements of information and operational technologies, some are less suited than others to meeting the unique operational technology demands, especially "always on" availability and minimizing the negative impacts of changes. Patching firmware and rebooting on "Patch Tuesday" every month are not viable for many critical infrastructure systems. In these cases, a more passive approach can provide greater threat intelligence while minimizing the operation impact. Honeypots have been used very effectively in information technology environments. These deceptive systems show promise for defending operational technology environments.

Over the last fifteen years, honeypots – systems designed to be attacked in order to learn attacker tactics, techniques and motives – have been proposed, developed, improved and implemented with great success [3, 5, 9, 20, 25, 26, 29, 33, 36, 37, 44, 51], including in detecting and analyzing the celebrated Stuxnet attack [30]. By their nature, activity in honeypot systems is malicious, or at best unintended, except for any background replay traffic or activity. Because all system resources are devoted to intrusion discovery and the background activity should be relatively easy to filter out, higher levels of system logging and other instrumentation can be provided that are not always possible in production environments. Also, false positive and false negative intrusion alerts can be drastically reduced if not eliminated. For these reasons, honeypots are well suited to defending critical infrastructure systems.

However, recent years have seen only incremental advances in honeypot technologies. Many tools are starting to show their age, incompatible with current versions of operating systems and dependent software. Tried-and-true tools have had little need to change when supporting traditional information technology systems (e.g., virtual honeypots for Windows and Linux operating systems such as honeyd), but they are not necessarily suited to industrial control systems, SCADA (supervisory control and data acquisition) environments and large-scale networks of embedded devices that are coupled to physical processes.

The intelligence gathering capabilities of the proposed honeypot framework can dramatically enhance the security of industrial control networks. The framework is lightweight, highly scalable and designed specifically to protect industrial control systems.

Several requirements for next generation honeynet technologies are proposed in this chapter. Many of these requirements are already assumed by current technologies and approaches; however a formal set of requirements is necessary to drive metric-based advancement. A proof-of-concept architecture is presented to meet these requirements. The architecture links process simulation tools, an advanced network simulator and a complete monitoring system to present a complex attack surface for virtualized industrial cyber-physical systems.

The next six sections discuss industrial control systems, honeypots and honeynets, Security Onion, high-interaction honeypot data collection, virtual networks and the Shodan search engine.

2. Industrial Control Systems

Industrial control systems is a general term that describes engineering process support systems in industrial settings. Modern industrial control systems generally comprise physical components (e.g., gauges, pumps, valves and other sensors and actuators) and digital computer components (e.g., embedded systems). Because of their dual nature, these systems are often referred to as cyber-physical systems. Nearly all modern critical infrastructure assets (e.g., electric grids, water treatment facilities, transportation management systems, and oil and gas pipelines) are managed by cyber-physical systems, which are increasingly being interconnected using traditional information technology networks.

A SCADA system is a distributed system where digital devices connected to a process through sensors and actuators communicate over a network to drive a physical process to a desired state or set point. The idea of using computing devices to monitor and control physical systems is not new. Digital computers were used as early as 1959 when computer control was introduced at Texaco's Port Arthur refinery [55]. These early systems were supervisory in nature. Plant loops were controlled by conventional pneumatic or electrical controllers, but monitored and optimized by computers.

Programmable logic controllers, introduced by Modicon (now Schneider Electric) in the 1960s, were originally designed to replace circuits used in sequential control. Modern programmable logic controllers can implement control loops

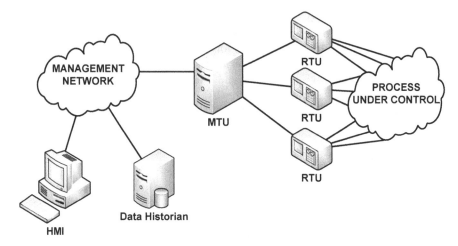

Figure 1. Typical process control network.

such as proportional-integral-derivative (PID) as well as logic functions and sophisticated algorithms.

Communications capabilities were introduced in programmable logic controllers as early as 1979. The Modbus protocol started as a proprietary protocol for Modicon equipment, but is now maintained by the Modbus Organization, a vendor-independent non-profit entity. The Modbus specifications [31] provide a simple communications mechanism for transmitting commands and data between a master terminal unit (MTU) at a control center and remote terminal units (RTUs) at field sites. The original protocol specification defines framing, encoding and error control for transmission over serial lines such as EIA-232 and EIA-485. It also defines standard operations and parameters for MTU-RTU interactions. More recently, the Modbus Organization defined a version of the protocol that uses TCP for transmission [31].

Most modern programmable logic controllers carry control and data messages over TCP/IP using industrial control protocols such as Modbus (widely used in the oil and gas industry), DNP3 (widely used in the electric power industry) and closely-related protocols such as Profibus and IEC 61850. Figure 1 shows a typical process control network and its supporting components.

JAMOD is used for prototyping Modbus-based SCADA systems. JAMOD is a Java Modbus library that supports three transport mechanisms: (i) TCP;(ii) UDP; and (iii) serial (UDP transport is experimental and is not part of the Modbus standard). JAMOD can be used to develop three key components of a SCADA system: (i) a Java class that emulates Modbus-capable programmable logic controllers with the four types of variables that Modbus defines: discrete inputs, discrete outputs, analog inputs and registers; (ii) control logic; and (iii) the process to be controlled. A typical operation cycle has a programmable logic controller read process variables, use the control logic to compute a control action and then pass it to a programmable logic controller output (e.g., an actuator) to perform an action on the process (e.g., close a valve). Using the JAMOD functionality and library of configuration settings and capabilities, many types of programmable logic controllers can be emulated in software.

3. Honeypots and Honeynets

Spitzner [44] defines a honeypot as a "security resource whose value lies in being probed, attacked or compromised." While Spitzner formally proposed honeypots in 1999 as trap systems for discovering information about attackers, credit is also assigned to Stoll, who published *The Cuckoo's Egg* in 1989 [45] and Cheswick, who authored "An evening with Berferd" in 1992 [8]. These two works describe how clever system administrators lured and studied attackers in order to understand their techniques and ultimately discover their identities. Since the formal creation of the Honeynet Project in 1999 [44], a number of technologies have been introduced to perform this type of intelligence gathering.

A honeypot is the most basic type of attacker trap – a non-production system that is set up to record user and software activities that are assumed to be malicious. Additional terminology has been coined following the "honey" theme to describe various levels of complexity and interactivity. The simplest is a "honeytoken" [43], which can be an unused file, registry key, database entry or email address with some level of additional monitoring to alert when the file is read, the key or database entry is modified or the email address is stolen and added to a spammer's target list.

A "honeyfarm" combines multiple honeypot systems in a cluster or server farm. A more complex setup, which includes honeypots or honeyfarms networked together with out-of-band management and monitoring systems, is referred to as a "honeynet." A honeynet is a complete system of systems with specific goals of attacker control and data collection. In order to fully monitor and control hacker interactions with a number of components in a honeyfarm, a specialized pass-through chokepoint system called a "honeywall" is deployed.

A common way to classify honeypot technologies is according to their levels of interactions with attackers. A honeytoken is generally a low-interaction system that simply waits for someone to come along and access it, upon which it triggers an alarm. Other low-interaction honeypots provide some responses to attacker stimuli. A common low-interaction honeypot tool is honeyd [37], which can emulate thousands of networked systems by faking IP addresses and listening on various ports. It provides various banners to attackers who scan the IPs and ports, and it may launch other services and scripts in order to customize responses.

High-interaction honeypots are often deployed as fully functional operating systems within virtual machines or on "bare metal." Virtual machines offer the advantage of being able to scale up more honeypots while limiting the hardware resources that are required. They also offer a means for taking snapshots of system state and rolling back the honeypot systems after compromises. However, they cannot be scaled beyond a handful of systems.

In order to support the management of a honeynet and contain attackers that break into honeypots, a modified approach to a firewall – called a "honeywall" is employed. Although several systems or tools can be used to construct a honeywall, Honeywall, developed by the Honeynet Project, is a specific system build with supporting tools on a single CD-ROM that runs as a live operating system (i.e., read-only). Two major versions of Honeywall have been released – Eeyore and Roo. Honeywall Roo [7] was designed to embody the requirements for GenIII honeynet technologies (discussed later in this chapter). Note that the general term, honeywall, is used to define the proposed data control and collection gateway system.

The first explicit requirement – data control – for a honeynet is to ensure that a compromised honeypot system does not cause harm to other systems in the network. One of the main concerns with deploying a honeypot is the liability and legality of deploying a known-vulnerable system that is intended to be hacked. As stated by Cheswick [8], "[d]ata control always takes priority over data capture." Specific requirements include having both automated and manual control mechanisms and two-deep protection to safeguard against the failure of any one control.

Honeywall Roo is designed to work on a system with three physical network interface cards. Two network cards are configured to bridge two networks, one is the upstream connection to the Internet and the other is the honeynet. The third network card is designated for connections to manage the system and is "out of band" from the other two networks.

Honeywall Roo handles data control using iptables for routing and firewall functions and `snort_inline`, a tool that is no longer actively supported. The `snort_inline` tool is a modified version of Snort[41], an open-source intrusion detection system, that reads packets from iptables and, based on the configured rules, updates the firewall to drop unwanted connections. Note that iptables is configured to provide rate limits for connections outbound from the honeynet to minimize the effects of denial-of-service attacks. As described later, the proposed approach incorporates these design elements, but also makes some significant improvements.

The second explicit requirement for GenIII honeynets is data capture. Capture is the recording of all (or as much as possible) activity in a honeynet. This includes system activity as well all the data entering and leaving the honeynet. An important part of the data capture requirement is that it should be done "without attackers knowing they are being watched" [19].

The third closely related requirement for honeynets is information sharing between disparate honeynets in a standardized way. This supports a community via the disclosure of pertinent threat information. It can lead to shared details about specific malware or targeted attacks from advanced attackers that can benefit other organizations. Honeywall Roo supports data captures and analyses in a number of ways. The primary method is via two Snort processes that listen on the bridge interface, one configured to perform full packet captures and the other configured to match traffic against the enabled rules to generate alerts. It also provides Argus [39], a network flow processing tool that provides connection summaries and statistics such as bandwidth and packets per second for each observed network flow. This data is tracked in a database managed by Hflow2 so that complete network sessions of flows that match a Snort signature can be reviewed in a web-based tool called Walleye.

Although Honeywall Roo provides excellent support for GenIII honeynets along with a menu-driven system-wide configuration capability [1], there are several problems with the current distribution that render it unusable. The first problem is that Honeywall Roo is based on Fedora Core v3, which reached its end-of-life in January 2006. It also uses Snort v2.6 (which has no available rulesets) and `snort_inline` for data control (which is no longer supported). For these reasons alone, the deployment of Honeywall Roo is ill-advised. Additionally, the Walleye web-based management and analysis interface must be run on the honeywall system, but it only enables data from the single honeywall system to be collected and reviewed. It is not currently possible to separate data control, data capture and data analysis functions on different systems.

A key contribution of this research is a honeywall system design that provides much-improved data analysis capabilities while meeting the data control requirement.

4. Security Onion

Several advanced intrusion detection and network security monitoring techniques and tools [2] can be leveraged to study honeynet data, especially when dealing with unknown attacks. Security Onion is a Linux distribution that combines many tools in a single platform to support out-of-the-box network security monitoring capabilities.

Security Onion provides a network sensor and storage system with utilities for PCAP recording and manipulation, stream identification and flow analysis, passive host identification, payload parsing and signature-based intrusion detection. Two core tools included with Security Onion are Snort and Argus, similar to Honeywall Roo. However, Security Onion offers many advanced management tools and a slew of analysis tools that make the difficult task of network security analysis more manageable.

A significant feature of Security Onion is its three-tier architecture that provides separation and secure communications between sensors, the server and the client. Security Onion Sensor provides applications, libraries and kernel modules for performing full network data captures. Network streams are fed to Bro, Snort or Suricata, Argus and others for processing against policies and signatures that can be updated daily. Security Onion Server provides centralized storage and processing for many sensors. Alerts and connection summary data are written to a MySQL database. Apache hosts multiple web-based applications for presenting data to analysts. Security Onion Client provides the front-end graphical user interface and command-line tools for processing PCAP files and analyzing network flows. In addition to the Sguil monitoring tool, the Security Onion Client includes Wireshark and NetworkMiner for browsing through network traces and reviewing embedded artifacts. Together with the web-based analysis and visualization tools of the ELK stack (Elasticsearch, Logstash and Kibana), tremendous capabilities are provided for network data analysis in an environment that is much more scalable and manageable than Honeywall Roo.

However, Security Onion is not designed to control a honeynet in an in-line deployment – it supports network data collection on a receive-only network interface card connected to a SPAN port or network tap. Another contribution of this research is a design for deploying Security Onion in an in-line manner.

5.   High-Interaction Honeypot Data Collection

A full packet capture in a network is invaluable, but it does not offer complete visibility of system activity. Just as network and systems administrators have migrated from cleartext to encrypted protocols (e.g., from Telnet to SSH), so have attackers who often connect to vulnerable sshd systems or use stolen or guessed user credentials to gain access. Once in, the attackers install their own, sometimes highly modified, versions of sshd or other encrypted remote access tools. This is done deliberately to obfuscate attacks from conventional network monitoring.

The Honeynet Project provides a solution to this problem in a tool called Sebek [18]. Sebek runs on a target honeypot system and collects attacker keystrokes and filesystem access data. Because this is done at the end node, it is possible to view and process data after it has been decrypted by the network software. This provides a critical monitoring capability that is not possible with network-only approaches. Sebek operates stealthily – like a rootkit, it runs in kernel space on a honeypot, hides from users and sends logs covertly to a Sebek server.

However, Sebek is detectable as an unlinked kernel module and because network statistics are increased significantly when keystroke logs are transmitted. Fortunately, many of these shortcomings have been addressed in other tools. For example, Qebek [42] adds hooks to the Qemu system emulator and Ether [13] does the same for Xen. These tools provide the necessary stealth logging in honeynets by addressing data capture in virtual machines.

6.   Virtual Networks with IMUNES

Virtual networks of communicating nodes can be generated quickly using the Integrated Multiprotocol Network Emulator and Simulator (IMUNES), a general-purpose network simulation architecture for large-scale real-time experiments [38]. Built on FreeBSD, the simulator offers kernel-level network stack virtualization without the overhead associated with frameworks that make extensive use of virtual machines. This is achieved using virtual nodes in chroot jails that have the same capabilities as the underlying kernel. Each IMUNES node can run an independent replica of the FreeBSD network stack as well as unique instances of user-level applications.

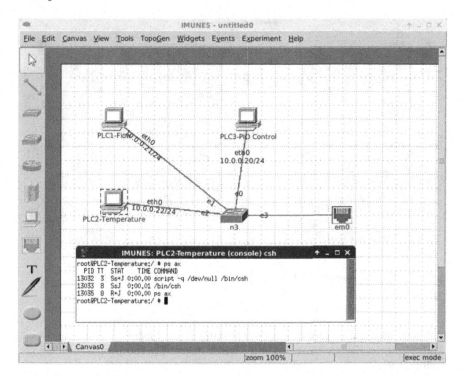

Figure 2. IMUNES graphical user interface.

IMUNES has a user-friendly graphical user interface (Figure 2) that enables arbitrary network topologies to be designed and deployed rapidly. The interface provides seven basic building blocks: (i) workstations; (ii) servers; (iii) hubs; (iv) switches; (v) routers; (vi) physical communications links (i.e., wires); and (vii) connectors for associating physical networks on host systems with virtual networks. Each building block can be reconfigured quickly by right-clicking a node and modifying it in a pop-up window.

Figure 3 shows a more complex model of an advanced metering infrastructure (AMI). IMUNES models can scale to 10,000+ nodes on a moderately powered workstation.

After a network topology has been defined and configured in IMUNES, the simulation is instantiated and executed. During the execution, it is possible to open a shell on any node and run installed applications. Wireshark and the Links web browser run by default on any node. Router nodes use Quagga to fully emulate routers while server nodes can be configured to run DHCP, an HTTP server and other services. It is then possible, by manipulating configuration scripts in IMUNES, to install additional FreeBSD packages in the root virtual filesystem used by each node. This mechanism has been used in this research to incorporate Java and JAMOD, additional industrial control protocols

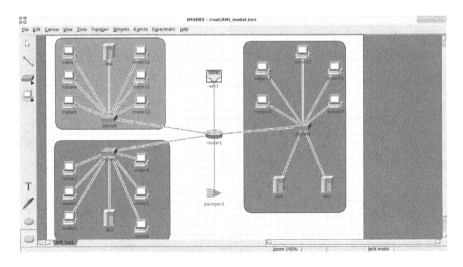

Figure 3. Advanced metering infrastructure model.

and network security tools for system monitoring and logging, including Sebek. Additional details are provided later when discussing the proposed honeynet architecture.

7.   Shodan Search Engine

The Shodan search engine (www.shodanhq.com) finds Internet-facing systems of certain types (e.g., by manufacturer, operating system, application and configuration) using web-crawling and system fingerprinting techniques. The crawlers scan the Internet for ports 80 (HTTP) and 443 (HTTPS) like most search engines, but also port 22 (SSH), port 53 (DNS), port 161 (SNMP), port 502 (Modbus/TCP) and many others. They query the ports for banners and elicit other responses (e.g., performing an SNMP-walk), and display the results in a searchable format.

For example, if the search term "Debian port:22" is entered, results for thousands of systems that are listening on port 22 and run the Debian operating system are presented. Shodan then creates clickable links to the IP addresses and, if available, provides latitude and longitude coordinates from GeoIP data.

When Shodan scans an IP address and finds an open Modbus port 502, it follows up with two Modbus queries to identify the system via its device ID and other string outputs. Often, the results show "DEVICE FUNCTION FAILURE." However, a quick search using "port:502" can actually discover systems, such as when they return responses like "Schneider Electric BMX P342020." Details from the whois database for IP addresses are also provided in the Shodan results, letting a searcher know, for example, that one such device is available on AT&T's U-Verse home fiber optic service. This may suggest that the programmable logic controller is at a home with a smart meter installed. A click on the GeoIP coordinates takes the searcher to a Google Maps satellite image of the home.

The Shodan search engine is powerful and it actively scours the Internet. As discussed later, these facts should be considered when building cyber-physical system honeynets.

8. Requirements and Prototype Architecture

This section presents the architecture of a next generation hybrid cyber-physical honeynet.

8.1 Next Generation Honeynet Requirements

The formal requirements adopted by the Honeynet Project for GenIII honeynets (third-generation technology) incorporate the essentials of successful honeypotting [19]. These are: (i) data control; (ii) data capture; and (iii) data collection. Additionally, several informal requirements are taken for granted or included as sub-requirements. While these requirements are certainly met by the most successful honeynets, they are not formally specified in the literature.

Therefore, three additional requirements are proposed for next generation honeynets: (iv) realism; (v) scalability; and (vi) detection resistance. These requirements are met by the proof-of-concept design; but they are likely met by other technologies as well. The three additional requirements are essential to updating honeynet deployments to make them viable as an additional network defense layer and as valuable research tools:

- **Realism:** GenIV honeynets should appear to would-be attackers as real production systems that are worth investigating. This requirement is prioritized based on the types of attacks that are desired to be attracted. Some systems on the Internet are very clearly set up as honeypots. While these systems may be effective at catching automated malware and initial reconnaissance scans, they would not fool active attackers who are seeking targets for manual exploitation. An attacker could find such systems by searching for "honeyd" in Shodan and avoid their IP addresses altogether.

  Realism in the context of industrial control systems suggests that a honeypot should have basic services such as HTTP, SSH and Telnet, but that the fake programmable logic controllers should be indistinguishable from real ones in network scans. This would mean constructing systems with the same open ports and providing the same responses that real systems provide to Shodan.

  Another aspect of realism is consistency. Specifically, each service must be realistic and the services running together in a honeynet must be consistent. An example honeypot system that is easily discoverable by Shodan would present a Microsoft IIS FTP server on port 21, Debian SSH server listening on port 22 and an open webserver on port 80 that lists pages for all manner of PHP and database management tools (e.g., different versions of `phpmyadmin` running simultaneously). Potential attackers would avoid this system because it is obviously a honeypot.

CryPLH [5] effectively imitates a Siemens S7 programmable logic controller by providing proper SNMP responses, HTTP and HTTPS pages and an emulation of the SIMATIC Step7 protocol over ISO-TSAP. The techniques used for reverse engineering a real programmable logic controller to create a honeypot are easily replicated for other cyber-physical systems. Another approach involves using Ettercap to record traffic to a real programmable logic controller and then automatically generate a system that provides the same or similar responses [50].

- **Scalability:** GenIV honeynets scale to realistic sizes. Attackers would expect to see dozens or hundreds of programmable logic controllers, not just one or two. However, when deploying full virtual machines it is difficult to meet the realism and consistency requirements – especially if 100 systems in the network are seen to have the same hostname or other identical features. Thus, scalability implies not simply running many virtual systems in the honeynet, but configuring diversity in the deployed systems, possibly by automatically changing configuration files that dictate their "personality" or appearance in the network.

- **Detection Resistance:** GenIV honeynets should not be detectable by attackers. In the official requirements for GenIII honeynets [19], a subrequirement under data control says to "control connections in a manner as difficult as possible to be detected by attackers." Because of the significance of this need and the tools and methods by which it may be met, this item is upgraded to a stand-alone requirement.

  Much research has focused on detecting the presence of a virtual machine versus a physical computer. It has also been shown that many of the GenIII honeynet technologies are identifiable by attackers. For example, `honeyd` and Sebek are technologies used exclusively in honeynets and are key components for meeting the monitoring and data capture requirements. However, research has shown that, with some effort, these systems can be identified by attackers, possibly redirecting them to other production systems [17, 37].

  Thus, a critical requirement for GenIV honeynets is detection resistance. Artifacts are bound to be present in any production system. However, the artifacts should, by design, present themselves in the absolute minimum way. For example, `honeyd` users must replace the initial configuration to hide basic facts that are presented by default, such as known timestamps of filesystem artifacts, protocol unimplemented functions and service banners that present the string "`honeyd`." Detection resistance also stipulates that software used in honeynets must be updated to address new research that publishes how to fingerprint a service such as Sebek, which led to the release of version 3.

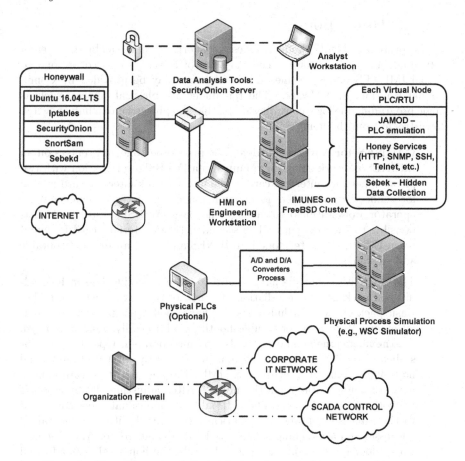

Figure 4. Next generation industrial control system honeynet architecture.

8.2 Proposed Honeynet Design

The proposed honeynet architecture has five components: (i) honeyfarm, comprising a number of virtual honeypots generated by the IMUNES network emulator; (ii) physical honeypot components (e.g., programmable logic controllers); (iii) simulated physical process, which is kept separate from the cyber components of the network; (iv) modernized honeywall running updated data collection tools and providing control of the environment; and (v) management network segment providing separated data analysis tools and access for honeynet operators to connect in an out-of-band manner to the various components. Figure 4 shows the proposed next generation industrial control system honeynet architecture.

8.3   Honeypots

The prototype GenIV honeynet design incorporates a scalable number of individual honeypot systems. The majority of these systems correspond to virtual IMUNES nodes. Some additional hosts may be provided by Qemu, Virtual Box and/or VMware. The remainder are physical devices, such as single programmable logic controller units, that are plugged into a hub or switch downstream from the honeywall.

■ **IMUNES for Virtual Nodes:** The prototype honeynet centers on an IMUNES network emulator running on a FreeBSD workstation with two physical network interface cards. The first network interface card is used for connections from the honeypot management network segment (e.g., operator workstations) to manage the base FreeBSD system, which is invisible to the honeynet. The second network interface card is bound to an Ethernet adapter node in IMUNES and given an Internet-routable address range.

The IMUNES script `prepare_vroot_10.sh` was modified to include additional packages for installation in `vroot` of the virtual network nodes. Basic packages were included, such as `bash` shell, Quagga for router emulation and Wireshark for troubleshooting. Additionally, `netcat`, `honeyd`, `ftelnetd`, `kojoney` and other tools were incorporated. OpenJDK was installed as the Java runtime environment. The script prepared the virtual node filesystems in `chroot` jails. IMUNES was used to create default network configurations for the nodes. After adjusting the first node's network with a publicly-available IP address, additional nodes connected to the same subnet were automatically configured with incremental IP addresses and a matching subnet mask and default route. After the network topology was configured in IMUNES, the honeywall was adjusted to enable packets to be forwarded to this range of IP addresses.

IMUNES meets the scalability requirement by enabling additional tools to be quickly added to each `vhost` node in the environment. As a honeypot operator decides to expand or modify the services offered, additional packages can be installed on all `vhost` nodes or individual files may be added instantly while the system is operating. These files are created by IMUNES in each virtual node filesystem; changes in each node are isolated to the node, including file deletions, additions and modifications. Additional nodes may be added by simply dragging and dropping nodes into the network topology. This makes it possible to rapidly modify the state of the honeynet and maintain customizations unique to each node or groups of nodes. This is far more manageable than running fully separate virtual machines; indeed, it is a key benefit of the proposed approach.

■ **IMUNES Honey Tools and Realism:** The goal of the proof-of-concept honeynet is to obtain information about threats to critical infrastructure systems. While providing general-purpose honeypots with a variety of services to entice attackers, the main focus is on attracting attackers interested in launching Modbus attacks. In order to meet the realism requirement, supplemental services typically found in cyber-physical systems must be incorporated. Full services such as `telnetd` and `sshd` can run on each `vhost`, providing high-interaction honeypot functionality.

The initial proof-of-concept experiments sought to emulate only a realistic network fingerprint. Therefore, it was decided to implement `ftelnetd` (fake Telnet) and `kojoney` (fake SSH) [10]. The two services present the usual banners to attackers upon initial connection and proceed to log the usernames and passwords; the login attempts always fail. Web-based management tools were scraped from real programmable logic controllers and hosted in the IMUNES nodes using `lighttpd`.

The first step in this effort is to mimic the TCP/IP stack options used by the real devices, which is accomplished using FreeBSD `pf`. Also, by scraping any web-based management interfaces, these tools can be recreated and deployed with `lighttp` in running IMUNES nodes.

Another aspect of realism and enticement is the context in which a honeypot is deployed. A honeypot must blend into its surroundings. Thus, the prototype honeynet was deployed on an Internet-reachable subnet of the university network. If the goal is to masquerade as an oil refinery or water treatment facility, the honeynet should certainly not be located in the network address block of a university's computer science department. A realistic honeynet should be deployed in the IP address space of an actual industrial facility to maintain realism and consistency. This is accomplished using a layer-2 virtual private network to forward traffic bound to an unused IP address range at an asset owner's site to the honeynet laboratory environment, which would be invisible to the attacker.

- **JAMOD for Modbus Slave Devices:** JAMOD is a critical component of the honeynet design because it can emulate a production cyber-physical system. The library enables customized ladder logic to run on multiple IMUNES virtual nodes, simulating master and slave devices in a working implementation of the Modbus/TCP protocol. A master program on one node is configured to connect to slave programs on other nodes, querying and setting various data registers. Slave devices can be configured to be "vulnerable" to remote queries and set points to be writeable by any remote master process. Attackers may then interact with any of the slave devices in the network by sending Modbus/TCP commands to the open ports of the nodes. It is also important to write JAMOD code that implements Modbus functions such as Slave ID, which are used in Shodan queries and by other scanning methods. Other tools such as Conpot [9], OpenPLC [40] and `opendnp3` [11] can also be deployed at IMUNES nodes to emulate other programmable logic controller platforms.

■ **HMI on a Windows XP Virtual Machine:** Documented attacks on industrial control systems, including Stuxnet [14] and others, often attempt to compromise the human-machine interfaces (HMIs) used by operators to manage cyber-physical components. A human-machine interface running on a full Windows XP virtual machine was employed to meet the realism and detection resistance requirements; this is not much different from what is used by other honeypots. The proof-of-concept honeynet has a custom interface built in LabVIEW [32]. The virtual machine executes on the same FreeBSD cluster that hosts IMUNES, but it is managed by the VirtualBox hypervisor.

■ **Physical Switch/PLCs and Scalability:** Another important design element incorporated in the prototype honeynet is a switch or hub downstream from the honeywall so that multiple systems can be added to the honeynet quickly and easily. This also provides a rapid manual data control mechanism – a system can be physically separated from the network if needed. The design element contributes to scalability because additional devices can be added to the honeynet without modifying the honeywall significantly; only the iptables rules need to be updated in order to forward traffic to the new honeypots.

The initial experiments employed a Direct Logic programmable logic controller. This device provides an Ethernet connection and includes a web server on port 80 and Modbus listener on port 502. The web server provides access to a configuration interface that requires no authentication so that values can be set via an HTTP form using POST commands. The Modbus listener provides responses to valid queries. All network traffic to and from the programmable logic controller is automatically recorded by the honeywall system without any extra configuration effort.

8.4   Simulated Physical Process

While simply positioning a Windows XP virtual machine in the cloud or connecting a typical programmable logic controller to the Internet would certainly draw attacks, they would not attract advanced threat actors who specifically target industrial processes. The honeynet architecture leverages a research simulation to construct a physical process that can be controlled via digital automation. This method for representing a real physical process is a significant contribution to the honeynet literature. The deployment of simulation software is shielded in a unique way from attacks – by converting signals from digital to analog and back again, which emulates real-world sensors and actuators.

Established methodologies and tools are available for modeling and simulation: (i) continuous process control systems, which typically involve differential equations and have real-time constraints; (ii) discrete systems, which keep a process under control using feedback from sensors to send commands to actuators; and (iii) communications networks, which use TCP/IP or direct-link serial lines. While the distributed nature and communications of a large-scale cyber-

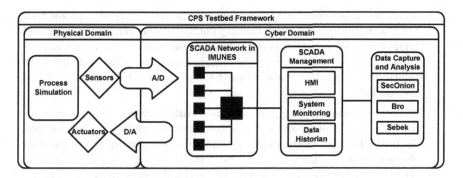

Figure 5. Cyber-physical system testbed for simulation and analysis.

physical system are handled by IMUNES, the honeynet implements a process simulator with an API for programmed sensors and actuators associated with real-world process components.

Models of power system buses and breakers (e.g., IEEE test buses [15]) have been created using software packages such as MATLAB and Simulink. Human-machine interface and power system simulators have been developed in LabVIEW [32] or acquired from entities such as Western Services Corporation [53]. Modelica, an object-oriented, equation-based language has been used to model complex physical systems [12, 16]. However, modeling and simulation tools do not always scale well and do not prioritize the goal of mimicking a physical process in a manner that deceives attackers.

Several testbeds have been developed for modeling and simulating physical systems such as electricity generation and transmission facilities, as well as cyber-physical systems that provide virtual representations of physical components [27, 28]. Simulators require modifications or new interfaces that share control and sensor feedback information with the virtual network. Simulations developed using MATLAB with Simulink [23, 46] and other platforms can be adapted for this purpose. Simulink modules provide the physical equations to create virtual systems that masquerade as a real physical process to attackers. Programmed transformations implementing digital-to-analog (D/A) and analog-to-digital (A/D) conversions provide an interface and convert data from the physical simulator to the cyber (relay) domain, enabling the modeled physical process to remain separate and unexposed, except via instrumentation. Figure 5 shows the cyber-physical system testbed for simulation and analysis.

8.5   Honeywall Design

Three novel aspects of the honeywall design are: (i) honeynet control; (ii) honeynet data capture; and (iii) honeynet data analysis:

- **Honeynet Control:** A GenIII honeynet should not be compromised by attackers to wreak more havoc on other unsuspecting users. However, the honeynet should also capture the full range of attacker techniques, which often involve making outbound connections to command-and-control servers that contain tools for download. Outbound connections from the honeypots to the Internet must be permitted, but automatic and manual intervention mechanisms must cut off attackers if they go too far.

Honeywall Roo was designed to be used with a layer-2 bridge interface to provide data control and data capture, sniffing traffic as it is forwarded from the Internet to the honeynet internals. Support for in-line monitoring and control using a network bridge interface is not supported by Security Onion. Nevertheless, it is possible to install the Security Onion Sensor package and tools such as network bridge support and SnortSam [22] to provide data capture and data control. The honeywall provides this control using Linux `netfilter` capabilities via iptables and SnortSam, a tool that dynamically adds firewall rules based on Snort alerts. The design incorporates an Ubuntu Server v16.04-LTS on a hardware configuration that mirrors that of Honeywall Roo and requires three network interface cards. The first network interface card provides the management connections; the other two cards are then bridged together using `bridge-utils` at layer 2 as in the case of Honeywall Roo.

- **Honeynet Data Capture:** The Security Onion Sensor package was installed on the Ubuntu system in order to perform data capture and collection. After manually modifying the network configuration for bridging two interfaces, the `br0` interface was selected to monitor inbound and outbound traffic on the bridge. This enables the installed tools to operate in an in-line manner, although this configuration is officially unsupported by Security Onion. The `sebekd` tool was then installed from the Honeywall Roo distribution with the necessary modifications to run on the Ubuntu platform. A Perl script was written to parse the `sebekd` data received by the honeywall without modification. The Sebek client was ported to FreeBSD and compiled into the honeypot kernel. It was then made available on every `vhost` node running in IMUNES.

- **Honeynet Data Analysis:** Data analysis employs a second system configured and installed with the Security Onion Server and Client packages. The system provides the database and web-based applications, and receives data from a sensor over an encrypted SSH tunnel. This enables data collection, offline storage and detailed analysis to be performed without impacting the honeywall. Additionally, multiple honeywall sensors may be deployed across a network and data can be securely aggregated for analysis at a primary system. This design supports the scalability requirement while maintaining good data control.

Because the new honeywall analysis system includes Bro and ELSA [34], analyses can leverage many more queries than are supported by Walleye, which relies entirely on Snort to generate intrusion alerts. However, to further support analyses, several customized Snort signatures were incorporated to alert to connections to open ports (e.g., 22, 23, 80 and 502), as well as connection attempts (e.g., SYN packets without the full connection-establishment handshakes indicative of scans) with messages such as "HONEYNET Connection established to port 80." This enables quick investigations of all attacker connections whether or not the connections match intrusion signatures. Analysis can be performed on all signatures matching "HONEYNET" and the sessions can be extracted quickly from the stored PCAP files via CapMe for offline examination using tools such as Wireshark or NetworkMiner.

9. Results and Analysis

A prototype honeynet conforming to the proposed architecture was constructed and deployed on the university development network from whence it was exposed directly to the Internet. Attackers began probing the honeynet almost immediately – the first scan was detected just 19 minutes after the Internet connection was made. The results presented in this section do not provide new insights into attacker tactics or techniques; rather, they demonstrate the utility of the prototype.

9.1 Modbus Scanning via Shodan

Within two days of deploying the honeynet on an IP address range that was not used on the Internet for several years, the Shodan web crawler engines found the honeynet, scanned it for the primary list of ports – including Modbus port 502 – and performed fingerprinting techniques (e.g., banner grabbing) to make data about the honeynet available in its search results.

Over the course of two weeks, the honeynet received connections from most of the systems `census1.shodan.io` through `census12.shodan.io`. These systems are located in the United States based on GeoIP and `whois` database records.

The fact that Modbus was scanned so quickly suggests that attackers can reliably search for industrial control system victims before performing any direct system reconnaissance or fingerprinting them. This should be taken into account when planning honeypot deployments as well as operational network defenses. No other systems connected to port 502 during the two-week period of the experiments.

9.2 Brute Force Login Attacks

The `ftelnetd` tool logged the usernames and passwords presented by attackers during Telnet connection attempts. More than 22,300 Telnet-only logins were attempted from 333 unique IP addresses in 55 countries. Because the connections may have come from Tor network exit nodes or addresses from

Table 1.   Top ten brute force Telnet attacks by country.

Source Country	IP Addresses	Login Attempts
China	356	6,456
India	59	1,927
Viet Nam	48	1,245
Mexico	35	1,414
United States	31	1,321
Columbia	24	723
Malaysia	20	1,425
Turkey	18	506
Korea	16	67
Russia (tied)	8	1,394
Taiwan (tied)	8	8

other proxies and privacy networks, correctly attributing the countries of origin and unique attackers would be difficult to impossible.

Table 1 provides a breakdown of the Telnet connection attempts during the two weeks of experiments. The most login attempts (744) came from a single IP address in Belarus. It is notable that only 419 distinct username-password combinations were recorded; many of them were attempted hundreds of times. Since automated attack tools tend to draw from the massive stolen username-password lists posted on the Internet, the small number of distinct username-password combinations suggests that a specialized list of login credentials has been tailored for industrial control systems that may be reachable via their Telnet ports while also listening on Modbus port 502.

Table 2.   Most common usernames and passwords.

Username	Count	Password	Count
admin	2,229	password	709
root	2,138	<blank>	612
cusadmin	343	admin	572
MGR	253	1234	455
support	168	12345	393
FIELD	96	123456	385
Administrator	91	Root	248
MANAGER	77	smcadmin	217
guest	60	dreambox	195
OPERATOR	55	highspeed	178

Table 2 lists the most common usernames and passwords used in the Telnet connection attempts. Note that limited results are reported here because future research with the honeynet would be impacted by the publication of detailed information. Published information about the honeynet would likely lead potential attackers to deliberately change their tactics.

10. Conclusions

Honeypots and other deception technologies have long been used to study malicious activity in networks, but clear requirements for honeypots that implement active defenses of industrial control systems have not been discussed. Existing honeynet requirements as well as new requirements for next generation honeynets specified in this chapter have been employed to develop a realistic, scalable and detection-resistant GenIV honeynet with an advanced honeywall and three-tier data collection subnet. The architecture incorporates a physical process simulation that is lacking in existing honeynets for cyber-physical-systems. It also supports the inclusion of additional physical systems to present a robust, hybrid cyber-physical target for attackers. Indeed, deployments of this honeynet architecture could provide valuable advanced threat intelligence for securing critical infrastructure assets.

References

[1] F. Abbasi and R. Harris, Experiences with a Generation III virtual honeynet, *Proceedings of the Australasian Telecommunications Networks and Applications Conference*, 2009.

[2] R. Bejtlich, *The Tao of Network Security Monitoring: Beyond Intrusion Detection*, Addison-Wesley, Boston, Massachusetts, 2004.

[3] J. Briffaut, J. Lalande and C. Toinard, Security and results of a large-scale high-interaction honeypot, *Journal of Computers*, vol. 4(5), pp. 395–404, 2009.

[4] C. Bronk and E. Tikk-Ringas, The cyber attack on Saudi Aramco, *Survival*, vol. 55(2), pp. 81–96, 2013.

[5] D. Buza, F. Juhasz, G. Miru, M. Felegyhazi and T. Holczer, CryPLH: Protecting smart energy systems from targeted attacks with a PLC honeypot, *Proceedings of the Second International Workshop on Smart Grid Security*, pp. 181–192, 2014.

[6] E. Byres, The air gap: SCADA's enduring security myth, *Communications of the ACM*, vol 56(8), pp. 29–31, 2013.

[7] G. Chamales, The Honeywall CD-ROM, *IEEE Security and Privacy*, vol. 2(2), pp. 77–79, 2004.

[8] B. Cheswick, An evening with Berferd in which a cracker is lured, endured and studied, *Proceedings of the Winter USENIX Conference*, pp. 163–174, 1992.

[9] Conpot Development Team, Conpot ICS/SCADA Honeypot (`conpot. org`), 2019.

[10] J. Coret, Kojoney – A Honeypot for the SSH Service (`kojoney.source forge.net`), 2006.

[11] I. Darwish, O. Igbe and T. Saadawi, Experimental and theoretical modeling of DNP3 attacks on smart grids, *Proceedings of the Thirty-Sixth IEEE Sarnoff Symposium*, pp. 155–160, 2015.

[12] P. Derler, E. Lee and A. Vincentelli, Modeling cyber-physical systems, *Proceedings of the IEEE*, vol. 100(1), pp. 13–28, 2012.

[13] A. Dinaburg, P. Royal, M. Sharif and W. Lee, Ether: Malware analysis via hardware virtualization extensions, *Proceedings of the Fifteenth ACM Conference on Computer and Communications Security*, pp. 51–62, 2008.

[14] N. Falliere, L. O'Murchu and E. Chien, W32.Stuxnet Dossier, Version 1.4, Symantec, Mountain View, California, 2011.

[15] C. Grigg, P. Wong, P. Albrecht, R. Allan, M. Bhavaraju, R. Billinton, Q. Chen, C. Fong, S. Haddad, S. Kuruganty, W. Li, R. Mukerji, D. Patton, N. Rau, D. Reppen, A. Schneider, M. Shahidehpour and C. Singh, The IEEE reliability test system-1996, A report prepared by the reliability test system task force of the application of probability methods subcommittee, *IEEE Transactions on Power Systems*, vol. 14(3), pp. 1010–1020, 1999.

[16] D. Henriksson and H. Elmqvist, Cyber-physical systems modeling and simulation with Modelica, *Proceedings of the Eighth Modelica Conference*, pp. 502–509, 2011.

[17] T. Holz and F. Raynal, Detecting honeypots and other suspicious environments, *Proceedings of the Sixth Annual IEEE SMC Information Assurance Workshop*, pp. 29–36, 2005.

[18] Honeynet Project, Know Your Enemy: Sebek – A Kernel Based Data Capture Tool (`old.honeynet.org/papers/sebek.pdf`), 2003.

[19] Honeynet Project, Honeynet Definitions, Requirements and Standards (`old.honeynet.org/alliance/requirements.html`), 2004.

[20] P. Huang, C. Yang and T. Ahn, Design and implementation of a distributed early warning system combined with intrusion detection system and honeypot, *Proceedings of the International Conference on Hybrid Information Technology*, pp. 232–238, 2009.

[21] Industrial Control Systems Cyber Emergency Response Team (ICS-CERT), Trends in Incident Response in 2013, Idaho Falls, Idaho, 2013.

[22] F. Knobbe, SnortSam – A firewall blocking agent for Snort (`www.snort sam.net`), 2001.

[23] V. Koganti, Cyber-Attack Simulation in MATLAB/Simulink, M.S. Thesis, Department of Computer Science, University of Idaho, Moscow, Idaho, 2017.

[24] B. Krebs, Cyber incident blamed for nuclear power plant shutdown, *The Washington Post*, June 5, 2008.

[25] S. Kuman, S. Gros and M. Mikuc, An experiment in using IMUNES and Conpot to emulate honeypot control networks, *Proceedings of the Fortieth International Convention on Information and Communications Technology, Electronics and Microelectronics,* pp. 1262–1268, 2017.

[26] T. Lengyel, J. Neumann, S. Maresca, B. Payne and A. Kiayias, Virtual machine introspection in a hybrid honeypot architecture, *Proceedings of the Fifth USENIX Workshop on Cyber Security Experimentation and Test,* 2012.

[27] J. Mahseredjian, V. Dinavahi, and J. Martinez, An overview of simulation tools for electromagnetic transients in power systems, *Proceedings of the IEEE Power Engineering Society General Meeting,* 2007.

[28] J. Mahseredjian, V. Dinavahi and J. Martinez, Simulation tools for electromagnetic transients in power systems: Overview and challenges, *IEEE Transactions on Power Delivery,* vol. 24(3), pp. 1657–1669, 2009.

[29] A. Mairh, D. Barik, K. Verma and D. Jena, Honeypot in network security: A survey, *Proceedings of the International Conference on Communications, Computing and Security,* pp. 600–605, 2011.

[30] S. McLaughlin, C. Konstantinou, X. Wang, L. Davi, A. Sadeghi, M. Maniatakos and R. Karri, The cybersecurity landscape in industrial control systems, *Proceedings of the IEEE,* vol 104(5), pp. 1039–1057, 2016.

[31] Modbus Organization, Modbus Application Protocol Specification, V1.1b3, Hopkinton, Massachusetts (www.modbus.org/specs.php), 2012.

[32] National Instruments, LabVIEW, Austin, Texas (www.ni.com/en-us/shop/labview.html), 2019.

[33] S. Nunes, Web Attack Risk Awareness with Lessons Learned from High Interaction Honeypots, M.S. Thesis, Information Networking Institute, Carnegie Mellon University, Pittsburgh, Pennsylvania, 2009.

[34] V. Paxson, Bro: A system for detecting network intruders in real-time, *Computer Networks,* vol. 31(23-24), pp. 2435–2463, 1999.

[35] N. Perlroth, Hackers are targeting nuclear facilities, Homeland Security Dept. and FBI say, *The New York Times,* July 6, 2017.

[36] V. Pothamsetty and M. Franz, SCADA HoneyNet Project: Building Honeypots for Industrial Networks (scadahoneynet.sourceforge.net), 2008.

[37] N. Provos, A virtual honeypot framework, *Proceedings of the Thirteenth Annual USENIX Security Symposium,* 2004.

[38] Z. Puljiz and M. Mikuc, IMUNES based distributed network emulator, *Proceedings of the International Conference on Software in Telecommunications and Computer Networks,* pp. 198–203, 2006.

[39] QoSient, Argus: Network Audit Record Generation and Utilization System, New York (qosient.com/argus), 2014.

[40] T. Rodrigues Alves, M. Buratto, F. de Souza and T. Rodrigues, OpenPLC: An open source alternative to automation, *Proceedings of the IEEE Global Humanitarian Technology Conference,* pp. 585–589, 2014.

[41] M. Roesch, Snort – Lightweight intrusion detection for networks, *Proceedings of the Thirteenth USENIX Conference on System Administration*, pp. 229–238, 1999.

[42] C. Song, B. Hay and J. Zhuge, Know Your Tools: Qebek – Conceal the monitoring, The Honeynet Project (`www.honeynet.org/sites/default/files/files/KYT-Qebek-final_v1.pdf`), 2010.

[43] L. Spitzner, Honeytokens: The other honeypot, *Symantec Connect* (`www.symantec.com/connect/articles/honeytokens-other-honeypot`), July 16, 2003.

[44] L. Spitzner, The Honeynet Project: Trapping the hackers, *IEEE Security and Privacy*, vol. 1(2), pp. 15–23, 2003.

[45] C. Stoll, *The Cuckoo's Egg: Tracking a Spy Through the Maze of Computer Espionage*, Doubleday New York, 1989.

[46] H. Tsai, C. Tu and Y. Su, Development of a generalized photovoltaic model using MATLAB/Simulink, *Proceedings of the World Congress on Engineering and Computer Science*, 2008.

[47] U.S. Department of Homeland Security, Common Cybersecurity Vulnerabilities in Industrial Control Systems, Washington, DC, 2011.

[48] U.S. Department of Homeland Security, NCCIC Year in Review 2017: Operation Cyber Guardian, Washington, DC (`www.us-cert.gov/sites/default/files/publications/NCCIC_Year_in_Review_2017_Final.pdf`), 2018.

[49] C. Valli and A. Woodward, SCADA security – Slowly circling a disaster area, *Proceedings of the International Conference on Security and Management*, pp. 613–617, 2009.

[50] T. Vollmer and M. Manic, Cyber-physical system security with deceptive virtual hosts for industrial control networks, *IEEE Transactions on Industrial Informatics*, vol. 10(2), pp. 1337–1347, 2014.

[51] S. Wade, SCADA Honeynets: The Attractiveness of Honeypots as Critical Infrastructure Security Tools for the Detection and Analysis of Advanced Threats, M.S. Thesis, Department of Electrical and Computer Engineering, Iowa State University, Ames, Iowa, 2011.

[52] D. Watson and J. Riden, The Honeynet Project: Data collection tools, infrastructure, archives and analysis, *Proceedings of the WOMBAT Workshop on Information Security Threats Data Collection and Sharing*, pp. 24–30, 2008.

[53] Western Services Corporation, Power Plant Simulation Overview, Frederick, Maryland (`www.ws-corp.com/default.asp?PageID=1&PageNavigation=Simulation-Overview`), 2019.

[54] K. Wilhoit, Who's really attacking your ICS equipment, *Trend Micro Security Intelligence Blog* (`blog.trendmicro.com/trendlabs-security-intelligence/whos-really-attacking-your-ics-devices`), March 15, 2013.

[55] T. Williams, Computer control technology – Past, present and probable future, *Transactions of the Institute of Measurement and Control*, vol 5(1), pp. 7–19, 1983.

Chapter 12

DYNAMIC REPAIR OF MISSION-CRITICAL APPLICATIONS WITH RUNTIME SNAP-INS

J. Peter Brady, Sergey Bratus and Sean Smith

Abstract   This chapter proposes a solution that provides reliable, non-disruptive updates to critical systems using a novel design pattern called a "snap-in," which is able to install replacement routines embedded in shared libraries during system execution. Most system updates are performed in a static or maintenance state. However, dynamically updating software reduces the time required for adding functionality and applying security upgrades. The proposed snap-in solution improves on previous work by adopting the novel approach of using the target's application binary interface to first load shared libraries that contain replacement routines into a running application, supplanting the original routines with replacement routines without having to modify the existing code. An automated toolkit is provided for scanning application binaries and determining where the replacement routines are to be added.

1.   Introduction

In 1992, researchers studied the software faults discovered during integration testing of the Voyager and Galileo spacecraft code at the Jet Propulsion Laboratory [17]. The bulk of the faults were directly attributed to errors in understanding or implementing requirements, and to miscommunications between development teams. Not surprisingly, "there's no such thing as a bug-free application" [32].

Not all faults in modern computing systems are found during internal integration and testing. As a result, faults found during field deployments become part of the maintenance cycle. Maintaining software during its lifetime is a significant and costly problem.

A NIST report [22] reveals that the costs to repair system defects increase rapidly after the requirements stage. Table 1, taken from the report, shows

© IFIP International Federation for Information Processing 2019
Published by Springer Nature Switzerland AG 2019
J. Staggs and S. Shenoi (Eds.): Critical Infrastructure Protection XIII, IFIP AICT 570, pp. 235–252, 2019.
https://doi.org/10.1007/978-3-030-34647-8_12

Table 1. Repair costs during various lifecycle stages.

Lifecycle Stage	Repair Cost
Requirements	$1x$
System Testing	$90x$
Installation Testing	$90x$ to $440x$
Acceptance Testing	$440x$
Operation and Maintenance	$470x$ to $880x$

that the cost of repairing a defect in the field is up to 880 times the cost of repair during the requirements stage (x denotes a normalized unit of cost).

Standard application maintenance generally has the following cycle:

- **Revision:** Decide what is to be changed, such as repairs based on bug reports from users or the addition of new functionality.

- **Development:** Make the changes to the application, rebuild and test in the engineering environment, and pass a release candidate to configuration management.

- **Testing:** Run the release candidate through a quality assurance process to ensure that it is ready for release.

- **Deployment:** When the new application release is ready to be installed, shut down the old version of the application, execute an installer program that loads the new release and start the new application.

This maintenance cycle does not work well for all systems. The ability to do dynamic updating as opposed to a restart-style deployment is necessary, especially in the case of mission-critical systems that cannot have any downtime. For example, a communications satellite, the Mars Rover or a power grid cannot be switched off entirely to update their software. While the Mars Rover had extensive planning and infrastructure to allow for software updates [6], not all systems have the level of resources needed for repairs, so devising an alternative technique is imperative.

Examples of other systems that do not have the standard maintenance lifecycle are those that are obsolete or that were created by vendors who are no longer in business. An inability to update system software can have disastrous consequences, such as not being able to contain a virus like Stuxnet [13] or a potential wide-spread failure.

Industrial control systems, which operate complex and dispersed infrastructures such as electric grids, oil and gas pipelines, and power plants, are good examples of critical systems with challenging maintenance cycles. Several guides for securing industrial control systems have been published (e.g., [27]). However, concerns have been raised about hardware obsolescence [9] and that industrial control systems became operational before the latest security techniques were developed [7]. Additionally, some industrial control systems may run on old or obsolete platforms that no longer have vendor support for their hardware and/or operating systems.

Internet of Things (IoT) devices have similar maintenance problems. Many consumer devices – as well as some industrial Internet of Things (IIoT) devices – have non-upgradeable firmware, meaning that there are no easy system upgrade paths. Additionally, integrators often incorporate low-cost circuit boards in their systems with no opportunities for firmware updates. Internet of Things software systems often have security issues. For example, developers may put together software from various sources in an *ad hoc* manner, resulting in security holes such as default or non-changeable administrative passwords [18] and buffer overflows such as those exploited by the Mirai botnet [12].

To address these challenges, this chapter presents a new design pattern called a "snap-in" that facilitates the insertion of new or modified software in a running system. Information in the application binary interface (ABI), in this case in the Linux executable linkable format (ELF), is leveraged to find faulty routines that are subsequently replaced with updated versions even while the system is operational. This novel approach ascertains information about an application and uses it to replace routines without changing the structure of the application. This is an important point because modifying application code directly can leave it in an inconsistent state.

Snap-ins are designed to quickly repair faulty code (e.g., validating SSL certificates in Internet of Things devices [15]) or to make rapid repairs to programs that experience "zero-day blooms" [24] (i.e., latent errors that can affect a wide range of programs, and program or operating system versions). Snap-ins also enable the layering of security proactively at a global control point in a piece of unmodified software [23]. For example, secure input-handling parsing of command inputs to Internet of Things devices via the application of language-theoretic security [1] can avert potential security holes by creating parser-combinators that enforce input validation to prevent malicious data manipulation.

2.   Snap-in Overview

The snap-in system has three major components:

- **Shared Libraries:** Shared libraries contain the patches to be installed. The patches modify or augment the operation of the target application. Shared libraries are employed to leverage standard software engineering techniques for aggregating custom routines or for modifying later versions of shared libraries used by the target application that is being repaired.

- **Mapping Data:** This data maps system executables to the repaired routines.

- **Snap-In Controller:** The snap-in controller reads the mapping data, searches for running target executables, pauses the execution of the target

Table 2. ELF segments used by snap-ins.

Segment	Writable	Definition
.header	No	ELF header and segment table
.hash	No	Symbol hash table
.dynsym	No	Dynamic linking symbols
.dynstr	No	Dynamic linking strings
.plt	No	Procedure linkage table
.text	No	Executable code
.rodata	No	Read-only data
.data	Yes	Initialized data
.got	Yes	Global offset table
.got.plt	Yes	Global offset table for procedure linkage table
.dynamic	Yes	Dynamic linking information
.bss	Yes	Uninitialized data

application, injects the new libraries, modifies the function addresses to point to the new libraries and then resumes the target application.

Details about the operation of the snap-in toolkit are provided later in this chapter. However, in order to understand how snap-ins work, it is necessary to discuss the binary format underling Linux applications, specifically, ELF.

2.1   ELF Files

Snap-ins require the ELF ABI [28], the current standard binary executable format for Unix and Linux systems. An ELF file is a dual-use object. It initially serves as a container for a compiler to store machine code and data and for the linker to assemble all the selected files into an executable program. The compiler creates a set of sections that contain the compiled code, data, relocation information and external references to other routines. ELF establishes a section header table that is accessed by the linker to resolve and update the reference sections in each file.

When a linker creates an executable file, it writes a program header table into the resulting ELF file. The program header table points to a set of segments. A segment has zero or more sections; for example, a read-only segment may contain code in an executable text section while constants reside in a read-only section.

An ELF file is also used when a loader reads the program header table of an executable file to map the file segments into memory and resolve run-time symbols via the shared libraries. As discussed later, the file segments are also used by the snap-in program to modify the software. Table 2 lists the ELF segments used by snap-ins. Interested readers are referred to [14] for more information about ELF.

Most Linux binaries are dynamically linked – they rely on a loader to connect required external system calls or functions to the correct shared libraries. For example, if an application wishes to call function `read()`, the linker writes information into the application that says it is located in the GNC C library `libc` along with the offset in the library. The linker does not write the actual address into the application for reasons of flexibility – if one or more libraries are upgraded, then all the applications that use the libraries would have to be re-linked to work properly.

Modern Linux systems use address space layout randomization (ASLR) [26] to map the shared libraries required by an application at randomized locations in the application memory space. This approach prevents malicious applications from using memory corruption to access resources that are denied to them. Attempting to write a hard-coded address into an application would make this feature unusable.

Since a loader must ascertain the memory space at runtime and resolve the connections just before the application runs, it needs to do its job quickly. The design of the ELF file makes this possible by establishing connections to the shared library as and when they are needed.

Continuing with the example, the first time that function `read()` is called by the executable, the mainline code calls some interlude code in the procedure linkage table (PLT) that triggers the loader to connect function `read()` to `libc`. The loader places the address entry in the `.got.plt` segment following which the function `read()` is called in `libc`. Subsequent calls made to `read()` automatically use the address written in segment `.got.plt`, so only the first call to the shared library function incurs a small time penalty. This procedure is crucial to the operation of snap-ins.

2.2 Mapping Data

Since the ELF ABI underpins the target applications to be repaired as well as the shared libraries to be installed, this research has a designed a toolkit containing a program that can read either. The toolkit extracts from the ELF data the entry point name, its relocatable address and, in the case of an application, the library name pointed to by the entry. It also identifies writable data that has to be relocated.

If the target application is multi-threaded, then additional data is collected to find the best places to stop code execution safely, primarily in blocking routines such as `select()`, `sleep()`, `fork()` and `pthread_cond_wait()`. These points, which are referred to as "thread markers," are stored in the mapping data.

The collected data is then used by the snap-in controller to match the repaired routines with target applications.

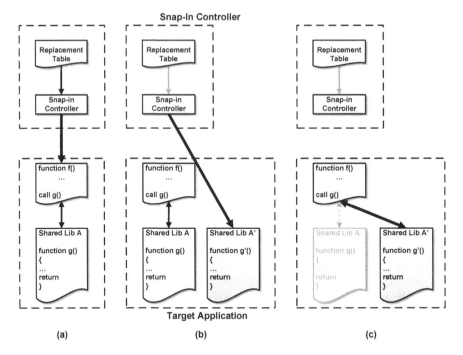

Figure 1.   Snap-in controller in operation.

2.3   Snap-In Controller

The snap-in controller is a daemon that runs on the system that is to be updated. The controller uses the collected mapping data to insert shared libraries into an operator-selected set of running programs.

The controller runs in a loop to query all the running applications on the system. If an application matches the pattern in the mapping data and has not already been updated, then the controller checks to see which shared libraries need to be loaded. After the shared library information is found, the controller briefly pauses the program *in situ* in the case of single-threaded applications. In the case of multi-threaded applications, it uses thread markers in the stored data to identify the appropriate places to pause.

Figure 1 clarifies the operation of the snap-in controller. Note the controller does not perform any modifications when the target application is executing; in such a situation, the controller pauses and it tries again after a timeout period.

The controller first reads the replacement table to find the target application that is running without modifications. The running target application initially uses function g() in shared library A (Figure 1(a)). Function g() has a bug and will, therefore, be replaced with the repaired function g'() located in a new shared library A'. Note that if multiple shared libraries are to be installed, all of them are installed into the process memory during this step.

Next, the ELF structure is used to connect the new library calls. In Figure 1(b), the controller installs the new snap-in library **A'** into the target address space and modifies the address pointers and data to point to the new function **g'()**.

The controller first checks if the loader has completed a lazy or a full binding to the entry points in the original library. If the routine is fully bound, then the controller checks the saved program counter to ensure that **g()** is not being accessed; if it is being accessed, then the controller restarts the executable and checks the state at an alternate quiescent point or thread marker to ensure that **g()** is not running.

After the controller is sure that **g()** is not in the execution stream, the ELF segment .got.plt is modified to change the address of **g()** in the old shared library routine to **g'()** in the new shared library; all future calls in the executable point to **g'()**. The address also gets the proper offset to match the address space layout randomization used for the application. Interested readers are referred to [14, 29] for details about this technique.

The controller loops through all the calls to be modified using the same technique. Certain libraries, such as DIABLO [31] and ERESI [5], facilitate the rewriting of ELF binaries. However, these libraries were not employed in this work.

On the other hand, if the loader has performed a lazy binding of the library call (i.e., the dependency is loaded when referenced for the first time), the controller does an explicit binding to the new version of the call by loading its address in the .got.plt segment.

After the snap-in controller completes the changes, it releases its connection to the target executable, updates its internal table to mark the executable as repaired and searches for the next executable to be repaired. The target application runs with the new library (Figure 1(c)). Calls to **g()** now go to **g'()**.

3. Snap-In Toolkit

A snap-in toolkit was created as part of this research. The toolkit contains utilities for source control and for system administrators to install snap-ins on target systems.

The toolbox supports the following functions:

- **Searching Executable Targets for Patch Points:** An automated scanner reads a selectable set of executables on a target system and saves entry point and patch point data in the XML format for each executable in an executable descriptor file (EDF).

- **Creating Patches for Executable Targets:** Software engineers develop patches, which they link to shared libraries for each target executable. The automated scanner is executed on the shared libraries to create a patch control file (PCF) with XML data for each library.

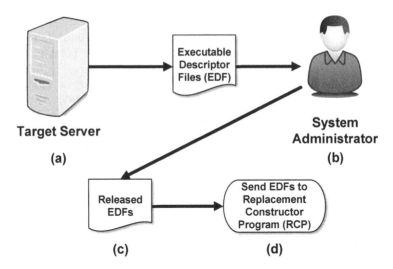

Figure 2.   Creating an executable descriptor file.

■ **Creating a Replacement Table:** A source code administrator obtains the patch control files for the released patches and selects the executable descriptor files associated with the target executables to be patched. A replacement constructor program (RCP) takes the two files and generates a replacement table.

■ **Installing Patches on Running Executables:** A system administrator receives and loads the patches and replacement tables for each target system. The snap-in controller, which runs as a daemon on the target system, reads the replacement table and checks if the applications listed in the table are running. The patch or patches of each running application are installed automatically.

3.1   Searching Executables

A Python-based program named `snapdata` was developed to scan and read the ELF symbol table information of an executable and output the executable descriptor file. The executable descriptor file contains specifics about the executable, such as the architecture for which it is built, the system libraries and names of external entries it calls and, optionally, the location of re-entrant or threaded code.

Figure 2 shows the process of creating an executable descriptor file. The target server executes `snapdata -e` to create the executable descriptor files (Step (a)). The system administrator pulls the descriptor files (Step (b)). The system administrator decides which programs need updates and releases the descriptor files (Step (c)). Finally, the released descriptor files are sent to

```
<?xml version='1.0' encoding='utf-8'?>
<edf version="1">
<!--Executable Descriptor File (EDF)-->
<info>
<!--File location and information-->
<!--File: /usr/bin/apt-->
<path>/usr/bin</path>
<filename>apt</filename>
<class>ELFCLASS64</class>
<OS>ELFOSABI_SYSV</OS>
<type>ET_DYN</type>
<machine>EM_X86_64</machine>
<entry>0x1890</entry>
<ABI>3.2.0</ABI>
<buildID>e4e5bbe239a65880c6b7d1b9f51bfded6c61220d</buildID>
</info>
<!--External entry points-->
<entries>
<entry name="strlen"/>
<entry name="dgettext"/>
</entries>
<!--External shared libraries-->
<libraries>
<library name="libapt-private.so.0.0"/>
<library name="libapt-pkg.so.5.0"/>
<library name="libstdc++.so.6"/>
<library name="libgcc_s.so.1"/>
<library name="libc.so.6"/>
</libraries>
</edf>
```

Figure 3. Sample executable descriptor file.

another system administrator for processing with the replacement constructor program.

Figure 3 shows a sample executable descriptor file output from /usr/bin/apt on a Ubuntu Linux system.

Applying snap-ins while pausing all the threaded code is important to prevent state changes; therefore, it is necessary to identify locations where code execution can be stopped safely. If snapdata determines that an executable is threaded, it looks for natural pauses in the code – the most straightforward places are at blocking calls such as select(), sleep(), fork() and pthread_cond_wait(). These thread markers are stored by snapdata in the executable descriptor file. The snap-in controller uses the thread markers to pause the program when installing the replacement library.

3.2   Creating Patches

As mentioned above, patch files are standard shared libraries that contain the modified routines for a particular target library. They enable the use of a pre-built, later version of an application library as a patch, which reduces the time required to repair a critical program. For example, if a new version of an application has a bug fix and it is not possible to upgrade to this version, a library from the new version could be used without any modifications.

A shared library is just a particular type of file that contains one or more compiled object files that were built in a positionally-independent way; this enables it to be loaded into the address space of any executable when the executable is running. Building a new shared library is straightforward; interested readers are referred to [3] for details. It is important to note that the patches must line up with entry points (subroutines) for this technique to be successful.

Another way to create a patch for an old or obsolete executable with no source code is available is to translate or "lift" the target. Lifting is a process that creates an intermediate representation (IR) bytecode from the machine code of the executable. After this is done, the patch is created by modifying the intermediate representation bytecode and recompiling the fixes into a shared library for use. Lifting executables to an intermediate representation is outside the scope of this work; interested readers are referred to [8, 16, 30] for additional details.

After the shared libraries containing the patches have been created, the snapdata program is used to scan and read the ELF symbol table information of the executable, run with a patch scanner flag set in order to scan the libraries and create a patch control file that maps the routines in each library. The first section of the control file gives the name and version range of the target library that is modified (it can be allowed to operate on all or selected versions of the target). The second section of the descriptor file lists the routine names in the target library to be replaced. The names in the patch file should typically match those in the target library, but a command developer may map the target name to another routine name in the patch library.

Figure 4 shows the process for creating patch control files. Developers select patches and create snap-in libraries and store the completed patches on a patch server in preparation for transfer (Step (a)). A configuration manager decides when to apply the set of patches and executes snapdata -p on the patch server to create the patch control files (Step (b)). The configuration manager decides which patch control files are to be included in a specific release (Step (c)) and sends the released patch control files to another administrator for processing with the replacement constructor program snaprcp. This process enables the targeted servers to receive the new shared libraries.

The snap-in shared libraries are installed in the /lib/snapin directory on the target system. Keeping them in a single location is straightforward for an operator; the directory tree is protected so that only the superuser can make modifications. An operator can install all the released snap-ins on a target system, but their use by the snap-in controller is determined by the installed

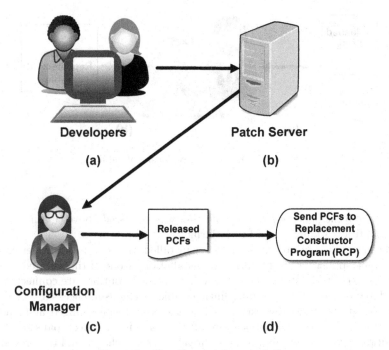

Figure 4. Creating patch control files.

replacement table, which is unique for each system. In fact, as described below, the installed replacement table may optionally be protected with encryption.

3.3 Creating a Replacement Table

The `snaprcp` tool creates a set of mappings between system executables and the created patches. The mapping data is used by the snap-in controller to decide which routines should be overridden in a program. The `snaprcp` tool reads the executable descriptor and patch control files created by parsing the executables and patches, respectively. It stores the routine of each executable and its matching patch in the replacement table for the snap-in controller.

Figure 5 shows the process involved in creating a replacement table. A system administrator receives the released executable descriptor and patch control files for a target system (Step (a)). The system administrator then executes the `snaprcp` program to produce the replacement table for the target system (Step (b)).

3.4 Installing Patches

The snap-in controller inserts new libraries into running programs and uses the replacement table to connect the appropriate subroutines to the repaired

Figure 5.   Creating a replacement table.

code. The basic operation of the controller was discussed above (Figure 1), but some additional points need to be clarified.

When a shared library or libraries are installed, the snap-in controller pauses the target application to perform the installation at one of the selected thread markers and then restarts the code. When the new routines are connected via the global offset table/procedure linkage table mechanism, checks are made to ensure that the thread marker is not in the code to be changed and, in the case of a multi-threaded application, all the threads have been paused. If the conditions are not met, an alternate thread marker is chosen and the procedure is repeated until the conditions are met. If the replaced code section has static, non-constant variables, then the current states of the variables are preserved in the data section of the new routine.

3.5   Authorizing Updates

The snap-in approach enables patching without taking applications down. Mission-critical systems, such as those running in operational technology environments, require extra diligence to ensure that the snap-ins are not corrupted accidentally or maliciously. Additionally, it is important to ensure that the target system receives the correct set of snap-ins. Authorization of patches is an orthogonal question; however, the toolkit provides an option for public-key authentication [25] of updates.

Specifically, a set of unique public/private key pairs is created – one for each target machine on which the snap-in toolkit executes, one for the configuration manager to sign snap-in patches and one for the replacement table constructor. Table 3 shows how the public/private key pairs are used for signing and verification.

The following operations are available:

- **Signing Executable Descriptor Files:** The target system signs each executable descriptor file with its private key. Each target system has its own set of keys to ensure that only patches assigned to it can be loaded on the system.

Table 3. Use of public/private key pairs.

System Function	Signer	Verifier
Target Machine	Executable descriptor file	Replacement table
Configuration Manager	Patch control file	N/A
Replacement Table	Replacement table	Executable descriptor file, patch control file

- **Signing Patch Control Files and Patches:** The configuration manager uses its private key to sign each patch control file and patch that are to be delivered.

- **Signing and Encrypting a Replacement Table:** The administrator who creates a replacement table first verifies the executable descriptor and patch control files with the respective public keys. If all the files are verified, the administrator runs the replacement constructor tool as described above.

  The final operation of the replacement constructor tool is to sign the replacement table with its private key, compress the table and all the patches into a single compressed archive file, and encrypt the output with the public key of the target system.

- **Installing Snap-Ins:** When a snap-in controller detects a new compressed archive file on a target system, it attempts to decrypt the file with its private key. If this is successful, the snap-in controller attempts to install snap-ins on running applications. It then verifies the signed replacement table with its public key and continues the installation if the verification is successful.

4. Related Work

Updating software dynamically is not a new problem. Several solutions have been proposed over the past decade.

Systems such as JavAdapter [20], a runtime replacement agent for Java systems, use features of the Java Virtual Machine (JVM) along with a system of containers and proxies to replace running Java classes. While JavAdapter is platform independent, it only works with Java-based applications. In contrast, snap-ins operate on ELF binaries; they are device hardware and language agnostic and can be recompiled for any platform that uses ELF. Other formats that have defined ABIs, such as the Windows x64 ABI [19], are easily incorporated.

Ksplice [2] is an object-code layer patching system for a running Linux kernel. One or more patch files are merged with kernel source code to create a new object segment, which is loaded into kernel memory. The existing code is modified with a trampoline to jump to the new object. However, this system only works with a Linux kernel and requires the original source code.

POLUS [4] also uses a trampoline mechanism to jump from an old function to a new one. In contrast, a snap-in modifies the pointers at the ELF level, which precludes having to modify existing code and potentially makes it easier to roll-back changes.

Kitsune [11] employs application source code and programmer-supplied transformation files to facilitate the migration of a complete process from an older to a newer version. This requires access to the original source code and the insertion of Kitsune-specific functions to control the migration. Snap-ins do not require any modifications to the original source code.

Katana [21] is the closest to the snap-in concept in that it uses ELF to do its modifications. However, it relies on source code to build patch objects whereas a snap-in does not require source code. Katana also uses a trampoline mechanism to modify the functions in running code. An advantage of Katana is cleaner migration of modified data from old to new functions; this feature will be incorporated in a future version of snap-ins.

5.   Next Steps

The snap-in project is currently moving from a prototype to an initial release of the toolkit. The toolkit includes all the utilities, installation guides and sample use cases. The utilities, which are written in Python (version 2.7), are approximately 1,000 lines of code. The snap-in controller is written in C; its compiled executable is 75 KB. All releases of the toolkit will be available on GitHub (github.com/jpbdart/snapin).

Future versions of the snap-in toolkit will include:

- **New Algorithm for Collecting Thread Markers:** The snapdata collection application uses a brute-force approach to search for thread markers and data that needs to be moved. A new algorithm will be incorporated that creates a network graph of the ELF binary; this should make the algorithm faster and more accurate.

  Developers of new applications may add "quiescent points" as discussed in [10]. This would simplify the work of the snapdata collection application because it would only have to search for the quiescent points in code instead of looking for thread markers. The developers would be implicitly guaranteeing that the quiescent points are safe places to stop the target executables as opposed to snapdata making educated guesses that stopping at thread markers would not cause execution problems.

- **Rollback of Application Repairs:** The current toolbox programs collect all the data necessary to perform rollbacks. Additional code will be incorporated to enable snap-in controllers to return applications to their original running states.

- **Repairs to Statically-Linked Code:** Small Internet of Things devices and many real-time operating systems have code that is statically-linked to applications (i.e., no calls are made to external shared libraries). Efforts are underway to collect the internal program calls to facilitate code repairs.

- **Other Hardware Architectures:** The current implementation targets the Intel x86 platform. The next hardware target will be ARM. The toolbox code, which is written in Python and C, should be portable to most hardware platforms.

Another area of research is the operation of snap-ins in highly-regulated systems, such as those used in the energy sector. For example, snap-ins cannot be incorporated in a power plant control system without evaluating the changes to be made and the liability incurred in making the changes. One possibility is to obtain approval from the regulator for repairs made using snap-ins. In such a scenario, the regulator would sign off on each snap-in, adding its own authorization key to the final code along with the entity that created the code. Thus, the power plant operator would only be able to install authorized snap-ins.

Future research will also investigate the compatibility of snap-ins with real-time operating systems. As mentioned above, research is currently focusing on repairs to statically-linked applications. Once this feature is added, the toolkit collection programs should obtain the target application data that is needed. However, research has to be conducted to see how the snap-in controller can make changes to systems with hard timing constraints.

6. Conclusions

Attacks on operational technology systems, especially those that provide essential services, are increasing in scope and frequency. Even the best systems and software age from a security point-of-view, enabling attackers to discover and exploit previously-unknown holes. Quickly repairing these systems and software is of prime importance.

Snap-ins are a powerful mechanism for quickly updating system applications that cannot be shut down or that do not have traditional maintenance plans in place. Emergency repairs such as vulnerability patches and program enhancements can be seamlessly delivered in real time by snap-ins without any downtime. Security measures that prevent tampering with the patches ensure that only the correct patches are delivered to the targeted hardware.

ufacturer or otherwise does not necessarily constitute or imply its endorsement, recommendation or favoring by the United States Government or any agency thereof. Additionally, the views and opinions of the authors expressed herein do not necessarily state or reflect those of the United States or any agency thereof.

Acknowledgement

This research was supported by the Office of Cybersecurity, Energy Security and Emergency Response of the U.S. Department of Energy and by the Directorate of Security Science and Technology of the U.S. Department of Homeland Security under Award No. DE-OE0000780.

References

[1] P. Anantharaman, M. Locasto, G. Ciocarlie and U. Lindqvist, Building hardened Internet-of-Things clients with language-theoretic security, *Proceedings of the IEEE Symposium on Security and Privacy Workshops*, pp. 120–126, 2017.

[2] J. Arnold and M. Kaashoek, Ksplice: Automatic rebootless kernel updates, *Proceedings of the Fourth ACM European Conference on Computer Systems*, pp. 187–198, 2009.

[3] H. Arora, Intro to Linux shared libraries (How to create shared libraries), *The Geek Stuff Blog* (www.thegeekstuff.com/2012/06/linux-shared-libraries), June 11, 2012.

[4] H. Chen, J. Yu, R. Chen, B. Zang and P. Yew, POLUS: A powerful live updating system, *Proceedings of the Twenty-Ninth International Conference on Software Engineering*, pp. 271–281, 2007.

[5] ERESI Team, The ERESI Reverse Engineering Software Interface (www.eresi-project.org), 2016.

[6] K. Finley, NASA pulls off 160-million-mile software patch, *Wired*, August 16, 2012.

[7] S. Gold, The SCADA challenge: Securing critical infrastructure, *Network Security*, vol. 2009(8), pp. 18–20, 2009.

[8] P. Goodman, Heavy lifting with McSema 2.0, *Trail of Bits Blog* (blog.trailofbits.com/2018/01/23/heavy-lifting-with-mcsema-2-0), January 23, 2018.

[9] H. Guzman-Miranda, L. Sterpone, M. Violante, M. Aguirre and M. Gutierrez-Rizo, Coping with the obsolescence of safety- or mission-critical embedded systems using FPGAs, *IEEE Transactions on Industrial Electronics*, vol. 58(3), pp. 814–821, 2011.

[10] C. Hayden, K. Saur, M. Hicks and J. Foster, A study of dynamic software update quiescence for multithreaded programs, *Proceedings of the Fourth International Workshop on Hot Topics in Software Upgrades*, pp. 6–10, 2012.

[11] C. Hayden, E. Smith, M. Denchev, M. Hicks and J. Foster, Kitsune: Efficient, general-purpose dynamic software updating for C, *Proceedings of the Twenty-Eighth Annual ACM SIGPLAN Conference on Object-Oriented Programming Systems, Languages and Applications*, pp. 249–264, 2012.

[12] C. Kolias, G. Kambourakis, A. Stavrou and J. Voas, DDoS in the IoT: Mirai and other botnets, *IEEE Computer*, vol. 50(7), pp. 80–84, 2017.

[13] R. Langner, Stuxnet: Dissecting a cyberwarfare weapon, *IEEE Security and Privacy*, vol. 9(3), pp. 49–51, 2011.

[14] J. Levine, *Linkers and Loaders*, Morgan Kauffmann Publishers, San Francisco, California, 1999.

[15] J. Leyden, Samsung smart fridge leaves Gmail logins open to attack, *The Register*, August 24, 2015.

[16] LLVM Compiler Infrastructure, Getting Started with the LLVM System (llvm.org/docs/GettingStarted.html), 2019.

[17] R. Lutz, Analyzing software requirements errors in safety-critical, embedded systems, *Proceedings of the IEEE International Symposium on Requirements Engineering*, pp. 126–133, 1993.

[18] D. Palmer, Is 'admin' password leaving your IoT device vulnerable to cyberattacks? *ZDNet*, April 26, 2017.

[19] M. Pietrek, Everything you need to know to start programming 64-bit Windows systems, *Microsoft Developer Network Magazine*, May 2006.

[20] M. Pukall, C. Kastner, W. Cazzola, S. Gotz, A. Grebhahn, R. Schroter and G. Saake, JavAdaptor – Flexible runtime updates of Java applications, *Software – Practice and Experience*, vol. 43(2), pp. 153–185, 2013.

[21] A. Ramaswamy, S. Bratus, S. Smith and M. Locasto, Katana: A hot patching framework for ELF executables, *Proceedings of the International Conference on Availability, Reliability and Security*, pp. 507–512, 2010.

[22] RTI International, The Economic Impacts of Inadequate Infrastructure for Software Testing, Planning Report 02-03, RTI Project No. 7007.011, Research Triangle Park, North Carolina, 2002.

[23] S. Ruoti, K. Seamons and D. Zappala, Layering security at global control points to secure unmodified software, *Proceedings of the IEEE Secure Development Conference*, pp. 42–49, 2017.

[24] S. Smith, *The Internet of Risky Things – Trusting the Devices That Surround Us*, O'Reilly Media, Sebastopol, California, 2017.

[25] S. Smith and J. Marchesini, *The Craft of System Security*, Pearson Education, Boston, Massachusetts, 2008.

[26] B. Spengler, PaX: The guaranteed end of arbitrary code execution, presented at *G-Con2*, 2003.

[27] K. Stouffer, V. Pillitteri, S. Lightman, M. Abrams and A. Hahn, Guide to Industrial Control Systems (ICS) Security, NIST Special Publication 800-82, Revision 2, National Institute of Standards and Technology, Gaithersburg, Maryland, 2015.

[28] The Santa Cruz Operation, System V Application Binary Interface, Edition 4.1, Santa Cruz, California, 1997.

[29] D. Tomaschik, GOT and PLT for pwning, *System Overlord Blog* (`sys temoverlord.com/2017/03/19/got-and-plt-for-pwning.html`), March 19, 2017.

[30] Trail of Bits, McSema, GitHub (`github.com/trailofbits/mcsema/blob/master/README.md`), 2019.

[31] L. van Put, D. Chanet, B. De Bus, B. De Sutter and K. De Bosschere, DIABLO: A reliable, retargetable and extensible link-time rewriting framework, *Proceedings of the Fifth IEEE International Symposium on Signal Processing and Information Technology*, pp. 7–12, 2005.

[32] R. Varshneya, There's no such thing as a bug-free app, *Entrepreneur*, October 22, 2015.

Chapter 13

DATA-DRIVEN FIELD MAPPING OF SECURITY LOGS FOR INTEGRATED MONITORING

Seungoh Choi, Yesol Kim, Jeong-Han Yun, Byung-Gil Min and Hyoung-Chun Kim

Abstract   As industrial control system vulnerabilities and attacks increase, security controls must be applied to operational technologies. The growing demand for security threat monitoring and analysis techniques that integrate information from security logs has resulted in enterprise security management systems giving way to security information and event management systems. Nevertheless, it is vital to implement some form of pre-processing to collect, integrate and analyze security events efficiently. Operators still have to manually check entire security logs or write scripts or parsers that draw on domain knowledge, tasks that are time-consuming and error-prone.

To address these challenges, this chapter focuses on the data-driven mapping of security logs to support the integrated monitoring of operational technology systems. The characteristics of security logs from security appliances used in critical infrastructure assets are analyzed to create a tool that maps different security logs to field categories to support integrated system monitoring. The tool reduces the effort needed by operators to manually process security logs even when the logged data generated by security appliances has new or modified formats.

Keywords: Security, event logs, integrated system monitoring

1.   Introduction

The vulnerabilities of industrial control systems used in critical infrastructure assets and the sophistication of attacks have increased significantly in recent years. In 2016, the U.S. Department of Homeland Security's ICS-CERT reported 257 new vulnerabilities in industrial control systems [9]. Meanwhile,

© IFIP International Federation for Information Processing 2019
Published by Springer Nature Switzerland AG 2019
J. Staggs and S. Shenoi (Eds.): Critical Infrastructure Protection XIII, IFIP AICT 570, pp. 253–268, 2019.
https://doi.org/10.1007/978-3-030-34647-8_13

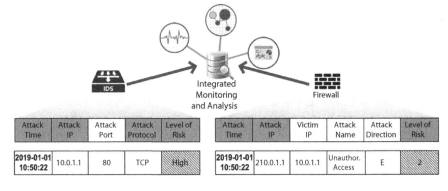

Attack Time	Attack IP	Attack Port	Attack Protocol	Level of Risk		Attack Time	Attack IP	Victim IP	Attack Name	Attack Direction	Level of Risk
2019-01-01 10:50:22	10.0.1.1	80	TCP	High		2019-01-01 10:50:22	210.0.1.1	10.0.1.1	Unauthor. Access	E	2

Figure 1.   Challenges involved in integrating security log data of different formats.

new operating environments and wireless technologies used in industrial control systems are increasing their attack surfaces.

Security devices are being incorporated in operational technology environments to combat cyber threats to industrial control systems and the critical infrastructure assets they manage. The growing demand for security threat monitoring and analysis techniques that integrate information from security logs has resulted in enterprise security management systems giving way to security information and event management (SIEM) systems, whose security logs contain valuable information about the security status and traceability of the operating environments. The information, which is in structured or unstructured formats, helps detect anomalies and analyze the causes of security incidents, contributing to the development of appropriate countermeasures. Big data technologies are actively being applied to security log datasets to enhance attack detection, security incident investigations and mitigation techniques.

However, operators of critical infrastructure assets have great difficulty integrating the diverse formats of security data in multiple device logs to perform security monitoring and analyses. Figure 1 shows the challenges involved in integrating security log data of different formats. The fields in white are specific to security devices whereas the fields in grey are common to security devices. However, the levels of risk have different data types and semantics.

Although standards exist for presenting security event information from individual devices, the standards may not be supported by device manufacturers and/or the formats may differ considerably. Even in the case of the Common Event Format (CEF) [1], which is designed to support interoperability in security information and event management systems, different manufacturers use different extension fields. Manufacturers that use the Syslog standard often add new fields according to their needs. The formats and contents of security events also differ based on the security policies applied at field sites where the devices are configured and operated.

Additionally, even when security logs have data fields with the same semantics, the logs are difficult to integrate because the data is in different formats. For example, data in an attack severity field may be expressed numerically as 1, 5 and 10 in one log, but may expressed using the strings "caution," "severe" and "serious" in another log. Such correspondences cannot be solved simply by identifying the same expression type in order to analyze the fields correctly.

Furthermore, depending on the nature of the infrastructure assets, various security devices are employed to enhance security or monitor the operating environments; this requires the integration of diverse security logs. The problems are acerbated because it is often difficult to acquire data specifications from manufacturers. As a result, operators require pre-processing modules for the security logs or they have to apply manual efforts that draw on their knowledge and experience.

In order to overcome these problems and support integrated security monitoring, security logs were examined to identify the target fields needed for security analysis and context awareness. The results were used to create a tool that derives the characteristics of security logs and identifies fields that match the target fields. The tool enhances security monitoring by enabling the integration of security logs and new formats in security logs from newly added or replaced security devices while minimizing the manual effort required on the part of developers.

2. Related Work

RFC 4765 [6] published in 2007 by the Internet Research Task Force (IETF) specifies the Intrusion Detection Message Exchange Format (IDMEF) as an information exchange standard for operating and managing security devices and systems (e.g., intrusion detection systems (IDSs) and intrusion prevention systems (IPSs)). IDMEF specifies the heartbeats that pass status information between equipment and systems, and alerts that pass network attack detection information. In 2008, MITRE released the Common Event Expression (CEE) format [11] that expresses and standardizes log exchanges between systems and end users, log providers and security information and event management system vendors. CEE provides a common representation language through the profile, Common Log Syntax (CLS) and Common Log Transport (CLT) throughout event handling, including event structuring, event encoding/decoding and event transmission. In 2013, MITRE introduced the Structured Threat Information Expression (STIX) format for organizing and expressing cyber threat information. STIX has been adopted for the trusted automated exchange of indicator information about cyber threats in real time.

Other entities have developed and released common event specifications. Some of the important specifications are:

- **Common Event Format (CEF):** ArcSight [1] designed CEF for logging and audits, and for security information and event management. CEF is primarily used with Syslog and provides custom fields for scalability.

- **Log Event Extended Format (LEEF):** IBM [7] developed LEEF as a custom event format for its Security QRadar products.

- **Cisco Intrusion Detection Event Exchange (CIDEE):** The Cisco CIDEE format [5] extends the Security Device Event Exchange (SDEE) standard that provides specifications for the formats and protocols used to exchange events. CIDEE is a custom event format that is used by Cisco intrusion prevention systems to exchange intrusion information.

Commercial vendors of security appliances typically do not comply strictly with the standards for security log formats. There are some similar fields and formats, but the details are different for each vendor, product and version. Since security devices are not designed to interoperate with devices from other manufacturers, the formats of individual fields in the security information they generate are not disclosed.

Plaintext protocol reversing efforts have been conducted to extract information from communications protocols [4, 8]. Most research efforts have focused on open-text protocols such as SMB and HTTP. However, recent studies have attempted to obtain information about private communications protocols between command and control servers and bots in order to detect and respond to distributed denial-of-service (DDoS) attacks by botnets [2, 3, 10]. These studies concentrate on the field separation of communications data and analyzing the context or state from server-client conversations. As a result, this work cannot be applied to map different security log formats to a single field required for monitoring purposes.

3.   Analysis of Field Characteristics

Four security appliances that are widely used in critical infrastructure assets were employed to analyze the characteristics of the fields in security logs. Ixia's Ixload, which can reproduce security violation situations, was used to enable the appliances to generate security logs.

Table 1 summarizes the attacks used in this research. They include 13 well-known flooding attacks and 6,740 vulnerabilities and malware attacks.

A total of 1,146,019 security logs were collected in the experimental environment over a ten-hour period. Table 2 shows a summary of the security logs. Note that the number of collected security logs differs from one security device to another due to differences in the types, numbers and detection methods of the security policies supported by the device vendors.

3.1   Target Fields in Security Logs

Analysis of the four types of security logs collected in the experimental environment confirmed that structural differences exist, e.g., for field numbers, types and contents. For security reasons, only limited information – not the detailed field structures – are described in this chapter.

Table 1. Summary of attacks.

Protocol	Attack
ARP	ARP flooding attack
ICMP	Fragmented ICMP message attack
	Ping of death attack
	Smurf attack
IGMP	Fragmented IGMP message attack
IP	Fragmented IP message attack
	Teardrop attack
TCP	Fragmented ACK flooding attack
	LAND attack
	SYN flooding attack
	Xmas tree attack
UDP	UDP flooding attack
	UDP fragment attack

Table 2. Summary of security logs.

Manufacturer	Device	Security Logs	
		Format	Total (Proportion)
A	IDS/IPS	I	117,850 (0.10)
B	IDS/IPS	II	672,624 (0.59)
C	IDS/IPS	III	52,801 (0.05)
C	Firewall	IV	302,744 (0.26)

Table 3. Target fields in security logs.

Manufacturer	Device	Security Log Fields		
		Format	Number	Targets
A	IDS/IPS	I	13	10
B	IDS/IPS	II	34	17
C	IDS/IPS	III	27	12
C	Firewall	IV	18	8

Table 3 shows the target fields in the security logs. Note that the IDS/IPS from A has the fewest fields (13) whereas the IDS/IPS from B has the most fields (34), more than 2.6 times more fields than A. The IDS/IPS from C has more fields (27) because its manufacturer uses various field structures in its devices according to their models and functions. Furthermore, even if each security log has the same field name, the field type or content may be different. For example, the Protocol field is represented differently by case-sensitive strings or numbers, such as "TCP" or "Tcp" or 6, depending on the manufacturer.

It is not necessary to use all the fields because other fields in a log may contain the associated information. For example, when ID-Rule and Name-Rule have the same meaning, ID-Rule is the key value that uniquely distinguishes the security policy whereas Name-Rule is an annotation used by administrators for easy recognition.

There may be unnecessary fields in terms of the semantics when performing integrated security monitoring. For example, Type-CategoryAttack is mainly used to classify detection results. However, it does not precisely classify and identify the attack type because the classification is too broad. In the case of Length-RawPacket, there are some difficulties in deriving a security threat by only examining the packet length.

Therefore, original field structure analyses were performed for three IDS/IPS devices and one firewall from the perspective of security monitoring and analysis. This resulted in the exclusion of three (minimum) to 17 fields (maximum). A field that was not included in all the security logs was excluded, but it was retained if it was deemed necessary for security monitoring and analysis.

3.2   Field Categories in Security Logs

In order to categorize the target fields listed above, the meanings of the 47 target fields in the security logs were analyzed. The target fields could be represented using 17 field-category-consolidated fields. Table 4 shows the categories of fields included by the manufacturers along with their contents. Seven categories of fields were included in all the security logs – Time-Sent, IP-Attacker, IP-Victim, Port-Attacker, Port-Victim, Type-AttackProtocol and Type-Action. The other categories of fields were included in some of the security logs.

The analysis also confirmed that the field categories depended on the types of security devices. The field categories of the security logs generated by IDS/IPS devices mainly deal with attack-related information such as the attack name, type and direction. On the other hand, certain categories of log fields were common regardless of the types of security devices. For example, ID-Rule was generated by IDS/IPS devices for the signature-based detection function. In the case of the firewall with an access-control-list-based security policy, ID-Rule was used even in the deny rules.

3.3   Syntax of Field Categories

The data types and main features of the fields in the security logs were analyzed in order to map field information such as field name and field meaning based on the field categories.

First, the field data types were analyzed and classified as String and Number as shown in Table 5. The String type is divided into Word (single length of text that does not contain spaces) and Sentence (collection of words separated

Table 4. Categories of fields in the security logs.

Field Category		Security Log Format				Information
Major	Minor	I	II	III	IV	
Time	Sent	✓	✓	✓	✓	Time of sent log
	Attack	–	✓	–	–	Time of attack start
	AttackEnd	–	✓	–	–	Time of attack end
IP	Detector	–	✓	–	–	IP address of device that detected attack
	Attacker	✓	✓	✓	✓	IP address of attacker
	Victim	✓	✓	✓	✓	IP address of victim
Port	Attacker	✓	✓	✓	✓	Port number of attacker
	Victim	✓	✓	✓	✓	Port number of victim
Name	Machine	–	✓	–	–	Name of device that detected attack
	Attack	✓	✓	✓	-	Name of detected attack
Type	Attack	–	✓	✓	–	Type of detected attack
	AttackDirection	-	✓	✓	–	Type of detected attack
	AttackProtocol	✓	✓	✓	✓	Type of transport protocol
	Action	✓	✓	✓	✓	Type of action against detected attack
Level	Risk	✓	✓	✓	–	Level of severity of detected attack
Count	TotalAttack	–	✓	✓	–	Total number of detected attacks
ID	Rule	✓	✓	–	✓	Rule ID that detected attack

by spaces). The Keyword type is a subtype of the Word type when the text is unique. In addition, special subtypes such as Time and IP are included for the String type. The Number type has the subtypes Constant (fixed numerical value) and Variable (variable numerical values).

Second, the field data was analyzed based on the field categories. The analysis yielded the data types shown in Table 6. To enhance understanding, each field category is arranged according to its type. The analysis confirmed that the field categories and types cannot be matched uniquely due to the different data formats in the security logs produced by the appliances.

Table 5.   Field type categories.

Type	Subtype	Context
String	Word	Single text
	Keyword	Single unique text
	Sentence	Multiple text
	Time	Timestamp
	IP	IP address
Number	Constant	Single fixed numerical value
	Variable	Variable numerical values

Table 6.   Mapping between field categories and types.

Field Category		Time	IP	Word	Keyword	Sentence	Constant	Variable
Major	Minor							
Time	Sent	✓	–	–	–	–	–	–
Time	Attack	✓	–	–	–	–	–	–
Time	AttackEnd	✓	–	–	–	–	–	–
IP	Detector	–	✓	–	–	–	–	–
IP	Attacker	–	✓	–	–	–	–	–
IP	Victim	–	✓	–	–	–	–	–
Port	Attacker	–	–	–	–	–	–	✓
Port	Victim	–	–	–	–	–	–	✓
Count	TotalAttack	–	–	–	–	–	–	✓
Type	AttackProtocol	–	–	✓	–	–	–	✓
Level	Risk	–	–	✓	–	–	–	✓
Type	Action	–	–	✓	–	–	–	✓
ID	Rule	–	–	✓	–	–	–	✓
Name	Attack	–	–	✓	–	✓	–	–
Type	Attack	–	–	✓	–	✓	–	–
Type	AttackDirection	–	–	✓	–	–	–	–
Name	Machine	–	–	–	✓	–	–	–

3.4   Semantics of Field Categories

The data characteristics are prominent in the case of a field category that maps to the Number type. To clarify the semantics, features were extracted from predefined information such as the communications protocol. The fields Port-Attacker and Port-Victim use numbers in the range 1 to 65,536 corresponding to two bytes of storage. On the other hand, Type-AttackProtocol has values from 0 to 255 because its values are represented by one byte in the IP headers.

Next, a situation was considered where a security event was generated in the operational environment as a result of an attack. Count-TotalAttack is always greater than zero because a security event occurs during an attack. Also, the

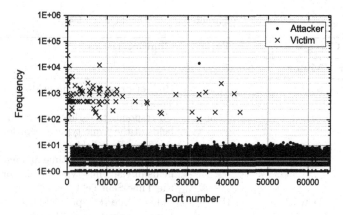

Figure 2. Field characteristics in security log format II.

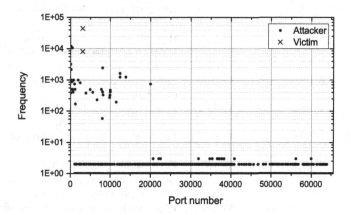

Figure 3. Field characteristics in security log format III.

number of attacks detected per unit time varies, so various values (including zero) could result.

Finally, characteristics were extracted from statistical patterns. The fields Port-Attacker, Port-Victim and Count-TotalAttack, which are mapped only to the Variable type, have different characteristics in terms of distributions of values (e.g., variance, skewness and kurtosis). Figures 2 and 3 show the significant differences that exist in the value distributions.

Tables 7 and 8 summarize the characteristics of the field categories.

4. Mapping Security Logs to Field Categories

This section demonstrates how security logs are mapped to field categories via data-driven analysis of the security logs.

Table 7.   Characteristics of field categories.

Field Category		Type	Characteristics
Major	Minor		
Time	Sent	Time	Highest priority among fields of the Time type
Time	Attack	Time	Corresponds to earlier time among fields of the Time type, except for the Time-Sent field
Time	AttackEnd	Time	Corresponds to later time among fields of the Time type, except for the Time-Sent field
IP	Detector	IP	Value of the IP type field is one (unique); predefined IP address resolution is required
IP	Attacker	IP	Does not include a specific string (.1, .255); predefined IP address resolution is required
IP	Victim	IP	IP fields except for IP-Detector and IP-Attacker; predefined IP address resolution is required
Port	Attacker	Variable	Fields with range 0–65,536; occurrence distribution is forward
Port	Victim	Variable	Fields with range 0–65,536; occurrence distribution is backward
Count	TotalAttack	Variable	Fields with 1–max range; kurtosis is high
Type	AttackProtocol	Word	Fewer word values and higher frequencies of occurrence; predefined protocol name verification is required
		Variable	Fields with range 0–255; fewer numbers of values and higher frequencies of occurrence

4.1   Overview

The data-driven mapping of security logs to field categories involves three phases:

- **Phase 1: Field Preparation:** During this phase, the security log that is the subject of the field mapping is received as input. The security log is parsed to remove delimiters and produce individual fields.

- **Phase 2: Field Analysis:** During this phase, the type of each field in the security log is classified. The classification results are mapped to the data characteristics. Details about the fields are presented in Section 3.2.

Table 8. Characteristics of field categories (continued).

Field Category		Type	Characteristics
Major	**Minor**		
Level	Risk	Word	Distribution is biased
		Variable	Fields with range 1–5 (10); distribution is biased
Type	Action	Word	Distribution is biased; predefined information verification is required
		Variable	Number of field values is low; distribution is biased
ID	Rule	Word	Meaningless text; no predefined information
		Variable	Fields with range 65,536–max; lowest priority among fields of the Variable type
Name	Attack	Word	Predefined attack name verification is required
		Sentence	Highest priority among fields of the Sentence type
Type	Attack	Word	Low priority among fields of the Word type
		Sentence	Longest text among fields of the Sentence type
Name	Machine	Keyword	Highest priority among fields of the Keyword type
Type	AttackDirection	Word	Predefined string (E,I) verification is required

- **Phase 3: Field Mapping:** During this final phase, a field category is identified by combining the mapped type and data characteristics. The output is a candidate field category for each field.

4.2 Phase 1: Field Preparation

During the field preparation phase, the raw security log is processed as an input for the subsequent field analysis phase (Figure 4). Since raw security logs have different formats depending on the manufacturer and device model, they have to be grouped into the same format. The grouped security logs are separated into fields based on delimiters. The data is organized in a structure (e.g., matrix or data frame) that simplifies the analysis based on the field type that is conducted in the next phase.

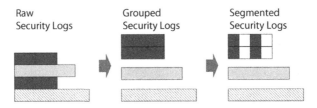

Figure 4. Field preparation using security logs.

Table 9. Results of mapping security logs to field categories.

Security Log Format	Total Fields	Correctly Mapping to Field Category		
		1st Candidate	2nd Candidate	Total (%)
I	10	9	0	9 (90)
II	17	16	1	17 (100)
III	12	9	3	12 (100)
IV	8	6	1	7 (87.5)
Total	47	40	5	45 (95.74)

4.3   Phase 2: Field Analysis

During the field analysis phase, the field type is first analyzed based on the field data. Following this, the field characteristics are analyzed to assign the field characteristics based on Tables 7 and 8.

After the field data type analysis is complete, field category candidates are identified and mapped according to the individual field types. However, as described above, there could be multiple candidates for a given field. For this reason, the field data characteristics also have to be analyzed.

The priority and frequency of data are assigned to each field of the String type (e.g., Word, Sentence, Keyword, IP and Time). Because the Variable type has multiple numerical values, the minimum and maximum, variance and skewness of the values are as recorded as characteristics.

4.4   Phase 3: Field Mapping

During the field mapping phase, the final type of each field is considered according to the priority of the candidate field category by analyzing the field type and characteristics provided by the field analysis phase. Upon applying the proposed method to the four security logs considered in this work, the field types were mapped as shown in Figures 5 through 8. The mapped candidates are presented in order of priority according to the data characteristics.

Table 9 summarizes the results of mapping security logs to field categories. As seen in the table, when the correct field categories were mapped to the first

Format I	Type	Label	1st Candidate	2nd Candidate
Field 1	Sentence	Name-Attack	Name-Attack	
Field 2	Time	Time-Sent	Time-Sent	
Field 3	IP	IP-Attacker	IP-Attacker	
Field 4	IP	IP-Victim	IP-Victim	
Field 5	Word	Type-AttackProtocol	Type-AttackProtocol	
Field 6	Variable	Port-Victim	Port-Victim	
Field 7	Word	Level-Risk	Level-Risk	Type-AttackProtocol
Field 8	Keyword	Type-Action	Type-Action	Type-AttackDirection
Field 9	Variable	Port-Attacker	Port-Attacker	
Field 10	Variable	ID-Rule	Type-AttackProtocol	Type-Attack

Figure 5. Results of mapping field categories in the security log with format I.

Format II	Type	Label	1st Candidate	2nd Candidate
Field 1	Time	Time-Sent	Time-Sent	
Field 2	IP	IP-Detector	IP-Detector	
Field 3	Time	Time-Attack	Time-Attack	
Field 4	Time	Time-AttackEnd	Time-AttackEnd	
Field 5	Keyword	Name-Machine	Name-Machine	
Field 6	Word	Type-AttackDirection	Type-AttackDirection	
Field 7	IP	IP-Attacker	IP-Attacker	
Field 8	IP	IP-Victim	IP-Victim	
Field 9	Variable	Port-Attacker	Port-Attacker	
Field 10	Variable	Port-Victim	Port-Victim	
Field 11	Word	Type-AttackProtocol	Type-AttackProtocol	
Field 12	Variable	Count-TotalAttack	Count-TotalAttack	
Field 13	Variable	ID-Rule	ID-Rule	
Field 14	Sentence	Name-Attack	Name-Attack	Type-Attack
Field 15	Sentence	Type-Attack	Name-Attack	Type-Attack
Field 16	Variable	Level-Risk	Level-Risk	
Field 17	Keyword	Type-Action	Type-Action	Type-AttackDirection

Figure 6. Results of mapping field categories in the security log with format II.

candidates, 40 field categories correspond to approximately 85.11% of the total 47 fields. When the ranges of the choices are extended to the second candidates, 45 field categories correspond to 95.74% of the total 47 fields. Note that ID-Rule, Type-Action and Level-Risk are generally not found in the security logs

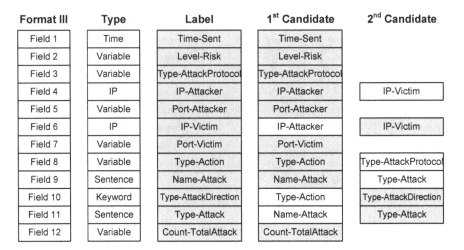

Format III	Type	Label	1st Candidate	2nd Candidate
Field 1	Time	Time-Sent	Time-Sent	
Field 2	Variable	Level-Risk	Level-Risk	
Field 3	Variable	Type-AttackProtocol	Type-AttackProtocol	
Field 4	IP	IP-Attacker	IP-Attacker	IP-Victim
Field 5	Variable	Port-Attacker	Port-Attacker	
Field 6	IP	IP-Victim	IP-Attacker	IP-Victim
Field 7	Variable	Port-Victim	Port-Victim	
Field 8	Variable	Type-Action	Type-Action	Type-AttackProtocol
Field 9	Sentence	Name-Attack	Name-Attack	Type-Attack
Field 10	Keyword	Type-AttackDirection	Type-Action	Type-AttackDirection
Field 11	Sentence	Type-Attack	Name-Attack	Type-Attack
Field 12	Variable	Count-TotalAttack	Count-TotalAttack	

Figure 7. Results of mapping field categories in the security log with format III.

Format IV	Type	Label	1st Candidate	2nd Candidate
Field 1	Time	Time-Sent	Time-Sent	
Field 2	Constant	Type-Action	Type-Action	Type-AttackProtocol
Field 3	Constant	Type-AttackProtocol	Type-Action	Type-AttackProtocol
Field 4	IP	IP-Attacker	IP-Attacker	
Field 5	Variable	Port-Attacker	Port-Attacker	
Field 6	IP	IP-Victim	IP-Victim	
Field 7	Variable	Port-Victim	Port-Victim	
Field 8	Variable	ID-Rule	Level-Risk	

Figure 8. Results of mapping field categories in the security log with format IV.

because the fields have the same semantics but different types. The limitations are discussed in the following section.

5. Discussion

The three principal discussion points are:

- **Dictionary for Semantics:** The semantics of the same fields in the security logs must be reconciled. Fields may be semantically equivalent based on predefined information that is commonly used, such as standards and specifications, but there may be differences in the field categories. For example, in the case of the Type-AttackProtocol field, "HTTP" in the String type and 80 in the Number type have to be considered as having the same meaning. However, the semantics of fields can be different regardless of the field types according to the predefined information from the manufacturer. For example, in the case of the Type-Action field, even if the field type is Number and the value is 1, then the field meaning can be changed by the "Deny" or "Allow" characteristics, depending on the predefined information. In the case of the Level-Risk field, a value of 1 for the Number type may correspond to "Low" or "High" depending on the predefined information.

- **Correlated Analysis of Fields:** *A priori* information and the analysis results can support field inference. The analysis of security logs produced by the IDS/IPS device created by manufacturer A confirms that security events are configured in a key-value manner. In other words, since the key is already known, it is possible to derive the characteristics of the value corresponding to the key and to apply it to infer the fields in the same or other security logs with similar characteristics. The fields can be more accurately inferred using security log fields that are related to each other. For example, it is possible to apply association analysis between an IP (address) field type and a Variable field type such as Port-Number with the range 1 to 65,536 for more precise classification of an attacker or a victim.

- **Manual Field Mapping Process:** This research is a preliminary attempt to support integrated monitoring of critical infrastructure assets because only four major security appliances were considered. In a real-world environment, monitoring personnel must handle all the formats in the security logs maintained in critical infrastructure assets. This is a highly manual process that relies on domain knowledge and experience. Although the proposed approach has involved some manual analysis, it is still a useful first step to removing dependencies and providing useful information that can reduce operator error.

6. Conclusions

The data-driven mapping of security logs can support the integrated monitoring of operational technology systems in the critical infrastructure. The characteristics of security logs from security appliances used in critical infrastructure assets have been analyzed to create a tool that maps different security logs to field categories based on their field types and characteristics. This enables events in multiple security logs to be integrated automatically. Moreover, it reduces the effort on the part of operators to manually process security logs for integrated security monitoring when the logged data generated by existing or new security appliances have diverse formats. Future research will focus on improving the field mapping tool by considering a variety of security appliances and critical infrastructure assets and applications.

References

[1] ArcSight, Common Event Format, Revision 15, ArcSight Technical Note, Cupertino, California, 2009.

[2] J. Caballero, P. Poosankam, C. Kreibich and D. Song, Dispatcher: Enabling active botnet infiltration using automatic protocol reverse-engineering, *Proceedings of the Sixteenth ACM Conference on Computer and Communications Security*, pp. 621–364, 2009.

[3] J. Caballero and D. Song, Automatic protocol reverse-engineering: Message format extraction and field semantics inference, *Computer Networks*, vol. 57(2), pp. 451–474, 2013.

[4] J. Caballero, H. Yin, Z. Liang and D. Song, Polyglot: Automatic extraction of protocol message format using dynamic binary analysis, *Proceedings of the Fourteenth ACM Conference on Computer and Communications Security*, pp. 317–329, 2007.

[5] Cisco Systems, Cisco Intrusion Detection Event Exchange (CIDEE) Specification, San Jose, California (`www.cisco.com/c/en/us/td/docs/security/ips/specs/CIDEE_Specification.html`), 2009.

[6] H. Debar, D. Curry and B. Feinstein, The Intrusion Detection Message Exchange Format (IDMEF), RFC 4765, 2007.

[7] International Business Machines, IBM QRadar: Log Event Extension Format (LEEF), Version 2, Armonk, New York (`www.ibm.com/support/knowledgecenter/SS42VS_DSM/b_Leef_format_guide.pdf`), 2016.

[8] H. Li, B. Zhang, B. Shuai, J. Wang and C. Tang, Automatic protocol feature word construction based on machine learning, *Proceedings of the IEEE International Conference on Progress in Informatics and Computing*, pp. 93–97, 2015.

[9] National Cybersecurity and Communications Integration Center, ICS-CERT – Year in Review, Department of Homeland Security, Washington, DC (`ics-cert.us-cert.gov/Year-Review-2016`), 2016.

[10] A. Sood, R. Enbody and R. Bansal, Dissecting SpyEye – Understanding the design of third generation botnets, *Computer Networks*, vol. 57(2), pp. 436–450, 2013.

[11] The CEE Board, Common Event Expression, MITRE, McLean, Virginia (`cee.mitre.org/docs/Common_Event_Expression_White_Paper_June_2008.pdf`), 2008.

[12] Z. Wang, X. Jiang, W. Cui, X. Wang and M. Grace, ReFormat: Automatic reverse engineering of encrypted messages, *Proceedings of the Fourteenth European Conference on Research in Computer Security*, pp. 200–215, 2009.

VI

INDUSTRIAL CONTROL SYSTEMS SECURITY

Chapter 14

MODELING AND MACHINE-CHECKING BUMP-IN-THE-WIRE SECURITY FOR INDUSTRIAL CONTROL SYSTEMS

Mehdi Sabraoui, Jeffrey Hieb, Adrian Lauf and James Graham

Abstract This chapter describes the formal modeling and machine-checking of a bump-in-the-wire device that secures field device communications in industrial control networks. Field devices serve as the connection points between computer-based control systems and the physical processes being controlled. Industrial control network traffic is routinely checked for transmission errors, but limited mechanisms are available for combating attacks that exploit industrial control protocols to target critical infrastructure assets.

This chapter focuses on a bump-in-the-wire solution that can be retrofitted on field devices to provide security functionality. The TLA+ formal specification language in combination with the isolation guarantees provided by the seL4 microkernel are used to demonstrate that the bump-in-the-wire solution provides important security and liveness properties. The resulting machine-checked system correctly applies hash-based message authentication to verify the authenticity of incoming messages while being resistant to attacks.

Keywords: Industrial control systems, security, formal methods, verification

1. Introduction

In 2014, the National Institute of Standards and Technology (NIST) released a cyber security framework [36] intended to enhance the cyber security postures of critical infrastructure assets. Industrial control systems are used across the critical infrastructure sectors, including chemical, critical manufacturing, dams, energy, food and agriculture, nuclear facilities, transportation systems and water treatment systems. These installations are often unpatched, offer low resilience to unexpected network traffic and incorporate few mechanisms that protect against malicious activities [43]. The NIST framework –

© IFIP International Federation for Information Processing 2019
Published by Springer Nature Switzerland AG 2019
J. Staggs and S. Shenoi (Eds.): Critical Infrastructure Protection XIII, IFIP AICT 570, pp. 271–288, 2019.
https://doi.org/10.1007/978-3-030-34647-8_14

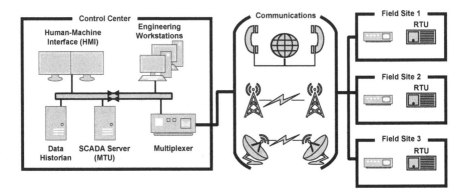

Figure 1. Typical industrial control system.

and the executive order that drove it [38] – highlight the need for strong cyber security in critical infrastructure assets that have historically focused on safety and physical security.

A secure system, like a safe system, should be designed to preserve certain properties and the implementation should satisfy these properties. Thus, the problem of developing a secure system involves two sub-problems: (i) formally express the core security properties of the system; and (ii) prove that the core security properties hold for every possible system state. Whether the system is a virtual banking application or a water treatment plant control system, high degrees of trust in the system design and implementation are paramount.

An industrial control system is a general term that describes myriad configurations of networked computer systems that operate and control physical equipment and processes in infrastructure assets. These systems make heavy use of mature, low-power and low-overhead technologies such as RS-232 communications and decades-old networking protocols to pass control commands and data between devices [21].

Figure 1 shows a typical industrial control system with three major components: (i) central control unit (or master terminal unit (MTU)) at the control center; (ii) remote control units (or remote terminal units (RTUs) or more generally field devices) at field sites; and (iii) communications equipment and protocols that link the central and remote units. The central control unit has a human-machine interface (HMI) used for plant operations. The field devices, which perform sensing and control, range from simple circuit boards powered by embedded controllers to expensive programmable logic controllers (PLCs) with racks of components. Since the master or central control unit gathers data from the field devices and sets operating parameters and issues commands to field devices to orchestrate plant operations, the overall system is often referred to as a supervisory control and data acquisition (SCADA) system.

Unlike typical enterprise information technology networks where confidentiality is a priority, industrial control networks value availability and integrity

Table 1. Modbus ASCII protocol data unit.

Start	Address	Function	Data	LRC	End
":"	2 bytes	2 bytes	Up to 504 bytes	2 bytes	"\r\n"

above confidentiality [33] – keeping the data in the system private is not as important as keeping the system running properly. Cyber threats to industrial control systems reflect this priority – attackers seek to disturb and disrupt the controlled processes rather than exfiltrate sensitive data. Attacks that disrupt network flows in industrial control systems can be devastating from the financial and safety perspectives [14, 42, 44, 46]. The importance of maintaining availability disincentivizes regular system changes or updates for fear of unscheduled downtime.

Attacks on SCADA protocols are often trivial because the protocols have few, if any, security features. Modbus, one of the most popular SCADA protocols, was developed in 1979 [35]. Modbus is a simple, connectionless protocol that can be modeled rigorously. This research considers the Modbus ASCII protocol [35].

Figure 1 shows the layout of a Modbus ASCII protocol data unit (PDU). It comprises a colon ":" to signal a new packet, two bytes for the recipient address, two bytes for the function code; up to 504 bytes for payload data, two bytes for a longitudinal redundancy check (LRC) that helps detect transmission errors and an ending character sequence "\r\n."

A fully verified microkernel such as seL4 [27] provides a platform for constructing software solutions for high assurance environments. Instead of a security statement such as "this system works for my expected inputs," seL4 enables a high-assurance statement to be made about the system: "this system works as expected for every possible input at an affordable cost." The platform provides process isolation through isolated address spaces. This supports the development of logically-contained processes, where each component acts on its own accord and communications between each component are controlled strictly.

The seL4 architecture enables a properly-designed microkernel environment to be treated as a distributed system on a single chip. A concurrency modeling language such as TLA+ [30–32] can be used to model the states and interactions of components, and each trace of state transitions can be machine-checked to conform to the modeled security properties (e.g., the secret key is confined to a certain component and only valid packets can reach the inner components). PlusCal, an algorithm language translatable to TLA+, can be used to model the sequential steps in the operation of each component.

This research focuses on a bump-in-the-wire solution that can be retrofitted on SCADA field devices to provide security functionality. It leverages TLA+ and PlusCal to model the components of the Modbus-based bump-in-the-wire security device that is designed with the seL4 microkernel in mind. The TLA+ formal specification language in combination with the isolation guarantees provided by the seL4 microkernel are used to demonstrate that the bump-in-the-wire device provides the desired security and liveness properties. The resulting machine-checked system correctly applies hash-based message authentication to verify the authenticity of incoming messages while being resistant to attacks. In particular, the verified specification assures that only valid, authenticated Modbus packets flow across a field device, that a compromised component cannot break the security properties of adjacent components, that the device is not vulnerable to replay and spoofing attacks, and that the device is resilient to malformed and malicious traffic.

2.   Background

The threats to traditional information technology infrastructure are well documented, but when industrial control systems merge with traditional information technology networks, the threats become even more significant in their scope and magnitude. Attacks such as the 2000 Maroochy Water breach [1] and the 2010 Stuxnet worm [3, 14, 15] demonstrate that even isolated industrial control systems are vulnerable to external threats. A Kaspersky Lab report [24] states that more than 10% of all blocked threats on industrial control computers originated from removable media such as USB drives. An attacker who gains access to an industrial control network finds little in the way of security mechanisms. Industrial communications protocols have limited, if any, security mechanisms and the SCADA protocols often lack basic authentication and integrity checking [34]. Meanwhile research has demonstrated that certain interactions involving industrial control protocols (e.g., Modbus TCP) and their carrier protocols (e.g., TCP/IP) can defeat security and integrity guarantees [13].

The longevity and uptime requirements imposed on industrial control systems present unique challenges to keeping them secure. Physical systems can be difficult to test, upgrade and replace. Thus, the ages of physical systems and their software are often measured in decades and the downtime costs are significant. Fragile, out-of-date firmware and protocol stacks are common and they exhibit anomalous behavior with non-conforming, let alone, malicious, traffic. Unexpected network traffic can cause heavy machinery to act in unpredictable ways. Any system state that has not been explicitly evaluated during the design phase poses a risk of disruption.

2.1   Industrial Control System Security

Efforts to address industrial control system security are generally aligned with the categories defined in the NIST framework [36] – detect, protect, identify, recover and respond. Detection leverages monitoring methodologies and tools for generating logs for low-performance field devices in SCADA systems, exporting logging data without fear of opening new attack vectors and conducting analyses without impacting system operations (see, e.g., [18, 41]). Protection involves the development and application of security mechanisms in software [2] or hardware [8]. Identify involves cataloging system assets and potential risks with efforts concentrating on the system as a whole [18] as well as on individual components such as vendor software and hardware [23–25]. Recovery involves picking up the pieces after an incident (accident or malicious) and incorporating the lessons learned in preparing for future incidents [6, 45]. Finally, response involves all activities that follow the detection of an incident (whether successful or not), including communication, analyses and mitigation [9, 39]. The work described in this chapter falls in the protection and detection categories, with the cryptographic signing mechanism supporting both forgery protection and detection.

2.2   seL4 and CAmkES

The seL4 microkernel has been fully verified from design to implementation to provide an exceptionally high level of assurance [26, 27]. It has evolved from the OKL4 family of microkernels that were reduced in size to the point where guarantees of bug-free code could still be realized. The seL4 microkernel has the verified ability to logically separate processes and implement highly-specified channels of communications between components in an architecture. If a cell in the kernel is compromised, it is shown that the other cells still maintain their desired security properties. This enables an abstract implementation of Rushby's separation kernel [40] for reducing a large security kernel into smaller, more easily provable, components that mimic a distributed system.

CAmkES is a component platform designed to address the increasing complexity and unreliability of embedded systems by facilitating the modular design of system services [16, 29]. CAmkES supports microkernel development; its design favors a low-overhead approach to accommodate the challenges involved in microkernel development. The CAmkES architecture provides a component model, standard interfaces (including support for user-defined interfaces) and user-defined interactions between components using these interfaces.

2.3   TLA+ and PlusCal

TLA+ is a formal language for modeling and reasoning about concurrent systems [30–32]. PlusCal is a language for modeling algorithms in a much more expressive manner than typical programming languages. TLA+ and PlusCal use mathematical notation to expand their reach beyond programming languages to allow for rigorous definitions and descriptions of algorithms and systems. The mathematical notation also facilitates model checking and proofs of properties of algorithms and systems.

PlusCal, which is a programmer-friendly option in the TLA+ toolchain, can be automatically translated to TLA+ and used with the TLC model checker provided by TLA+. TLC is a brute-force model checker that explores states up to a certain number of transitions, raises alerts about properties that have been violated and provides traces where the violations occurred. This research has employed TLA+ for two categories of checks that are defined and performed for each state and transition reached by the model checker: (i) invariants; and (ii) liveness properties.

Invariants are statements are always true regardless of the system state. An invariant in a simple banking example is: an account balance is never less than zero. This invariant is expressed in TLA+ as follows:

$$\forall\, acct \in Accounts : acct.balance \geq 0 \tag{1}$$

The initial state of a system might satisfy all the invariants, but then the system may never leave its initial state. A system that never changes its state is not useful. Therefore, liveness properties are specified. A liveness property – or temporal property – checks that a property is eventually true. A liveness property for a binary clock that alternates between zero and one is: if the clock bit is currently one, then it will eventually be zero. An example liveness property that is applicable to this research is: if an incoming message is a valid communications packet, then it will eventually be processed and forwarded. This liveness property is specified as follows:

$$message.valid = True \rightsquigarrow forward = True \tag{2}$$

3.   Related Work

The DNP3 SCADA communications protocol is commonly used to transmit commands and data between a central operations center and remote substations [10–12]. DNP3 Secure Authentication [19] adds security mechanisms to the basic DNP3 protocol to provide authentication and authorization. Amoah et al. [2] have conducted a formal behavioral analysis of DNP3 Secure Authentication. They employed colored Petri Nets to model common replay, modification and spoofing attacks on the DNP3 Secure Authentication specification, in the process, discovering a previously-unknown attack that could be launched by an attacker with access to data in motion, but without access to the secret key. Their modeling of the communicating entities and an attacker revealed that the snooping of non-aggressive challenge response sessions by the attacker could modify the sequence number and issue a request in the aggressive mode of DNP3 communications. This resulted in the attacker being able to spoof a valid request and replay previous messages sent in the network. This attack specifically targeted critical requests that changed system operations by modifying set-points and setting parameters.

Kuhn and Dray [28] have applied formal modeling and verification techniques to a microprocessor-based device to create a smart token system for controlling access to network hosts. Their objective was to create a civilian security-critical system where formal methods could be used to improve the system; this system could then serve as a testbed for applying formal methods for securing larger projects. The application of formal methods contributed to correcting inconsistencies in the smart token design, improving its resilience and finding a subtle, but critical, bug that could have completely compromised the security provided by the smart token. Kuhn and Dray noted that the application of formal methods to their project had tangible benefits despite its limited focus and small budget.

The DARPA-funded High-Assurance Cyber Military Systems (HACMS) Program [17] has worked with Boeing to increase the security of an unmanned H-6U helicopter in a practical manner using formally-verified code and the seL4 microkernel. Engineers were able to separate the components of the H-6U into different virtual machines running on an seL4 hypervisor and then convert certain components from the virtual machines to fully-verified native components. Although verifying the entire H-6U system was infeasible, the effort was able to verify select components to expand the trusted computing base of the system and enhance its reliability. The upgraded H-6U was able to stay in flight and complete its test mission despite being actively attacked by multiple compromised components and a professional red team. The attackers were unable to pivot from the compromised components to affect H-6U flight control or mission control.

4. Security Preprocessor Checking Using TLA+

Hieb and Graham [20] have proposed a bump-in-the-wire solution that enhances communications security between control centers and field sites that employ legacy systems. The solution introduces an inline security preprocessor that retrofits raw communications packets with authorization and authentication; the encapsulations are stripped at the field sites. The bump-in-the-wire design does not impact control and configuration operations because the preprocessor is transparent to the control center and field devices. The approach adds some latency; however, since the timing requirements for control systems range from microseconds to seconds, the latency provided by the added security is acceptable in many industrial control systems [19, 20].

The preprocessor of Hieb and Graham [20] incorporates three components: two for communications and a middle component that performs the authorization and authentication checks. This section extends the design by adding higher assurance via guarantees provided by seL4 and model verification using TLA+. The desired properties of the preprocessor are first translated into TLA+. Following this, a model is built that preserves the security properties.

4.1 System Modeling

The new system model has four components that logically separate the security functions: (i) checking that messages conform to the Modbus specification; (ii) signing messages with SHA-2; (iii) networking with raw Modbus messages in a trusted network; and (iv) networking with encapsulated/signed Modbus messages in an untrusted network. The separation isolates critical decisions,

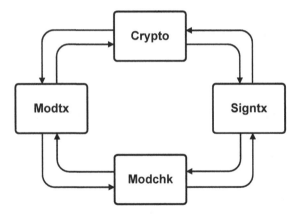

Figure 2.   CAmkES components.

rendering exploitation more difficult and supporting parallelism to improve performance should the need arise.

Each of the four components runs as a separate process, confining each critical decision-making block of code to its own memory space. Each component was also modeled separately in TLA+, following which all the components were modeled together to explore the security properties of the system as a whole. Figure 2 shows the four components. Each component provides a message interface and consumes messages from two other components.

Each thread component was specified separately using PlusCal and then collectively as an asynchronous system. An example is the signature checking thread of the Crypto component in Figure 2. Each thread is provided with a queue from which it dequeues a message and performs its processing. The Modtx component can place messages in the queues of Modchk and the message signing thread of Crypto. The Signtx component can place messages in the queue of Modchk and the signature verification thread of Crypto. This system of message passing to queues is an abstraction of the interprocess communications between the four CAmkES components.

TLA+ and its TLC model checker enable sets to be defined and each element of the sets to be used when exploring model states. It would make sense to define a set that includes every possible input for every thread. However, in the case of network communications, it is impossible to specify the set of all possible bits that can be read from or written to a serial port. This task is infeasible even when the message size is restricted to the Modbus specification. Therefore, this work uses specially-crafted packets to test the typical cases and edge cases of valid and invalid messages that could be encountered with the goal of showing that every message is covered by these cases. The serial port was also abstracted as receiving and sending messages one byte at a time to limit the search spaces of incoming and outgoing data to single bytes at a time.

Table 2. Desired system properties.

System	Property
A message in an internal queue has a valid length	Invariant
A message in a networking queue waiting to be printed has been validated	Invariant
Only a well-formed, valid Modbus message reaches the trusted network	Invariant
Only a well-formed, signed Modbus message reaches the untrusted network	Invariant
A message entering the system reaches the opposite component and is eventually consumed	Liveness
A component queue is eventually emptied	Liveness

The checking begins when a set of messages arrive at the Modtx component and a different set of messages arrive at the Signtx component. The simulation ends when all the queues are empty and there are no further states to explore. Microsoft's specification of Cosmos DB [5] is a similar message passing system that uses TLA+.

4.2 Invariants and Liveness Guarantees

Table 2 shows the desired system properties. The four invariants ensure that: (i) only messages with valid lengths make it to the inner components; (ii) messages in the queues of the networking components are checked for validity by the components from where they came and the valid messages are printed to the screen; (iii) only well-formed and properly-verified Modbus messages reach the trusted network; and (iv) only well-formed and properly-signed Modbus messages reach the untrusted network.

Liveness properties are more difficult to check in a large model. However, the two liveness properties in Table 2 ensure that: (i) messages entering the preprocessor from a networking component eventually reach the opposite networking component and are eventually consumed; and (ii) all queues are eventually emptied.

The messages selected to push through the system drive the model. Since it is not possible to model every possible input to the networked components, only certain amounts and types of messages that exercise every state in the model are employed. The TLC model checker keeps track of the number of times each state is reached; states that are reached zero times are of particular interest. Although a concise set of messages has not been found to hit every state in a single run without running out of memory, each state can be reached over multiple runs with different sets of inputs. The inputs include messages that are too short to be valid, messages that are too long to be valid, messages that are valid, messages that contain incorrect characters, messages that cause restarts, and all possible single-byte inputs.

4.3   Specifying and Checking Properties

Two components interface with an output (i.e., printing to the screen in a virtual machine and printing to a serial port on hardware). The first component, Modtx, reads and transmits Modbus messages while the second component, Signtx, reads and transmits signed Modbus messages.

The Modtx component has a read thread and a write thread. The component reads a byte at a time from the serial buffer until its buffer is full or a colon (:) is received to signal a new Modbus packet or a carriage return/line feed (\r\n) is received to signal the end of a Modbus packet. The Modtx buffer is large enough to hold the largest Modbus packet as defined in the Modbus specification. When the buffer fills without the \r\n, it is cleared and its index is reset. If a colon is received, then the buffer is cleared and the colon is placed at the head of the buffer. When a \r\n is received, the Modtx component interprets its buffer as containing a completed Modbus packet. The packet is assigned an ID and is simultaneously passed to both the cryptography component and the Modbus checking component.

The Modtx write thread gathers messages from the Modbus checking component and Crypto component. If a new message with a unique ID comes from the Crypto component, it is stored until a message with the same ID is also received from the Modbus checking component. After the two messages have been received, both messages are checked for validity. If the Crypto component was able to validate the message signature and the Modbus checking determined that the message contained a correctly-formed Modbus packet, then the raw Modbus message is printed to the output. Thus, a message is printed only if both the checking components agree the message is valid.

The invariants and liveness properties in the Modtx specification ensure that only well-formed, verified packets are printed, that the data to be transmitted is eventually transmitted and only whole (not necessarily well-formed) messages reach the inner components.

The top half of Table 3 shows the two invariants and two liveness checks for the Modtx read thread, which reads bytes from the trusted serial port. The fist invariant stipulates that the receiving buffer never exceeds the maximum size of a Modbus message. The second invariant stipulates that the application buffer (holding data to be forwarded to the inner components) never exceeds the maximum size of a Modbus message. The two liveness checks ensure that if a complete Modbus message is received (starting with a colon and ending with \r\n) and is under the maximum size, then the message is eventually processed and forwarded to the inner components.

The bottom half of Table 3 shows the two invariants and three liveness checks for the Modtx write thread. The first invariant stipulates that a byte is only sent if the original message is a valid Modbus message. The second invariant stipulates that only valid Modbus characters reach the sending register. The

Table 3. Desired Modtx component properties.

Modtx Read Thread	Property
A receiving buffer containing bytes read from the serial port does not hold more than a Modbus message	Invariant
A buffer containing bytes to be forwarded to inner components does not hold more than a Modbus message	Invariant
A well-formed Modbus message in the receiving buffer is eventually processed	Liveness
A well-formed Modbus message is eventually forwarded to inner components	Liveness

Modtx Write Thread	Property
A byte is printed to the serial port only if the entire Modbus message is valid	Invariant
Only valid Modbus characters are stored in the serial port register	Invariant
A sending buffer containing a valid Modbus message is eventually emptied	Liveness
A valid Modbus message to be printed is eventually printed	Liveness
A transmit flag that is raised is eventually lowered	Liveness

first liveness check ensures that if there is a message to send (transmit flag is raised) and the message is a valid Modbus message, then the buffer is eventually emptied. The second liveness check ensures that if there is a valid Modbus message to send, then the bytes are eventually sent. The third liveness check ensures that if the transmit flag is raised, then it is eventually lowered to allow a new message to start the process again.

The Signtx component works in a similar manner as the Modtx component, but with two exceptions. Its reading thread looks for a complete encapsulated message instead of a complete Modbus message and it utilizes the Crypto component to validate signatures instead of its signing functionality. The Signtx component assigns ID numbers to incoming messages and forwards decapsulated messages to the Modbus checking component.

4.4 Checking Modbus Properties

The Modbus protocol is modeled within TLA+ and a mechanism is incorporated to check that a given stream of bytes conforms to the Modbus standard [35]. These are necessary to ensure that only valid Modbus packets can traverse the preprocessor.

The Modbus specification is more a definition than a model of behavior. As shown in Table 1, a Modbus message has five simple fields and a longitudinal redundancy check for determining transmission errors. The lengths and character sequences in the fields in a Modbus packet are clearly defined, so it is straightforward to analyze each field. The head of the packet is checked to be the colon. The address and function fields are both checked to be two-byte hexadecimals. The data field is checked to be between zero and 504 bytes long and all the characters are hexadecimal. The end of the data field is found by taking every character from its start to the length of the packet and subtracting four. The longitudinal redundancy field is checked to be two hexadecimal characters and that the value in the packet matches the computed value. The end field is checked to contain exactly \r\n.

The Modbus message definition is used as an invariant in other specifications. This requires checking that the length of a received message is within the Modbus size limits. Next, each field of the message is examined individually to determine if it matches its definition. A message is a valid Modbus message when all the components match the definitions in Table 1. The Modchk component passes its decision (valid or invalid) along with the message itself to the opposite component from which the message was received.

4.5   Checking Cryptographic Properties

The Crypto component has two functions: (i) message signing; and (ii) signature verification. The seL4 architecture makes the signing capabilities available only to the Modtx component and the verifying capabilities available only to the Signtx component. This means that signed data only flows one way and unsigned data only flows the other way.

When Modtx receives a raw Modbus message to be signed, it passes the message and message ID to the message signing function in the Crypto component. The Crypto component generates a hash-based message authentication code (HMAC) using the Beringer-Appel verified HMAC and SHA-256 implementations [4, 7] with a preshared key, then forwards the raw Modbus message, the generated HMAC and the message ID to the Signtx component. Alternatively, when Signtx receives a signed message from the untrusted network, it passes the message and the message ID to the signature verification function. The signature verification function separates the raw Modbus message from the received HMAC, generates its own HMAC and compares the two HMACs. It then passes the raw Modbus message, the message ID and the Crypto component decision (valid or invalid) to the Modtx component.

Modeling the Crypto component hides the cryptographic techniques behind a Boolean abstraction as the verification work for the target implementation of HMAC has been done elsewhere [4, 7]. The specification uses an HMAC comparison function that simply returns true or false regardless of the strings being compared. When checking the model, the TLA+ model checker expands the state space for both possibilities, ensuring that the safety or liveness properties are not violated regardless of the decision made by the Crypto component.

Table 4. Desired Crypto component properties.

Message Signing	Property
A macMessage is empty or contains a well-formed packet	Invariant
The input and output of the signing function are different	Invariant
A password does not change	Invariant
A message that is received is eventually processed	Liveness
A message that is processed is eventually forwarded	Liveness

Signature Verification	Property
A password does not change	Invariant
A message that is flagged as valid is, in fact, valid	Invariant
A message that is invalid is never flagged as valid	Invariant
A message that is received is eventually flagged as valid or invalid	Liveness
A message that is received is eventually forwarded	Liveness

The message signing function has three invariants and two liveness checks (top half of Table 4). The buffer that holds the processed string to be forwarded, macMessage, is checked in all the invariants. The first invariant stipulates that macMessage is either empty or contains a well-formed packet. The second invariant stipulates that the information received and passed by the message signing function are different, demonstrating that processing has taken place. The third invariant stipulates that the password variable is never changed. The two liveness check ensure that a message that is received is eventually processed and forwarded.

The signature verification function has three invariants and two liveliness checks (bottom half of Table 4). As in the case of the message signing function, the first invariant stipulates that the password variable is never changed. The second invariant stipulates that a message marked as valid when it is forwarded to the Modtx component has a validated HMAC. The third invariant stipulates that an invalid message is never flagged as valid. The two liveness checks ensure that, if a message is received, then it is eventually flagged and forwarded to the Modtx component.

5. Discussion

An attacker who targets the network in which the bumper-in-the-wire device operates may attempt to forge messages, or tamper with or replay captured messages. Alternatively, the attacker may attempt to exploit the trust relationship between the internal network and the device by assuming control and generating malicious traffic that originates from the device as described in [22]. However, the device is immune to these types of attacks because invariants ensure that, regardless of the model state, only valid Modbus messages (whether encapsulated or not) can be printed. Further, if the assumptions described above hold, then the system would not accept messages that have been tampered with (i.e., messages that do not match the attached HMACs). A nonce is included in each encapsulated message to prevent replay attacks.

Restricting the model checking to a feasible state-space required a few tricks. The simplest incarnation of the model completed in roughly ten minutes, but the number of states extended to the tens of millions. Modeling each thread individually enabled around 10,000 states to be explored to verify the invariants and perform the liveness checks. Relying on the verification work applied to the seL4 component architecture enabled the component models to be kept separate while maintaining the queue-based message passing structure of the general model. While these strategies may change according to the project, researchers have shown that even larger projects can see benefits when the state space is restricted to a manageable size [5, 37]

6. Conclusions

Industrial control network traffic is routinely checked for transmission errors, but limited security mechanisms are available for combating attacks that exploit industrial control protocols to target field devices. The bump-in-the-wire solution considered in this research is designed to be retrofitted on field devices to provide the needed security functionality. The TLA+ formal specification language in combination with the isolation guarantees provided by the seL4 microkernel are used to demonstrate that the bump-in-the-wire device provides the desired security and liveness properties. Indeed, the resulting machine-checked system correctly applies hash-based message authentication to verify the authenticity of incoming protocol messages while being resistant to attacks. In particular, the verified specification assures that only valid, authenticated Modbus packets flow across a field device, that a compromised component cannot break the security properties of adjacent components, that the device is not vulnerable to replay and spoofing attacks, and that the device is resilient to malformed and malicious traffic.

Future research will focus on formal proofs at the code level and a verified implementation targeting the seL4 microkernel. The modular design would be conducive to full formal verification because the components are limited in how they interact with other components (if they interact at all). The seL4 proof work provides the isolation and interprocess communications guarantees, facilitating a component-based architecture. The component-based architecture can be abstracted to a distributed system of critical decision points, which TLA+ excels at modeling and checking. Thus, the important next step is to move from a TLA+ specification to executable, verified C code. The verified C code could be incorporated in the CAmkES build and deployed in a native seL4 application.

References

[1] M. Abrams and J. Weiss, Malicious control system cyber security attack case study – Maroochy Water Services, presented at the *Twenty-Fourth Annual Computer Security Applications Conference*, 2008.

[2] R. Amoah, S. Camtepe and E. Foo, Formal modeling and analysis of DNP3 Secure Authentication, *Journal of Network and Computer Applications*, vol. 59, pp. 345–360, 2016.

[3] N. Anderson, Confirmed: US and Israel created Stuxnet, lost control of it, *Ars Technica*, June 1, 2012.

[4] A. Appel, Verification of a cryptographic primitive: SHA-256, *ACM Transactions on Programming Languages and Systems*, vol. 37(2), article no. 7, 2015.

[5] Azure, Azure Cosmos TLA+ specifications, GitHub (`github.com/Azure/azure-cosmos-tla`), 2018.

[6] M. Bartock, J. Cichonski, M. Souppaya, M. Smith, G. Witte and K. Scarfone, Guide for Cybersecurity Event Recovery, NIST Special Publication 800-184, National Institute of Standards and Technology, Gaithersburg, Maryland, 2016.

[7] L. Beringer, A. Petcher, K. Ye and A. Appel, Verified correctness and security of OpenSSL HMAC, *Proceedings of the Twenty-Fourth USENIX Security Symposium*, pp. 207–221, 2015.

[8] Blue Coat Systems, Blue Coat ICS Protection, Scanner Station Version, USB Malware Defense for Industrial Computers, User Guide, Version 5.3.1, Sunnyvale, California (`docplayer.net/18790337-Blue-coat-ics-protection-scanner-station-version.html`), 2014.

[9] P. Cichonski, T. Millar, T. Grance and K. Scarfone, Computer Security Incident Handling Guide, NIST Special Publication 800-61, Revision 2, National Institute of Standards and Technology, Gaithersburg, Maryland, 2012.

[10] Control Microsystems, DNP3 User and Reference Manual, Kanata, Canada, 2007.

[11] K. Curtis, A DNP3 Protocol Primer (Revision A), DNP3 Users Group, Calgary, Canada (`www.dnp.org/Portals/0/AboutUs/DNP3%20Primer%20Rev%20A.pdf`), 2005.

[12] S. East, J. Butts, M. Papa and S. Shenoi, A taxonomy of attacks on the DNP3 protocol, in *Critical Infrastructure Protection III*, C. Palmer and S. Shenoi (Eds.), Springer, Berlin Heidelberg, Germany, pp. 67–81, 2009.

[13] J. Edmonds, M. Papa and S. Shenoi, Security analysis of multilayer SCADA protocols, in *Critical Infrastructure Protection*, E. Goetz and S. Shenoi (Eds.), Springer, Boston, Massachusetts, pp. 205–221. 2007.

[14] N. Falliere, Stuxnet introduces the first known rootkit for industrial control systems, *Symantec Security Response Blog* (`www.symantec.com/connect/blogs/stuxnet-introduces-first-known-rootkit-scada-devices`), August 6, 2010.

[15] N. Falliere, L. O'Murchu and E. Chien, W32.Stuxnet Dossier, Version 1.4, Symantec, Mountain View, California, 2011.

[16] M. Fernandez, G. Klein, I. Kuz and T. Murray, CAmkES Formalization of a Component Platform, National Information and Communications Technology Research Centre of Excellence (NICTA), Sydney, Australia, 2012.

[17] K. Fisher, J. Launchbury and R. Richards, The HACMS Program: Using formal methods to eliminate exploitable bugs, *Philosophical Transactions, Series A, Mathematical Physical and Engineering Sciences*, vol. 375(2104), article no. 20150401, 2017.

[18] T. Gary, ICS/SCADA smart scanning: Discover and assess IT-based systems in converged IT/OT environments, *Tenable Blog*, June 12, 2018.

[19] G. Gilchrist, Secure authentication for DNP3, *Proceedings of the IEEE Power and Energy Society General Meeting – Conversion and Delivery of Electrical Energy in the 21st Century*, 2008.

[20] J. Hieb, J. Graham, J. Schreiver and K. Moss, Security preprocessor for industrial control networks, *Proceedings of the Seventh International Conference on Information Warfare and Security*, pp. 130–137, 2012.

[21] V. Igure, S. Laughter and R. Williams, Security issues in SCADA networks, *Computers and Security*, vol. 25(7), pp. 498–506, 2006.

[22] Industrial Control Systems Cyber Emergency Response Team (ICS-CERT), Advisory (ICSA-12-231-01B), Sixnet Universal Protocol Undocumented Function Codes (Update B), Idaho Falls, Idaho (`www.us-cert.gov/ics/advisories/ICSA-13-231-01B`), September 17, 2013.

[23] Industrial Control Systems Cyber Emergency Response Team (ICS-CERT), ICS-CERT Advisories, Idaho Falls, Idaho (`ics-cert.us-cert.gov/advisories`), 2019.

[24] Kaspersky Lab ICS CERT, Threat Landscape for Industrial Automation Systems in the Second Half of 2016, Kaspersky Lab, Moscow, Russia, 2017.

[25] Kaspersky Lab ICS CERT, Threat Landscape for Industrial Automation Systems in H2 2017, Kaspersky Lab, Moscow, Russia, 2018.

[26] G. Klein, P. Derrin and K. Elphinstone, Experience report: seL4: Formally verifying a high-performance microkernel, *Proceedings of the Fourteenth ACM SIGPLAN International Conference on Functional Programming*, pp. 91–96, 2009.

[27] G. Klein, K. Elphinstone, G. Heiser, J. Andronick, D. Cock, P. Derrin, D. Elkaduwe, K. Engelhardt, R. Kolanski, M. Norrish, T. Sewell, H. Tuch and S. Winwood, seL4: Formal verification of an OS kernel, *Proceedings of the Twenty-Second ACM Symposium on Operating Systems Principles*, pp. 207–220, 2009.

[28] D. Kuhn and J. Dray, Formal specification and verification of control software for cryptographic equipment, *Proceedings of the Sixth Annual Computer Security Applications Conference*, pp. 32–43, 1990.

[29] I. Kuz, Y. Liu, I. Gorton and G. Heiser, CAmkES: A component model for secure microkernel-based embedded systems, *Journal of Systems and Software*, vol. 80(5), pp. 687–699, 2007.

[30] L. Lamport, The temporal logic of actions, *ACM Transactions on Programming Languages and Systems*, vol. 16(3), pp. 872–923, 1994.

[31] L. Lamport, *Specifying Systems: The TLA+ Language and Tools for Hardware and Software Engineers*, Addison-Wesley, Boston, Massachusetts, 2002.

[32] L. Lamport, The TLA Home Page (`lamport.azurewebsites.net/tla/tla.html`), December 6, 2018.

[33] H. Mackenzie, SCADA security basics: Why industrial networks are different than IT networks, *Tofino Security Blog*, October 31, 2012.

[34] L. Martin-Liras, M. Prada, J. Fuertes, A. Moran, S. Alonso and M. Dominguez, Comparative analysis of the security of configuration protocols for industrial control devices, *International Journal of Critical Infrastructure Protection*, vol. 19, pp. 4–15, 2017.

[35] Modbus Organization, Modbus over Serial Line: Specification and Implementation Guide, V1.02, Hopkinton, Massachusetts (`www.modbus.org/docs/Modbus_over_serial_line_V1_02.pdf`), 2006.

[36] National Institute of Standards and Technology, Framework for Improving Critical Infrastructure Cybersecurity, Version 1.1, Gaithersburg, Maryland, 2018.

[37] C. Newcombe, T. Rath, F. Zhang, B. Munteanu, M. Brooker and M. Deardeuff, Use of Formal Methods at Amazon Web Services, Amazon, Seattle, Washington (`lamport.azurewebsites.net/tla/formal-methods-amazon.pdf`), 2014.

[38] B. Obama, Presidential Policy Directive 21: Critical Infrastructure Security and Resilience (PPD-21), The White House, Washington, DC, February 12, 2013.

[39] M. Permann, K. Lee, J. Hammer and K. Rohde, Mitigations for security vulnerabilities found in control system networks, presented at the *Sixteenth Annual Joint ISA POWID/EPRI Controls and Instrumentation Conference*, 2006.

[40] J. Rushby, Design and verification of secure systems, *Proceedings of the Eighth ACM Symposium on Operating Systems Principles*, pp. 12–21, 1981.

[41] K. Scarfone and P. Mell, Guide to Intrusion Detection and Prevention Systems (IDPS), NIST Special Publication 800-94, National Institute of Standards and Technology, Gaithersburg, Maryland, 2007.

[42] U. Shamir, Analyzing a New Variant of BlackEnergy 3: Likely Insider-Based Execution, SentinelOne, Mountain View, California, 2016.

[43] K. Stouffer, J. Falco and K. Scarfone, Guide to Industrial Control Systems (ICS) Security, NIST Special Publication 800-82, National Institute of Standards and Technology, Gaithersburg, Maryland, 2011.

[44] J. Sullivan and D. Kamensky, How cyber-attacks in Ukraine show the vulnerability of the U.S. power grid, *The Electricity Journal*, vol. 30(3), pp. 30–35, 2017.

[45] United Nations Security Council Counter-Terrorism Committee Executive Directorate (CTED) and United Nations Office of Counter-Terrorism, The Protection of Critical Infrastructure against Terrorist Attacks: Compendium of Good Practices, Geneva, Switzerland, 2018.

[46] D. Wagner, Infrastructure under attack, *Risk Management*, vol. 63(8), pp. 28–33, 2016.

Chapter 15

DEFINING ATTACK PATTERNS FOR INDUSTRIAL CONTROL SYSTEMS

Raymond Chan, Kam-Pui Chow and Chun-Fai Chan

Abstract   Attack patterns have been used to specify security test cases for traditional information technology systems in order to mitigate cyber attacks. However, the attack patterns for traditional information technology systems are not directly applicable to industrial control systems. This chapter considers the differences between traditional information technology systems and industrial control systems, discusses why attack patterns for traditional information technology systems are inadequate for industrial control systems, and specifies attack patterns for industrial control systems. The attack patterns are useful for creating security test cases for assessing the security levels of industrial control systems. An elevator system case study is used to demonstrate the utility of industrial control system attack patterns in specifying security test cases.

Keywords: Industrial control systems, attack patterns, security testing

1.   Introduction

A large-scale industrial control system (ICS) can comprise hundreds or even thousands of programmable logic controllers (PLCs) and sensors interconnected in a network. Information technology networks at large corporations do not have control devices and sensors, but they may have similar workstations and servers as industrial control systems. Additionally, the network architectures of industrial control systems and information technology networks are similar. The interconnections of industrial control systems and information technology networks expose the control systems and the infrastructure assets they operate to cyber attacks.

The Stuxnet worm, which attacked Iran's uranium hexafluoride centrifuges, demonstrated how a cyber weapon could enter a conventional information technology asset and eventually move into a highly-secure industrial control system [15]. In 2015, BlackEnergy, an HTTP-based toolkit, enabled hackers to

© IFIP International Federation for Information Processing 2019
Published by Springer Nature Switzerland AG 2019
J. Staggs and S. Shenoi (Eds.): Critical Infrastructure Protection XIII, IFIP AICT 570, pp. 289–309, 2019.
https://doi.org/10.1007/978-3-030-34647-8_15

launch distributed denial-of-service (DDoS) attacks on industrial control systems and supervisory control and data acquisition (SCADA) systems [2]. In 2017, the WannaCry malware infected workstations at the Chernobyl nuclear power plant, which had to switch to manual radiation monitoring as a result of the attack [5]. The Shodan search engine enables users to discover and gain information about thousands of Internet-facing industrial control systems around the world; the information collected can be used by hackers to enter the industrial control systems and disrupt, perhaps even damage, the physical assets they operate.

Attack patterns have been used to specify security test cases for traditional information technology systems in order to mitigate cyber attacks. However, the attack patterns for traditional information technology systems are not directly applicable to industrial control systems. This chapter considers the differences between traditional information technology systems and industrial control systems, discusses why attack patterns for traditional information technology systems are inadequate for industrial control systems, and specifies attack patterns for industrial control systems. The attack patterns are useful for creating security test cases for assessing the security levels of industrial control systems. An elevator system case study is used to demonstrate the utility of industrial control system attack patterns in specifying security test cases.

2. Related Work

Attack pattern research has largely focused on specifying and discovering attack patterns for information technology systems. Zhu [16] has proposed an algorithm that determines network attack patterns by mining network traffic logs. The resulting patterns are used to identify and detect network attacks.

Rahaman et al. [11] have developed an attack pattern framework for identifying and mitigating attacks on enterprise information systems. Li et al. [7] have proposed an attack pattern mining algorithm that extracts attack patterns from security logs.

Other researchers [8] have analyzed attacks using attack patterns in a comprehensive attack knowledge repository. Bozic and Wotawa [1] have proposed a formalization of attack patterns from which test cases can be generated and executed automatically to conduct security testing.

Limited attack pattern research has concentrated on industrial control systems. Pricop and Mihalache [10] have proposed a fuzzy-logic-based approach for modeling cyber attack patterns on data transfers in industrial control systems. They classified adversaries into profiles ranging from script kiddies to cyber warriors. They also introduced an adversary profile score that can be used to rate adversary skills. However, they do not discuss the types of industrial control system attacks that an adversary could perform. Indeed, from the security point of view, identifying an adversary profile may not be adequate to develop an industrial control system protection plan.

In summary, research on attack patterns has focused primarily on information technology systems and related adversary knowledge. Since attacking industrial control systems is quite different from attacking traditional information technology systems, it is necessary to define attack patterns that are specific to industrial control systems. Attack patterns for industrial control systems can help understand the underlying security issues and assist in creating security test cases for industrial control systems.

3. Attack Patterns

An attack pattern is an abstraction mechanism for describing how a specific type of attack can be executed. An attack pattern describes the context where the attack type is applicable along with its working principle. It also defines the nature of the attack and provides general recommendations for mitigating the attack. In short, an attack pattern is a blueprint of an attack.

According to Sethi and Barnum [12], attack patterns define a series of repeatable steps that can be applied to simulate an attack against the security of a system. The Common Attack Pattern Enumeration and Classification (CAPEC) [9] specifies cyber attack patterns for information technology systems. Although some of these attack patterns can be applied to industrial control systems, it is important to define attack patterns that are specific to industrial control systems. In fact, absent attack patterns that are customized to industrial control systems, it is not possible to cover all the attack types that target industrial control systems. This means that a complete set of security test cases cannot be defined. Security testing that does not cover all possible attacks prevents proper assessments of the risk levels of industrial control systems.

3.1 Design Patterns

Gamma et al. [3] have specified design patterns for software and operating systems. These design patterns can be applied to specify attack patterns for industrial control system that are related to software, operating system and network architectures. Design patterns define common models or problems whereas attack patterns define cyber attacks that occur frequently.

Unfortunately, attack patterns for information technology systems do not cover the fact that an adversary can change the physical environment of an industrial plant. For example, sensors that monitor industrial plant equipment and environments are not covered by attack patterns for information technology systems. Because industrial control devices always trust sensor data, which is easily tampered with, the attacks cannot be mitigated by software or program logic. As a result, it is necessary to specify attack patterns for industrial control systems using the design patterns of Gamma et al. [3].

3.2 Attack Pattern Usage

Attack patterns are useful for defining and developing application security and security-related actions for information technology systems. The attack patterns help understand the possible threats and their impacts [4]. Additionally, attack patterns are useful for testing applications and systems to identify and mitigate potential vulnerabilities.

For example, a security engineer can study attack patterns corresponding to man-in-the-middle and replay attacks before an application is designed. The security engineer would know in advance the possible attacks that the application may face. Furthermore, he/she would know the security testing that should be conducted based on the attack patterns. Last, but not least, the application can be planned and developed to achieve security by mitigating the attacks specified by the attack patterns.

Since industrial control systems do not have security testing standards, it is essential to define attack patterns for these systems. Many industrial control systems do not receive security patches or have application and operating system update policies in place for fixing vulnerabilities [14]. Attack patterns are needed to propose a security testing standard that forces industrial control system operators to define security patches and policies. Indeed, attack patterns are vital to preparing and defining test cases for assessing the security levels of industrial control systems.

3.3   System Comparison

This section discusses the common characteristics and the differences between information technology and industrial control systems.

An industrial control network hierarchy has three layers [13]. The top layer is the enterprise layer, which is similar to that of an information technology system. This layer usually comprises servers and workstations that are necessary to support operations. Examples are the mail server and the database server that stores information. The workstations are typically connected to industrial control devices, which means they can access the control devices and impact the physical equipment. Below the enterprise layer is the control layer that contains industrial control devices that monitor and manage physical equipment located in the lowest physical plant layer. The physical plant layer is maintained and managed by technicians and engineers who usually do not have a role in securing industrial control devices.

The differences between information technology and industrial control systems can be understood in terms of their architectures, constituent devices, attack goals and attack methods. As mentioned above, the enterprise layers of information technology and industrial control systems are similar. However, the bottom two layers of the network hierarchy – the control layer and the physical plant layer – are unique to industrial control systems.

In the case of industrial control systems, the control layer comprises industrial control devices while the physical plant layer comprises physical equipment and sensors. Information technology systems do not have such devices. The devices in the bottom two layers of industrial control systems are attractive cyber attack targets because they are more vulnerable than devices in the enterprise layer. Moreover, successful attacks can disrupt plant operations, and possibly damage or destroy plant equipment.

Attackers of information technology systems and industrial control systems generally have different goals, although some goals may be similar. In the case of information technology systems, an attacker may wish to steal sensitive or proprietary data, disrupt business operations or collect ransom [6]. Attackers of industrial control systems typically have political or terrorist motivations, but they may also be interested in accessing proprietary information, disrupting plant operations or collecting ransom [15].

Information technology systems are generally attacked via malware or by exploiting software or operating system vulnerabilities to gain system access. Industrial control system attackers typically leverage unauthenticated and unencrypted communications protocols to target workstations, human-machine interfaces, industrial control devices and sensors.

4. Attack Pattern Classification

This section defines common attack patterns for industrial control systems using the attack pattern classification profiles suggested by Sethi and Barnum [12]. The adversary profiles defined by Pricop and Mihalache [10] are used to specify the skill levels of adversaries.

The following subsections describe five industrial control system attack patterns. The Information Collection and Analysis attack pattern describes how an adversary can gather information about an industrial control device before launching an attack. The Injection attack pattern describes how the behavior of an industrial control device can be controlled or modified. The Denial-of-Service attack pattern describes how an industrial control device can be the source or target of a denial-of-service attack and how denial of service increases the vulnerability of the industrial control system. The System Resource Manipulation attack pattern describes how a software application or workstation in an industrial control system can be attacked. Finally, the Sensor Manipulation attack pattern describes how an adversary can use a sensor to alter the behavior of an industrial control device.

4.1 Information Collection and Analysis

- **Description:** A programmable logic controller periodically sends commands to and receives data from devices in its industrial control network. An adversary can collect and analyze this information to gain knowledge about the industrial control network and its devices.

- **Attack Prerequisites:** An adversary can access the internal industrial control network and capture communications traffic between the programmable logic controller, human-machine interfaces (HMIs) and workstations.

- **Targeted Vulnerabilities or Weaknesses:** The attack leverages the weakness where devices in an industrial control network do not encrypt their communications. The communications information includes MAC addresses, IP addresses, device model numbers and firmware versions. Industrial control devices also respond to the Link Layer Discovery Protocol (LLDP) and Internet Control Message Protocol (ICMP), which enables an adversary to locate the devices quickly.

  An industrial control network does not incorporate security devices such as firewalls and intrusion detection systems to isolate the control and physical plant layers, and to alert operators to intrusions. An industrial control network also may not have proper access control policies in place, enabling an adversary to utilize the available protocols to query devices. An adversary who controls a workstation can locate and connect to any and all industrial control devices in the network.

- **Attack Method:** An adversary gains access to a workstation in an industrial control network. The adversary then captures network communications and issues queries to obtain information about devices in the industrial control network.

- **Attacker Goal:** An adversary desires to collect information about devices in an industrial control network to understand the operation of the industrial control system.

- **Required Attacker Skill Level:** An adversary only requires basic hacking skills in order to gain access to the industrial control system and capture network traffic to obtain industrial control device information. The attack can be performed by all the adversary profiles defined by Pricop and Mihalache [10].

- **Example:** An adversary sniffs Link Layer Discovery Protocol messages in an industrial control network and analyzes them to obtain information about industrial control devices in the network. The adversary can use the device information to launch more sophisticated attacks on the industrial control system.

4.2   Injection

- **Description:** Industrial control device communications are insecure. The network communications are seldom protected by authentication and encryption. An adversary who knows how industrial control devices communicate with each other can inject communications messages that alter the behavior of the devices or crash the devices.

- **Attack Prerequisites:** An adversary needs to understand the working principles of industrial control devices, and how they are managed and manipulated using communications protocols (e.g., Siemens STEP 7 and

Modbus). In some cases, the adversary may issue a command to download a program from an industrial control device and understand the program logic in order to fully control the device.

- **Targeted Vulnerabilities or Weaknesses:** In order to ensure compatibility, industrial control devices use standard communications protocols. Devices often communicate using an older version of a protocol to ensure compatibility with other devices in the network. Also, protection mechanisms for information technology systems are not customized to industrial control systems; for example, they may not understand industrial control protocols. The firmware and software of industrial control devices may rarely or never be updated or patched because vendors may not support the devices or the devices have to operate continuously and cannot accommodate the downtime required to install updates. An adversary could employ an older version of a protocol to query and attack industrial control devices. Additionally, the adversary could upload altered firmware or control programs to the devices to conduct attacks.

- **Attack Method:** An adversary accesses a workstation in an industrial control network. A malicious program is installed on the workstation to inject commands and upload malicious programs or firmware to industrial control devices.

- **Attacker Goal:** An adversary desires to change the behavior of industrial control devices to crash the entire industrial control system, or to control industrial control devices in order to make the industrial control system operate in an abnormal or unsafe manner.

- **Required Attacker Skill Level:** An adversary needs to understand the industrial control network architecture, industrial control device operation and the communications protocol in order to control and change the behavior of the devices. Examples include making an elevator motor move the elevator car much faster than normal or switching off the elevator light.

- **Example:** A false command injection attack can change the behavior of an industrial control device. Based on the commands that an industrial control device sends or receives, a security testing professional can specify feasible attacks on the device.

4.3 Denial-of-Service

- **Description:** An industrial control network interface does not require a fast Ethernet connection. Unlike a traditional information technology network, the amount of network traffic is relatively low in an industrial control network. An adversary does not need to generate a massive volume of traffic to launch an effective denial-of-service attack on an industrial control network. Indeed, launching a denial-of-service attack from just one workstation is enough to affect the performance of industrial control devices.

Attack traffic can be sent from the control center, human-machine interfaces or network devices. Attack traffic can also be generated by industrial control devices.

- **Attack Prerequisites:** An adversary installs and executes malware on an industrial control device that generates malicious network traffic.

- **Targeted Vulnerabilities or Weaknesses:** The bandwidth of an industrial control network is generally much lower than that of an information technology network; the typical throughput of an Ethernet connection interface of an industrial control device is low (e.g., 10 to 100 Mbps). Moreover, network security devices such as firewalls and intrusion prevention systems are often not installed to protect industrial control devices.

- **Attack Method:** A denial-of-service attack on an industrial control network can be launched from three types of devices:

  - *Workstation:* An adversary installs malware on a workstation to disrupt the communications channels between a human-machine interface and industrial control devices to render the industrial control system out of control.

  - *Industrial Control Device:* An adversary installs malware on an industrial control device, which generates attack traffic that crashes workstations and/or human-machine interfaces.

  - *Human-Machine Interface:* An adversary installs malware on a human-machine interface, which sends attack traffic to workstations and industrial control devices that causes them to malfunction.

- **Attacker Goal:** An adversary desires to render industrial control devices uncontrollable. The malfunctioning industrial control system disrupts the industrial process and potentially damages plant equipment.

- **Required Attacker Skill Level:** An adversary needs knowledge about the industrial control network architecture and needs to know how to generate network traffic. All types of adversaries can execute denial-of-service attacks.

- **Example:** An adversary prevents a human-machine interface from communicating with an elevator programmable logic controller, causing the elevator to go out of control. Figure 1 shows a human-machine interface screen after the execution of a denial-of-service attack on an elevator programmable logic controller.

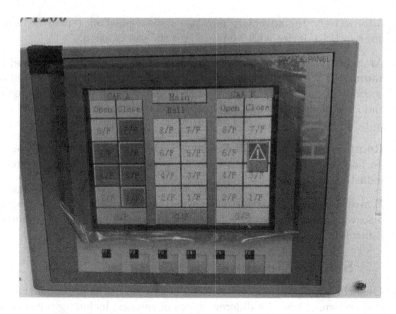

Figure 1. Human-machine interface screen after a denial-of-service attack.

4.4 System Resource Manipulation

- **Description:** Security patch management is typically not in place for workstation operating systems and applications. In many cases, a workstation may use an older operating system (e.g., Windows XP) that has never been updated because of the 24/7 operational requirement. Additionally, updated antivirus software may not be installed on the workstation. Again, because of the 24/7 operational requirement, industrial control system applications may not have been updated for years, which means they may have critical vulnerabilities that enable an adversary to access and modify industrial control devices.

- **Attack Prerequisites:** An adversary gains access to a workstation in an industrial control network and determines the vulnerable software systems and applications installed on the workstation.

- **Targeted Vulnerabilities or Weaknesses:** An adversary targets operating system and industrial control application vulnerabilities, and leverages the absence of antivirus software on a workstation. Access to the workstation enables the adversary to control and modify industrial control devices.

- **Attack Method:** An adversary exploits operating system and industrial control application vulnerabilities to gain control of a workstation.

Alternatively, the adversary may use a spear phishing (email) attack or insert a USB device with malware into the workstation.

- **Attacker Goal:** An adversary desires to disrupt a workstation and the automated operation of control devices, and ultimately disrupt plant operations or damage plant equipment. Operators would have to monitor and control the plant manually; in the worst case, the plant would have to be shut down.

- **Required Attacker Skill Level:** Attacking a workstation requires basic hacking skills. The attack can be performed by a hacker, terrorist, industrial spy or cyber warrior.

- **Example:** An attacker installs malware on a workstation. The malware discovers and issues commands that impact the behavior of industrial control devices in the network.

4.5   Sensor Manipulation

- **Description:** A sensor attack targets the sensors in an industrial control system. There are different types of sensors, including temperature sensors, light sensors and touch sensors. In general, there are two types of sensor attacks:

  - *Physical Attack:* This attack tampers with sensors or causes them to send incorrect responses. For example, an adversary can manually cover a light sensor, causing it to send an incorrect signal. Incorrect sensor values would cause an industrial control device such as a programmable logic controller to send incorrect commands to the physical plant.

  - *Wireless Attack:* This attack involves the wireless injection of incorrect sensor responses. Communications between sensors and industrial control devices rarely employ authentication and encryption. An adversary can pretend to be a sensor and send false values to industrial control devices. The industrial control devices would be unable to verify the correctness of the inputs they receive.

- **Attack Prerequisites:** An adversary must know where the sensors are located and how they are connected to industrial control devices. The adversary also has to know how to modify sensor signals that are sent to industrial control devices.

- **Targeted Vulnerabilities or Weaknesses:** Sensors are used to monitor a physical plant. Because sensor communications with industrial control devices are neither authenticated nor encrypted, an adversary can capture and modify the signals sent to industrial control devices.

- **Attack Method:** In the case of wired sensors, physical access is required on the part of an adversary to launch an attack that affects sensor signals.

In the case of wireless sensors, an adversary can capture sensor signals to industrial control devices and perform wireless signal injection and replay attacks.

- **Attacker Goal:** An adversary desires to change sensor signals to induce industrial control devices to behave incorrectly. Consider, for example, an elevator that has a light sensor to detect if an object is blocking the door of the elevator car. The adversary could modify the light sensor signal from on to off, causing the door to keep opening. Also, touch sensors in the elevator detect if the car has moved to the upper or lower limit. The elevator will not move if the adversary alters these sensor signals.

- **Required Attacker Skill Level:** An adversary needs a good understanding of how industrial devices operate a physical plant. The adversary also must know how sensors and industrial control devices are connected and how the devices behave after receiving sensor signals. The attack can be performed by a terrorist, industrial spy or cyber warrior.

- **Example:** An attacker modifies sensor signals and causes an industrial control system to behave in an incorrect manner.

5. Elevator System Case Study

This section defines the security test cases for an elevator system based on the industrial control system attack patterns described in the previous section.

An elevator system operator asked the authors of this paper to design and conduct a security test of a newly-deployed elevator system. The operator wanted an assessment of the security level of the elevator system and to determine if an adversary could exploit vulnerabilities in the workstation, industrial control devices and sensors to launch attacks that would interrupt elevator service or seize control of the elevator system.

5.1 Security Test Cases

The following security test cases are based on the industrial control system attack patterns defined in the previous section:

- **Information Collection and Analysis:** The security test cases in this category evaluate whether or not device information can be obtained by an adversary. This information could be used by the adversary to develop sophisticated attacks that interrupt elevator service or seize control of the elevator system.

  Table 1 shows five security test cases for the Information Collection and Analysis attack pattern based on the elevator system architecture.

- **Injection:** The security test cases in this category evaluate whether or not elevator system communications are protected by authentication and encryption. Additionally, the security test cases evaluate whether or not

Table 1. Security test cases for Information Collection and Analysis.

Objective	Description/Actions	Expected Result
Obtain elevator controller information – passive	1. Plug attack device into the elevator system 2. Use `tcpdump` or Wireshark to capture traffic 3. Analyze traffic to obtain elevator controller information	Elevator controller information cannot be obtained
Obtain elevator controller information – active	1. Plug attack device into the elevator system 2. Use Nmap to scan the elevator controller 3. Analyze traffic to obtain elevator controller information	Elevator controller information cannot be obtained
Obtain control device information – passive	1. Plug attack device into the elevator system 2. Use `tcpdump` or Wireshark to capture traffic 3. Analyze traffic to obtain control device information	Control device information cannot be obtained
Obtain control device information – active	1. Plug attack device into the elevator system 2. Use Nmap to scan the control device 3. Analyze traffic to obtain control device information	Control device information cannot be obtained
Obtain sensor information	1. Plug attack device into the elevator system 2. Use `tcpdump` or Wireshark to capture traffic 3. Analyze traffic to obtain sensor information	Sensor information cannot be obtained

the control protocol is vulnerable and whether or not modified control system commands and responses can be injected into elevator system communications.

Tables 2 and 3 show five security test cases for the Injection attack pattern.

■ **Denial-of-Service:** The security test cases in this category cover possible TCP and UDP denial-of-service attacks on the elevator controller, control devices and sensors.

Table 2. Security test cases for Injection.

Objective	Description/Actions	Expected Result
Test authentication between the elevator controller and control devices	1. Plug attack device into the elevator system 2. Stop the communications between the elevator controller and control devices 3. Use `tcpdump` or Wireshark to capture traffic 4. Start the communications between the elevator controller and control devices 5. Analyze traffic to check if the authentication between the elevator controller and control devices is vulnerable	Communications between the elevator controller and control devices are authenticated Authentication is secure
Test for encrypted communications between the elevator controller and control devices	1. Plug attack device into the elevator system 2. Stop the communications between the elevator controller and control devices 3. Use `tcpdump` or Wireshark to capture traffic 4. Start the communications between the elevator controller and control devices 5. Analyze traffic to check if encrypted communications exist between the elevator controller and control devices and if they are vulnerable	Communications between the elevator controller and control devices are encrypted Encryption is secure
Test if the control protocol is vulnerable	1. Plug attack device into the elevator system 2. Stop the communications between the elevator controller and control devices 3. Use `tcpdump` or Wireshark to capture traffic 4. Start the communications between the elevator controller and control devices 5. Analyze traffic to check if the control protocol version used is vulnerable	Control protocol is not vulnerable

Table 3.   Security test cases for Injection (continued).

Objective	Description/Actions	Expected Result
Test command injection into the elevator controller	1. Plug attack device into the elevator system 2. Stop the communications between the elevator controller and control devices 3. Use `tcpdump` or Wireshark to capture traffic 4. Start the communications between the elevator controller and control devices 5. Capture commands sent to the elevator controller 6. Modify and send commands from the attack device 7. Test if the commands are executed by the elevator controller	Commands cannot be injected into the elevator controller
Test response injection into the control devices	1. Plug attack device into the elevator system 2. Stop the communications between the elevator controller and control devices 3. Use `tcpdump` or Wireshark to capture traffic 4. Start the communications between the elevator controller and control devices 5. Capture responses sent to the control devices 6. Modify and send responses from the attack device 7. Test if the responses are accepted by the control devices	Responses cannot be injected into the control devices

Table 4 shows six security test cases for the Denial-of-Service attack pattern.

■ **System Resource Manipulation:** The security test cases in this category relate to performing penetration testing on the control devices and workstation in the elevator system. Since the workstation connects to the elevator system, some security test cases assess the security levels of the workstation and network configuration.

Table 4. Security test cases for Denial-of-Service.

Objective	Description/Actions	Expected Result
Test if TCP DoS attacks can be launched on the elevator controller	1. Plug attack device into the elevator system 2. Use **hping** or LOIC to send TCP packets to the elevator controller 3. Check if the elevator controller operates properly	TCP DoS attacks cannot affect the elevator controller
Test if UDP DoS attacks can be launched on the elevator controller	1. Plug attack device into the elevator system 2. Use **hping** or LOIC to send UDP packets to the elevator controller 3. Check if the elevator controller operates properly	UDP DoS attacks cannot affect the elevator controller
Test if TCP DoS attacks can be launched on the control devices	1. Plug attack device into the elevator system 2. Use **hping** or LOIC to send TCP packets to the control devices 3. Check if the control devices operate properly	TCP DoS attacks cannot affect the control devices
Test if UDP DoS attacks can be launched on the control devices	1. Plug attack device into the elevator system 2. Use **hping** or LOIC to send UDP packets to the control devices 3. Check if the control devices operate properly	UDP DoS attacks cannot affect the control devices
Test if TCP DoS attacks can be launched on the sensors	1. Plug attack device into the elevator system 2. Use **hping** or LOIC to send TCP packets to the sensors 3. Check if the sensors operate properly	TCP DoS attacks cannot affect the sensors
Test if UDP DoS attacks can be launched on the sensors	1. Plug attack device into the elevator system 2. Use **hping** or LOIC to send UDP packets to the sensors 3. Check if the sensors operate properly	UDP DoS attacks cannot affect the sensors

Table 5. Security test cases for System Resource Manipulation.

Objective	Description/Actions	Expected Result
Scan control devices using a vulnerability scanner	1. Plug vulnerability scanner into the elevator system 2. Use the vulnerability scanner scanner on the control devices 3. Check the results provided by the vulnerability scanner	No critical vulnerabiliies are found
Scan the workstation using a vulnerability scanner	1. Plug vulnerability scanner into the elevator system 2. Use the vulnerability scanner scanner on the workstation 3. Check the results provided by the vulnerability scanner	No critical vulnerabilities are found
Check the network configuration in the elevator system	1. Use the administration console to check the network configuration	Network is configured properly
Extract the elevator program from the elevator controller	1. Plug attack device into the elevator system 2. Use the IDE (e.g., Siemens TIA Portal) to connect to the elevator controller 3. Send the download command to the elevator controller 4. Check if the elevator program can be downloaded	Elevator program cannot be extracted from the elevator controller
Modify the elevator program in the elevator controller	1. Plug attack device into the elevator system 2. Use the IDE (e.g., Siemens TIA Portal) to connect to the elevator controller 3. Send the upload command to the elevator controller 4. Check if the modified elevator program can be uploaded and execute properly	Modified elevator program cannot be uploaded to the elevator controller and execute properly
Check the elevator controller firmware version	1. Plug attack device into the elevator system 2. Use the IDE (e.g., Siemens TIA Portal) to connect to the elevator controller 3. Check the firmware version	Elevator controller firmware is the latest version

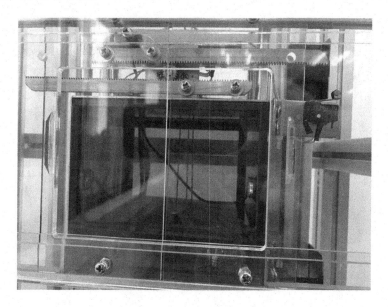

Figure 2. Elevator light sensor.

Table 5 shows six security test cases for the System Resource Manipulation attack pattern.

■ **Sensor Manipulation:** The security test cases in this category relate to potential compromises of sensors. In the case of wired sensors, the sensors have to be located and attacked by physical means. In the case of wireless sensors, a Wi-Fi sniffer and/or Bluetooth sniffer are required. The security test cases for the Sensor Manipulation and Injection attack patterns are similar. However, the two attack pattern categories are treated separately for effective security testing.

The elevator system has light sensors and touch sensors that connect to the elevator controller (Figures 2 and 3, respectively). The security test cases check whether or not it is possible to change the sensor values and the behavior of the elevator.

Table 6 shows five security test cases for the Sensor Manipulation attack pattern.

5.2   Results

The attack patterns enabled the security testing team to define elevator system security test cases. Also, the attack patterns helped identify the types of attacks, vulnerabilities exploited by the attacks, and methods for detecting and mitigating the attacks.

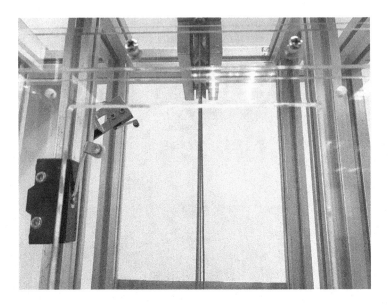

Figure 3.   Elevator touch sensor.

6.   Conclusions

The interconnections of industrial control systems and information technology networks expose the control systems and the infrastructure assets they operate to cyber attacks. Attack patterns have been used to specify security test cases for traditional information technology systems in order to mitigate cyber attacks. However, because of differences in the architectures, constituent devices, attack goals and attack methods, the attack patterns for traditional information technology systems are not directly applicable to industrial control systems.

Five attack patterns have been specified for industrial control systems – Information Collection and Analysis, Injection, Denial-of-Service, System Resource Manipulation and Sensor Manipulation. Each industrial control system attack pattern has six components – description, attack prerequisites, targeted vulnerabilities or weaknesses, attack method, attacker goal and required attacker skill level.

As demonstrated in the elevator system case study, the attack patterns help understand the possible threats and their impacts to an industrial control system and the physical plant it operates. The attack patterns are also useful for creating security test cases for assessing the security levels of the industrial control system, and for developing and implementing attack mitigation mechanisms.

Table 6. Security test cases for Sensor Manipulation.

Objective	Description/Actions	Expected Result
Test authentication between the elevator controller and sensors	1. Plug attack device into the elevator system 2. Use `tcpdump` or Wireshark to capture traffic 3. Analyze traffic to check if the authentication between the elevator controller and sensors is vulnerable	Authentication is secure
Test encryption between the elevator controller and sensors	1. Plug attack device into the elevator system 2. Use `tcpdump` or Wireshark to capture traffic 3. Analyze traffic to check if the encryption between the elevator controller and sensors is vulnerable	Encryption is secure
Test if the sensor signals can be modified	1. Plug attack device into the elevator system 2. Use `tcpdump` or Wireshark to capture signals sent by the sensors 3. Modify and send signals from the attack device 4. Check if the signals are accepted by the elevator controller	Sensor signals cannot be modified
Test if the sensors can be accessed physically and replaced	1. Gain physical access to the elevator system 2. Locate the sensors 3. Attempt to remove and replace the sensors 4. Check if the elevator system is still operational	Sensors cannot be accessed physically and replaced
Test if the wireless sensor signals can be tampered with	1. Use `tcpdump` or Wireshark to capture wireless signals sent by the sensors 2. Modify and send wireless signals from the attack device 3. Check if the signals are accepted by the elevator controller	Wireless sensor signals cannot be tampered with

References

[1] J. Bozic and F. Wotawa, Security testing based on attack patterns, *Proceedings of the Seventh IEEE International Conference on Software Testing, Verification and Validation Workshops*, pp. 4–11, 2014.

[2] Z. Flom, Shedding light on BlackEnergy with open source intelligence, *Recorded Future Blog* (`www.recordedfuture.com/blackenergy-malware-analysis`), March 3, 2016.

[3] E. Gamma, R. Helm, R. Johnson and J. Vlissides, *Design Patterns: Elements of Reusable Object-Oriented Software*, Addison-Wesley, Boston, Massachusetts, 1994.

[4] M. Gegick and L. Williams, Matching attack patterns to security vulnerabilities in software-intensive system designs, *Proceedings of the Workshop on Software Engineering for Secure Systems – Building Trustworthy Applications*, 2005.

[5] M. Havis, Chernobyl under attack: Computers "shut down" at nuclear disaster plant, *Daily Star*, June 27, 2017.

[6] P. Jie and L. Li, Industrial control system security, *Proceedings of the International Conference on Intelligent Human-Machine Systems and Cybernetics*, vol. 2, pp. 156–158, 2011.

[7] K. Li, Y. Li, J. Liu, R. Zhang and X. Duan, Attack pattern mining algorithm based on security logs, *Proceedings of the IEEE International Conference on Intelligence and Security Informatics*, p. 205, 2017.

[8] T. Li, E. Paja, J. Mylopoulos, J. Horkoff and K. Beckers, Security attack analysis using attack patterns, *Proceedings of the Tenth IEEE International Conference on Research Challenges in Information Science*, 2016.

[9] MITRE, Common Attack Pattern Enumeration and Classification (CAPEC), McLean, Virginia (`www.capec.mitre.org/about/index.html`), 2019.

[10] E. Pricop and S. Mihalache, Fuzzy approach for modeling cyber attack patterns on data transfer in industrial control systems, *Proceedings of the Seventh International Conference on Electronics, Computers and Artificial Intelligence*, pp. SSS-23–SSS-28, 2015.

[11] M. Rahaman, C. Hebert and J. Frank, An attack pattern framework for monitoring enterprise information systems, *Proceedings of the Twenty-Fifth IEEE International Conference on Enabling Technologies: Infrastructure for Collaborative Enterprises*, pp. 173–178, 2016.

[12] A. Sethi and S. Barnum, Introduction to Attack Patterns, Cigital, Dulles, Virginia (`www.us-cert.gov/bsi/articles/knowledge/attack-patterns/introduction-to-attack-patterns`), 2006.

[13] K. Stouffer, V. Pillitteri, S. Lightman, M. Abrams and A. Hahn, Guide to Industrial Control Systems (ICS) Security, NIST Special Publication 800-82, Revision 2, National Institute of Standards and Technology, Gaithersburg, Maryland, 2015.

[14] C. Valli, Issues common to Australian critical infrastructure providers' SCADA networks discovered through computer and network vulnerability analysis, *Proceedings of the Sixth Australian Digital Forensics Conference*, 2008.

[15] K. Zetter, *Countdown to Zero Day: Stuxnet and the Launch of the World's First Digital Weapon*, Broadway Books, New York, 2014.

[16] Y. Zhu, Attack pattern discovery in forensic investigations of network attacks, *IEEE Journal on Selected Areas in Communications*, vol. 29(7), pp. 1349–1357, 2011.

Chapter 16

AN INCIDENT RESPONSE MODEL FOR INDUSTRIAL CONTROL SYSTEM FORENSICS BASED ON HISTORICAL EVENTS

Ken Yau, Kam-Pui Chow and Siu-Ming Yiu

Abstract   Cyber attacks on industrial control systems are increasing. Malware such as Stuxnet, Havex and BlackEnergy have demonstrated that industrial control systems are attractive targets for attackers. However, industrial control systems are not limited to malware attacks. Other attacks include SQL injection, distributed denial-of-service, spear phishing, social engineering and man-in-the-middle attacks. Additionally, methods such as unauthorized access, brute forcing and insider attacks have also targeted industrial control systems. Accidents such as fires and explosions at industrial plants also provide valuable insights into the targets of attacks, failure methods and potential impacts.

This chapter presents an incident response model for industrial control system forensics based on historical events. In particular, representative industrial control system incidents – cyber attacks and accidents – that have occurred over the past 25 years are categorized and analyzed. The resulting incident response model is useful for forensic planning and investigations. The model enables incident response teams and forensic investigators to decide on the expertise, techniques and tools to be applied to ensure sound evidence acquisition, analysis and reporting.

Keywords: Industrial control systems, incident response, forensics

1.   Introduction

The critical infrastructure is defined as processes, systems, facilities, technologies, networks, assets and services that are essential to the health, safety security or economic well-being of citizens and the effective functioning of government [14]. Critical infrastructure assets can be stand-alone or interconnected, and interdependent within and across cities, states and nations. Disruptions or

© IFIP International Federation for Information Processing 2019
Published by Springer Nature Switzerland AG 2019
J. Staggs and S. Shenoi (Eds.): Critical Infrastructure Protection XIII, IFIP AICT 570, pp. 311–328, 2019.
https://doi.org/10.1007/978-3-030-34647-8_16

damage to critical infrastructure assets could result in the loss of life, adverse economic effects and loss of public confidence [14].

Industrial control systems are indispensable to the safe and efficient operation of critical infrastructure assets. An industrial control system can be a single embedded system such as a programmable logic controller (PLC) that controls an automatic door or an elevator; or it could be a large and complex distributed control system connected to multiple supervisory control and data acquisition (SCADA) systems in a nuclear power plant [24].

Modern industrial control systems are increasingly connected to corporate networks and the Internet over TCP/IP and wireless protocols to improve their performance and effectiveness [22], exposing the previously-isolated systems to myriad remote attacks. According to an IBM report [12], cyber attacks on industrial systems in 2016 increased by 110% over the previous year (2015). Because of the importance of industrial control systems, it is crucial to protect them from remote cyber attacks as well as from undesirable incidents such as hardware failures, malicious intruders, accidents and natural disasters [23].

Digital forensics is an important part of an incident investigation. It helps reconstruct past events and activities based on timelines in order to prevent recurring attacks and undesirable incidents from occurring. Industrial control systems may comprise hundreds to thousands of interconnected devices. The devices include programmable logic controllers and remote terminal units (RTUs), which are highly specialized embedded systems that often have limited computational and memory resources, and functionality. As a result, it can be difficult to acquire data from industrial control systems. Traditional digital forensic techniques are also inadequate for industrial control systems. Moreover, standard forensic guidelines, procedures and tools are not as yet available for investigating incidents involving industrial control systems.

Several frameworks, processes and tools have been developed for industrial control system security and forensics; these are primarily based on attack patterns of real or synthetic industrial control system malware. However, only a portion of industrial control system incidents involve malware attacks. This chapter presents an incident response model for industrial control system forensics based on historical events. In particular, representative industrial control incidents – cyber attacks and accidents – that have occurred over the past 25 years are categorized and analyzed. The resulting incident response model is useful for forensic planning and investigations. The model enables incident response teams and forensic investigators to decide on the expertise, techniques and tools to be applied to ensure sound evidence acquisition, analysis and reporting.

2.   Forensic Challenges

Digital forensic techniques and tools are required to collect evidence for legal proceedings and internal investigations, as well as to handle malware incidents and unusual operational problems. Regardless of the application, digital forensics involves four basic processes: (i) collection; (ii) examination;

Figure 1. Digital forensic process [10].

(iii) analysis; and (iv) reporting (Figure 1). The implementation details of these processes vary based on the specific forensic needs.

Although digital forensics is becoming a mature domain, investigators need to modify traditional digital forensic processes for use in industrial control system environments. The following forensic challenges are encountered in industrial control environments [7]:

- The availability of industrial control systems is a top priority. Therefore, it is often not possible to shut down devices such as programmable logic controllers for evidence collection and forensic investigations.

- Most modern industrial control environments provide only some of the required data collection features (e.g., identifying, recording, copying and labeling materials from a variety of data sources in the information architecture). Many industrial control systems do not support forensic data collection.

- Contemporary forensic tools, such as those used to examine running processes and services, automate evidence collection through precompiled scripts or programs, bit copy processes and programs that generate checksums for image verification, are often not designed to accommodate industrial control system technologies. Many forensic tools cannot be adapted to operate in industrial control environments.

3. Industrial Control Networks

Operational technology (OT) refers to the hardware and software that monitor and/or control industrial processes. Industrial control systems and SCADA systems are examples of operational technology. The protection of critical infrastructure networks is commonly considered to fall in the domain of SCADA security [4]. However, this is not necessarily true.

In fact, critical infrastructure networks are hybrids of operational technology and information technology [4]. Industrial control systems are often connected to corporate networks (Figure 2). Whether they reside in large critical infrastructure assets or small localized controller-run assets, industrial control systems integrate operational and information technologies.

Stuxnet, a most sophisticated and complex malware, was designed to target industrial control systems. It was launched from a conventional information technology network to attack programmable logic controllers in an operational

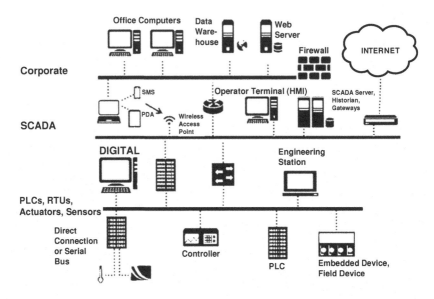

Figure 2. Example industrial control network [4].

technology network. The Stuxnet attack demonstrated that an air gap between information technology and operational technology can be breached [4].

4.   Literature Review

Research on industrial control system and programmable logic controller security and forensics significantly ramped up after Stuxnet was discovered in 2010. The research has generally focused on vulnerabilities in industrial control systems and protocols. Several types of simulated cyber attacks have been investigated to advance security and forensic efforts.

Spenneberg et al. [20] developed a worm that propagates to programmable logic controllers. The worm scans a network for programmable logic controllers, attacks the targets and then replicates itself on the targets. Spenneberg and colleagues have analyzed the impacts of the worm on various targets and have suggested possible mitigations.

Abbasi and Hashemi [1] have investigated the security implications of embedded system input/output pin control. They demonstrate how an attacker can affect the integrity and availability of embedded system inputs and outputs by exploiting pin control operations. Such attacks on programmable logic controllers can be difficult to detect.

Ben Aloui [2] has demonstrated the ease with which dynamic code injection can be executed on a Siemens S7-300 programmable logic controller without shutting down or restarting the device. The program, which is written in the C language and uses the Snap7 library, pushes a new program segment (organization block) into the CPU. A small human-machine interface (HMI) was developed to illustrate dynamic modifications of the execution flow. Several countermeasures and protection strategies were proposed to combat dynamic code injection.

All these research efforts are useful for industrial control system threat analysis and forensics, but they focus on simulated, not real, cyber attacks. Thus, the results do not reflect real situations. Indeed, realistic solutions for industrial control system forensics are unlikely to be developed by considering only simulated attacks.

Eden et al. [6] have proposed a forensic incident response model for industrial control systems. The model has four stages: (i) prepare; (ii) detect; (iii) triage; and (iv) respond. Eden and colleagues outline the forensic triage process and highlight the differences and challenges involved in performing forensic incident responses on industrial control systems compared with traditional systems. The forensic incident response model is useful, but is generic as opposed to incident-specific.

5.   Classification of Incidents

In order to develop a practical methodology for industrial control system forensics, representative incidents since 1992 discussed in newspaper articles, technical reports and research papers were examined. The incidents were first organized into two types: (i) attacks; and (ii) accidents. They were then classified into four categories: (i) general computer malware; (ii) unauthorized access; (iii) industrial control system malware; and (iv) accidents.

The classification model is based on categories of malicious activity [3] and accidents. Tables 1 and 2 summarize the incidents.

5.1   General Computer Malware

General computer malware targets traditional information technology systems such as office computers and human-machine interfaces. However, malware attacks can indirectly shut down or otherwise impact industrial control system operations.

A variant of the Sobig worm was introduced into the CSX Railroad headquarters in Jacksonville, Florida in August 2003 [3]. The malware installed applications and created backdoors while continuing to spread by infecting e-mail attachments. Although the worm was not specifically designed to target railroad systems, it propagated to the control center and proceeded to disrupt signaling, dispatch and other related systems. Reports indicated that Amtrak trains in the area were also affected by the malware in CSX Railroad systems. The malware attack caused multiple train delays and expensive clean-up activities.

Table 1. Selected incidents classified into four categories [3, 12].

Type	Category	Year	Representative Incident
Attacks	**General Computer Malware**	2003	The SQL Slammer worm disabled a nuclear power plant in Ohio, USA
		2003	The Sobig worm was introduced in the CSX Railroad headquarters in Florida, USA
		2005	The Zotob worm infected 13 automobile plants in Ohio, USA, causing shutdowns and delays
		2006	An attacker penetrated a water treatment facility network in Pennsylvania, USA
		2014	The modified Gh0st RAT Trojan infected a fast-breeder nuclear reactor in Tsuruga, Japan
Attacks	**Unauthorized Access**	1992	A fired employee hacked into Chevron systems in New York and California, USA, and reconfigured the emergency alert network
		1997	A teenager connected to a dial-up loop carrier system servicing an airport in Massachusetts, USA and sent a series of commands that disabled the system
		2000	A former consultant attacked a sewage treatment plant in Maroochy, Australia
		2007	Striking workers (insiders) penetrated a traffic system in California, USA
		2008	An attacker used a homemade device to remotely derail a train in Lodz, Poland
		2009	A disgruntled former IT contractor hacked into leak detection systems on multiple oil platforms off the coast of California, USA
		2011	A hacker used Shodan to access HMIs in a water utility network in Texas, USA
		2013	A sophisticated attacker penetrated the U.S. Army Corps of Engineers National Inventory of Dams, USA
		2014	A hacker accessed a SCADA server in the USA that operated mechanical equipment

5.2 Unauthorized Access

These incidents involve unauthorized persistent access of control center systems or field devices from another network such as a corporate network or

Table 2.   Selected incidents classified into four categories [3, 12] (continued).

Type	Category	Year	Representative Incident
Attacks	Industrial Control System Malware	2003	An attacker sabotaged a marine terminal in Venezuela
		2010	The Stuxnet worm destroyed uranium hexa-fluoride centrifuges in Natanz, Iran
		2014	The Havex Trojan entered OPC servers and tried to exfiltrate data from industrial control systems in the USA and Europe
		2016	The BlackEnergy Trojan caused power outages in the Ivano-Frankivsk region of Ukraine
Accidents	Accidents	2013	Two mechanics died in a fire in the nacelle of a wind turbine in The Netherlands [12]
		2013	An elevator dropped on its way up a building in North Point, Hong Kong [11]
		2014	Nickel sulfate was discharged into a river from a mine in Harjavalta, Finland [13]
		2015	Water mixed with molten metal in a foundry in Feurs, France to cause an explosion [13]
		2015	Pressurized flammable gas leaked into a petrochemical complex in Gonfreville-l'Orcher, France [13]
		2017	An escalator suddenly accelerated and then reversed its direction in a mall in Mong Kok, Hong Kong [15]

the Internet. The attackers can be insiders (e.g., employees, contractors and vendors) or outsiders.

One of the most famous SCADA system breaches occurred at Maroochy Water Services on Queensland's Sunshine Coast in Australia [18]. Vitek Boden, a former Maroochy consultant, used a laptop computer and a radio transmitter to take control of 150 sewage pumping stations. Over a three-month period, he released one million liters of untreated sewage into a water drain from where it flowed into local waterways. Mr. Boden launched the attack because he was denied a fulltime position with the Maroochy Shire Council.

5.3   Industrial Control System Malware

Industrial control system malware specifically targets field devices such as programmable logic controllers. The incidents may involve firmware tampering or exploiting device vulnerabilities.

Stuxnet is a most sophisticated industrial control system malware that leveraged four zero-day vulnerabilities and two compromised digital certificates in its attacks on Iran's uranium hexafluoride centrifuges [3]. The malware exploited

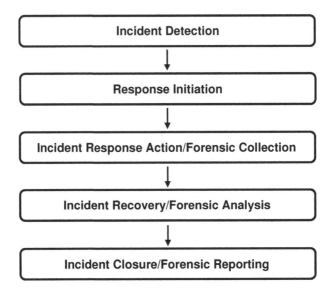

Figure 3. Cyber incident response model with an embedded forensics component.

application software to control Windows systems that could modify the control programs of Siemens programmable logic controllers, inducing abnormal operations and eventually destroying several centrifuges.

5.4   Accidents

Accidents include incidents such as incorrect control, power disruptions, hardware failures and fires that are not due to cyber attacks or cyber criminal activities [5]. They are typically caused by design flaws, human error and natural phenomena.

A fire in the nacelle of a wind turbine in The Netherlands in October 2013 killed two service engineers [24]. Investigators working in collaboration with the Netherlands Forensic Institute, Department of Digital Technology and the wind turbine manufacturer were able to remove the controller located at the base of the turbine to extract evidence.

6.   Refined Incident Response Model

Incident response requires substantial planning and resources. [19]. Digital forensics, which is a core component of incident response capabilities, covers the collection, examination, analysis and reporting of incident data [7]. A forensic program is typically initiated after incident response processes such as restoration, mitigation and initial reporting. Many organizations integrate the forensic function in incident response processes, especially when the start of the forensic function cannot be defined clearly.

Fabro and Cornelius [7] have studied the integration trend and have defined a cyber incident response model with an embedded forensics component as shown in Figure 3. In this approach, forensic collection is embedded in incident response, forensic analysis in incident recovery and forensic reporting in incident closure.

The study of historical industrial control system incidents reveals that special skills and techniques are not always required for digital forensic examinations of industrial control systems. Some incidents can be investigated using traditional forensic techniques and tools, especially when the incidents fall in the general computer malware and unauthorized access categories. In the case of an industrial control system incident, the incident response team typically incorporates industrial control system specialists and applies special techniques and tools in the investigation. However, the historical incident data reveals that traditional forensic techniques and tools are adequate for investigating incidents in the general computer malware and unauthorized access categories, eliminating the need to use specialized techniques and tools.

Therefore, in order to increase the efficiency of forensic processes, the core components of cyber incident response in Figure 3 are refined by inserting a new incident categorization component after the incident detection component during the early stage of preparing a forensic response plan. Figure 4 shows the refined incident response model with an embedded industrial control system forensics component.

Additionally, two types of response are incorporated: (i) traditional forensics; and (ii) industrial control system forensics. Depending on the classification assigned to an incident, the investigation can employ either traditional forensics or industrial control system forensics during the early stage. This saves time, effort and resources while ensuring more precise and effective incident response.

6.1　Traditional Forensics

This section discusses the application of traditional forensics to industrial control systems in incidents involving general computer malware and unauthorized access. Since traditional information technology computers, networks and protocols are targeted, traditional forensic methods are adequate for digital investigations. Normal hard drive analysis, log analysis and network tools can be used to examine what was running on the systems and reveal the causes of the incidents.

- **General Computer Malware:** In the case of the virus attack on CSX Railroad, traditional digital forensics would have been sufficient because the incident did not involve industrial control equipment or field devices. The incident mainly involved general computer systems. Therefore, the investigation would have identified the hosts that were infected by malware, and appropriate containment, eradication and recovery ac-

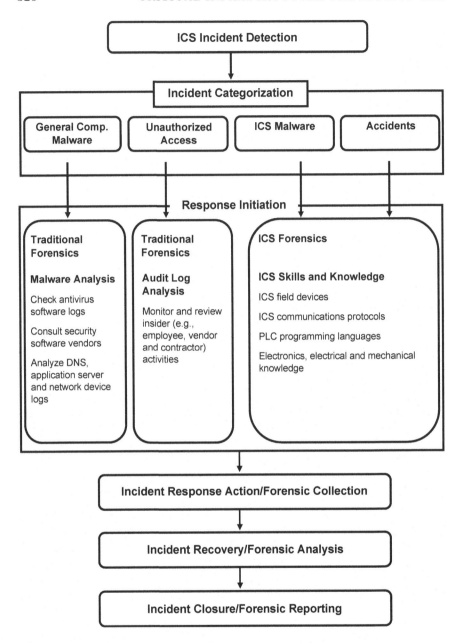

Figure 4. Refined incident response model with an ICS forensics component.

tions would have been applied to the infected hosts. Evidence would then have been collected from the domain name server (DNS) logs, application server logs and network device logs. Traditional network forensic logs would also have been analyzed to reveal detailed information about the malware activity [19].

- **Unauthorized Access:** In the case of the unauthorized access incident at Maroochy Water Services, a PDS Compact 500 process controller, two-way radio and computer laptop were found in Mr. Boden's automobile. Mr. Boden stated that he owned all the items and was using them for study, personal correspondence and work related to his family business. However, law enforcement discovered that the PDS Compact 500 controller and two-way radio were stolen from Hunter Watertech, a company contracted to install PDS Compact 500 units at pumping stations belonging to Maroochy Shire.

  The software installed in Mr. Boden's laptop computer was developed by Hunter Watertech and was required to communicate with the SCADA system at Maroochy Water Services; the software had no other practical use. The two-way radio was set to the same frequency as two of the three available repeater stations. The laptop computer startup and shutdown times were consistent with the logged intrusions. The PDS Compact 500 process controller had the same address as the one logged during the intrusions. Moreover, Mr. Boden was arrested at a location that was within radio range of the pumping station repeater and close enough to connect to the SCADA network.

  All the evidence in the Maroochy Water Services incident was collected by applying traditional digital forensic techniques and tools with the assistance of Hunter Watertech personnel. Mr. Boden was ultimately sentenced to two years in jail on 30 charges of computer hacking, theft and causing environmental damage [17].

  Industrial control system attacks are not limited to malware. Other attacks include advanced persistent threats (APTs), spear phishing, SQL injection, distributed denial-of-service (DDoS), social engineering and man-in-the-middle (MITM) attacks. However, less sophisticated methods such as unauthorized access, brute forcing and insider attacks can be just as effective [17]. As in the case of the CSX Railroad and Maroochy Services attacks, many incidents can be handled using traditional forensic methods because the incidents did not involve industrial control equipment or field devices.

6.2 Industrial Control System Forensics

Traditional forensic techniques and tools do not provide data collection functionality for programmable logic controllers, remote terminal units, intelligent electronic devices and other field devices encountered in industrial control environments [24]. Therefore, incidents that fall in the industrial control system

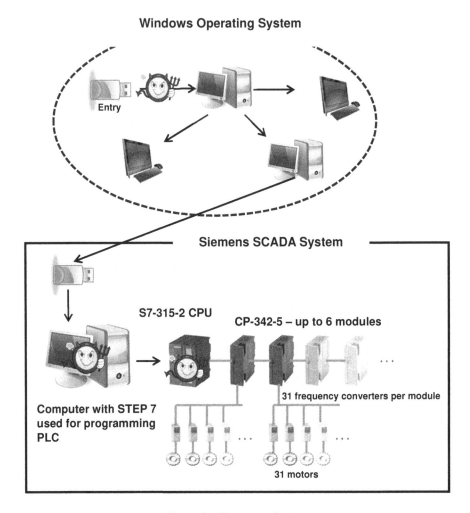

Figure 5. Stuxnet infection.

malware and accidents categories require the application of industrial control forensic expertise and tools.

- **Industrial Control System Malware:** The Stuxnet malware was developed to target specific industrial control systems. The malware conducted a layered attack against three systems: (i) Windows operating system; (ii) Siemens PCS 7, WinCC and STEP 7 industrial software applications that run on Windows (SCADA system); and (iii) Siemens STEP 7 programmable logic controllers (SCADA system).

  Figure 5 provides an overview of the Stuxnet infection. The malware entered and infected a target system via a USB flash drive, following which it searched for, propagated to and infected other target systems. It originally leveraged four zero-day Windows vulnerabilities to propagate and infect systems. Stuxnet was designed to sabotage centrifuges that employ Siemens SCADA systems by reprogramming the programming logic controllers to command the centrifuges to operate outside their designed parameter ranges [8].

In order to conduct a forensic investigation of a Stuxnet-type incident, incident response personnel must have substantial knowledge about SCADA systems, especially programmable logic controller and field device hardware, firmware and software (applications) as well as SCADA communications protocols. Furthermore, highly specialized techniques and tools are required to collect and analyze data from industrial control devices in a forensically-sound manner.

- **Accidents:** In the case of an accident like the wind turbine fire in The Netherlands discussed above, investigators were required to have adequate industrial control system expertise and sophisticated tools because evidence pertaining to the accident had to be collected from the RAM chip in the programmable logic controller located at the base of the turbine. Therefore, the accident investigators worked closely with professionals from the Netherlands Forensic Institute, Department of Digital Technology and the wind turbine manufacturer to collect and analyze the evidence.

On March 25, 2017, a serious escalator accident occurred in a busy Mong Kok, Hong Kong shopping mall. A 45-meter escalator linking the fourth and eighth floors and carrying about 120 patrons malfunctioned and suddenly moved in the reverse direction, injuring 18 people [16].

The technical investigation report [9] stated that the escalator accident was due to the failure of the main drive chain and a broken chain safety device. There was no overloading of the escalator. The investigators worked closely with escalator workers, a registered escalator engineer, the escalator contractor and personnel from the mall management company to collect evidence for examination.

Investigating incidents involving industrial control systems is not only about finding evidence about potential criminal activities. This is because incidents are often the result of accidents such as equipment malfunctions and fires [24]. Accident investigators must have adequate technical expertise and the appropriate tools to collect and analyze evidence from industrial control systems that are directly or indirectly connected to accidents, or are proximal to the accidents [24].

7. Discussion

This study has some limitations. A large number of industrial control system incidents go unreported and, in other cases, details about the incidents are not published. The number of incident categories proposed depends on the representative incidents considered in the study and different selections of incidents would likely yield different incident categories. Moreover, information about the incidents considered in the study was collected from various sources, and may have various assumptions and biases. All these factors are expected to affect the results of the analysis.

This study reveals that a large proportion of industrial control system incident investigations can be conducted using traditional forensic processes. However, some incidents are more difficult to handle because embedded systems such as programmable logic controllers are specialized devices with their own communications protocols, connection interfaces, operating systems and programming languages [24]. Therefore, in the case of incidents related to embedded systems, investigators may have to work with experts who have the appropriate tools to collect and analyze data from industrial control equipment. Some tools are able to extract evidence from RAM chips in the devices, but this may not always be done in a forensically-sound manner [24].

Programmable logic controllers are arguably the most important components in industrial control systems. They are attractive targets because successful attacks on programmable logic controllers can result in significant industrial process malfunctions and equipment damage. Each vendor usually provides custom software for programming, communicating and configuring its programmable logic controllers. For example, STEP 7 software running in Windows environments is used to program, communicate with and configure Siemens programmable logic controllers.

The following STEP 7 features are useful in forensic investigations of programmable logic controllers:

- **Logging communications between a programmable logic controller and STEP 7 software:** Communications events of interest include Program Change, Start PLC and Stop PLC (Figure 6). For example, the logged information enables an investigator to identify who changed the control program and when it was changed.

- **Checking the integrity of the control program in a programmable logic controller:** The control program in a programmable logic controller and the source program in the device used to program it can be compared to identify alterations to the program logic.

- **Monitoring programmable logic controller inputs/outputs and control program memory addresses:** The inputs/outputs and memory address values provide valuable information about malicious activity.

- **Monitoring execution time:** A programmable logic controller executes in a cyclic manner. Every cycle has three phases: (i) read inputs; (ii) execute the control program; and (iii) update outputs [16]. A change in the execution time can indicate control program alteration.

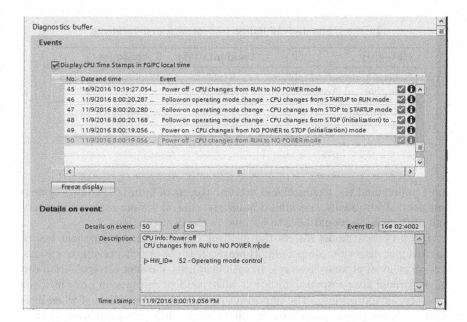

Figure 6. STEP 7 event activity log.

Other vendors (e.g., Allen Bradley) provide similar software (RSLogix) for their programmable logic controllers. The software is useful for investigating industrial control system incidents involving industrial control system malware and accidents.

The official investigative report [9] on the escalator incident in the Mong Kok, Hong Kong shopping mall attributed the cause to the failure of the main drive chain as well as a broken chain safety device. The main drive chain failure was due to metal fatigue, and the chain safety device malfunction was due to the presence of grease on the sliding surface of the moving part of the device and an improper setting of the compression springs. The incident was classified as an accident and the investigators cooperated with the escalator contractor and manufacturer to collect evidence for analysis. However, the focus was on the mechanical parts of the escalator. Clearly, the investigation would have been more comprehensive by applying digital forensic processes to extract and analyze evidence residing in the controllers.

In order to prepare an efficient plan for industrial control system forensics, incidents should be classified at an early stage if possible. In the case of incidents involving general computer malware or unauthorized access, the investigations can be handled just like they are for incidents involving conventional information technology systems. In the case of incidents involving industrial control system malware and accidents, the investigations must incorporate industrial control system experts, including vendor personnel. The investigators

Table 3. Summary of industrial control system incidents.

Category	Incidents (%)	Techniques
General Computer Malware	5 (19%)	Traditional forensics
Unauthorized Access	9 (35%)	
ICS Malware	6 (23%)	ICS forensics
Accidents	6 (23%)	

must understand the technical and tactical aspects of industrial control system forensics. Additionally, specialized industrial control system evidence recovery and analysis tools would have to be used in the investigations.

The proposed model inserts the incident categorization component before the incident detection component. However, it is not always possible to categorize an incident at an early stage. In such instances, incident categorization can be performed after response initiation, after incident response or after incident recovery, as appropriate. The important point is that, regardless of when incident categorization is performed, it enhances the efficiency of the investigation.

8.   Conclusions

The incident response model presented in this chapter is useful for forensic planning and investigations of industrial control system incidents. The model enables incident response teams and forensic investigators to decide on the expertise, techniques and tools to be applied to ensure sound evidence acquisition, analysis and reporting.

Most investigations of industrial control system incidents tend to focus on malware attacks; this could obscure determinations of other causes of the incidents. The majority of the representative incidents considered in this work (19% + 35% = 54% in Table 3) fall in the general computer malware and unauthorized access categories, which means that they could be investigated using traditional forensic techniques. In the other words, industrial control system experts and specialized tools are not required for all investigations of industrial control system incidents. Robust guidelines and tools are available for such investigations, which greatly simplify incident response.

Another key point is that performing incident categorization early in incident response renders the entire process more effective and efficient. Based on the incident categorization, forensic investigators can decide on the industrial control system expertise, techniques and tools that are required, which reduces the time, effort, costs and resources.

Future research will analyze a comprehensive collection of industrial control system incidents. This research will provide valuable insights into incident handling, enabling the creation of a robust forensic investigation model for industrial control systems.

References

[1] A. Abbasi and M. Hashemi, Ghost in the PLC: Designing an undetectable programmable logic controller rootkit via pin control attack, presented at *Black Hat Europe*, 2016.

[2] N. Ben Aloui, Industrial Control Systems Dynamic Code Injection, Cybersecurity Labs, DCNS Toulon, Toulon, France (`grehack.org/files/ 2015/Grehack%202015%20-%20Paper%20-%20Industrial%20Control%20 Systems%20Dynamic%20Code%20Injection.pdf`), 2015.

[3] N. Carr, Development of a Tailored Methodology and Forensic Toolkit for Industrial Control Systems Incident Response, M.S. Thesis, Cyber Systems and Operations, Naval Postgraduate School, Monterey, California, 2014.

[4] A. Dar, Protecting industrial control networks – It's not just about SCADA security, *Cyberbit Blog*, February 10, 2017.

[5] M. Dzwiarek, An analysis of accidents caused by improper functioning of machine control systems, *International Journal of Occupational Safety and Ergonomics*, vol. 10(2), pp. 129–136, 2004.

[6] P. Eden, A. Blyth, P. Burnap, Y. Cherdantseva, K. Jones, H. Soulsby and K. Stoddart, A forensic taxonomy of SCADA systems and approach to incident response, *Proceedings of the Third International Symposium for ICS and SCADA Cyber Security Research*, pp. 42–51, 2015.

[7] M. Fabro and E. Cornelius, Recommended Practice: Creating Cyber Forensic Plans for Control Systems, INL/EXT-08-14231, Idaho National Laboratory, Idaho Falls, Idaho, 2008.

[8] N. Falliere, L. O'Murchu and E. Chien, W32.Stuxnet Dossier, Version 1.4, Symantec, Mountain View, California, 2011.

[9] Government of the Hong Kong Special Administrative Region, EMSD releases technical investigation report on escalator incident at Langham Place, Press Release, Hong Kong, China (`www.info.gov.hk/gia/ general/201706/09/P2017060900449.htm`), June 9, 2017.

[10] K. Kent, S. Chevalier, T. Grance and H. Dang, Guide to Integrating Forensic Techniques into Incident Response, NIST Special Publication 800-86, National Institute of Standards and Technology, Gaithersburg, Maryland, 2006.

[11] S. Lau and J. Ngo, Seven injured in lift accident in North Point building, *South China Morning Post*, March 3, 2013.

[12] D. McMillen, Security Attacks on Industrial Control Systems: How Technology Advances Create Risks for Industrial Organizations, IBM Security, International Business Machines, Somers, New York, 2015.

[13] Ministry of the Environment, Energy and the Sea, Lessons Learnt from Industrial Accidents, 12th Seminar, Paris, France (`www.impel.eu/ wp-content/uploads/2018/01/Brochure_IMPEL2017_EN.pdf`), 2017.

[14] Public Safety Canada, Critical Infrastructure, Ottawa, Canada (`publicsafety.gc.ca/cnt/ntnl-scrt/crtcl-nfrstrctr/index-en.as px`), 2018.

[15] Radio Television Hong Kong, Langham Place escalator malfunctions, injuring 18, *RTHK News*, March 25, 2017.

[16] K. Sacha, Translatable finite state time machine, in *Design for Dependable Systems*, E. Gaudin, E. Najm and R. Reed (Eds.), Springer, Berlin Heidelberg, Germany, pp. 117–132, 2007.

[17] N. Sayfayn and S. Madnick, Cybersafety Analysis of the Maroochy Shire Sewage Spill, Working Paper CISL# 2017-09, Cybersecurity Interdisciplinary Systems Laboratory, Sloan School of Management, Massachusetts Institute of Technology, Cambridge, Massachusetts, 2017.

[18] J. Slay and M. Miller, Lessons learned from the Maroochy water breach, in *Critical Infrastructure Protection*, E. Goetz and S. Shenoi (Eds.), Springer, Boston, Massachusetts, pp. 73–82, 2007.

[19] M. Souppaya and K. Scarfone, Guide to Malware Incident Prevention and Handling for Desktops and Laptops, NIST Special Publication 800-83, Revision 1, National Institute of Standards and Technology, Gaithersburg, Maryland, 2013.

[20] R. Spenneberg, M Bruggemann and H Schwartke, PLC-Blaster: A worm living solely in the PLC, presented at *Black Hat USA*, 2016.

[21] B. Sperber, Solutions emerge to prevent control system cyber-attacks, *Automation World*, May 23, 2012.

[22] T. Spyridopoulos, T. Tryfonas and J. May, Incident analysis and digital forensics in SCADA and industrial control systems, *Proceedings of the Eighth IET International System Safety Conference Incorporating the Cyber Security Conference*, 2013.

[23] K. Stouffer, J. Falco and K. Scarfone, Guide to Industrial Control Systems (ICS) Security, NIST Special Publication 800-82, National Institute of Standards and Technology, Gaithersburg, Maryland, 2011.

[24] P. van Vliet, M. Kechadi and N. Le-Khac, Forensics in industrial control system: A case study, in *Security of Industrial Control Systems and Cyber Physical Systems*, A. Becue, N. Cuppens-Boulahia, F. Cuppens and S. Katsikas (Eds.), Springer, Cham, Switzerland, pp. 147–156, 2016.

[25] C. Wueest, Targeted Attacks Against the Energy Sector, Version 1.0, Symantec, Mountain View, California, 2014.

Printed in the United States
By Bookmasters